The Single Market Review

AGGREGATE AND REGIONAL IMPACT

TRADE, LABOUR AND CAPITAL FLOWS:
THE LESS DEVELOPED REGIONS

The Single Market Review series

Subseries I — Impact on manufacturing
Volume:
1 Food, drink and tobacco processing machinery
2 Pharmaceutical products
3 Textiles and clothing
4 Construction site equipment
5 Chemicals
6 Motor vehicles
7 Processed foodstuffs
8 Telecommunications equipment

Subseries II — Impact on services
Volume:
1 Insurance
2 Air transport
3 Credit institutions and banking
4 Distribution
5 Road freight transport
6 Telecommunications: liberalized services
7 Advertising
8 Audio-visual services and production
9 Single information market
10 Single energy market
11 Transport networks

Subseries III — Dismantling of barriers
Volume:
1 Technical barriers to trade
2 Public procurement
3 Customs and fiscal formalities at frontiers
4 Industrial property rights
5 Capital market liberalization
6 Currency management costs

Subseries IV — Impact on trade and investment
Volume:
1 Foreign direct investment
2 Trade patterns inside the single market
3 Trade creation and trade diversion
4 External access to European markets

Subseries V — Impact on competition and scale effects
Volume:
1 Price competition and price convergence
2 Intangible investments
3 Competition issues
4 Economies of scale

Subseries VI — Aggregate and regional impact
Volume:
1 Regional growth and convergence
2 The cases of Greece, Spain, Ireland and Portugal
3 Trade, labour and capital flows: the less developed regions
4 Employment, trade and labour costs in manufacturing
5 Aggregate results of the single market programme

Results of the business survey

EUROPEAN COMMISSION

The Single Market Review

AGGREGATE AND REGIONAL IMPACT

TRADE, LABOUR AND CAPITAL FLOWS: THE LESS DEVELOPED REGIONS

The Single Market Review

SUBSERIES VI: VOLUME 3

OFFICE FOR OFFICIAL PUBLICATIONS
OF THE EUROPEAN COMMUNITIES

KOGAN PAGE . EARTHSCAN

This report is part of a series of 39 studies commissioned from independent consultants in the context of a major review of the Single Market. The 1996 Single Market Review responds to a 1992 Council of Ministers Resolution calling on the European Commission to present an overall analysis of the effectiveness of measures taken in creating the Single Market. This review, which assesses the progress made in implementing the Single Market Programme, was coordinated by the Directorate-General 'Internal Market and Financial Services' (DG XV) and the Directorate-General 'Economic and Financial Affairs' (DG II) of the European Commission.

This document was prepared for the European Commission

by

Centre for Economic Research and Environmental Strategy (CERES)

It does not, however, express the Commission's official views. Whilst every reasonable effort has been made to provide accurate information in regard to the subject matter covered, the Consultants are not responsible for any remaining errors. All recommendations are made by the Consultants for the purpose of discussion. Neither the Commission nor the Consultants accept liability for the consequences of actions taken on the basis of the information contained herein.

The European Commission would like to express thanks to the external experts and representatives of firms and industry bodies for their contribution to the 1996 Single Market Review, and to this report in particular.

Office for Official Publications of the European Communities
2 rue Mercier, L-2985 Luxembourg
ISBN 92-827-8808-3   Catalogue number: C1-72-96-003-EN-C

Kogan Page . Earthscan
120 Pentonville Road, London N1 9JN
ISBN 0 7494 2340 4

Table of contents

List of tables   **viii**

List of figures   **xii**

List of abbreviations   **xiii**

Acknowledgements   **xiv**

1. Summary   **1**

1.1.   Introduction and methodological approach   1
    1.1.1. Qualitative indicator analysis   2
    1.1.2. Regression analysis   2
1.2.   The main strengths and limitations   3
    1.2.1. The main limitations   3
    1.2.2. The main strengths   3
1.3.   The main results   4
    1.3.1. Static effects   4
    1.3.2. Location effects   5
    1.3.3. Factor accumulation and growth effects   6
    1.3.4. Other related issues   6
1.4.   Specific results for each country   6
    1.4.1. The main results for Ireland   6
    1.4.2. The main results for Italy   7
    1.4.3. The main results for Greece   8
    1.4.4. The main results for Portugal   10
    1.4.5. The main results for Spain   11
    1.4.6. The main results for East Germany   12
1.5.   The main results regarding convergence   13

2.   Review of literature and methodological background   **15**

2.1.   Introduction   15
    2.1.1. The single market measures   17
2.2.   The impact of economic integration: theoretical predictions   18
    2.2.1. Allocation effects   18
    2.2.2. Accumulation effects   18
    2.2.3. Location effects   19
    2.2.4. Technical change effects   20
2.3.   The impact on trade flows   20
    2.3.1. Introduction   20
    2.3.2. Trade creation/diversion   21
    2.3.3. Intra-industry trade   22
    2.3.4. Relative international competitiveness and specialization   26

2.4.	The impact on factor flows	27
	2.4.1. Short- to medium-run effects	28
	2.4.2. Long-run effects	28
3.	**Methodological approach to the empirical analysis**	**29**
3.1.	Introduction	29
3.2.	Indicator analysis	30
3.3.	Regression analysis	33
	3.3.1. Theoretical foundations of the model	35
	3.3.2. The panel data approach	36
	3.3.3. The measurement of technical progress	37
	3.3.4. Co-integration and aggregation	40
	3.3.5. Instrumental variables	41
	3.3.6. Structural breaks and time-dependent parameters	41
	3.3.7. The *antimonde*	42
	3.3.8. Convergence analysis	42
3.4.	The trade liberalization index	44
4.	**Empirical analyses of the less developed regions of the European Union**	**53**
4.1.	Ireland	55
	4.1.1. Background	55
	4.1.2. Data	57
	4.1.3. Indicator analysis	60
	4.1.4. Main conclusions	67
	4.1.5. Appendix A1 to Section 4.1	69
4.2.	Italy	75
	4.2.1. Background	75
	4.2.2. Data	83
	4.2.3. Indicator analysis	87
	4.2.4. Regression analysis	96
	4.2.5. General conclusions	106
	4.2.6. Appendix A1 to Section 4.2	109
	4.2.7. Appendix A2 to Section 4.2	119
	4.2.8. Appendix A3 to Section 4.2	126
4.3.	Greece	133
	4.3.1. Background	133
	4.3.2. Data	134
	4.3.3. Indicator analysis	138
	4.3.4. Main conclusions from the indicator analysis	165
	4.3.5. Regression analysis	167
	4.3.6. Appendix A1 to Section 4.3	176
	4.3.7. Appendix A2 to Section 4.3	178
	4.3.8. Appendix A3 to Section 4.3	185
4.4.	Portugal	187
	4.4.1. Background	187
	4.4.2. Data	191
	4.4.3. Indicator analysis	196

4.4.4.	Main conclusions from the indicator analysis	207
4.4.5.	Regression analysis for Portugal and Ireland	208
4.4.6.	Appendix A1 to Section 4.4	217
4.4.7.	Appendix A2 to Section 4.4	220
4.5.	**Spain**	**228**
4.5.1.	Background	228
4.5.2.	Data	232
4.5.3.	Indicator analysis	234
4.5.4.	The main conclusions drawn from the indicator analysis	278
4.5.5.	Regression analysis	281
4.5.6.	Appendix A1 to Section 4.5	290
4.6.	**East Germany**	**295**
4.6.1.	Background	295
4.6.2.	Data	296
4.6.3.	Indicator analysis	297
4.6.4.	The main conclusions drawn from the indicator analysis	302
4.6.5.	Appendix A1 to Section 4.6	304
5.	**Comparative analysis and the issue of convergence**	**305**
5.1.	**Comparative analysis**	**305**
5.1.1.	Static effects	307
5.1.2.	Location effects	308
5.1.3.	Factor accumulation and growth effects	308
5.1.4.	Other related issues	309
5.2.	**An introduction to the convergence issue**	**309**
5.3.	**Methodology**	**310**
5.4.	**A test of the impact of the SMP on convergence**	**312**
5.5.	**Conclusions**	**314**
5.6.	**Appendix A1 to Chapter 5**	**316**
5.7.	**Appendix A2 to Chapter 5**	**318**
Bibliography		**321**

List of tables

Table 2.1.   The fundamental effects of economic integration   16

Table 3.1.   Relationship between the SMP and the nature and extent of trade flows   31
Table 3.2.   The SMP and factor flows   32
Table 3.3.   SMP measures   47
Table 3.4.   Trade and factor liberalization measures for Germany   48
Table 3.5.   Trade and factor liberalization measures for Spain   48
Table 3.6.   Trade and factor liberalization measures for Greece   49
Table 3.7.   Trade and factor liberalization measures for Italy   49
Table 3.8.   Trade and factor liberalization measures for Ireland   50
Table 3.9.   Trade and factor liberalization measures for Portugal   50
Table 3.10.   The values of the trade liberalization index for all six countries
                    studied in this review   51

Table 4.1.1.   The correspondence between the different kinds of industrial
                    classifications adopted for the indicator analysis for each country
                    and the classification (TPFF classes) used for all countries
                    in the regression analysis   54
Table 4.1.2.   NACE sectors for the analysis of Irish trade flows   59
Table 4.1.3.   Comparison of domestically and foreign-owned manufacturing
                    exports   60
Table 4.1.4.   Labour migration trends, 1987–94   66
Table 4.1.5.   FDI flows, 1985–92   67
Table A1.4.1.1.   Ireland: trade creation   69
Table A1.4.1.2.   Ireland: trade diversion   70
Table A1.4.1.3.   Ireland: Grubel-Lloyd indicator   71
Table A1.4.1.4.   Ireland: absolute IIT indicator   71
Table A1.4.1.5.   Ireland: scaled IIT indicator   72
Table A1.4.1.6.   Ireland: RCAs   72
Table A1.4.1.7.   Ireland: specialization indicator   73
Table A1.4.1.8.   Ireland: export market share indicator   73
Table A1.4.1.9.   Ireland: explanatory variables   74
Table A1.4.1.10.   Ireland: capital/labour ratio   74
Table 4.2.1.   Regional economic accounts, ISTAT (1980–92) classifications   84
Table 4.2.2.   External trade statistics, ISTAT (1985–92) classifications   85
Table 4.2.3.   Matched classifications and sector labels   86
Table A1.4.2.1.   The main economic indicators   109
Table A1.4.2.2.   Trade creation index: best-performing sectors   111
Table A1.4.2.3.   Trade diversion index: best-performing sectors   112
Table A1.4.2.4.   Grubel-Lloyd index: best-performing sectors   113
Table A1.4.2.5.   IIT index: best-performing sectors   114
Table A1.4.2.6.   RCA index: best-performing sectors   115
Table A1.4.2.7.   Shares of FDI from the EU   116
Table A1.4.2.8.   Shares of migration from and into the EU   117
Table A1.4.2.9.   Regional employment flows (Herfindahl index)   118
Table A1.4.2.10.   Regional investment flows (Herfindahl index)   118

Table A2.4.2.1.	Correlation between trade indicators and sectoral characteristics (1985–92)	119
Table A2.4.2.2.	Correlation between correlation of trade indicators and the liberalization index and sectoral characteristics (1985–92)	121
Table A2.4.2.3.	Correlation between factor flow indicators and the liberalization index (1985–92)	123
Table A2.4.2.4.	Average of the percentage growth rate/level of the key economic indicators (1985–92)	123
Table A2.4.2.5.	Difference of the percentage growth rate/level of the factor flow indicators (1987–92 minus 1985–87)	124
Table A2.4.2.6.	Difference of the percentage growth rate/level of the key economic indicators (1987–92 minus 1985–87)	124
Table A2.4.2.7.	Correlation referred to in Tables A2.4.2.3 and A2.4.2.4 (1985–92)	125
Table A2.4.2.8.	Correlation referred to in Tables A2.4.2.5 and A2.4.2.6 (1985–92)	125
Table A3.4.2.1.	Sectoral regression parameters for Italy	127
Table A3.4.2.2.	Non-sectoral regression parameters for Italy	132
Table 4.3.1.	Strong-performing Greek industries in terms of exports to the EU and the rest of the world	134
Table 4.3.2.	NACE 70 codes	135
Table 4.3.3.	Greek regions at NUTS 2 level	135
Table 4.3.4.	NACE 70 codes revised according to Greek data availability	137
Table 4.3.5.	Trade creation and trade diversion indices for national data	139
Table 4.3.6.	RCA and Grubel-Lloyd indices for national data	141
Table 4.3.7.	Output by manufacturing sector for Greece in 1985 and 1992	142
Table 4.3.8.	Manufacturing output by region for Greece in 1985 and 1992	142
Table 4.3.9.	Regional specialization	143
Table 4.3.10.	Sectors to be studied in each of the 13 Greek regions	144
Table 4.3.11.	Region 11: Anatoliki Makedonia and Thraki	145
Table 4.3.12.	Region 12: Kentriki Makedonia	146
Table 4.3.13.	Region 13: Dytiki Makedonia	147
Table 4.3.14.	Region 14: Thessalia	148
Table 4.3.15.	Region 21: Ipeiros	149
Table 4.3.16.	Region 22: Ionia Nisia	150
Table 4.3.17.	Region 23: Dytiki Ellada	151
Table 4.3.18.	Region 24: Sterea Ellada	152
Table 4.3.19.	Region 25: Peloponnisos	153
Table 4.3.20.	Region 30: Attiki	154
Table 4.3.21.	Region 41: Voreio Aigaio	155
Table 4.3.22.	Region 42: Notio Aigaio	156
Table 4.3.23.	Region 43: Kriti	157
Table 4.3.24.	Trade creation indicator	158
Table 4.3.25.	Trade diversion indicator	159
Table 4.3.26.	The Grubel-Lloyd indicator	160
Table 4.3.27.	The RCA indicator	161
Table 4.3.28.	The export specialization indicator	162
Table 4.3.29.	The Herfindahl indices of employment concentration	164
Table 4.3.30.	Total FDI by region, 1988–92 (US$ million)	165
Table A2.4.3.1.	Sectoral regression parameters for Greece	179
Table A2.4.3.2.	Non-sectoral regression parameters for Greece	184

Table A3.4.3.1.   Trade creation indices for national data   185
Table A3.4.3.2.   Trade diversion indices for national data   185
Table A3.4.3.3.   Grubel-Lloyd indices for national data   186
Table A3.4.3.4.   RCA indices for national data   186
Table 4.4.1.   Regional gross value added per capita (% mainland value added
                  per capita)   187
Table 4.4.2.   Regional convergence for the period 1980–86   188
Table 4.4.3.   Regional convergence for the period 1986–90   188
Table 4.4.4.   Annual growth rates for GDP (%)   189
Table 4.4.5.   Net financial flows between Portugal and the EU (in billions
                  of escudos)   189
Table 4.4.6.   Increase in trade with the EU: sectors with higher growth (in
                  decreasing order of growth rates)   197
Table 4.4.7.   Increase in trade with non-EU countries: sectors with non-negative
                  growth (in decreasing order of growth rates)   197
Table 4.4.8.   Sectors showing trade creation and trade diversion on the mainland   198
Table 4.4.9.   Correlation between external trade growth and product, investment
                  and productivity growth on the mainland   198
Table 4.4.10.   Regions   198
Table 4.4.11.   Regions   198
Table 4.4.12.   European intra-industry specialization (B_j)   199
Table 4.4.13.   Correlation between IIT growth and value added, investment and
                  productivity growth for the mainland   200
Table 4.4.14.   Changes in comparative advantage and disadvantage for the
                  mainland   202
Table 4.4.15.   Comparative advantage   202
Table 4.4.16.   Competitiveness of the Portuguese tourism industry relative to EU
                  and non-EU countries   203
Table 4.4.17.   The mainland's shares of the export market   203
Table 4.4.18.   The specialization process on the mainland   203
Table 4.4.19.   Correlation between growth in share of the export market and
                  specialization and valued added growth   204
Table 4.4.20.   Correlation between FDI growth and product and productivity
                  growth for the mainland   205
Table 4.4.21.   Inward FDI   205
Table 4.4.22.   Herfindahl index for employment   206
Table 4.4.23.   Herfindahl index for investment   207
Table 4.4.24.   Correlation between changes in the Herfindahl index and product
                  and productivity growth   207
Table A1.4.4.1.   Grubel-Lloyd coefficient (GL_i), NCN 4   217
Table A1.4.4.2.   Grubel-Lloyd coefficient (GL_i), NACE 2)   218
Table A1.4.4.3.   NACE-CLIO RR17   219
Table A2.4.4.1.   Sectoral regression parameters for Portugal and Ireland   221
Table A2.4.4.2.   Non-sectoral regression parameters for Portugal and Ireland   227
Table 4.5.1. β convergence in Spanish CCAA (1991–95)   230
Table 4.5.2. β convergence in product/employment   231
Table 4.5.3.   Regional specialization from capital stock   234
Table 4.5.4.   Regional shares of private capital stock (%)   238

Table 4.5.5.	Ranking and impact on the capital/labour ratio	239
Table 4.5.6.	The Herfindahl index of sectoral employment	242
Table 4.5.7.	The Herfindahl index of regional employment	244
Table 4.5.8.	The Herfindahl index of sectoral investment	245
Table 4.5.9.	The Herfindahl index of regional investment	246
Table 4.5.10.	Madrid's trade indicators change 92/88	248
Table 4.5.11.	Competitive position of Spain's sensitive sectors	249
Table 4.5.12.	Catalonia's trade indicators change 92/88	254
Table 4.5.13.	País Vasco's trade indicators change 92/88	258
Table 4.5.14.	All other regions' trade indicators change 92/88	263
Table 4.5.15.	The impact of the SMP on the specialization index change 92/88	270
Table 4.5.16.	The impact of the SMP on the RCAs change 92/88	271
Table 4.5.17.	The impact of the SMP on IIT (the Grubel-Lloyd index) change 92/88	273
Table 4.5.18.	The effect of the SMP on trade creation (Xie/Qi) change 92/88	274
Table 4.5.19.	The effect of the SMP on trade creation (Mei/Ci) change 92/88	275
Table 4.5.20.	The effect of the SMP on trade diversion (Moi/Ci) change 92/88	277
Table 4.5.21.	The effect of the SMP on trade diversion (Xoi/Qi) change 92/88	277
Table A1.4.5.1.	Sectoral regression parameters for Spain	291
Table A1.4.5.2.	Non-sectoral regression parameters for Spain	294
Table 4.6.1.	IIT in East Germany, 1989–94 (Grubel-Lloyd index)	298
Table 4.6.2.	RCAs for East Germany, 1989–94	299
Table 4.6.3.	The specialization index for East Germany, 1989–93	299
Table 4.6.4.	East Germany's shares of the export market to the EU (in %), 1989–93	300
Table 4.6.5.	East Germany's sectoral distribution of exports and imports (in %), 1989–94	301
Table 4.6.6.	FDI in East Germany, 1991–93 (stocks in billion DM)	302
Table 4.6.7.	Migration flows for East Germany, 1989–94	302
Table A1.4.6.1.	The components of ten commodity aggregates	304
Table A1.5.	The estimates of Equation 1 used to measure convergence	316
Table A2.5.	The estimates of Equation 3 used to measure convergence	318

List of figures

Figure 2.1. Summary of the determinants of the rate of output growth   19

List of abbreviations

CSF	Community Structural Funds
EC	European Community
EMU	Economic and Monetary Union
EU	European Union
FDI	Foreign direct investment
GATT	General Agreement on Tariffs and Trade
GDP	Gross domestic product
GL	Grubel-Lloyd index
GNP	Gross national product
ICSO	Irish Central Statistical Office
IIT	Intra-industry trade
IIT-E	European intra-industry trade
LI	Liberalization index
MNC	Multinational company
NSSG	National Statistical Service of Greece
OECD	Organization for Economic Cooperation and Development
RCA	Revealed comparative advantage
RCA-E	European revealed comparative advantage
R&D	Research and development
SEM	Single European Market
SI	Specialization index
SIC	Standard industrial classification
SITC	Standard International Trade Classification
SMP	Single market programme
VA	Value added
XMS	Export market shares

Sectoral abbreviations used in the regression analysis

AGR	Agriculture, forestry and fisheries
ENP	Energy products
MEM	Ferrous and non-ferrous ores and metals, other than radioactive
NMM	Non-metallic minerals and mineral products
CHP	Chemical and pharmaceutical products
MEP	Metal products, machinery, equipment and electrical goods
TRE	Transport equipment
FBT	Food, beverages and tobacco
TEC	Textiles and clothing, leather and footwear
PAP	Paper and printing products
WOR	Wood, rubber and other products

Acknowledgements

The project was directed by Professor Y. Katsoulacos of the Centre for Economic Research and Environmental Strategy (CERES), Greece, in collaboration with Professor C. Carraro of GRETA Econometrics, Italy.

Country experts who worked on the project were: Brendan Shiels, Fitzpatrick Associates, Ireland; Paola Fasulo and Pierantonio Rosso, GRETA Econometrics, Italy; Manolis Antoninis, Athanasios P. Papadopoulos, Gr. Papanikos, Centre for Economic Research and Environmental Strategy, Greece; Joao Confraria, Universidade Catolica Portuguesa, Portugal; Juan Castillo and Amparo Roca, Instituto Valenciano de Investigaciones Económicas, Spain; and Peter Hohlfeld, Rheinisch-Westfäliches Institut für Wirtschaftsforschung (RWI), Germany.

1. Summary[1]

1.1. Introduction and methodological approach

The single market programme (SMP) has raised many theoretical and empirical (policy-related) questions. An important set of questions relates to the impact of the 'single market' created by the programme on trade and factor flows from and into the less developed regions of the European Union (EU).

Economic theory suggests that we can categorize the impact on trade and factor flows of the SMP in terms of allocation, accumulation and location effects (Baldwin and Venables, 1995). It also suggests that economic growth will be affected (indirectly) by the SMP by means of the more efficient use of factors of production in specific sectors and regions (allocation effects) as a result of their relocation in other sectors or regions (location effects) and by the additional effects of integration on factor accumulation (accumulation effects). It is also possible that the impact of the SMP on economic growth will contribute to increased convergence between the different countries and regions of the EU.

This review has two main objectives. The first is to evaluate empirically the above effects of the SMP on trade and factor flows between the regions and sectors of the less developed countries of the EU. The second is to try to assess to what extent these effects, via their impact on economic growth, have contributed to increased real convergence.[2]

The methodology we have used towards achieving these objectives is based on two complementary types of analysis:

(a) descriptive qualitative indicator analysis of trade and factor flows;
(b) regression analysis of trade and factor flows and of the extent to which growth of per capita income and real convergence have been affected.

Subject to some important caveats, the data used for both types of analysis are data at the NUTS 2 level of regional disaggregation and NACE 2 level of sectoral disaggregation, covering the years 1985 to 1992. To some extent, the local research teams have managed to obtain data at these levels of disaggregation (including export and import data). Thus, such data were obtained for Ireland (considered as one region), Italy and Spain (not all regions and years). For Greece and Portugal, however, the local teams have had to 'construct', or estimate, regional export and import data as described in the relevant county reports for these countries (Sections 4.3 and 4.4 respectively). The researchers faced severe problems with data for the case of (East) Germany (Section 4.6) – indeed, for this reason, this region could not be examined in a satisfactory manner.[3] We now turn to a brief description of our methodological approach.

---

[1] The Summary and Chapters 2, 3 and 5 were prepared by the contractor (CERES, Athens) in collaboration with GRETA Econometrics, Venice, and their work was coordinated by Professors Y. Katsoulacos and C. Carraro. The regression analysis contained in each of the country reports (Chapter 4) was prepared by GRETA Econometrics.

[2] The exact meaning we give to the word 'convergence' in this review will become apparent below.

[3] Also, it became part of the EU much later than the other countries analysed.

1.1.1. Qualitative indicator analysis

Main hypotheses regarding effects on trade flows

We can distinguish three fundamental aspects in the relationship between the effects of the SMP and the nature and extent of a country's/region's trade flows:

(a)   trade creation/diversion;
(b)   intra-industry trade (reflecting the relative significance of scale effects);
(c)   relative international (or EU) competitiveness/specialization.

Table 3.1 (in Section 3.2) describes in detail the indicators we use to measure these aspects.

As indicated in Sections 2.3 and 3.2, economic theory suggests, though not unambiguously, that the SMP will have positive effects on 'internal' trade creation and negative effects on trade diversion, and that it will increase intra-industry trade. Concerning relative competitiveness/specialization, it is not possible to make *a priori* predictions for specific sectors or regions of any given country, but a number of issues can be addressed concerning sectoral and regional relative competitiveness and specialization (see in particular Section 3.2, Table 3.1).

Main hypotheses regarding effects on factor flows

As detailed in Sections 2.4 and 3.2 (in particular, Table 3.2), the anticipated effects concerning factor flows are the following:

(a)   factor flows between countries:
        (i)   labour: little effect anticipated;
        (ii)   foreign direct investment (FDI): an increase is anticipated;
(b)   capital/labour ratio is expected to increase (though the effect is not unambiguous; see also Table 3.2);
(c)   employment and investment flows into sectors of new intra-industry or inter-industry specialization is expected to increase.

1.1.2. Regression analysis

The regression analysis is considered as complementary to the indicator analysis. It is undertaken in parallel with it and the results from the two types of analyses are carefully cross-checked. The regression analysis is considered particularly useful in addressing the following issues:

(a)   the second fundamental objective of the study, concerning effects on growth and real convergence;
(b)   the issue of the *antimonde* (in this respect an important innovation of this review is the construction and use of a 'trade liberalization index' that is based on the actual implementation of the measures of the SMP in each country, so the values of the index change over time (between 1985 and 1992) and across countries);
(c)   disentangling other effects (an effort has been made in this review to disentangle the effects of the SMP from other effects to the extent possible and, in particular, from:
        (i)   accession effects – in the cases of East Germany, Portugal and Spain;
        (ii)   Community Structural Fund (CSF) support;

(iii) cyclical effects;

(iv) globalization effects.

1.2. The main strengths and limitations

1.2.1. The main limitations

The most serious difficulty in undertaking the analysis presented in this review has been that of obtaining regional (NUTS 2) data, especially the data required to construct trade flow indicators. As a result of this difficulty, the analysis suffers from two limitations:

(a) as already noted, trade flow indicators for Greece and Portugal are largely based on 'estimated' data, and, further, the lack of pre-1988 regional trade data for Spain has meant that it has had to be excluded from the analysis of the effect of the SMP on convergence in Chapter 5;

(b) as the data availability difficulties were different and uneven across countries, the data sets varied in terms of their sectoral coverage (see also the explanatory note at the beginning of Chapter 4).

This last limitation, plus the difficulty in comparing regions in different countries, has meant that there is little room for 'horizontal' comparisons of the basic trade and factor flow effects of the SMP across regions of different countries. An attempt at such a horizontal comparative analysis is nevertheless made in Section 5.1, which concentrates on trying to identify the strength of the main SMP effects in terms of their consistency across regions.

1.2.2. The main strengths

This review should primarily be seen as providing, for the first time, some extremely useful descriptive information about what is happening to trade and factor flows for the vast majority of each of the Objective 1 regions of the EU post-1985. This information will provide the basic starting point for any future study on trade and factor flows with a regional dimension. Second, this information has important interpretative value. Of course, one may think of various ways of interpreting this information. Our primary concern has been to use this information to check whether or not support can be provided for the main hypotheses about the effects of the SMP on the trade and factor flows of the Objective 1 regions as described in our methodology.

What, then, is the overall message that emerges from this review? More specifically, what is the added value of this review relative to those using national data? The added value comes from the interpretative power of the regional information we generated and the overall message it delivers. To see this, note that a study on the effect of the SMP based on national data can, at best, be interpreted as indicating what is happening, on average, across the regions or economic sectors of the country. However, it can never be used to interpret how strong the SMP effect has been as this can only be done by looking at its consistency across regions.[4]

Additionally, we provide important evidence on the impact of the SMP on factor accumulation, growth and convergence at sectoral level, which is useful in understanding convergence among regions as these sectors are likely to drive convergence at the aggregate level.

In the next section, we summarize the main results of the review concerning the strength or consistency of the effects of the SMP across the Objective 1 regions of the EU.

1.3. The main results

For expositional reasons, we divide the effects of the SMP into three broad categories:

(a) **Static effects.** Under this heading we consider the movements of all trade and factor flow indicators other than those we use to measure location effects, the capital/labour ratio and the factor accumulation movements. Thus, we consider that the importance of the static (mainly allocation) effects of the SMP can be captured by looking at the movements of:
  (i)   trade creation/diversion indicators;
  (ii)   intra-industry trade indicators;
  (iii) revealed comparative advantage;
  (iv)   FDI and other factor flows.
(b) **Location effects.** We have used movements in indices of regional and sectoral concentrations of employment and investment to try to capture these effects.
(c) **Factor accumulation and growth effects.** To discover the effects of the SMP on factor accumulation and growth, we have used qualitative analysis of movements in the capital/labour ratio and the regression analysis.

Below we outline each of these three categories of the effects of the SMP in turn. We also outline, briefly, a number of other related 'horizontal' issues, such as the relative strength of trade versus factor flows and the effects of the Community Structural Funds (CSF).

1.3.1. Static effects

Trade creation/trade diversion

The overall picture that emerges here is, to a large extent, consistent with theoretical anticipations, though the effects are rarely very strong and there are also some surprises, especially with regard to some aspects of trade diversion. The latter, as measured by exports to 'other countries', has increased in some instances (sectors), and is true, though with differing

---

[4]   However, using the information we generated to make direct cross-regional comparisons additional to those provided in this review would require a data set far richer (at sectoral and regional level), far more reliable and homogeneous than that which was available to the researchers involved in this review. More specifically, the reasons that make even cross-country comparisons of average movements across regions or sectors particularly difficult are given in the introduction to 'horizontal' analysis, Chapter 5 (Section 5.1). These difficulties are multiplied when one attempts to make direct regional/sectoral comparisons, given the differences between, for example, the same sector across regions of different countries.

significance, for all countries. There is, however, a positive 'internal' trade creation effect, as anticipated, that is more significant for Spain, Ireland and Portugal than for Greece and Southern Italy.

Intra-industry trade

Results are, again, broadly consistent with theoretical expectations, and, in this case, they are consistently strong, at least for Spain, Greece, Southern Italy and, more doubtfully, for Portugal. The exception is Ireland, but this is likely to reflect fundamental inter-industry specialization forces that have been dominant in the Irish economy for much longer and which generally continued to be strong up to 1992.

Revealed comparative advantage (RCA)

Here results are mostly negative. This said, in Southern Italy there is an effect in a few sectors that may be the result of a cyclical upswing. In Ireland, the RCA has increased for all manufacturing, but notably in high-tech sectors dominated by foreign-owned firms. In Greece, the effect on the RCA across most sectors is not particularly encouraging, though there are some important exceptions (such as in the non-metallic minerals sector, which is very important to Greece's external trade). The effect is also discouraging, if anything more so, for Spain and Portugal.

FDI

While there are indications that the SMP has affected FDI positively, as we would anticipate, in Portugal and Spain it has boosted economic growth and convergence, but no such conclusion can be reached for Southern Italy, Greece and Ireland. Thus, there is no consistently strong effect of the SMP on FDI in the Objective 1 regions of the EU.

Other factor flows

There is quite a large divergence in data availability concerning other factor flows across countries. Labour migration flows could be measured only in Ireland, Italy and Spain,[5] and, very tentatively, we can say that in all these cases, in the period 1985 to 1992, these flows have increased, though we could not show that these increases are linked to the SMP.

1.3.2. Location effects

The picture concerning movements in regional and sectoral concentrations of employment and investment is also mixed, suggesting that the location effects of the SMP have not, until 1992, been consistently strong for the less developed regions of the EU. There are quite strong effects in just Portugal and Spain but in opposite directions: towards increased concentration in Portugal, but towards decreased concentration in Spain (more pronounced in investment than in employment).

---

[5]   As already noted, the distinct case of East Germany is not included in the analysis in this chapter.

1.3.3. Factor accumulation and growth effects

The capital/labour ratio does not show significant changes in Ireland, but it does so for many sectors in Greece and Spain, suggesting, at least tentatively, that the SMP has provided a modernizing stimulus for these countries.

Finally, concerning factor accumulation and growth effects, the regression analysis suggests that for both human and physical capital there was an overall positive effect for Portugal and Southern Italy, but for Spain an effect on physical capital only (not human capital) is discernible for only some of the sectors[6] and such a conclusion cannot be reached for Greece (these being the four countries for which we could provide credible tests for such effects). Some additional information on the effects of the SMP on growth are given in the next subsection and in Section 5.1 as well as, in more detail, in the specific country reports.

1.3.4. Other related issues

Trade flows versus factor flows

Do the results suggest that the SMP had a stronger and/or more consistent effect on trade or on factor flows? The answer is that it depends on the country. For Southern Italy, the SMP affected more trade flows than factor flows (for the latter, effects were negative or statistically insignificant), while exactly the reverse is true for Portugal. For Spain and Greece, the results are mixed and, for the latter, not significant.

The effects of the CSF

Finally, we comment on the rather uneven effects the CSF has produced in each country. For Southern Italy, the overall effect is positive, while a positive effect is found in Greece only for textiles and clothing, and in Portugal and Ireland only for wood and rubber, food, beverages and tobacco. This clearly does not reflect any differences in the methodological approach as the same methodology was used for all regions and countries. Data availability problems may, however, explain, at least in part, the different effects, as a lack of data diminished the quality of the regression analysis.

1.4. Specific results for each country

1.4.1. The main results for Ireland

As detailed in the relevant country report (Section 4.1), there are some unique features of the Irish economy and its economic history that we regard as central to the degree to which trade and factor flows may have changed over the period 1985–92. Notably, the increase in the numbers of multinational companies (MNCs) operating in Ireland, and their effect on total, and more importantly, sectoral intra-EU trade, are expected to have influenced the outcome considerably, although by exactly how much is uncertain. Given that increases in intra-EU trade reflect regional competitiveness, these MNCs will have undoubtedly enhanced the outcome for Ireland. However, there is, of course, ambiguity as to the extent to which this

---

[6]   However, for Spain, there is an indication that the SMP has indirect effects on factor accumulation via its effect on trade flows.

regional competitiveness is a reflection of growing competitiveness among Irish firms resulting from the SMP.

The second feature is Ireland's close trade relations with the UK. While indigenous firms continue to rely heavily on the UK market for export earnings, free trade has been in place for much longer than that which is emerging currently under the SMP.

We have faced a number of data constraints for Ireland that are detailed in Section 4.1. Because of these, we advise caution when drawing substantive conclusions.

The data support the premise of there being an effect of trade creation occurring as a result of the SMP. While the evidence suggests that this is strongest in sectors characterized by a high level of MNC activity, there are interesting exceptions. In relation to trade diversion, however, the evidence is somewhat mixed.

Contrary to expectations, the analysis showed intra-industry trade (IIT) between Ireland and the EU declining in the period, but this seems likely to reflect increases in inter-industry specialization that has been characteristic of Irish manufacturing over the period. The data suggest that the trend of declining IIT in Ireland during the late 1980s, exposed by Brülhart and McAleese (1995) and earlier studies, has generally continued up to 1992. These findings are expected to reflect a process of inter-industry specialization involving a move away from traditional labour-intensive industry towards high-tech capital-intensive activity continuing in Irish manufacturing. This process, driven strongly by direct investment into Ireland by MNCs, has been (and continues to be) the central development within Irish manufacturing since the early 1980s, and the central reason for the findings being contrary to expectations in the Irish case.

As we would have expected, the data show Ireland as having an increased RCA over the period – for all manufacturing, but notably for high-tech sectors dominated by foreign-owned firms.

In relation to factor flows, the data show increased levels of Ireland-EU labour migration during the period. This trend holds true even when the UK is not included as part of the EU. This is a somewhat surprising finding given that the language and cultural differences that are expected to suppress such increased mobility remain in abundant evidence in Ireland. On FDI, the data do not confirm increases in intra-EU capital mobility, and the analysis does not apparently indicate a significant change in the Irish capital/labour ratio over the period.

1.4.2. The main results for Italy

The empirical analysis for Italy (Section 4.2) leads, in many cases, to results that are consistent with the previous literature, though carrying out an extended regional and sectoral analysis, with both statistical and econometric tools, enabled us to provide not only a more complete and internally consistent picture of economic development in Southern Italy, but also some new results.

From the indicator analysis, we obtained some evidence supporting existing conclusions. In particular, in the sample period of 1985–92, the increase in trade diversion and trade creation is very small and limited to a few sectors, but there is evidence of an increase in IIT. This increase seems to be linked also to the implementation of the SMP. The positive impact of the

SMP on IIT concerns most sectors and regions. It is, however, larger in those sectors in which the accumulation rate is larger.

Concerning the effect on RCA, the SMP may have had a positive effect in a few sectors, but, generally, this seems to be associated with an upswing of the business cycle (which may itself have been produced partly by the SMP).

In contrast with the Onida (1987) and Sestito (1991) indications, the accumulation of physical capital is still the main engine to economic growth in Southern Italy, and is likely to be the main transmission mechanism through which the SMP implementation can affect economic growth and convergence. This conclusion is further supported by the regression analysis.

Among the regions of Southern Italy, the one in which we can observe the largest increase of trade flow indicators in most sectors is Basilicata. In the other ones, the post-1987 change in trade flow indicators concerns only a few sectors. Still, the regions in which we can observe the highest average economic performance are Puglia, Campania and Abruzzi. As far as sectors are concerned, post-1987 changes are relevant mainly in traditional sectors in which niche effects can be singled out (textiles and clothing, transport equipment, food, beverages and tobacco).

These results are largely confirmed by the regression analysis. Both the indicator and the regression analysis lead to one important conclusion. The implementation of the SMP affected more trade flows than factor flows. In particular, the SMP had a generalized positive impact on IIT, whereas the impact on trade creation has been weak and limited to a few sectors (mainly paper, wood, rubber and metal products). Negative or statistically insignificant effects were instead found for factor flows (including FDI).

Did this positive effect of the SMP on trade flows (mainly on IIT) affect economic growth? And if the answer is yes, through which channels? Our analysis shows that liberalization had a positive impact on capital accumulation (mainly through the increase in IIT). However, this impact of the SMP was transmitted to per capita income growth in only a few sectors (metal minerals, chemical products, metal products and food, beverages and tobacco).

As a consequence, only in 6 of the 11 sectors do we observe a positive impact of the implementation of the SMP on per capita income growth. These are through the effects of the SMP on the accumulation of physical capital in the four sectors of metal minerals, chemical products, metal products and food, beverages and tobacco; through a direct structural effect in agriculture; and through a positive effect on the accumulation of human capital in the wood and rubber sector.

1.4.3. The main results for Greece

The first comment concerning the Greek country report (Section 4.3) is that many of the Greek regions have manufacturing bases that are too narrow for effects to be of any significant order. It can be said that Greek regions, except in a few cases, lack any particular characteristics of regional specialization of the type one comes across in other parts of the EU. Linkages between different activities are poor and this is probably the outcome of an emphasis on activities with low value added and technological content.

However, a few interesting changes have apparently occurred as a result of the SMP. The food, beverages and tobacco sector dominates Greek manufacturing and has been characterized by differing performances between the northern and the southern regions. The first displayed declining trade activities (both to EU and non-EU countries) while the others increased their volume of export trade. A split pattern with a gap between the northern and the southern regions also took place in the minerals extraction sector, the second most important sector of Greek manufacturing. In this case, the northern regions performed better than the southern ones in increasing trade creation and trade diversion (something that is contrary to what would be expected in a single market), RCA and export specialization, but worse than them with regard to IIT.

Another example of erratic behaviour of the northern regions in traditional industries is the footwear and clothing sector (5% of output in 1992), as the regions of Anatoliki Makedonia and Thraki and of Kentriki Makedonia suffered more from diminution of their export trade and relative competitive position than did Attiki and Dytiki Ellada, which are located in the southern part of the country.

The SMP seems to have benefited the non-metallic minerals sector especially, a sector which has traditionally formed a large part of Greece's external trade. Two regions have even managed to turn the negative sign of the RCA indicator into a positive one. The other major Greek industry, textiles, has experienced hard times during this period as its competitive position has been eroded. The volume of exports increased mainly towards third countries and not so much towards the EU.

Finally, the signs concerning RCA across most sectors and regions do not seem particularly encouraging – a result confirmed by our regression analysis.

In conclusion, it may be said that the SMP has had a beneficial, though not substantial, trade creation effect in the majority of Greece's manufacturing activities and has contributed to an increase in IIT relationships. However, no important specialization trends seem to have occurred. The sectors based on more complicated technology have remained stagnant and insignificant. Despite some isolated signs, we are left with the impression that Greek manufacturing will continue to concentrate on activities deriving their competitiveness from static comparative advantage factors.

As explained in Section 4.3.3, not much can be said about the effects, if any, of the SMP on factor flows. The increase of the capital/labour ratio in the vast majority of sectors and regions may be attributed to a modernizing stimulus in Greek manufacturing that occurred because of the competitive pressures that grew within the single market. Its consequences remain to be seen. The employment concentration indices capturing location effects did not reveal any significant regional or sectoral reorderings. That is also the conclusion stemming from an analysis of the FDI data.

We can also conclude from the analysis of the Greek regions that almost no positive impact on capital accumulation from the implementation of the SMP is likely to have occurred and there is no evidence of any impact on growth, with the exception of the paper sector.

1.4.4. The main results for Portugal

The country report for Portugal (Section 4.4) suggests that, from 1986 to 1992, import penetration growth rates have been higher than export/production growth, this trend being more obvious after 1990. Several factors contributed to this: EU membership, implying both trade liberalization with partner countries and lower degrees of protection from imports from third countries, the SMP, and adjustments following the progressive reversal of exchange rate policies, aiming at greater exchange rate stability in the early 1990s.

In general, this process has led to decreasing comparative advantages for domestic firms, which may be related to the role of IIT. In sectors such as paper and textiles, clothing and footwear, increasing IIT led to decreasing positive comparative advantages. In agriculture and in most of the other industrial sectors, starting from initial positions of negative comparative advantages, decreasing shares of IIT reinforced the comparative disadvantages of domestic firms. Products of non-metallic minerals and energy were the exceptions to the general trend. In the first case, positive comparative advantages were reinforced and, in the second, comparative disadvantages weakened.

At the same time, domestic firms increased their share of many EU exports, and this is related to a process of specialization centred on textiles, clothing and footwear, non-metallic mineral products, timber and furniture, electrical engineering and motor vehicles. Foreign investment seems to have played a role in the development of this specialization pattern, mainly in electrical engineering, and motor vehicles and components. However, in the case of motor vehicles and components, several large foreign projects benefited from government support, and it remains to be seen if that was enough to build a sustainable motor industry at the domestic level.

There were important differences in labour productivity changes among the regions. In Norte, Centro and Lisboa e Vale do Tejo, growth in trade seems to have been positively related to growth in value added and in labour productivity. The regions of Norte and Centro seem to have a greater variety of industries with positive comparative advantages, although this conclusion is sensitive to assumptions made to estimated trade data. It seems clear that the same regions have a greater number of industries with positive changes in regional specialization patterns. In Lisboa and Algarve, the concentration of economic activity in terms of employment increased, which has to be explained by the growth of services sectors. Moreover, increased concentration seems to be closely related to increased labour productivity, suggesting a fast concentration of resources in higher productivity (non-tradable) activities. On the other hand, this is positively related to growth in value added. Concentration of investment flows may well reinforce this pattern, having increased everywhere, although this result may well be sensitive to assumptions made to estimated investment data.

Turning more specifically to effects on factor flows and on growth, the regression analysis, which for the case of Portugal was undertaken by considering this country together with Ireland (see Section 4.4.5), suggests that the implementation of the SMP had a larger impact on factor flows than on trade flows. Also, a generalized positive effect is found only with FDI from EU countries.

The change in FDI had a generalized positive effect on both physical and human capital accumulation. That is, liberalization had a positive impact on capital accumulation through an increase in FDI. A positive stimulus to physical capital accumulation was also provided by CSFs (at least in some sectors).

Only physical capital seems to have had a positive impact on growth in some sectors (paper, non-metal minerals, wood and rubber, metal products, food, beverages and tobacco, and agriculture). Therefore, in these sectors, the implementation of the SMP, through its effects on FDI, also had a positive impact on growth.

1.4.5. The main results for Spain

Our analysis for the case of Spain (Section 4.5) has shown, in general, important changes occurring in most Spanish regions and sectors, changes which were particularly important for the trade flows and of less significance for the factor flows.

However, it would be premature to state that the impact of the SMP was very significant in the case of Spain as it is necessary to take into account at least two types of factors that limit the explanatory capacity of the analysis, namely the simultaneous process of integration of the Spanish economy into the EU, beginning in 1986 and culminating precisely in the years covered in this report, and the level of aggregation used in the analysis. The latter concerns not just the fact that, as for the other countries, the analysis was based on the NACE 2 level of sectoral disaggregation but also that, due to non-availability of data, in the case of Spain, all regions other than Madrid, Catalonia and the Basque country were aggregated into a single region for the purposes of constructing trade (though not factor) flow indicators. Taking these caveats into account, the main conclusions that can be drawn on the impact of the SMP in the case of Spain are as follows.

The specific impact of the SMP on factor flows does not seem to have been very intense, although a process of moderate structural change is clearly perceptible. All the regions showed increases in the capital/labour ratio for the period 1978–92, evidence of the effort made in capitalization and modernization of the industrial fabric to improve competitiveness in view of the single market. The analysis carried out on regional and sectoral concentration of employment and investment (by means of Herfindahl indices) has enabled us to conclude that:

(a)   there was a trend towards diversification in both employment and investment, although the decrease in concentration was more pronounced in investment than in employment (however, in most sectors and regions, this change cannot be attributed to the impact of the SMP, as this trend had been observed since 1978);

(b)   nevertheless, there was a localized increase of concentration in certain regions (Extremadura, Asturias) and sectors;

(c)   Spain's entry into the single market seems to have influenced investment, but not decisively.

The different impacts from one region to another (strong growth in three of them and a notable increase of diversification in five of them) was not on a large enough scale to substantially alter the regional ranking of sectoral concentration.

More specifically, concerning effects on trade flows the following points were noted:

(a)   The export specialization index fell most in the sectors described as sensitive and for which there was weak demand, as in the case of the food, beverages and tobacco (41-42) and leather, footwear and clothing (44-45) sectors, the specialization in which decreased in all regions. On the other hand, the steep rise of specialization in the automobiles (35) sector confirms that the sectors with greater intensity of technology and for which there is high demand have performed better.

(b)   The RCA indicator shows a worsening of competitiveness of many Spanish manufacturing sectors, confirming the loss of importance of the IIT model. Catalonia and the other regions group reflect a greater loss of competitiveness against the increase in imports from EU countries and, by sectors, automobiles (35) stands out as having the greatest rise in its RCA, while textiles and clothing (43) and paper, printing and publishing (47) sectors are at the opposite extreme, with substantial falls in their competitiveness.

(c)   The IIT indices show that there was an intensification of the IIT model on entry into the EU, and the trend was towards specialization in sectors with strong or medium EU demand. In this sense, specialization implies differences in regional preferences, but, for all regions, the electrical machinery (34) sector experienced the greatest specialization.

(d)   The trade creation effect resulting from the process of integration of the Spanish economy into the EU was intense and widespread. There was high penetration of EU imports, as revealed by other studies made after entry, Catalonia and the all other regions group experiencing the greatest creation of trade. The growth of import penetration in the food, beverages and tobacco (41-42) sector stands out among the traditional sectors – the high level of trade creation in the electrical machinery (34), other means of transport (36) and instrument engineering (37) sectors being among those in which there was medium and high demand. There are, however, notable regional differences within single sectors. For example, in the chemicals (25) sector, intense trade creation was generated in Madrid, where this sector is one of the most competitive and important in regional exports, but not in the all other regions group.

(e)   Finally, in trade with third countries, the diversion of trade in industrial products was insignificant, and it can be confirmed that the internal trade creation effect has compensated for the trade diversion effect generated by the process of integration. Catalonia and Madrid are the regions where it is possible to detect most cases of diversion, and at sectoral level, non-metallic minerals (23) is the only one where a clear diversion effect can be distinguished.

Concerning the effect of CSFs in Spain, our regression analysis suggests that CSFs had a significant and positive influence on the accumulation of physical capital, but not on human capital. The effects on factor accumulation and growth are summarized in Section 5.1 and, in detail, in the relevant country report.

1.4.6.   The main results for East Germany

With respect to East Germany (see Section 4.6), we faced severe problems regarding the availability of data, documented in detail in Section 4.6.2. As a consequence, the indicator analysis is of limited scope, covering as it does only a very limited number of trade and factor flow indicators. The main tentative conclusions that emerge from this analysis are as follows.

At this point in time, East Germany is successfully driving on its integration into the EU and the world economy with its exports of mechanical engineering and chemical products. The changes in the structure of exports as well as imports since unification indicate that we may anticipate, as a result of a further reconstruction of the capital stock as well as relatively extensive use of high-quality human capital, that the comparative advantage of East Germany in the sectors of mechanical engineering and chemical goods can be strengthened even more in the medium term. Also, the still relatively more well-developed inter-industrial division of labour may turn more and more into an intra-industrial division of labour between East Germany and Western industrialized countries. This trend can already be observed on the basis of the calculated Grubel-Lloyd indices. In almost all groups of goods, a stronger increase in IIT is to be seen. If the change in the specialization and trade pattern takes place in the expected direction, it may encourage a speedier integration into the world economy than would otherwise occur as when a well-developed intra-industrial division of labour is in place during the course of integration processes, this tends to result in lower adjustment costs than is the case when there is a well-developed inter-industrial division of labour.

Concerning factor flows, overall, FDI grew between 1991 and 1993, but East Germany's FDI share still accounts for only 2% of the total FDI in Germany. Labour migration – after the large outflow following 1989 – has levelled out and is now increasingly influenced by foreigners.

1.5. The main results regarding convergence

As already noted the second important issue addressed in this report is the convergence issue (see Chapter 5). Is there a convergence process which is taking place for the less developed EU regions? Did the SMP provide a positive boost to this convergence process? Because of the data availability problems for Spain (trade flow data were not available prior to 1988) and East Germany, the convergence issue has been examined for the regions of Greece, Ireland, Italy and Portugal.

We should make clear here that, throughout this review, the term 'convergence' is used to refer to *sectoral* production (value added) per capita, and so it is only when this can be considered as a proxy of income per capita in a region that we actually provide a test of convergence of regional income per capita. It would be an adequate proxy if we accounted for all – rather than for a few manufacturing sectors – of the production in each region. Nevertheless, convergence in the sectors analysed is likely to drive convergence at the aggregate regional level.

The results from the convergence analysis regarding the effect of the SMP are rather negative, but, given that the analysis uses data up to 1993 (the year 1993 is not included), this should probably have been expected and the results should not be regarded as too disappointing. Especially for the less developed regions, any acceleration of the convergence process due to the SMP is likely to manifest itself some time after the completion of the programme in 1992.

Here are some more specific points that came out of the analysis:

(a) The convergence analysis provides evidence that a convergence process is taking place, particularly strongly in the sectors of textiles and clothing, chemical products, paper, metal minerals, transport equipment and wood and rubber. The only sector for which no convergence process is found is the metal products sector.

(b) The convergence process was found to have been speeded up by the implementation of the SMP in only a few sectors. Indeed, we get statistically significant evidence of a positive impact of the SMP on convergence only for the wood and rubber sector, while in transport equipment, metal products and energy products it is likely that convergence has also increased. A negative impact of convergence is likely in the non-metal minerals and the food, beverages and tobacco sectors.

(c)   When an increase in convergence due to the SMP occurs, it is induced mainly by a positive change in the effect of human capital on convergence.

2. Review of literature and methodological background

2.1. Introduction

The Treaty of Rome explicitly stated that its goal was to establish a single market in Europe with free movement of final goods, services and factors of production. In the preamble to the Treaty, the objective of reducing the economic disparities across regions of the European Union was also stated. In the mid-1980s, this objective of reducing regional inequalities was reinforced by the accession of Greece, Portugal and Spain. At about the same time (1985), the momentum towards further integration was revitalized by the European Commission, which adopted a programme aimed at increasing economic growth and convergence by reducing all trade and factor impediments. A single market would be created by 1992, permitting the free flow of goods and factors of production.

The single market programme (SMP) has raised many theoretical and empirical (policy-related) questions. An important set of questions relates to the impact of the single market created by the programme on trade and factor flows from and into the less developed regions of the EU. The free movement of final products and factors of production was expected to have positive static and dynamic effects on economic welfare and to provide a stimulus to the economic growth of the less developed regions of the EU. Economic theory suggests that we can categorize the effects of the single market in terms of allocation, accumulation and location effects (see Baldwin and Venables, 1995). There could also be an important effect on technical change and, thus, growth, as described in particular by Grossman and Helpman (1992).

The most important task undertaken by this review has been that of examining empirically these effects on trade flows and factor flows between the different regions and sectors of the less developed countries of the EU. The second important task has been to try to assess to what extent these effects have contributed to increased real convergence between the studied countries and regions of the EU. In order to undertake the latter task, we first examined how the economic integration that has been achieved by the SMP has affected economic growth per capita in the six less developed countries we studied and then we analysed the issue of real convergence. Table 2.1 summarizes the discussion that follows.

In the rest of this chapter we provide a theoretical review of the first six relationships indicated by the lines in Table 2.1. The issue of real convergence (relationship 7 in Table 2.1) is examined in Chapter 3, Section 3.3.8. First, however, before we move into the next section (2.2), we briefly describe the basic categories of the single market measures that constitute the core of the programme. Then, in the next section, we review the basic effects of the SMP on economic welfare as predicted by economic theory (relationship 1 in Table 2.1). Here we rely on the writings of Baldwin and Venables (1995), de la Fuente (1995a) and Grossman and Helpman (1994). These are set out in order to be able to relate subsequent analysis to these fundamental effects. In Sections 2.3 and 2.4 we describe, respectively, the anticipated impact on trade flows and factor flows that could be produced as a result of the fundamental economic effects of the SMP and we review the basic indicators that have been used to measure these impacts on these flows (relationships 2, 3 and 4 in Table 2.1).

Table 2.1.   The fundamental effects of economic integration

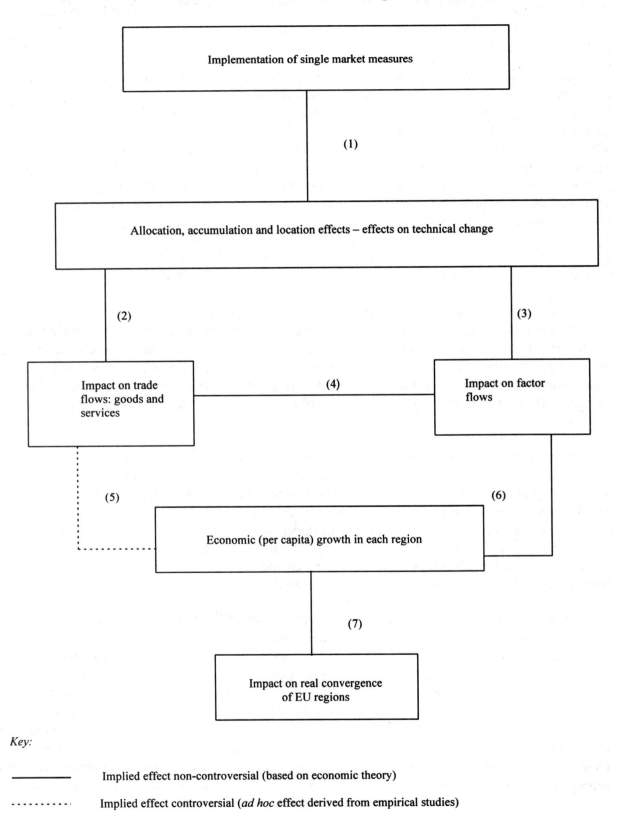

Key:

———————   Implied effect non-controversial (based on economic theory)

· · · · · · · · · ·   Implied effect controversial (*ad hoc* effect derived from empirical studies)

Economic growth is affected indirectly by trade liberalization, i.e. through the more efficient use of factors of production in specific sectors and regions or through their relocation in other sectors or regions and by the additional effects of integration on factor accumulation (relationships 4 and 5 in Table 2.1). There is a controversial direct link from trade flows to economic growth (relationship 6 in Table 2.1). The models in the empirical literature supporting such a direct link are surveyed in Edwards (1993). These are, however, *ad hoc* models and our approach concerning growth effects (described in detail in Chapter 3) is based on the view that trade promotes growth because of its effect on the allocation, location and accumulation of factors of production.

The final link in Table 2.1 concerns the issue of real economic convergence. A number of studies surveyed by Sala-i-Martin (1990) and the 1994 issue of the *Journal of Economic Perspectives* have examined the convergence hypothesis. This literature is relevant as the ultimate objective of this review concerns the assessment of real convergence between the less developed EU regions and between these and the rest of the EU. We discuss our approach to the issue of real convergence in Chapter 3, Section 3.3.8.

2.1.1. The single market measures

In 1985, the European Commission issued a White Paper listing almost 300 measures to be implemented in order to establish a single market. The SMP was ratified in January 1987 and became the Single European Act, with a mandate to abolish all national barriers to trade and factors flows. The single market was put into effect on 1 January 1993. The policy changes required for the implementation of the SMP were:

(a)　trade liberalization of goods and services:
　　(i)　removal of customs formalities;
　　(ii)　liberalization of public procurement;
　　(iii)　establishing common technical standards in production and distribution;
(b)　liberalization of factor flows:
　　(i)　unconstrained labour mobility;
　　(ii)　opening up the capital markets;
　　(iii)　mutual recognition of approvals by national regulatory agencies;
(c)　general deregulation:
　　(i)　lowering subsidies and anti-competitive regulation;
　　(ii)　enforcement of competition policy;
(d)　other arrangements:
　　(i)　qualified majority for all the Council decisions that relate to the completion of the single market, with the exception of tax issues that require anonymity;
　　(ii)　promoting economic and social cohesion[7] by allocating structural funds to less developed regions.

A number of other measures were also taken to complement the SMP, such as the Social Charter in 1989 and various harmonization policies that affect air transport, insurance and immigration from non-EU countries.

---

[7]　It should be noted here, however, that the structural funds are usually considered as a distinct measure from the other SMP measures mentioned.

2.2. The impact of economic integration: theoretical predictions

The impact of economic integration can be analysed in terms of allocation, location and accumulation effects. In addition, as has been shown by Grossman and Helpman (1992), economic integration could have powerful effects on technical change and innovation. This section discusses these four effects.

2.2.1. Allocation effects

By allocation effects is meant an increase in real income (welfare) due to more efficient allocation of factors of production that result from decreasing trade barriers and from the elimination of production and consumption (price) distortions (see de la Fuente (1995a), section B1 for an analytical discussion of this issue). However, the distribution of welfare gains may be uneven, with some larger countries experiencing net welfare losses (the optimal tariff argument).

Another possible source of welfare loss after removing trade barriers may be trade diversion as opposed to trade creation. Trade diversion occurs when there is a switch in trade from outside efficient suppliers to less efficient suppliers inside the EU. Originally, the literature on trade diversion/trade creation was developed by Viner (1950), Meade (1955), Lipsey (1960) and Michaely (1963). It was surveyed by Krauss (1972). However, Mundel (1964) and Kemp and Wan (1976) have developed theoretical frameworks that show how member countries can benefit from an economic union even if there is trade diversion. Further, empirical studies have reinforced the view that economic integration creates rather than diverts trade.

The above assumes perfectly competitive markets. The allocation effects on income and welfare could probably be larger if we allow for economies of scale (increasing returns) and imperfect competition (see Krugman and Obstfeld – 1994, Chapter 6 – for an introduction to this literature. This theoretical literature has not, however, reached unambiguous conclusions. The welfare impact on individual countries is difficult to evaluate *ex ante* and its size depends very much on the assumptions made by the specific model on the relevant importance of supply and demand elasticities, economies of scale, market size, the concentration of industry and other trade distortions. As it is reported by de la Fuente (1995a), empirical models show that the welfare gains are larger under imperfect competition and economies of scale than they would have been under situations of perfect competition.

Another source of efficiency gains comes from the reduction of internal organizational slack, termed X-inefficiency by Leibenstein (1966). Economic integration increases competition, forcing a better, more efficient allocation of the managerial resources of the firm.

The allocation effects discussed up to now are static, in the sense that they do not take into consideration the impact of the single market measures on factor accumulation. The next section discusses these other, dynamic effects of economic integration.

2.2.2. Accumulation effects

The accumulation effects of the SMP can be analysed in terms of factor accumulation through changes in savings and investment rates, on the one hand, and in terms of technical progress, on the other. Both affect output growth, as shown in Figure 2.1, taken from de la Fuente (1995a).

Figure 2.1. **Summary of the determinants of the rate of output growth**

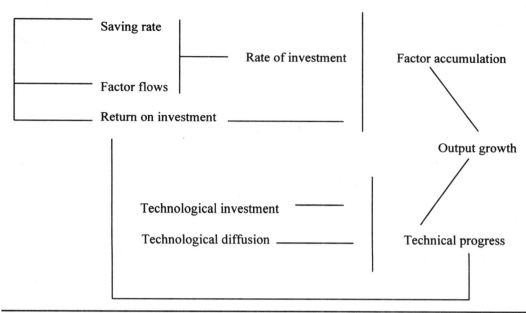

Source: De la Fuente (1995a).

The static effects (allocation effects), discussed in the previous section, assess the impact on the output of the SMP, assuming that there is no change in the stock of factors of production. The ultimate effect of the (static) increase in output due to the SMP will be an increase in savings, thus raising the steady state capital to labour ratio. This is the so-called induced capital formation argument or long-run impact on growth and output of economic integration (see Baldwin, 1989 and 1992, and de la Fuente (1995a) pp. 39–43).

This analysis of the effect on factor accumulation and growth of trade liberalization measures can be expanded to allow for permanent productivity-enhancing factor accumulation effects (endogenous growth). The new growth literature, initiated by Romer (1986), has made the accumulation of factors of production a ceaseless endogenous process of the economic system. This literature emphasizes the micro-foundations of factor accumulation, specifying the private costs and gains in new investment in human capital and technical progress. The conclusion reached by this 'new' literature is that continuous output growth can be achieved by sustained productivity growth generated, for example, by a continuous process of R&D investment and innovations.

2.2.3. Location effects

The elimination of trade barriers will affect the geographical concentration of economic (industrial) activity, as stressed in particular in recent work by Krugman (1991, 1991a, and 1991b) and Krugman and Venables (1990, 1993 and 1994). Two factors emphasized by this new literature are:

(a)   increasing returns to scale in production that are internal to the firm;
(b)   trade costs, such as transport, marketing and communication costs due to language and/or cultural differences.

The distribution of economic activity across regions cannot be determined *a priori*. It is true that for those industries that experience increasing returns (due to large fixed costs), the elimination of trade barriers makes it profitable to concentrate production in specific regions. On the other hand, if economies of scale are not large enough relative to regional demand and trade costs are large, then economic activity may spread in many regions. This effect may be reinforced by wage differentials that are due to labour immobility.

2.2.4. Technical change effects

As already suggested, the SMP is expected to affect the rates of return on savings and factors of production. In particular, the return on investment and the rate of capital accumulation are expected to be positively affected. These effects will be reinforced by technical progress via an increase in technological investment and diffusion.

Economic integration has a technical progress effect by means of its impact on the accumulation of technological knowledge. Grossman and Helpman (1992) have identified four mechanisms by which economic integration might affect the accumulation of technological knowledge.

First, economic integration will facilitate the communication of technical information. Second, competition, which is the expected result of economic integration, forces private agents to implement new ideas and technologies. Third, economic integration increases the size of the market, creating more profit opportunities. This can have a positive effect on the innovation process, even though increasing competition may have a negative effect on innovation. Fourth, innovation may be encouraged by the specialization fostered by economic integration.

Baldwin (1992) has also developed a theoretical argument that links the accumulation of human capital (knowledge) to the removal of trade barriers and economic growth. Nevertheless, it is quite possible that the impact of the SMP might negatively affect the incentives to invest in technological innovations and human capital accumulation and this may particularly be the case in relatively less developed countries. Grossman and Helpman (1992) give four reasons for this perhaps being the case.

First, more trade implies more competition and national firms might find that this reduces the anticipated profitability of their investment in knowledge. Second, opening up trade with a technologically advanced country may force the less advanced country to reduce investment in innovation. This might lead to a concentration of technological progress in a few regions that had an advantage in innovative production before economic integration. Third, countries with unskilled (manual) labour may be forced by economic integration to specialize in commodities that are low in technological content. Fourth, countries that invested relatively more in human capital before economic integration will experience a higher reward after economic integration, reducing the incentives to invest in research and development.

2.3. The impact on trade flows

2.3.1. Introduction

There are two fundamental reasons for countries to specialize and trade.

First, countries differ either in their resource endowments or in technology (or both) and specialize in producing the goods and services in which they have a comparative advantage. Second, the existence of economies of scale (or increasing returns) makes it advantageous for each country to specialize in the production of only a limited range of goods and services. This, together with the fact that consumers love variety (or have convex preferences), explains why countries specialize and trade in products of the same industry (IIT).

As noted in the previous section, economic integration has effects on both of these sources of specialization and trade. These effects will have important implications for a country's trade flows. We will distinguish between three fundamental aspects in the relationship between the effects of integration (discussed in the previous section) and the nature and extent of a country's trade flows:

(a)   trade creation/diversion;
(b)   IIT (reflecting the relative significance of scale effects);
(c)   relative international (or EU) competitiveness/specialization.

2.3.2. Trade creation/diversion

The simplest and most obvious aspect of this relationship concerns the aggregate volume of trade. As noted by Baldwin and Venables, 'one of the earliest, and most enduring, rules of thumb for evaluating the welfare impact of (economic integration) involves the aggregate volume of trade. According to this approach welfare increases if the volume of trade rises. The earliest evaluations of European integration employed very simple time-series models of imports. Following Viner (1950), these studies focused on measuring trade creation and trade diversion'. However 'the logical validity of connection between welfare gains and the sum of trade creation and diversion holds up only under a long list of unreasonable assumptions: only tariff cuts . . . or other DRC [domestic rest-creating] barriers are considered, tariff rates are uniform across all products and all trading partners initially, and finally scale, pure profit, variety and accumulation effects are unimportant'. Subsequent research has showed that these effects are important, so such an approach presents a very limited interest from the point of view of aggregate welfare analysis. Moreover, Haaland and Wooton (1992) show that quite often a welfare-raising increase in market integration may actually decrease the amount of trade by eliminating reciprocal dumping.

It was observed by Viner (1950), that 'despite these qualifications, it may be worth undertaking this sort of study simply because the notions of trade creation and diversion are so firmly fixed in the minds of many. Moreover, it is easy to do even if welfare conclusions cannot be made. Bilateral trade flows are intermediate variables that are of interest for positive as well as normative reasons.' An additional indirect benefit of measuring the extent of trade creation and diversion is that this can provide useful information concerning the impact of integration on a country's relative competitiveness and specialization.

Now, to measure trade creation and diversion, we can start with the following identity for the products of sector i for period t:

$$C_{it} = Q_{it} - X_{it} + M_{it}^{E} + M_{it}^{0}$$

where:

C_{it} = consumption of the products of sector i in t in the studied country;
Q_{it} = domestic production of the products of sector i in t;
X_{it} = exports of the products of sector i in t;
M_{it}^E = imports of the products of sector i in t from the EU;
M_{it}^0 = imports of the products of sector i in t from other (non-EU) countries.

Also, let $M_{it} = M_{it}^E + M_{it}^0$

Trade creation between the country and the rest of the EU can be measured by the movement over time of the following indices:

(i) M_{it}^E / C_{it} (or, $M_{it}^E / Q_{it} - X_{it} + M_{it}$)

and

(ii) $\dfrac{X_{it}^E}{Q_{it}}$

where X_{it}^E = exports of the products of sector i to other EU countries in t. The first index is sometimes referred to as 'internal' trade creation. These are expected to increase as a result of the SMP. Trade diversion between the country and non-EU countries can be measured by the movement over time of the indices:

(i) $\dfrac{M_{it}^o}{C_{it}}$

and

(ii) $\dfrac{X_{it}^o}{Q_{it}}$

where X_{it}^0 = exports of the products of sector i to non-EU countries. These indices (the first is sometimes referred to as 'external' trade diversion) are, all other things being equal, expected to be reduced by the SMP.

2.3.3. Intra-industry trade (IIT) $92 - 98$

As already hinted at above, a dominant distinction in modern trade theory is that between inter-industry and intra-industry trade. Inter-industry trade reflects comparative advantage. Even if countries had the same overall factor proportions, their firms would continue to produce differentiated products and the demand of consumers for differentiated products made abroad would continue to generate intra-industry trade. It is economies of scale that keep each country from producing the full range of products for itself; thus economies of scale can be an independent source of international trade. The relative importance of intra-industry and inter-industry trade depends on how similar countries are. If factor proportions are similar, then there will be little inter-industry trade, and intra-industry trade, based ultimately on economies of scale, will be dominant. On the other hand, if factor proportions are very different, all trade will be based on comparative advantage (there will be no intra-industry trade based on economies of scale). Concerning the empirical evidence, Greenway and Milner (1984) note that 'although there are considerable difficulties associated with the computation of a meaningful summary statistic of the importance of intra-industry trade, relative to total trade, a substantial amount of evidence now exists to suggest that intra-industry trade has increased in importance to the point where it may account for over 60% of total trade in most developed market economies'.

Economic integration can be expected to have a powerful positive impact on IIT by affecting positively a number of factors that are associated with high IIT. We can distinguish between short- to medium-run and medium- to long-run effects of integration on IIT.

Short- to medium-run effects

In the short to medium run, integration is expected to increase IIT for the following reasons.

(a) **Product differentiation** IIT will tend to be greater the more potential there is for product differentiation. Integration by increasing firms' possible market size increases the potential for product differentiation and this will tend to increase IIT.

(b) **Scale economies** IIT will tend to be greater in commodities where there is scope for scale economies. Integration, again by increasing market size, can, all other things being equal, increase the scope for scale economies and, hence, IIT.

(c) **Trade barriers (openness)** Empirical evidence suggests that IIT tends to be greater when trade barriers are low (see Greenway and Milner, 1984). This suggests a direct link between integration that eliminates trade barriers and the size of IIT. However, the effect may be due to long-run considerations: openness may eventually result in similarities in tastes and/or convergence of per capita income; both of these will lead to an increase in IIT.

The above need to be qualified for each country by taking into account the following:

(d) **Distance factors** IIT tends to decrease as the average distance from the country's trading partners increases. Thus, factors (a) to (c) are unlikely, all other things being equal, to have the same effect on IIT between Greece and the EU and on IIT between, say, Ireland and the EU.

Medium- to long-run effects

It is common to measure similarity in terms of 'taste overlap' (see, for example, Greenway and Milner, 1984) and/or by similarity in per capita income and to find that IIT is positively correlated with such similarity indicators. Integration is expected to increase 'similarity' in these senses in the long run, so it will also produce a positive effect on IIT.

Measurement of IIT

There is a variety of ways of measuring IIT (see Greenway and Milner, 1984), perhaps the best known of which is that proposed by Grubel and Lloyd (1975), which can be written (without a time subscript) as:

$$B_j = \left[1 - \frac{\left| X_j^E - M_j^E \right|}{\left(X_j^E + M_j^E \right)} \right] x\ 100,$$

where:

X_j^E = exports of industry j products to the EU
M_j^E = imports of industry j products to the EU
$j = 1 \ldots n$
$0 \le B_j \le 100$.

The closer the index is to its upper bound of 100 (occurring when $X_j^E = M_j^E$), the greater the proportion of total trade of sector j that is of an IIT type. The closer the index is to its lower bound of zero (occurring when X_j^E or M_j^E equal zero), the greater the extent to which inter-industry trade dominates.

The principal problem with any index of IIT, is the difficulty of unambiguously defining the term 'industry' for empirical purposes. The problem is not just one of defining the concept, but of actually operationalizing it. Thus, even if we could arrive at some critical degree of similarity in input requirements that would serve to distinguish activities within an 'industry' from those outside it, we would still face the difficulty of obtaining suitably classified data for empirical analysis. Regrouping data from established classifications such as the Standard International Trade Classification (SITC) or the UK Standard Industrial Classification (SIC) is, in principle, feasible but, in practice, difficult. The response of most researchers is to adopt a particular digit of the classification with which they are working and to assume that the categories classified as industries can reasonably be expected to contain activities with similar input requirements. A great many investigators have accepted the third digit of the SITC as a suitable level of statistical disaggregation to approximate the concept 'industry'. There is, however, no *a priori* reason for the third digit of either of these classifications to be more suitable than, say, the fourth digit. Indeed, it is likely that for some activities the third digit will be the 'appropriate' level, while for others it may be the second, fourth or fifth. Unless we regroup, though, which will probably necessitate breaking up the classification, we cannot be entirely certain. Some evidence for both the SITC (Finger, 1975) and the SIC (Rayment, 1976) exists which suggests that variability in input requirements *within* the third digit of each of these classifications could be greater than variability *between* third-digit categories. If this is the case, then there are grounds for arguing that at least some recorded IIT is simply the outcome of categorical aggregation, i.e. the grouping together into statistical categories of activities from different industries (this problem is discussed in detail in Greenway and Milner, 1984). One possible way of making an allowance for categorical aggregation is by computing an adjusted index of IIT as follows:

$$C_j = \left[1 - \frac{\sum \left| X_{ij}^E - M_{ij}^E \right|}{\sum \left(X_{ij}^E + M_{ij}^E \right)} \right] x\ 100,$$

where

j = SITC 001 . . . 899,
i = SITC (001.1 . . . 001.9) . . . (899.1 . . . 899.9)

$0 \leq C_j \leq B_j \leq 100.$

Thus, rather than summing exports and imports at the fourth digit, then taking their absolute difference for the numerator, which is in effect what happens in the computation of Bj, we sum the individual fourth-digit imbalances to obtain the numerator. To the extent that categorical aggregation manifests itself in a payments imbalance at the subgroup level, C_j makes some adjustment for it. We must note, of course, that offsetting imbalances at the fourth digit does not have to be the outcome of differing factor ratios. As long as we presume that the third digit is consistent with an 'industry', C_j provides a lower bound on our estimate of IIT. It might be objected that differing factor ratios need not manifest themselves in differing imbalances, hence the foregoing argument is circular. The point, however, is that if Finger's (1975) argument is to stand up, the ratios have to do this – after all, this is the essence of the Heckscher-Ohlin postulate. (For a fuller discussion of this and other approaches to evaluating the impact of categorical aggregation, see Greenway and Milner, 1984.)

The above remarks concern the measurement of ITT that has been practised in most of the empirical literature testing the determinants of ITT. In this literature, the indicator used is B_j, mentioned above, i.e. the *share* of IIT in each industry's gross trade. However, as indicated in a recent article by Greenway *et al.* (1994), the *absolute* amount of ITT in each industry may be a more appropriate measure for many purposes, especially when you are interested, as we are, in the adjustment implications of ITT. According to the authors, with research 'focusing increasingly on how greater integration affects [that is, changes] ITT and specialization at the margin . . . [for] the purposes of empirical research . . . it would seem more appropriate *to measure changes in the amount, than in the share, of ITT'*. This was also recognized by Hamilton and Kniest (1991), but their proposed new index of marginal IIT may, according to Greenway *et al.* (1984), 'introduce significant biases into any analysis where the purpose is to investigate the adjustment implications of changes in IIT'. Greenway *et al.* suggest that where the focus of attention is on identifying and explaining changes in IIT, a scaled or unscaled measure of absolute IIT may be most appropriate, i.e.:

$$IIT_j = (X_j^E + M_j^E) - \left| X_j^E - M_j^E \right|$$

Changes in IIT_j over time may be adjusted for the effects of inflation to obtain a real measure of the absolute change in IIT:

$$\ddot{A}IIT_j \ (real) = \ddot{A}IIT_j \ (1/deflator)$$

On the other hand, changes in intra-industry specialization, rather than trade *per se* may call for the use of scaling of (real) $\ddot{A}IIT_j$ relative to gross production.

Note that by using an absolute measure of a change in IIT ($\ddot{A}IIT_j$), we are able to compare the effects of changes in both inter- and intra-industry trade directly as $\ddot{A}IIT_j$ is the change in gross trade – $\ddot{A}(X_j^E + M_j^E)$ – less the change in net or inter-industry trade – $\left| X_j^E - M_j^E \right|$.

2.3.4. Relative international competitiveness and specialization

One of the most powerful anticipated effects of economic integration is, through the scale, variety and the other allocation and location effects identified above, the alteration in the relative international competitiveness and specialization of the countries affected by it. This will occur as firms in different sectors and regions adjust to more efficient capacities and to new optimal product lines. It is impossible to predict *a priori* exactly what the final effect of integration will be for each country's sectors and regions, in terms of their relative competitiveness and specialization and how this will be reflected in the pattern of the country's trade flows. This final effect will depend, to a large extent, on the strategic ability of firms in each country to adjust to the increased competition implied by integration and to exploit the opportunities created by larger potential markets and, among other things, on initial conditions as well as on the sector in question.

Nevertheless, a large number of indicators has been devised to measure relative competitive strength, specialization and their changes as conditions change. We have just described above how we could attempt to measure intra-industry specialization changes by $\ddot{A}IIT_j$ scaled by gross production.

The indicator which is probably best known and most often used to measure relative competitiveness is the Balassa or revealed comparative advantage (RCA) index, which is given for sector i in period t by:

$$RCA_{it} = \frac{(X_{it}^E - M_{it}^E)}{(X_{it}^E + M_{it}^E)} \, x \, 100$$

It is clear that $-100 < RCA < 100$ and that when exports grow faster than imports, there will be a positive change in RCA, indicating an increase in RCA. In the literature, values of RCA such as $100 > RCA > 0$ are broadly considered to indicate strong relative competitiveness, while values such as $0 > RCA > -100$ to indicate weak relative competitiveness.

Another index that has often been used to evaluate a country's export specialization in a particular sector relative to that of its EU partners is the specialization index (SI), given by:

$$SI = \frac{(X_i \, / \, X)}{(X_{iE} \, / \, X_E)} \, x \, 100$$

Where:

X_i = the total exports of the sector
X = the total exports of the country
X_{iE} = the total exports of sector i products from EU countries
X_E = the total exports of EU countries.

When $SI > 100$, this suggests relatively high specialization in sector i. If $SI < 100$, this suggests low specialization. Of course, we will be interested in the dynamics of sectoral export specialization, that is in $d\,(SI)$, which is the change in SI over time.

The export market shares – $XMS_i = X_i / X_{iE}$ – are also often used to provide information about competitiveness over the medium and longer term as they are a measure of the success that countries in the EU have had in capturing foreign markets.

Finally, we may use changes in the indices of trade creation given above.

$$\frac{M_{it}^E}{C_{it}}$$

and

$$\frac{X_{it}^E}{Q_{it}}$$

to get a picture of changes in the relative competitiveness of sector i. This is judged to increase if:

$$\frac{M_{it}^E}{C_{it}}$$

falls over time, while

$$\frac{X_{it}^E}{Q_{it}}$$

is increased over time. However, much the same information can be obtained by considering changes in the value of RCA, so our empirical investigation will only utilize changes in this latter indicator.

2.4. The impact on factor flows

The elimination of barriers to the mobility of factors that is part of the SMP implies that, within the EU, citizens of any member country have the legal right to live and work in any other member country. The removal of barriers to factor mobility should lead to an increase in factor flows between countries, where we may distinguish between flows of *labour* between countries and flows of *capital* (i.e. FDI).

Concerning the former – labour flows – there is very little prospect that labour mobility will rise to levels approximating those within countries any time in the foreseeable future. Language and cultural barriers remain high enough to make it hard to imagine that large-scale labour migration has been taking place even after the removal of all other barriers to mobility.

While there is little prospect of a large increase in labour mobility among countries, there may be increasing mobility of other factors. Specifically, FDI may be expected to increase – as indeed, it did following the free trade agreements in North America in the 1980s when there was a surge in FDI – as an important aspect of SMP has been the increased freedom for multinational firms to operate across borders.

Going on to predictions from theoretical models, the effects of integration on factor flows can be divided into those in the short to medium run and the long run.

2.4.1. Short- to medium-run effects

As integration increases the aggregate volume of trade, we anticipate an increase in the flows of capital and labour into the production of traded goods. However, scale and product differentiation effects lead to an increase in IIT and this will lead to movements of factors to new specializations. The important thing is to find out whether or not specialization shifts trade in an inter-industry or intra-industry direction. In the former case, the country will increase trade in which it has comparative advantage so there will be a relative increase in demand for factors it has in relative abundance.

All the above are effects on factor flows produced as integration affects a country's extent and nature of trade flows (relationship 4 in Table 2.1). Gasiorek, Smith and Venables (1993) study the effect of the single market on factor demands using a general equilibrium model in which production uses intermediate goods and four primary factors of production: capital, manual, non-manual/professional and non-manual/managerial and clerical. They work out how the single market will influence trade flows and outputs in each of 13 sectors and the implications of these changes for factor demands. They find that demand for all factors increases in France, Germany and the rest of the EU, while some factor demands decrease in Italy and the UK. Within each economy, the factor experiencing the largest increase in demand is capital in France, non-manual labour (type 1) in Germany and the UK and non-manual labour (type 2) in Italy. In no country does manual labour experience an increase in demand relative to all other factors.

2.4.2. Long-run effects

In the long run, the allocation and location effects of the SMP *Single Market Programme* will induce additional factor accumulation. As described by Baldwin and Venables (1995) and de la Fuente (1995a) and summarized above, as the increase in income from the allocation and location effects will be partly saved and invested, in the long run, we expect this to lead to an increase in the capital/labour ratio, leading to an increase in output that is a multiple of the original increase.

To summarize very briefly, we have outlined the following anticipated effects concerning factor flows:

(a)   factor flows between countries;
      (i)   labour – little effect anticipated;
      (ii)   FDI – increase anticipated;
(b)   capital/labour ratio is expected to increase (see also Table 3.2);
(c)   employment and investment flows into sectors of new intra-industry or inter-industry specialization are expected to increase.

3. Methodological approach to the empirical analysis

3.1. Introduction

Our methodology was chosen in order to achieve the twin objectives of:

(a) analysing the impact of the SMP on trade and factor flows for the less developed regions of the EU;

(b) assessing to what extent the observed pattern has affected real convergence within the EU, using a two-fold approach consisting of complementary types of analysis, namely:
  (i) descriptive, qualitative indicator analysis of trade and factor flows;
  (ii) regression analysis of trade and factor flows and of the extent to which growth of per capita income and real convergence have been effected.

The data used for both types of analysis are data at NUTS 2 level of regional disaggreggation and NACE 2 level of sectoral disaggreggation. Most of the local research teams have managed to obtain data at these levels of disaggreggation (including export and import data). Thus, such data were obtained for East Germany, Ireland (both of these are considered here as one region), Italy and Spain (not all regions). For Greece and Portugal, the local teams have had to 'construct' or estimate regional export and import data as described in the relevant reports for these countries. Of course, it is fully appreciated that, in these specific cases, the estimation of regional trade flows data must be very carefully executed as there is clearly a high risk that the underlying assumptions used for data estimation would otherwise undermine the desired objectives. The role of local expertise and qualitative analysis has been crucial in analysing and assessing these regional data.

In the next two sections, we provide details of, respectively, the indicator and regression analyses that have been undertaken for the purposes of this study. At this point, it is worth stressing that:

(a) the indicator analysis was complemented by extensive qualitative assessment that fully exploited the local knowledge of the relevant research team;

(b) the regression analysis should be considered as complementary to the indicator analysis (as it was undertaken in parallel with it and results from the two types of analyses were carefully cross-checked) and is particularly useful in addressing the following issues:
  (i)   the second fundamental objective of the study, concerning effects on growth and on real convergence;
  (ii) the issue of the *antimonde*;
  (iii) disentangling other effects.

An effort has been made in the study to disentangle the effects of the SMP from other effects as much as possible and, in particular, from:

(a) accession effects (in the cases of Germany, Portugal and Spain);
(b) CSF support;
(c) cyclical effects;
(d) globalization effects.

Our approach to disentangling these effects is described fully in Section 3.3.

3.2. Indicator analysis

As we presented the methodological background to the indicator analysis that was undertaken, including a discussion of the main hypotheses that were tested and the main theoretical predictions in Chapter 2 in some detail, here we simply have two tables that summarize the discussion there. Table 3.1 concerns trade flows and Table 3.2 factor flows.

It should be noted at this point that Tables 3.1 and 3.2 provide an exhaustive list of all indicators that potentially could be used. Given the data limitations for each specific case, the country reports cannot contain an analysis of all these indicators. However, in all cases, almost all trade flow indicators and most factor flow indicators have been computed and analysed. The notation used in the tables is as follows:

M_{it}^{E} = exports of products of sector i to EU countries in period t;
C_{it} = consumption of products of sector i in t;
X_{it}^{E} = exports of products of sector i to EU countries in t;
Q_{it} = production of products of sector i in t;
M_{it}^{0} = imports of products of sector i from countries outside the EU;
X_{it}^{0} = exports of products of sector i to countries outside the EU;
X_{i} = total exports of sector i from a given country;
X_{iE} = total exports of sector i products from all EU countries;
X = total exports from a given country;
X_{E} = total exports from all EU countries;
L_{r} = employment in region r;
L_{ir} = employment in sector i in region r.

Table 3.1. Relationship between the SMP and the nature and extent of trade flows

Aspects of the relationship	Predicted effect (or hypothesis to be tested)	Measurement	
		Indicator	Form (in all cases the change in the value of the revelant indicator is used)
Trade creation/ diversion	Aggregate trade volume between integrated countries is expected to increase (though the effect of this on welfare is not unambiguous).	Trade creation. Trade diversion.	(M_{it}^{E}/C_{it}), $(X_{it}^{E}/Q_{it})^{1}$ (M_{it}^{0}/C_{it}), $(X_{it}^{0}/Q_{it})^{1}$
Intra-industry trade (IIT)	IIT and intra-industry specialization are expected to increase, though the size of the increase depends on the scope for scale economies and product differentiation in specific sectors and may differ substantially between countries with countries furthest away from the core (e.g. Greece) affected least.	Grubel- Lloyd index. Absolute IIT indicator (to measure changes in IIT flows due to adjustment processes). Scaled IIT indicator (to measure intra-industry specialization).	$B_j = \left[1 - \dfrac{\left| X_j^{E} - M_j^{E} \right|}{(X_j^{E} + M_j^{E})} \right] x100$ $IIT_j = (X_j^{E} + M_j^{E}) - \left| X_j^{E} - M_j^{E} \right|$ (IIT_i / Q_i)
Relative competitiveness/ specialization	Not possible to make a priori predictions for specific sectors or regions of any given country. A number of issues are addressed, however: (a) how the competitive position of each sector developed over the period of the announcement and implementation of the SMP; (b) how the specialization position of each sector developed over the same period; (c) whether or not there have been significant changes in sectoral competitiveness and/or specialization – are they the strong performers the traditional sectors, are they sectors in strong international demand (what is their future growth potential)? (d) what the significance is of competitive sectors to the export performance of the country; (e) whether or not the sectoral concentration of exports has been increasing?	Revealed comparative advantage (RCA). Specialization index. Export market shares.	$RCA_{it} = \dfrac{(X_{it}^{E} - M_{it}^{E})}{X_{it}^{E} + M_{it}^{E}} \; x \; 100$ $SI_i = \dfrac{(X_i / X)}{(X_{iE} / X_E)} \; x \; 100$ $XMS_i = \dfrac{X_i}{X_{iE}}$

[1] In the terminology used by the Commission, these refer to (internal) trade creation and (external) trade diversion measures.

Table 3.2.   The SMP and factor flows

Aspects of the relationship		Predicted effect	Measurement
Factor flows	Labour	Little effect anticipated.	Labour flows from the less developed regions to other EU countries (we tried to use data identifying the regional source and destination of migrants).
	FDI	Positive effect anticipated.	FDI flows in each of the less developed regions from other EU countries.
Capital/labour ratio		Positive effect anticipated.[1]	Ratio of total investment in previous τ years to average employment in these years, where τ = number of years that the capital stock is renewed (usually τ is taken to be equal to 10). Capital stock data were used to compute the capital/labour ratio, whenever such data were available.
Inter-regional and inter-sectoral employment flows		If location effects are important, increased concentration of factors is expected in specific regions and sectors.	Measure changes in the sectoral and regional distribution of employment and investment by measuring changes in the Herfindahl indices of sectoral and regional employment and investment. For example: $$H_s^e = \sum_{i=1}^{n} h_i^2, h_i = \frac{L_{ir}}{L_r}$$ is the Herfindahl index of sectoral employment, where n is the number of sectors, L_{ir} is employment in sector i in region r, and L_r is total employment in region r.

[1] The effect is generally ambiguous, but is likely to be positive for the less developed regions under examination here for two reasons. First, increased competition is likely to force firms to rationalize and/or modernize in an effort to remain competitive and this is likely to lead to the use of more capital-intensive techniques. Second, assuming capital is much more mobile than labour, it is labour cost differences that are likely to be large to start with. So, labour costs are expected to rise relative to capital costs in the less developed regions that start with the lowest labour costs.

3.3. Regression analysis

The objective of this section is to explain why we chose the methodology we did to quantify the impact of the SMP on trade and factor flows and, hence, on growth in the studied regions. Moreover, we assessed whether or not a convergence process is taking place in the regions considered in this review and whether or not the SMP has made a positive contribution to such a process.

This sort of quantification required the comparison of two sets of time paths of key economic variables: the values observed as the SMP was implemented (the actual time paths), and the values that would have been observed if the SMP had just happened (the so-called *antimonde*). The latter are generally non-observable. It was therefore necessary to use a methodology that provided a reliable assessment of the *antimonde*, even if it was imperfect.

This issue is discussed in detail by Baldwin and Venables (1995) where the difficulty of quantifying *antimonde* variables is clearly stressed. Two problems are emphasized:

(a)   even if a perfect model of the economic systems under study were available, errors would arise because of:
    (i)   the impossibility of observing what policy decisions would have been made if the SMP had not happened;
    (ii)   the parameter estimation errors, which are magnified by small sample sizes;
(b)   available models are all imperfect, so additional sources of errors are:
    (i)   omitted exogenous and policy variables;
    (ii)   misspecified functional forms for the model equations;
    (iii) imperfect representation of the real economic system due to the 'poor state of economic theory which may lead to picking a wrong theoretical model' (Baldwin and Venables, 1995).

In addition to these problems, it is important to stress that a correct inference of the impact of the SMP could take place only if a micro-economic structural model were fully available. However, lack of data implies that aggregate time series or cross-sections are often used and that some equations may not include only free parameters. As a consequence:

(a)   aggregation biases may arise;
(b)   model parameters may depend on policy variables, which change over time (as in the case of the introduction of the SMP).

Among the 'imperfect models' that can be used to quantify the effects of the SMP on trade and factor flows and on economic growth, we selected the regression model. The benefits and costs of this approach compared to the others (CGE, macro-econometric models, time series analysis and so on) are discussed by Baldwin and Venables (1995)[8] and de la Fuente (1995a). The regression approach is certainly the most popular (even if it is not the most reliable as far as its theoretical properties are concerned). Several applications of this approach are discussed by Baldwin and Venables. In particular, they emphasize the difficulty of estimating

---

[8]   Baldwin and Venables (1995) distinguish between simulated, estimated and ad hoc *antimonde*. Simulated *antimondes* can be obtained from CGE and macroeconometric models, whereas estimated *antimondes* are provided by regression models of growth, firm size, trade variables. Ad hoc *antimondes* are the outcome of business surveys or of a mix of partial equilibrium estimates.

'structural' equations, which implies that regression analysis is more a tool for quantifying correlations among variables than the coefficients of behavioural equations. Here we also want to note that two further sources of errors are likely to emerge:

(a)   Variables in a regression model are usually the joint outcome of a more general economic model, which leads to biased estimates and difficult assessments of causality directions.

(b)   Variables are usually co-integrated. This may lead, at worst, to the discovery of an entirely spurious relationship. At best, the regression only provides consistent estimates of the elements of some co-integrating vector, but standard asymptotic theory does not apply to the estimates.

The objective of our analysis is to propose a methodology that minimizes the importance of the above errors and their impact on our economic analysis. The basic elements of the methodology we chose are as follows:

(a)   The regression model should be as close as possible to a theoretically founded model. In particular, following Baldwin and Venables' survey (1995) and the evidence contained in Levine and Renelt (1992), growth was assumed to depend only on factor accumulation and technical progress; these variables in turn depend on trade indicators. The dynamics of factor accumulation and trade indicators reflect, among other things, the introduction of the SMP.[9] As a consequence a multiple equation model must be estimated.[10]

(b)   The efficiency of our estimates was increased by using a panel data technique that would exploit both the time and the sectional variability of the available data. Sectional parameter differences (different economic structures in different regions) were accounted for appropriately.

(c)   Omitted or misspecified variables are often unobservable variables. In particular, in the existing literature on convergence (or on the impact of the SMP; see de la Fuente, 1995a), the main problem is the measurement of technical progress, which is a crucial variable in the growth equation (see below). We therefore proposed and implemented a latent variable approach (based on the Kalman filter technique) to measure technical progress.

(d)   Aggregation and co-integration biases were dealt with appropriately, using results contained in the work of Hall and Urga (1995), Engle and Granger (1987), and Sims, Stocka and Watson (1990).

(e)   The multi-equation approach and an instrumental variable estimation technique was used to minimize simultaneity biases.

(f)   However sophisticated, the regression approach is unlikely to identify free parameters. Therefore, a policy change such as the introduction of the SMP is likely to introduce a structural break of the parameters. This break cannot be assumed to have taken place in 1987 for two reasons: the SMP has been implemented slowly, and expectations of the

---

[9]   This approach is based on strong economic theory results (see Baldwin and Venables, 1995). It does, however, contrast with some empirical findings where trade flows directly affect growth (see Edwards' survey, 1993). The weakness of regression analyses in which trade flows directly affect growth is highlighted in Levine and Renelt, 1992.

[10]   In particular, we envisaged estimating a seven-equation model: one for growth, two for the accumulation of physical and human capital, and four for the main factor and trade flow indicators.

SMP implementation may have modified behavioural rules in the period pre-1987. On the one hand, these breaks make it difficult to identify the co-integration vector (Banerjee and Urga, 1995). On the other hand, these parameter changes, in addition to cross-regional parameter differences, may lead to an excessive number of parameters which prevent the equations from being identified (see Hsiao, 1987). To solve these problems, we imposed a time-dependent parameter structure[11] in which parameters depend, among other variables, on values of an indicator of the degree of implementation of the SMP. This indicator is constructed on the basis of the number and type of SMP directives implemented in each country (see below).

Let us now provide a more detailed description of the equations that will be used to quantify the effects on growth, factor and trade flows of the SMP.

3.3.1. Theoretical foundations of the model

There is extensive literature which attempts to identify the determinants of growth from cross-countries and time series data on macro-economic aggregates. This literature can be understood following the theoretical framework proposed in Baldwin and Venables (1995), where the following per capita growth accounting equation is derived from the usual Cobb-Douglas aggregate GDP function:

Equation 1 $\qquad y_t = a_t + \alpha k_t + \beta h_t - (1-\gamma)l_t$

where:

y_t = per capita GDP growth
a_t = the rate of growth of technical progress
k_t and h_t = physical and human capital respectively
l_t = the growth rate of unskilled labour.[12]

From Equation 1, it can be seen that growth only depends on technical progress and factor accumulation. Empirical evidence seems to support this conclusion, despite the few works showing that trade flows may enter Equation 1. In particular, Levine and Renelt (1992) show that trade variables are insignificant in their empirical specification of Equation 1. Therefore, the model must be complemented by two other equations explaining factor accumulation (l_t is assumed to be exogenous):

Equation 2 $\qquad k_t = s_0 + s_1 Y_t + s_2 K_t + s_3 \Delta XE_t/Y_t + s_4 \Delta B_t + s_5 \Delta RCA_t + s_6 \Delta FDI_t$
Equation 3 $\qquad h_t = r_0 + r_1 Y_t + r_2 H_t + r_3 \Delta XE_t/Y_t + r_4 \Delta B_t + r_5 \Delta RCA_t + s_6 \Delta FDI_t$

where we account for the standard stock flow law of motion (Baldwin and Venables, 1995) and for possible effects of changes (Δ) of trade creation (XE_t/Y_t), IIT (B_t), international competitiveness (RCA_t) and foreign (EU) direct investments (FDI_t).[13] As explained in

---

[11] Hsiao shows how to implement a time-dependent panel estimation technique.

[12] Notice that data at the regional and sectoral level are available only for y_t, k_t and l_t; a_t is proportional to an indicator of technical progress at country level (see Section 3.4), whereas h_t is proxied by the number of students in and above secondary school age whose observations are available at regional level.

[13] Note that all time series appearing in Equation 2 are available at the regional and sectoral levels, whereas Equation 3 was estimated at the regional level only.

Baldwin and Venables (1995), the rationale of Equations 2 and 3 is that capital accumulation is likely to be pro cyclical (this explains the introduction of Y_t into the equation; in the empirical specification we will also use the rate of change of Y_t) and faster when capital is small (i.e. regions with a low level of capital stocks are likely to grow more rapidly that those with high levels). This argument implicitly embodies the assumption of a technology characterized by decreasing returns. As this may not be the case in some sectors, we did not expect the coefficients r_2 and s_2 to be necessarily negative. The other variables in Equations 2 and 3 capture the impact of trade and factor flow indicators on growth. They are the main indicators described in the previous section. Note that, because of lack of degrees of freedom, we could not consider all indicators. Therefore, we focused on the main ones: trade creation, IIT, RCA and EU investments in the studied regions.

These trade indicators are also endogenous in the model. We assumed the following equations:

Equation 4 $b_{pt} = b_0 + X_t \psi + \rho I_t$ $p = 1,2,3,4,5$

where b_1, b_2, b_3, b_4 denotes trade creation, IIT, international competitiveness and EU FDI respectively; X_t contains proxies for cyclical and globalization effects (the growth rate of employment or of industrial production and world trade growth respectively) and dummies for accession effects (in Germany, Portugal and Spain). In the set of explanatory variables, X_t, we also included the other variables that are used in the descriptive and graphical analysis of the indicators, namely labour productivity, sectoral specialization and capital intensity (the capital/labour ratio). Finally, we also accounted for CSF support in all regions. Notice that all these variables should enable us to disentangle the effects of the SMP (quantified by the parameter ρ) on trade and factor flows, from the effects of cyclical and globalization variables and of variables capturing the specificity of each sector (capital intensity, labour productivity and specialization).

Note that human capital accumulation is proxied by the growth rate of high education labour force, whereas a_t is assumed to be proportional to the growth rate of the technical progress indicator, the measurement of which is explained in Section 3.4 ($a_t = \phi g_t$, $g_t = dT/T$). As in many other empirical studies (such as Mankiw *et al.*, 1992), the dynamics of k_t is captured by the dynamics of the growth rate of investments, whereas l_t is proxied by the growth rate of total labour force (including migrants), from which we have deducted the number of workers with a secondary school degree in order to obtain a proxy of the unskilled labour force.

3.3.2. The panel data approach

The data sample on which the above model has been estimated is formed by two-digit NUTS regional data and two-digit NACE sectoral data for a time horizon ranging from 1985 to 1992. Let i denote regions, j sectors and t the year. A generic equation of our regression model can be written as:

$$z_{ijt} = c_{ij} + x_{ijt}\theta_{ij} + u_{ijt}$$

where:

$i = 1, \ldots, m$
$j = 1, \ldots, n$
$t = 1, \ldots, N$

and where a constant, c_{ij}, has been added to all equations. As each sector is characterized by a specific technology, we dropped index j because the seven equations of the model were estimated for all sectors. Moreover, following Hsia (1987), we assumed that cross-regional parametric differences within a country were defined as a function of the initial level of the dependent variable (a proxy for the initial conditions of the accumulation process) plus an error term, v_i. For example, if the parameter vector, θ_i, were to be put into Equation 1, it would be a function of per capita GDP at the beginning of the sample period, a variable which was also used in Levine and Renelt (1992). Denoting the level (not the growth rate) of the dependent variable at the beginning of the sample period by $Z^\circ i$, then we have:

Equation 5 $z_{it} = cZ^\circ_i + x_{it}(Z^\circ_i\mu + v_i) + u_{it} + v_{ci} = cZ^\circ_i + w_{it}\mu + \varepsilon_{it}$

where:

$w_{it} = x_{it}Z^\circ_i$

$\varepsilon_{it} = u_{it} + x_{it}v_i + v_{ci}$

Equation 5 can be estimated using standard random coefficient panel data techniques (in practice, a modified GLS estimator was used to account for heteroscedasticity; see Hsia, 1987).

The advantages of using a panel approach are well known. First, they give us a sufficiently large number of data points, increasing the degrees of freedom and reducing the collinearity among explanatory variables, hence improving the efficiency of econometric estimates. Second, they make it possible to test whether or not there are structural differences across regions by testing the null hypothesis defined by Equation 5 against the alternative, $z_{it} = c + x_{it}\theta + u_{it}$.

3.3.3. The measurement of technical progress

The basic idea is that the dynamics of technical change cannot be observed, and that traditional approaches, in which technical change is proxied either by a time trend or by the computation of factor productivity indices (chiefly, the rate of change of total factor productivity), yield-biased and inconsistent estimates (Fuller, 1987).[14]

Here we used a latent variable structural equation model that employed data on total expenditures on research from public and private sources, on imports of patents and on business cycle indicators as cause variables for the latent technological variable. The latent variable approach extracts information from indicators and cause variables while being able to

---

[14]   The idea of treating technical change as an unobserved or latent variable is shared by the partial equilibrium approaches of Slade (1989) and Gao (1994), and by the general equilibrium model of Boone *et al.* (1992).

avoid using them as exact representations of technological change. The goal is to minimize measurement errors and thus the inconsistency of the estimation procedure.

In order to achieve this goal, we assumed that the capital stock is composed of two components: a new efficiency improving capital stock and the old one. Each year a new vintage of capital becomes operational. In this way, new capital is added to the two components. The characteristics of this new capital depend on a number of economic variables which affect the firms' decision to instal the more efficient capital (such as factor prices).

Let K be the capital stock and K_n and K_o the new, efficiency improving and the old capital stocks, respectively. By definition, $K = K_n + K_o$, which implies:

Equation 6 $k = k_o + (k_n - k_o)(K_n/K)$

where k, k_n and k_o are the growth rates of the overall new and old capital stocks respectively.

Suppose that:

Equation 7 $k_n - k_o = f(x)/(K_n/K) + \varepsilon$

where $f(x)$ is the capital growth rate in the long run, when all efficiency improving technological possibilities have actually been implemented, i.e. when $K_n = K$ and $k_o = 0$; x is a set of explanatory variables and ε is a stochastic error. The implicit assumption here is that diffusion of technical progress takes place at decreasing rates of growth. Finally, the following equation defines the dynamics of the old, traditional component of the capital stock:

Equation 8 $k_o = h(W,v)$

where W is a set of explanatory variables and v is a stochastic error term. In particular, the explanatory variables include R&D spending, output demand, factor prices and the number of imported patents. Everything else being equal, it is likely that more R&D spending increases the technological possibilities of the economic system, thereby inducing investment in efficiency-improving capital, which replaces investment in old capital. Similarly, higher energy or labour prices may induce firms to increase investments in factor-saving technologies.

Equations 6, 7 and 8 define the structure of the latent variable model. As k_n and k_o are not observable, they must be estimated by filtering the information contained in the observable variables. To do that, let us rewrite Equations 6-8 in a state space form as follows:

Equation 9a $k = Hs + \varepsilon$
Equation 9b $s = Fs(-1) + v$

where s is the state space vector, which contains the unobservable variable k_o and the parameter vectors β and δ associated with the variable vectors x and W respectively. More precisely:

$$H = [1 \ x \ 0], \quad s = \begin{bmatrix} k_0 \\ \beta \\ \delta \end{bmatrix} \qquad F = \begin{bmatrix} m & 0 & w \\ 0 & 1 & 0 \\ 0 & 0 & 1 \end{bmatrix}$$

The matrix H is called output matrix, while the matrix F is the transition matrix of the state space form of the model containing the parameters, which captures the adjustment speed of the components of the capital stock, the variable vector and the zeros and ones necessary to reproduce the identities concerning all time invariant coefficients. The error terms ε and v are assumed to be normally distributed and serially uncorrelated.

The state space form was estimated using the square root Kalman and information filters described by Carraro (1988). The covariance matrix of the error terms ε and v have been estimated using the maximum likelihood method. The initial values for the state vector has been estimated using the GLS procedure proposed in Carraro (1985). The results of our estimates of the state space transition matrix F, the output matrix H and of the state vector s (in particular, the vector δ) showed that the filtering procedure we used to decompose the capital stock yielded homogeneous results across different EU countries.

For example, the parameters of the vector δ reflecting the impact on the growth rate of the old capital stock induced by domestic R&D expenditures and by imported patents were negative and about -0.022 and -0.021 in all EU countries (the EU averages were -0.0226 and -0.0217). Moreover, the impact of output growth on the same growth rate ranged from 0.209 to 0.210 in all EU countries. Some differences were found in the speed of adjustment coefficient m of the composition of the capital stock to the desired value (the only unknown parameter in matrix F), and in the autonomous change of the growth rate of the old capital stock (the constant in the vector W).

The speed of adjustment ranged from 0.726 in France to 0.924 in Denmark and Ireland. The EU average was 0.768. The autonomous change of the growth rate of the old capital stock was higher (in absolute value) in Greece, Spain and Ireland, i.e. in the less developed European countries (values in these countries were -0.0082, -0.0044 and -0.0082 respectively). This implies that in less developed countries, the old capital stock has been replaced more quickly than in developed countries. By contrast, as more developed countries have already implemented a large number of efficiency improving technologies, the substitution between the two components of the capital stock has taken place more slowly in such countries (the best examples being Germany and the UK where the parameter values for the autonomous change were -0.0017 and -0.0012 respectively).

As expected, domestic R&D and imported patents reduced the growth rate of the old capital stock, which was therefore replaced by the new one. By contrast, when output grew, both types of capital stock grew. Finally, the speed of adjustment was quite high in all countries, thus showing little sluggishness in technological innovation.

Given the above results, the dynamics of the two time series K_n and K_o were reconstructed (notice that the method is close to the one used to decompose a time series into cyclical and seasonal components; see Harvey, 1987). Then, an indicator of technical change was provided by the ratio $T = K_n/K_o$. The average growth rate of this indicator ($g_t = dT/T$) was fairly low in the developed countries of the EU (about 2% in Germany, France and Italy, slightly lower in the UK), whereas it was much higher in the less developed countries (from 9% in Ireland to 30% in Greece). In all countries, the growth rate of the technical progress indicator became lower as the country grew (because the model objective is to capture the implementation of best available technologies in the short and medium run). Note that our indicator of technical progress was determined at the aggregate country level and thus did not differ across sectors or regions. Even with this limit (and others), it can still be considered a better proxy of technical progress than a deterministic trend or measures of R&D expenditure.

3.3.4.　Co-integration and aggregation

The time series appearing in Equations 1 to 4 may be co-integrated (usually $I(1)$). As previously stated, this could seriously distort the conclusion of our analysis. At worst, we could identify an entirely spurious relationship. At best, we could consistently estimate the elements of some co-integrating vector. As standard asymptotic theory does not apply, this could have led us to make incorrect inferences about the parameters that we estimated.

The classical approach to dealing with co-integrated variables, especially in the time series literature, has been to difference them as many times as needed to make them stationary. This is a quite simple solution. However, the problem with it is that differencing eliminates the opportunity to estimate the original relationships between the levels of the variables. Moreover, the general case is the one in which only a subset of the variables is co-integrated. Then, differencing the variables certainly modifies the model specification.

Therefore, more sophisticated approaches have been proposed (chiefly the two-step procedure by Engle and Granger, 1987, and the three-step procedure by Engle and Yoo, 1991). Engle and Granger estimated the following ECM:

Equation 10　　$\Delta z_{it} = cZ^{\circ}_i + w^{\circ}_{it}\mu^{\circ} + \chi(z_{it} - q_{it}\theta^{\circ}) + \Delta q_{it}\eta + \varepsilon_{it}$

where $w_{it} = [w^{\circ}_{it}\ q_{it}]$ and q_{it} is the vector of co-integrated variables, whereas w°_{it} includes either non-stochastic variables or $I(0)$. Then, a preliminary regression of z_{it} on q_{it} plus a constant term is used to identify θ° (estimates are super-consistent). Then, a second regression is used to identify the parameters of (10) where θ° is replaced by its first step estimate.

There is, however, a simple alternative to this approach. Sims, Stocka and Watson (1990) show that a correct inference on the parameters of a linear regression involving $I(1)$ variables can be obtained if the parameters can be written as the coefficient of an $I(0)$ variable with zero mean. As shown by Davidson and McKinnon (1993), this condition is satisfied by the parameter χ, η and $\lambda = -\chi\theta^{\circ}$ of the following regression:

Equation 11　　$\Delta z_{it} = cZ^{\circ}_i + w^{\circ}_{it}\mu^{\circ} + \chi z_{it} + q_{it}\lambda + \Delta q_{it}\eta + \varepsilon_{it}$

Therefore, if the analysis focuses on χ, η and λ, a simple one-step procedure can be used to estimate the parameters of Equations 1 to 4 even when time series are $I(1)$. In the actual regression analysis described below we will try both the one-step (just described) and the two-step approaches proposed by Engle and Granger (1987) in order to choose the most effective method (given the constraints in terms of data availability).

Aggregation and co-integration are also related problems. The panel data sample at our disposal is not formed by individual micro data at the firm level, but, rather, by aggregate micro data. In this case, if the micro time series are *I(1)*, Pesaran and Smith (1995) show that GLS estimators no longer provide consistent estimates of parameters of the aggregate sectoral model. There is, however, an exception to this negative conclusion. As shown by Hall and Urga (1995), if explanatory variables at the micro level are characterized by a common trend, then valid inference can still be obtained at the sectoral level. This is, therefore, the assumption that we used in the sequel.

3.3.5. Instrumental variables

Another important problem to be solved when tackling the estimation of Equations 1-4 is the presence of endogenous explanatory variables, which generally leads standard GLS techniques to yield inconsistent estimates (because of the so-called simultaneity bias). This problem can easily be solved by using an instrumental variables technique. The instrumental variable estimator must be designed in order to account for heteroscedasticity (as shown above), for structural changes of the parameters, and for co-integration. Beyond these technicalities, the real problem is the determination of adequate instrumental variables. Here we assumed that appropriate instruments could be found among lagged explanatory variables. This solution is certainly inefficient. However, again we need to account for the constraints on the data set. The time series available both at regional and sectoral level are quite limited and are used in Equations 1-4 either as endogenous or exogenous variables. Therefore, instruments other than lagged variables can hardly be found.

3.3.6. Structural breaks and time-dependent parameters

There is a last and important problem to be discussed. Equations 1-4 can hardly be considered structural equations where free parameters only are included – Equation 1 because of the specification given to technical progress, Equations 2 and 3 because they include, in an *ad hoc* fashion, measures of trade creation, IIT, international competitiveness, business cycles and globalization, Equation 4 because they are reduced forms. Therefore, as previously discussed, they are more a way of quantifying correlations among variables than a way of estimating behavioural parameters. As a consequence, we cannot expect parameters to be invariant to policy regime changes. Therefore, a policy change, such as the introduction of the SMP, is likely to introduce a structural break of the parameters. This break cannot be assumed to have taken place in 1987 for two reasons: the SMP has been implemented slowly, and the expectation of the implementation of the SMP may have modified behavioural rules in the period pre-1987. Therefore, we have constructed an index of the SMP implementation on the basis of the number and type of SMP directives implemented in each sector. This index is used to explain the variability over time of the model parameters (alternatively, expected values of this index can be used). As stressed in Hsia (1987), this is the best way of capturing parameter time variability without losing too many degrees of freedom. Let I_t be our index of SMP implementation in each country. Moreover, let the parameters c, χ, η and λ of Equation 11 be time-varying. Their dynamics are assumed to be described as follows:

Equation 12a $\quad c_t = c_0 + c_1 I_t + c_2 CSF_i + u_{1t}$

Equation 12b $\quad \chi_t = \chi I_t + u_{2t}$

Equation 12c $\quad \eta_t = \eta I_t + u_{3t}$

Equation 12d $\quad \lambda_t = \lambda I_t + u_{4t}$

Therefore, Equation 11 becomes:

Equation 13 $\Delta z_{it} = c_0 Z^{\circ}_i + c_1 I_t Z^{\circ}_i + c_2 CSF_i Z^{\circ}_i + w^{\circ}_{it} \mu^{\circ} + \chi I_t z_{it} + I_t q_{it} \lambda + I_t \Delta q_{it} \eta + \varepsilon^{\circ}_{it}$

where:

$\varepsilon^{\circ}_{it} = \varepsilon_{it} + Z^{\circ}_i u_{1t} + z_{it} u_{2t} + q_{it} u_{4t} + \Delta q_{it} u_{3t}$

Note that we account for both time and regional breaks in the constant c. What seems to us important is to verify whether cohesion structural funds modified the industrial structure in the studied region. This is why regional differences related to the amount of structural funds in a given region are considered in Equation 13. This equation can be consistently estimated using a generalized *IV* estimator (see Hsia, 1987; Chow, 1983), which takes into account the additional heteroscedasticity introduced by the error terms u_{it}, $i=1, 2, 3, 4$.

3.3.7. The *antimonde*

It is now possible to understand how the *antimonde* necessary to assess the impact of the SMP can be defined. Suppose no SMP was implemented in 1987. Then, from 1987 to 1993, we would have I_t equal to *1* and the model parameters would be constant over time. Moreover, the dynamics of trade and factor flow indicators (Equation 4) would not be affected by the SMP measures, thus inducing different dynamics of factor accumulation and of GDP growth. Therefore, we are able to account for the effects of no SMP both on the model variables (trade indicators and hence factor accumulation) and on the model parameters (which are no longer subject to changes over time).

Following Baldwin and Venables' (1995) guidelines, the *antimonde* thus constructed enabled us to compare actual data on the main economic variables (influenced by the SMP) with simulated observations in which the effects of the SMP were neutralized. The differences between the actual and simulated values (where business cycles and globalization effects have also been accounted for) determined the relative impact of the SMP on trade, factor accumulation and growth.

3.3.8. Convergence analysis

The last issue to be addressed by our regression analysis was the convergence issue. Is growth in the EU peripheral regions, as measured by the equations described above, such as to lead these economies to converge to the average European growth level? Did the SMP provide a positive boost to the convergence path, that is, did the SMP accelerate convergence?

To answer these questions, we first of all selected a convergence criterion. There is a wide debate in the economic literature (see Barro and Sala-i-Martin, 1992; de la Fuente, 1995a) on the merits of alternative definitions of convergence (β convergence, σ convergence, conditional versus unconditional convergence).[15] As far as this work is concerned, it seemed appropriate to select β rather than σ convergence as the criterion to be used to study convergence. The reasons can be summarized as follows:

(a) σ convergence, in which a regression is designed in order to identify whether or not and why the (root of the) variance (σ) of per capita income of a group of regions becomes

---

[15]   A formal comparison of different definitions of convergence is provided in Sala-i-Martin (1994).

smaller and smaller is probably the concept closest to the intuitive motion of convergence; moreover, β convergence, the alternative concept proposed in the literature, is only a necessary, but not sufficient condition for σ convergence (Friedman, 1992; Quah, 1993; Sala-i-Martin, 1994); however, for an appropriate analysis of σ convergence, much longer time series should be available. Moreover, the variability of per capita income among both the 44 regions considered in this review[16] and all the other EU regions should be accounted for.

(b)   β convergence has been designed to understand whether or not poorer countries tend to catch up with richer ones (Sala-i-Martin, 1994). This is indeed one of the two crucial pieces of information we would like to provide, that is, whether or not peripheral EU regions are catching up with the most developed EU regions. The second crucial piece of information is whether or not the implementation of the SMP helped the convergence process. Again, β convergence seems to be more appropriate than σ convergence as it can be analysed simply by using a cross-section of regions.[17]

Our methodological approach to the study of convergence therefore paralleled the one proposed by Barro (1991), Barro and Sala-i-Martin (1992) and used by Levine and Renelt (1992). First, as stated above, we considered the cross-section defined by the 44 regions analysed in this review. Second, we ran the following regression (see Levine and Renelt, 1992; Baldwin and Venables, 1995):

Equation 14 $(y_j - l_j)_{avg} = cost_j + \alpha INV_{j,avg} - \beta RGDP_{j.85} + \gamma GPO_{j,avg} - \delta SEC_{j,8}$
$+ \varphi TECH_{j,avg} + \theta DUMMIES_j + u_j$

where *INV*, *GPO*, *SEC*, *RGDP* and *TECH* are, respectively, the average (1987-92) investment to GDP ratio, the average population growth, the 1985 secondary enrolment rate, the 1985 GDP per capita, and the average indicator of technical progress described in Section 3.3. The dependent variable is the average growth rate of per capita income in region *j*. Notice that the introduction of the initial values for GDP and the enrolment rate implies that we are going to analyse conditional β convergence (as opposed to absolute convergence; see Sala-i-Martin, 1994)

As explained in Baldwin and Venables (1995), Equation 14, which is similar to the standard Barro-type equation, can be rationalized in terms of Lucas' (1988) endogenous growth model, where *SEC* is a proxy for human capital With respect to the specification used in Levine and Renelt (1992), we introduced into Equation 14 an indicator of technical progress to account for the remarks on omitted variables contained in Baldwin and Venables (1995), and a few dummies to capture accession effects.

As is well known, a positive value of β provides evidence that convergence is taking place among the studied regions and the EU average. Moreover, the speed of convergence increases with β. Alternatively, the engine of convergence may be human capital (as in Lucas' (1988)

---

[16]   The regions analysed are 4 in Spain, 8 in Italy, 13 in Greece, 5 in Portugal and Ireland (treated as a single region).

[17]   A good explanation of why β convergence may be more informative than σ convergence is contained in Sala-i-Martin (1994).

model and as suggested by Barro's (1991) results). In this case, the value of δ would be positive.

In order to verify whether or not the SMP had a positive impact on convergence, we considered the following regression:

Equation 15
$$(y^*_j - l^*_j)_{avg} = cost^*_j + \alpha^* INV^*_{j,avg} - \beta^* RGDP_{j,85} + \gamma^* GPO_{j,avg}$$
$$- \delta^* SEC_{j,85} + \varphi^* TECH_{j,avg} + \theta^* DUMMIES_j + v_j$$

where the dependent variable is the *antimonde* relative per capita income derived from the simulation described in Section 3.7. Note that we also consider the impact of the SMP on the explanatory variables. This is why the value of the investment/GDP ratio is also derived from the *antimonde* regression equations. However, we assumed that the effect of the SMP on technical progress would not to be significant.

The difference between Equations 14 and 15 leaves us with:

Equation 16
$$IM_{j,avg} = cost°_j + (\alpha-\alpha^*)INV_{j,avg} - (\beta-\beta^*)RGDP_{j,85} + (\gamma-\gamma^*)GPO_{j,avg}$$
$$- (\delta-\delta^*)SEC_{j,85} + (\varphi-\varphi^*)TECH_{j,avg} + (\theta-\theta^*)DUMMIES_j +$$
$$\alpha^*(INV_{j,avg} - INV^*_{j,avg}) + \eta_j$$

where the dependent variable is defined as the difference between the actual average relative rate of growth in per capita income and the average *antimonde* rate of growth determined as explained in Section 3.3.7.

The null hypothesis is that the coefficient $\pi_1 \equiv \beta-\beta^*$ (and/or $\pi_2 \equiv \delta-\delta^*$) is statistically significant and positive. This hypothesis can easily be tested using standard inference techniques.

Summing up, the convergence analysis was aimed at testing two hypotheses, which reflect the basic questions raised at the beginning of this section:

- H^1_0: $\beta > 0$ and/or $\delta > 0$;
- H^2_0: $\pi_1 < 0$ and/or $\pi_2 < 0$

Note that the above tests were performed for all sectors considered in this study.

We are certainly aware of the limits of the regression approach to the analysis of convergence. The usual criticisms refer to the possibility of omitting relevant variables, the *ad hoc* nature of the regression which can lead to the discovery of correlations rather than causality effects, the sample size, which may be too small, etc. However, we believe that the regressions described in this section are a complement to the analysis proposed in the previous sections. This complement helps us in summarizing information and makes explicit some of the correlations among the crucial variables covered in our study.

3.4.   The trade liberalization index

Our purpose in this section is to show how we constructed an index of trade liberalization that we included in the regressions for the econometric analysis of the impact of the SMP.

Generally, in analysing the impact of a policy change, the most common approach has been to incorporate a dummy in the regression analysis that takes the value of 0 (respectively, 1) before (respectively, after) the policy change. For our purposes this approach has two important disadvantages:

(a) the policy changes associated with the SMP consisted of a large set of measures, of differing importance for trade and factor flows or for growth, that were implemented gradually over time between 1985 and 1993, so the measure of trade liberalization must also change gradually (increase) over time;

(b) the policy changes were introduced at different times in the various EU countries; so, however, we decide to measure the extent of trade liberalization for the purposes of econometric analysis, and the measure must be different for each country.

In the present review an attempt is made to overcome these two disadvantages by constructing an index of trade liberalization that:

(a) increased gradually over time;

(b) was unique to each of the six countries under investigation.

The index we constructed was based on the yearly rate at which the policy changes associated with the SMP were introduced in each country.

Any index such as this, based on the actual introduction of policy changes, does not take into account the economic effects of the *expectations* concerning these policy changes. However, there are good reasons to believe that economic agents' actions were not much affected by expectations of the SMP measures, mainly due to the uncertainty associated with the following:

(a) Political factors specific to each country made things very uncertain and it was difficult to obtain precise information about the date of introduction of each specific measure in different countries. This is important, especially when combined with the fact that economic agents would act on the basis of information about implementation in other countries rather than just in their own.

(b) Even more importantly, perhaps, rarely has the introduction of the SMP measures been associated with actual enforcement and it is the very uncertain information about the time of enforcement that is pertinent if we want to make predictions concerning the SMP's effects on economic agents' behaviour.

The various categories of measures associated with the SMP are listed in Table 3.3. We have obtained information on the year each measure in Table 3.3 was introduced in each of the six countries under investigation.

Consider now the value of the trade liberalization index for country j in year t, LI_t^j. Let:

$\overline{m}_{it}^j$ = the number of measures of type i introduced up to year t in country j,

k = the total number of SMP measures,

$\overline{M}_i^j$ = the total number of measures of type i introduced in country j between 1985 and 1993,

w_i = the weight given to measures of type i.

Then, very generally:

$$LI_t^j = \sum_{i=1}^{k} w_i \frac{\overline{m}_{it}^j}{\overline{M}_i^j}$$

where:

$$\sum_{i=1}^{k} w_i = 1$$

However, examination of Table 3.3 reveals that it is possible to simplify this without damaging its interpretative value significantly. Two factors point to the need to simplify and to the types of simplification that we needed to, and did, undertake:

(a)   Clearly there are measures that seem particularly unimportant in terms of their implications for trade and factor flows and thus can be excluded from further consideration. In relation to this we decided to exclude measures 1.2 and 1.3.

(b)   It is impossible to assign relative weights to each one of the measures under each of the main categories of the SMP measures in Table 3.3, other than in a very arbitrary way – some aggregation of measures is required – so we aggregated the measures in subcategories 2.1, 2.4 and 2.6.

Following these two simplifications, we have constructed, for each country, tables indicating the number of measures in each subcategory introduced between 1985 and 1993. These are Tables 3.4 to 3.9. To construct the trade liberalization index for each country we used the *total* in each (of the three) categories indicated in these tables. Thus we let:

m_{it}^j = the total number of measures in category i - i = 1, 2, 3 introduced up to year t in country j;

M_i^j = the total number of measures in category i introduced between 1985 and 1993 in country j.

Thus:

$$LI_t^j = \sum_{i=1}^{3} w_i \frac{m_{it}^j}{M_i^j}$$

where: $\sum_{i=1}^{3} w_i = 1$

Concerning the weights, it is clear that category 2 is far more important than either categories 1 or 3. Given this, we, with some degree of arbitrariness, decided to use the values $w_2 = 0.6$ and $w_1 = w_3 = 0.2$. This of course means that, all other things being equal, if country j has introduced up to year t more measures in category 2 than another country that has introduced up to year t more measures in either of the other two categories, then country j will have a higher LI_t value than the other country.

Given these assumptions, we calculated the index 100 * *LI* for each country on the basis of the above formula. The results, normalized to the value of 1 for 1985, are shown in Table 3.10 (except for Portugal, which introduced no measures prior to 1986).

Table 3.3.   SMP measures

1. Abolition of physical barriers

1.1. Goods inspections
1.2. Veterinary inspection
      1.2.1. Animal health
      1.2.2. Public health
      1.2.3. Public and animal health
      1.2.4. Zootechny
1.3. Phytosanitary inspection
1.4. Persons' inspection

2. Abolition of technical barriers

2.1. Normalization
      2.1.1. New approach to harmonization
      2.1.2. Motor vehicles
      2.1.3. Agricultural machines
      2.1.4. Food products
      2.1.5. Pharmaceutical products
      2.1.6. Chemical products
      2.1.7. Construction
      2.1.8. Other sectors
2.2. Public calls for tender
2.3. Free circulation of dependent workers and self-employed persons
2.4. Common market of services
      2.4.1. Banks
      2.4.2. Insurances
      2.4.3. Market of movable values
      2.4.4. Transport services
      2.4.5. New technology and services
2.5. Capital flows
2.6. Cooperation among enterprises
      2.6.1. Society law
      2.6.2. Intellectual ownership
      2.6.3. Fiscal status of enterprises
      2.6.4. Competition
      2.6.5. Single energy market

3. Abolition of fiscal barriers

3.1. Value added tax
3.2. Production taxes

Source: 'Misure nazionale di recepimento' per l'applicazione del Libro Bianco della CEC sul completamento del mercato interno' (updated to 31 October 1993).

Table 3.4.   Trade and factor liberalization measures for Germany

Measures	1985	1986	1987	1988	1989	1990	1991	1992	1993	Total
1.1	5	3	1	2	2	1	4	3	0	21
1.4	0	0	0	1	2	1	1	0	0	5
Total 1	**5**	**3**	**1**	**3**	**4**	**2**	**5**	**3**	**0**	**26**
2.1 (total)	0	1	5	5	7	18	8	17	4	65
2.2	0	0	0	0	0	0	0	0	0	0
2.3	0	0	0	0	4	1	0	3	0	8
2.4 (total)	0	4	1	1	· 3	9	2	12	2	2
2.5	0	0	0	0	0	0	0	0	0	0
2.6 (total)	3	0	1	0	2	0	3	2	3	14
Total 2	**3**	**5**	**7**	**6**	**16**	**28**	**13**	**32**	**9**	**119**
3.1	1	0	0	0	0	1	0	3	0	5
3.2	0	0	0	0	0	0	0	9	0	9
Total 3	**1**	**0**	**0**	**0**	**0**	**1**	**0**	**12**	**0**	**14**
Grand total	**9**	**8**	**8**	**9**	**20**	**31**	**18**	**47**	**9**	
Cumulative total	**9**	**17**	**25**	**34**	**54**	**85**	**103**	**150**	**159**	

Table 3.5.   Trade and factor liberalization measures for Spain

Measures	1985	1986	1987	1988	1989	1990	1991	1992	1993	Total
1.1	0	7	2	1	2	1	6	3	0	22
1.4	0	0	0	1	2	1	1	0	1	6
Total 1	**0**	**7**	**2**	**2**	**4**	**2**	**7**	**3**	**1**	**28**
2.1 (total)	0	1	2	5	19	7	20	18	10	82
2.2	1	0	0	0	0	0	1	0	0	2
2.3	0	1	0	0	0	0	0	5	6	12
2.4 (total)	0	3	2	1	1	8	8	8	3	34
2.5	0	0	0	0	0	0	0	1	0	1
2.6 (total)	0	0	0	3	8	0	1	2	0	14
Total 2	**1**	**5**	**4**	**9**	**28**	**15**	**30**	**34**	**19**	**145**
3.1	1	0	1	0	0	0	1	1	3	7
3.2	0	0	0	0	0	0	0	7	2	9
Total 3	**1**	**0**	**1**	**0**	**0**	**0**	**1**	**8**	**5**	**16**
Grand total	**2**	**12**	**7**	**11**	**32**	**17**	**38**	**45**	**25**	
Cumulative total	**2**	**14**	**21**	**32**	**64**	**81**	**119**	**164**	**189**	

Table 3.6.   Trade and factor liberalization measures for Greece

Measures	1985	1986	1987	1988	1989	1990	1991	1992	1993	Total
1.1	4	3	1	3	2	1	3	3	0	21
1.4	0	0	1	0	1	1	1	0	0	4
Total 1	**4**	**3**	**2**	**3**	**3**	**2**	**4**	**3**	**0**	**24**
2.1 (total)	2	2	7	6	1	13	21	24	2	78
2.2	0	0	0	0	0	0	0	0	2	2
2.3	0	0	0	2	0	1	2	4	3	12
2.4 (total)	0	3	1	1	0	5	4	13	0	27
2.5	0	0	0	0	0	1	0	0	0	1
2.6 (total)	0	3	2	0	2	1	2	4	1	15
Total 2	**2**	**8**	**10**	**9**	**3**	**21**	**28**	**43**	**8**	**132**
3.1	0	1	1	0	0	1	0	3	0	6
3.2	0	0	0	0	0	0	0	4	5	9
Total 3	**0**	**1**	**1**	**0**	**0**	**1**	**0**	**7**	**5**	**15**
Grand total	**6**	**12**	**13**	**12**	**6**	**24**	**32**	**53**	**13**	
Cumulative total	**6**	**18**	**31**	**43**	**49**	**73**	**105**	**158**	**171**	

Table 3.7.   Trade and factor liberalization measures for Italy

Measures	1985	1986	1987	1988	1989	1990	1991	1992	1993	Total
1.1	4	3	1	3	2	1	3	3	0	20
1.4	0	0	0	0	0	0	3	3	1	7
Total 1	**4**	**3**	**1**	**3**	**2**	**1**	**6**	**6**	**1**	**27**
2.1 (total)	0	1	1	10	4	4	13	36	9	78
2.2	0	0	0	0	0	0	1	2	0	3
2.3	0	0	0	0	0	0	5	5	0	10
2.4 (total)	0	3	1	1	1	3	7	18	3	37
2.5	0	0	0	0	0	1	0	0	0	1
2.6 (total)	0	1	0	0	2	0	4	5	5	17
Total 2	**0**	**5**	**2**	**11**	**7**	**8**	**30**	**64**	**17**	**144**
3.1	1	0	0	0	0	0	2	1	3	7
3.2	0	0	0	0	0	0	0	9	0	9
Total 3	**1**	**0**	**0**	**0**	**0**	**0**	**2**	**10**	**3**	**16**
Grand total	**5**	**8**	**3**	**14**	**9**	**9**	**38**	**80**	**21**	
Cumulative total	**5**	**13**	**16**	**30**	**39**	**48**	**86**	**166**	**187**	

Table 3.8.   Trade and factor liberalization measures for Ireland

Measures	1985	1986	1987	1988	1989	1990	1991	1992	1993	Total
1.1	4	4	2	3	2	1	3	4	1	24
1.4	0	0	0	0	3	0	1	0	0	4
Total 1	**4**	**4**	**2**	**3**	**5**	**1**	**4**	**4**	**1**	**28**
2.1 (total)	0	1	1	8	9	6	19	20	4	68
2.2	0	0	0	0	0	0	0	3	3	6
2.3	0	0	4	0	1	0	1	1	3	10
2.4 (total)	0	3	1	1	2	4	9	15	0	35
2.5	0	0	0	0	0	1	0	0	0	1
2.6 (total)	0	1	2	1	2	0	3	4	1	14
Total 2	**0**	**5**	**8**	**10**	**14**	**11**	**30**	**24**	**11**	**131**
3.1	0	1	0	0	0	0	0	4	1	6
3.2	0	0	0	0	0	0	0	6	1	7
Total 3	**0**	**1**	**0**	**0**	**0**	**0**	**0**	**10**	**2**	**13**
Grand total	**4**	**10**	**10**	**13**	**19**	**12**	**34**	**56**	**14**	
Cumulative total	**4**	**14**	**24**	**37**	**56**	**68**	**102**	**158**	**172**	

Table 3.9.   Trade and factor liberalization measures for Portugal

Measures	1985	1986	1987	1988	1989	1990	1991	1992	1993	Total
1.1	0	7	1	1	3	3	3	3	0	21
1.4	0	0	0	0	2	0	1	2	0	5
Total 1	**0**	**7**	**1**	**1**	**5**	**3**	**4**	**5**	**0**	**26**
2.1 (total)	0	1	1	3	5	17	9	33	12	81
2.2	0	0	0	0	0	1	1	1	0	3
2.3	0	0	0	2	2	0	1	2	4	11
2.4 (total)	0	3	1	2	1	7	9	13	0	36
2.5	0	0	0	0	0	0	0	0	1	1
2.6 (total)	0	4	1	0	4	0	1	4	2	16
Total 2	**0**	**8**	**3**	**7**	**12**	**25**	**21**	**48**	**18**	**142**
3.1	0	0	1	0	0	1	0	2	0	4
3.2	0	0	0	0	0	0	0	5	4	9
Total 3	**0**	**0**	**1**	**0**	**0**	**1**	**0**	**7**	**4**	**13**
Grand total	**0**	**15**	**5**	**8**	**17**	**29**	**25**	**60**	**22**	
Cumulative total	**0**	**15**	**20**	**28**	**45**	**74**	**99**	**159**	**181**	

Table 3.10.   The values of the trade liberalization index for all six countries studied in this review

	1985	1986	1987	1988	1989	1990	1991	1992	1993
Germany	1.00	1.71	2.34	3.13	4.77	7.29	8.82	14.06	14.73
Spain	1.00	5.25	7.85	10.95	19.63	24.22	35.44	51.19	60.10
Greece	1.00	2.76	4.54	6.09	7.00	9.96	13.75	21.14	23.57
Italy	1.00	2.02	2.40	4.01	5.05	6.02	10.64	20.99	23.74
Ireland	1.00	3.34	5.12	7.48	10.97	12.98	18.79	31.91	35.00
Portugal	0.00	1.00	1.41	1.83	2.85	4.49	5.86	9.84	11.41

4. Empirical analyses of the less developed regions of the European Union

Explanatory note[18] regarding sectoral data coverage in the country reports

As mentioned earlier, the methodology used for each country report presented in this chapter is based on the two-fold approach of:

(a)   qualitative indicator analysis;
(b)   regression analysis.

The objective was to undertake both of these types of analysis using regional (NUTS 2) data covering all NACE two-digit manufacturing sectors. As mentioned before, it was not possible to obtain these regional data for all the countries we studied and, in particular, such data for trade had to be estimated for Greece and Portugal. In this note we explain the situation concerning the sectoral coverage achieved in the country reports.

Sectoral data coverage differs across countries. Thus, using as a base the NACE 70 classification, containing 20 sectors (shown in Table 4.3.2), data for almost all the sectors contained in this classification could be found only for Spain, while for Greece and Ireland 15 sectors could be covered (see Tables 4.3.4 and 4.1.2 respectively), and for Portugal 11 sectors could be covered (see Table 4.4.27). For Italy, emphasis was given to the fact that it was the only country for which good regional data could be obtained for all less developed regions of the country. This meant that some compromise had to be made with respect to sectoral coverage. Thus, for Italy, data for only 11 sectors could be obtained, and these were for the (somewhat different) NACE R44 classification (see Table 4.2.3). Thus, the indicator analysis for each country proceeded based on the (different) lists of sectors for which data could be obtained for each country.

Concerning the regression analysis, however, the need for homogeneity meant that the least common denominator had to be used, and this was given by the sectoral classification used in the indicator analysis of Italy. This, of course, implies that for all countries other than Italy, the sectoral coverage in the regression analysis was different (much more restricted) than the sectoral coverage achieved in the indicator analysis of that country. Only a limited number of sectors were covered in both the indicator *and* the regression analysis of each of these countries, as shown in detail in the table that follows.

---

[18]   This note does not concern the special case of the region of East Germany.

Table 4.1.1. The correspondence between the different kinds of industrial classifications adopted for the indicator analysis for each country and the classification (TPFF classes) used for all countries in the regression analysis[1]

The 'final' classification (TPFF) adopted in the regression analysis	How the TPFF classification has been constructed using the NACE R44 branches. This aggregation was used for the indicator analysis for Italy	The correspondence between the NACE 44 and the NACE 70 classifications used to reproduce the TPFF classification. This NACE 70 aggregation was used for the indicator analysis for Spain	The NACE 70 branches used in the indicator analysis for Ireland and the correspondence adopted for the TPFF classification	The NACE 70 aggregation that was used for the indicator analysis for Greece	The NACE-CLIO RR17 classification that was used for the indicator analysis for Portugal, which is the same as the TPFF classification
TPFF classes	NACE R44 branches	NACE 70 branches	NACE 70 branches	NACE 70 branches	NACE RR17 classes
Agriculture	1				01
Energy products	03+05+07+09+11				06
Metal minerals	13	2200	2200	2200	13
Non-metal minerals	15	2300+2400	2400	2300+2400	15
Chemical products	17	2500+2600	2500	2500	17
Metal products	19+21+23+25	3100+3200+3300+3400+3700	3100+3200+3300+3400+3700	3100+3200+3300+3400	24
Transportation equipment	27+29	3500+3600	3500+3600	3500	28
Food, beverages and tobacco	31+33+35+37+39	4100	4100	4100	36
Textiles and clothing	41+43	4300+4400+4500	4300+4400+4500	4300+4400+4500	42
Paper products	47	4700	4700	4700	47
Wood and rubber	45+49+51	4600+4800+4900	4600+4800	4600+4800+4900	50

[1] Note that for Spain, Ireland and Greece (the third, fourth and fifth columns respectively) the indicator analysis covers separately all sectors for which a code number is shown. For example, the Spanish indicator analysis covers sectors 2300 and 2400 separately.

4.1. Ireland

Fitzpatrick Associates, Dublin

4.1.1. Background

Integration and convergence

Economic integration is not a new phenomenon for Ireland. As a political and economic part of the United Kingdom since 1801, Ireland fully participated in Britain's move towards free trade after 1846. Over subsequent decades, Irish nationalists blamed free trade with Britain for Ireland's industrial decline in the nineteenth century, and a policy of protectionism seemed likely when the Independent Irish State was founded in 1922. However, free trade was maintained throughout the 1920s. In 1932, the country switched to severe protectionism, with an attempt being made to industrialize based on import substitution. This stemmed from a mix of both domestic policy and the international policy drift of the period. The policy seemed to work in the 1930s and continued, because of necessity, through World War Two, but the country stagnated in the 1950s. This was at a time when the rest of Europe was enjoying a GATT-led boom.

In 1958, coincidentally the year of the Treaty of Rome, a new, outward-looking policy was initiated. This began a period of Irish trade policy that laid the basis for all that has followed since – free trade with the UK in 1965, GATT entry in 1966, EC entry in 1973 and now impending EMU membership in 1999.

Steps were taken to encourage inward investment and expose the economy to international competition. Ireland entered the Anglo-Irish Free Trade Area with the UK in 1966. This was significant since it meant Ireland had free trade (and general close 'single market'-type links) to its major trade partner for many years. Both countries joined the EEC in 1973. Those industries – typically traditional domestic-oriented consumer goods industries, operating on an inefficiently small scale – that had been built up in the 1930s came under severe pressure during this period and subsequently. Indeed, the future of such industries is still a key issue in Irish industrial policy today and their needs are dominating the debate on EMU. Irish trade policy is, in many ways, a case of 'plus ça change, plus c'est la même chose'. None the less, the 1960s and early 1970s were Ireland's most economically successful years since independence: economic growth accelerated and emigration came to a halt for the first time since the Famine of the late 1840s. Indeed, in the 1970s, unusually, the economy experienced net immigration. However, the Irish government's borrowing in the late 1970s led to a fiscal crisis in the 1980s, during which time unemployment rose and emigration resumed.

Direct foreign investment has played a major role in transforming the structure of the Irish economy. Multinational companies (mostly from the US rather than from fellow EU members) have been particularly prominent, especially after 1973, and have used Ireland as an export base to the EU as a whole. Multinational companies have been particularly strong in high-tech sectors, notably electronics and pharmaceuticals. Many authors stress the dualistic nature of Irish manufacturing today, with large foreign export-oriented high-tech sectors existing alongside smaller Irish-aimed companies in more traditional sectors, selling to domestic and UK markets. This structural dimension of the economy is the key to any interpretation of its trade performance, including that concerning the single European market (SEM).

Ireland's post-war performance in comparative perspective

Ireland's post-war performance has been poor in light of the recent convergence literature. However, any assessment of Ireland's relative performance comes with a health warning: the data you use matter greatly. O'Grada and O'Rourke (1994) show that between 1950 and 1988, Ireland was a substantial negative outlier when they plotted growth rates against initial income levels. However, the OECD and Penn World Tables data sets tell very different stories about timing. Both show Ireland performing very poorly in the 1950s, and better in the 1960s when it opened up to trade. However, whereas OECD data show relatively good performance from 1973 on, with growth of 2.68% per annum, Heston-Summers show growth of only 0.85% per annum for the latest period.

Ireland's measured growth from 1988 to 1994 has been extremely high, although the suspicion persists that transfer pricing by multinational companies can explain some of the output growth. The ratio of GNP to GDP has declined from almost 100% in the early 1970s to 88% in 1994. Finally, Kennedy (1992) points out that Ireland's performance in terms of income or output per worker is superior to its performance in per capita terms. This difference is due to the declining share of the population at work. Unlike most other Member States, demographic factors still play a major role in Ireland's economic performance.

The bottom line, however, is that between 1950 and 1994, OECD data show Ireland growing (in terms of GDP per capita) at 1.9% per annum, the same rate as Europe as a whole. By contrast, Italy's growth rate was 3.6% per annum while Greece, Portugal and Spain grew at 3.8% per annum.

Intra-industry trade (IIT)

The most up-to-date analysis of IIT in Ireland is by Brülhart and McAleese (1994), who calculated IIT indices at a five-digit level from 1961 to 1990. They confirm the conclusions of earlier studies (McAleese, 1976, 1979; NESC, 1989) that, first, IIT is high in Ireland and, second, that IIT increased in the 1960s and 1970s, but declined slightly between 1985 and 1990. The same conclusion holds whether GL indices are Aquino-adjusted or not.

The small decline in IIT in the late 1980s reflects a move towards inter-industry specialization, in contrast to the intra-industry adjustment that occurred previously. In particular, Brülhart and McAleese conclude that Ireland specialized out of traditional labour-intensive sectors into capital-intensive, export-oriented sectors during this period. This process, they say, can help explain the much slower growth of manufacturing employment (3%) than manufacturing output (27%) or trade (33%) experienced in Ireland during this period. The adjustment is assessed using Brülhart's (1994) marginal IIT measure.

The single European market and convergence

Barro (1994) surveyed Ireland's adjustment to free trade in the light of theoretical arguments, in the growth and economic geography literature, that integration with core countries can, in some circumstances, be bad for the periphery. Barro asked whether or not, in the wake of Ireland's entry to the EEC in 1973, we could observe reductions in human capital formation; industry productivity growth; R&D activities; the output of increasing returns to scale industries. In each case the answer was 'No'. Indeed, Barro noted that, according to Neven (1990), Ireland has a revealed comparative advantage in human-capital-intensive goods! Barry argued that increasing levels of foreign direct investment help to explain why the gloomier predictions of some theorists (such as Young, 1991, Stokey, 1991, and Krugman and Venables, 1990) fail so spectacularly in the Irish case. In turn, Lyons and McCloughlan (undated) argue that Ireland has been so successful in attracting multinational companies because of tax incentives, grant awards, cheap, skilled labour, privacy of production with little risk of being imitated (due to the lack of indigenous high-tech firms), a stable political environment and because English is the main language. Clearly FDI in Ireland has been largely due to Ireland's position within the EU, and to the extent that the SMP affects the industries within which multinational companies operate (in fact, it does), Ireland can benefit. O'Malley (1990) examined the 39 industries that he considered most likely to be affected by the single market. These industries accounted for 53.6% of manufacturing employment and 60.9% of manufacturing value added. The discrepancy between the employment and value added figures arose largely because of four sensitive industries: office and data processing machinery (NACE 330), telecommunications equipment (NACE 344), medical and surgical equipment (NACE 372), and pharmaceuticals (NACE 257). These sectors have a very high value added per employee.

The SMP-sensitive sectors are more characterized by FDI than manufacturing as a whole: multinational companies account for 56% of employment in these sectors, 40% for manufacturing as a whole. This suggests that Ireland is well-positioned to benefit from the SMP. Moreover, O'Malley finds that those sensitive sectors in Ireland with high intra-EU export to import ratios (15 in all) have far higher levels of value added per employee than the 23 with low export/import ratios, and are quite competitive internationally. The latter are potentially vulnerable to increased competition, but they account for a far lower share of manufacturing employment (19% as opposed to 28%) and, in any case, tend to be in sectors that are growing less rapidly internationally than the sectors in which Ireland is competitive. Ireland's 'strong sensitive' sectors are, as expected, more likely to be dominated by multinational companies than the more vulnerable sectors.

These considerations led O'Malley to conclude that the prospects for Irish industry under the SMP are 'quite good'. The notion that the SMP is already having an impact is strengthened by Brülhart and McAleese (1994), who showed that the decline in IIT between 1985 and 1990 has been highest in industries that are highly sensitive to the SMP. In those industries least sensitive to it, IIT has actually continued to increase since 1985. This finding indicates that there has been a process of inter-industry adjustment in those sectors that have been most liberalized. Moreover, 85% of manufacturing jobs' growth occurred in the sensitive sectors. The decline in the GL index for sensitive sectors reflected Ireland's moving towards specializing *into* these sectors, rather than specializing *out* of them.

4.1.2. Data

Data on trade flows

Regarding trade flows, the data used for the study were from the VISA database, supplied by Eurostat. The principle advantage of VISA is that it has a breakdown of trade data by the NACE industrial classifications, which can correspond to domestic manufacturing statistics. VISA data are supplied to Eurostat by the Irish Central Statistics Office (CSO), with export and import statistics being supplied from the trade section, and manufacturing employment, production and investment figures coming from the industry section. The data are based on the annual Census of Industrial Enterprises, which covers all industrial enterprises employing 20 or more people.

We attempted to include as many NACE sectors in the analysis as possible. Some 15 two-digit sectors are included, as well as total manufacturing, while no three-digit data were supplied. The remaining two-digit sectors could not be included due to the differing classifications used by Eurostat and the CSO. For reasons of confidentiality, the CSO does not publish data on employment, production, investment and value added exactly according to the two-digit classification. As a result, for these sectors, VISA had no data for Ireland covering some two-digit sectors, and the analysis we had decided on was not possible in such cases.

For the 15 NACE two-digit sectors analysed, as well as NACE 9001 – total manufacturing – VISA data for Ireland cover almost all study variables for the period 1985–92. The missing data relate to investment in all sectors in the years 1991–92. The reason for this omission would seem to be that industrial employment and production statistics are gathered only from the full annual census, the most recently published version of which refers to 1990. In addition, the CSO publishes individual manufacturing output price indices for only 9 of the 15 NACE sectors and for *all* manufacturing. Analysis requiring deflated production figures was therefore possible for nine sectors as well as for all manufacturing.

Table 4.1.2 lists the NACE sectors that were included in the analysis of trade flows, the asterisks indicating those sectors for which deflation was possible.

As has been stated above, the distinction between 'high-tech' foreign-owned multinational affiliates and more 'traditional' Irish indigenous firms is important in any examination of Irish manufacturing. While not included in the indicator analysis, distinctions we made were based on data, both published and unpublished, from the CSO Census of Industrial Production. These data have limited years of coverage, and we have examined the balance in 1990, as well as the nominal export trend between 1987 and 1990. Table 4.1.3 compares the respective export performances for this period.

Data on factor flows

Regarding factor flows, a number of national sources were utilized. In addition to the sectoral employment and investment data from VISA, the following were used:

(a)   Figures for total employment in the economy were taken from the annual CSO Labour Force Survey.

(b)   Total investment in the economy was taken as total gross domestic fixed capital formation (nominal and real) from the annual CSO National Income and Expenditure releases.

(c)   With regard to labour migration, the CSO publishes official annual population and migration estimates, breaking down inward and outward migration figures by source and destination. These estimates are based on the population census (carried out every five years), annual labour force surveys and country of residence surveys. As they are estimates, the figures are presented in thousands with one decimal place, i.e. to the nearest 100 persons.

(d)   FDI data used in the analysis came from the OECD International Direct Investment Yearbook, which publishes Irish data based on figures received from the Industrial

Development Authority (IDA), the state body with responsibility for attracting foreign investment.

Data limitations

As with most empirical enquiries, the Irish element of this study has not been without its data-related problems. While we attempted to offset these as far as possible, a number of weaknesses are worthy of comment:

(a)   Trade data for some sectors suggested levels of exports above those of production and, while in theory this is possible, common sense suggests it is simply not the case at this level, but, in so far as we are concerned with changes as opposed to absolutes, this problem may not be as serious as it appears.

(b)   Because of the lack of production data that corresponds correctly to trade data, we were unable to include all the NACE two-digit sectors. Notably, the forced exclusion of the food and chemical manufacturing sectors meant we had to disregard a high proportion of total Irish manufacturing.

(c)   The numbers of sectors available for full analysis were further diminished by the lack of corresponding price indices.

(d)   FDI data was not included in the balance of payments statistics and as this is a variable of great importance in the Irish economy, particularly in manufacturing, the use of an indicator of FDI was unsatisfactory and unlikely to reflect reality as closely as would be desirable.

Table 4.1.2.   NACE sectors for the analysis of Irish trade flows

NACE sector	Sensitivity to	Sector
2200*	NS	Production and preliminary processing of metal
2400*	MS	Manufacture of non-metallic minerals products
3100*	NS	Manufacture of metal articles
3200*	MS	Mechanical engineering
3300	HS	Office and data processing machinery
3400*	HS	Electrical engineering
3500*	MS	Manufacture of motor vehicles and parts
3600	HS	Manufacture of other means of transport
3700*	HS	Instrument engineering
4300*	MS	Textiles
4400	NS	Leather and leather goods
4500	MS	Manufacture of footwear and clothing
4600*	NS	Timber and wooden furniture industries
4700	NS	Paper and paper products, printing
4800	MS	Processing of rubber and plastics
9001*		Total for manufacturing

*   The sectors for which deflation was possible according to Buigues *et al.* (1990) methodology. See in particular the study by O' Malley in the Buigues report.

Table 4.1.3.   Comparison of domestically and foreign-owned manufacturing exports

NACE sector	% export growth 1987–90		Contribution to total export growth	
	Irish	Foreign	Irish	Foreign
2200	64	-3	101.2	-1.2
2400	-12	28	-18.3	118.3
3100	43	48	30.0	70.0
3200	-4	16	-4.1	104.1
3300	674	14	10.3	89.7
3400	114	55	12.7	87.3
3500	5	56	2.4	97.6
3600	197	99	83.4	16.6
3700	3	30	0.3	99.7
4300	-20	24	-42.7	142.7
4400-4500	16	0	102.5	-2.5
4600	72	0	100.7	-0.7
4700	22	91	30.3	69.7
4800	34	42	16.9	83.1
9001	26	39	19.4	80.6

Source: CSO Census of Industrial Production, published and unpublished data, 1987-90.

4.1.3. Indicator analysis

Background

This section presents a descriptive examination of the results of the indicator analysis regarding the impact of the SMP on Irish trade and factor flows. The methodology adopted for the indicator analysis is described in the next section. Unlike for other countries, the analysis did not include regional specificity beyond the country as a whole.

The results of the analysis for trade flows and for factor flows are presented separately. For each, there is a brief description of the methodology, followed by sections describing the results for each type of indicator. Finally, there is a summary of the main results.

Trade flows – methodology

The examination of the relationship between the SMP and the nature and extent of trade flows to and from Ireland involved the calculation of the indicators, as specified in the methodology. In order to simplify the analysis of 9 indicators over 8 years and 16 sectors, the following approach was followed:

(a)   We divided the full study period (1985-92) into two subperiods, namely 1985-87 and 1988-92. We calculated the average value of each indicator within each of these two subperiods, together with the growth rate of each between the first subperiod and the second.

(b)   We then calculated the corresponding growth rate of a number of 'explanatory' variables that captured characteristics of each sector individually, which were:

(i)   the real growth in value added in each sector;

(ii)   the growth rate of the investment/value added ratio in each sector (with the second period average having been taken as the average of 1988-99 only due to data constraints);

(iii)   the real growth in labour productivity in each sector;

(iv)   the growth rate of a specialization index showing sectoral value added relative to all manufacturing value added.

(c)   We then examined sectoral trends in trade creation/diversion, IIT and relative competitiveness and specialization in the light of the above explanatory sectoral characteristics to identify actual trends relative to those predicted. The degree of comparison possible between sectoral indicator results and sectoral explanatory characteristics was, however, constrained by the lack of available price indices for some sectors.

Trade flows – results

Trade creation and diversion

In terms of trade creation, the data showed that, in Ireland, the proportion of total manufacturing production exported to the EU grew by 10% between the two subperiods. The proportion of apparent consumption of manufactured goods imported from the EU grew by 2.5%. This confirmed the prediction that aggregate manufacturing trade volume between Ireland and integrated countries grew over the period in question.

At sectoral level, 12 out of the 15 sectors analysed recorded positive growth in outward EU trade creation, while 8 sectors showed growth in inward trade creation as defined here. The strongest growth in outward trade came from the sector manufacturing means of transport other than motor vehicles and parts, which registered growth of 54%. A small manufacturing sector in Ireland both in absolute and relative terms, this industry is not characterized by a strong foreign multinational company presence, and the trade growth appeared to reflect a growing propensity to export to the EU among established indigenous producers.

Other sectors that registered strong growth in outward trade creation were motor vehicles and parts (40%), electrical engineering (38%) and footwear and clothing (26%). Of these, the growth in outward trade creation in electrical engineering concurred with strong growth in real value added and real labour productivity. A very large high-tech sector in Ireland, dominated by multinational companies, has seen its proportion of total manufacturing value added grow by almost 30%, the highest for all the sectors in the period analysed. In relation to inward trade, electrical engineering ranked first again, with intra-EU imports growing by 37% relative to apparent consumption. Also showing a strongly growing intra-EU import propensity was the sector manufacturing non-metallic mineral products, growth there being almost 20%. However, unlike the electrical engineering sector, where the growth was concurrent with growth in output, employment and exports, the non-metallic mineral products sector in Ireland was small and declining in importance, and the higher degree of intra-EU import penetration is likely to be a result of displacement rather than production processing and re-export. The performance in the footwear and clothing sector is worthy of comment. A traditional sector with relatively few multinational companies, the 26% growth in intra-EU export creation is strong when considered alongside a concurrent 33% drop in the value of the specialization indicator (sectoral value added/total manufacturing value added).

Turning to trade diversion – the degree to which the SMP may have acted to reduce the proportions of Irish manufacturing production and apparent consumption traded with non-EU countries – the evidence is mixed. Extra-EU exports as a proportion of production fell by 5%, but there was a 7% growth in the proportion of apparent consumption from outside the EU. Such growth in non-EU trade as a proportion of consumption is obviously contrary to expectations. An explanation is once more to be found in Ireland's high and growing multinational sector, particularly US multinationals. It has been shown that foreign-owned firms account for up to three quarters of Irish manufacturing exports. While similar figures on the import side are not available, they too are likely to be high. It is probable that growth in the level of imported goods from the US and Japan by Irish subsidiaries of multinational companies is the factor behind the apparent lack of import trade diversion over the period. An examination of trade diversion within sectors would tend to confirm this proposition. The office and data processing sector is large and growing in Ireland, and almost entirely made up of subsidiaries of multinationals, the majority of which originate from the US. The growing size and importance of this sector in Ireland means it is likely to be a strong driver behind the results for all manufacturing. Of all the sectors examined, this had the highest share of manufacturing production in 1992. While the sector displayed a decline in extra-EU exports relative to production of 4% over the two subperiods, it also displayed an increase of 5% in the proportion of consumption imported from outside the EU. As well as the actions of the subsidiaries of multinationals in Ireland, this is likely to be a reflection of the overall competitiveness of US firms in this industry.

In terms of export diversion, with the exception of motor vehicles and parts, all sectors examined displayed a decline in the proportion of output exported to non-EU countries over the subperiods. These declines ranged from a 47% drop in timber and wooden furniture to a decline of only 0.2% in paper and publishing. Again, the small absolute size of the motor vehicles and parts sector, from which total extra-EU exports amounted to only ECU 3.5 million in 1992, may account for its apparent lack of export trade diversion.

In terms of import diversion, only 8 of the 15 sectors displayed the expected decline. Of these, the sharpest decline was in non-metallic minerals, where non-EU imports as a proportion of consumption fell by almost 20%. As noted earlier, this sector also displayed one of the highest growth rates in import trade creation. The evidence therefore suggests that the SMP has been effective in increasing imports of non-metallic minerals into Ireland from within the EU in favour of those from elsewhere. Another sector that showed a strong degree of import diversion was that engaged in the manufacture of metal articles. Between the two subperiods, the value of the import trade diversion indicator declined by just over 15%, reflecting a declining degree of extra-EU import penetration. However, unlike the non-metallic minerals sector, this did not concur with growing intra-EU import penetration.

IIT and specialization

The average value of the Grubel-Lloyd indicator of IIT between Ireland and the EU for all manufacturing declined by 7% to 87.7 between the two subperiods, reflecting a trade surplus that grew as a percentage of total trade. However, at almost 88, the indicator shows that total trade with the EU remains reasonably equally balanced between exports and imports. This overall finding is not in accordance with the expectations regarding the impact of the SMP. However, at sectoral level, while the average Grubel-Lloyd indicator for manufacturing as a whole fell over the period, it actually increased for 10 of the 15 sectors examined.

The sectors that displayed the highest degree of growth in the Grubel-Lloyd index between the subperiods examined were motor vehicles and parts (24%) and other means of transport (29%). With regard to the former, the sector is dominated by imports, but, over the period, growth of exports exceeded that of imports. It is likely, however, that much of the growth in exports came from the small number of large subsidiaries of multinationals operating in the sector and as a result of indigenous firms not being sufficiently competitive to increase their market share during the implementation of the SMP. However, concerning the sector producing other means of transport, as noted earlier, there was significant export trade creation and the growth in the Grubel-Lloyd index reflected a growing competitiveness among Irish indigenous producers in EU markets.

The electrical engineering sector displayed the sharpest decline in the average value of the Grubel-Lloyd index over the period examined. From an average of 98 in the first subperiod, the Grubel-Lloyd index fell by 19% to an average of just under 80 in the second period. This has been the result of intra-EU export growth accelerating ahead of import growth, and largely reflects the activities of multinationals, which dominate exports from the sector, particularly in the telecommunications and electronics sectors. Of the nine sectors for which price indices were available, it emerged that the electrical engineering sector displayed the highest real growth in labour productivity and the highest real growth in value added.

Another sector that registered a declining Grubel-Lloyd indicator was the non-metallic mineral products sector (-10.5%). Unlike the electrical engineering sector, the decline here was a reflection of a growing trade deficit as a proportion of total trade. A declining sector with real value added growth well below that for all manufacturing, the SMP would seem to have led to increased competitive pressures from foreign producers and falling market shares among Irish firms.

In relation to intra-industry specialization, the analysis showed that 10 of the 15 sectors recorded growth in this area or growth in the absolute level of IIT relative to production. Among the sectors indicating highest growth were non-car transport (62%), motor vehicles and parts (40%), and footwear and clothing (26%). Prominent among the five sectors that recorded a declining average value of the intra-industry specialization indicator were office and data processing machinery (-10%), and timber and wooden furniture (-9%).

Competitiveness and specialization

Our analysis showed that the indicator of RCA for all manufacturing grew from a level of +5.6 to +12.3 in Ireland between the two subperiods in question. This growth in overall comparative advantage reflects Ireland's growing manufacturing trade surplus, which has been central to the country's strong economic performance over the period. However, again, much of the increased exports resulted from increased activity among affiliates of multinationals, and the degree to which the competitiveness of indigenous Irish manufacturers within the EU has changed during the SMP is a subject of debate. Furthermore, the extent of the presence of multinationals means that its effect is present in sectoral and subsectoral as well as aggregate data, although to varying degrees.

At sectoral level, 12 of our 15 sectors recorded positive intra-EU RCA growth over the period. The electrical engineering sector again ranked first. Over the two subperiods, the average intra-EU RCA in this sector grew from a level of +1.4 to +20.2. As noted, this is reflective of the growth in the activity of multinationals in the sector. On the other hand, the average RCA of the sector manufacturing non-car transport equipment improved from -39 to -20. While still at a comparative disadvantage, this improved competitiveness is less likely to be driven by the activity of multinationals. Similarly, the growth in intra-EU RCA of the leather and leather goods sector – which saw an average increase from -10 to -1 – is more likely to indicate growing competitiveness among established indigenous firms as multinationals do not figure prominently in this sector.

The sector that registered the steepest decline in RCA was non-metallic minerals. From an average level of -13 in the first subperiod, its RCA fell to -22 in the second. This again highlights the declining fortunes of Irish firms in this sector during the implementation of the SMP.

With regard to the indicator of sectoral export specialization (i.e. the importance of exports from different sectors in Ireland relative to the EU as a whole), among the sectors included the highest growth in the two subperiods was in the two sectors manufacturing motor vehicles and parts, and electrical engineering. In the case of the former, the sector remained a low contributor to total manufacturing exports. However, when compared to the sector at total EU level, its contribution grew strongly. With regard to the latter, Ireland's export specialization is, however, much higher, and the analysis also exposed it as a sector in which Ireland is specializing faster than the EU as a whole. Furthermore, assuming the criterion of $SI>100 =$ specialization and $SI<100 =$ non-specialization, it is the only sector in which Ireland became specialist over the period examined. In addition to these two, only 1 of the 15 sectors included – namely the metal production sector – registered growth in the average value of the specialization indicator over the period. In this case, the growth was much more modest, and the absolute value of the indicator showed that it still cannot be seen as one in which Ireland specializes.

Among the remaining 12 sectors, there was a decline in the average value of the specialization indicator. The non-metallic minerals sector recorded the biggest relative decline (-19.5%). Also significant were the footwear and clothing sector (-18.9%) and the leather and leather goods sector (-18.1%). However, in neither of these cases could Ireland be considered as specializing at any stage over the period analysed.

Reflective of Ireland's strong manufacturing export performance over the period of the implementation of the SMP was the 10% increase in the average share of the EU manufacturing export market over the two subperiods. Of the sectors included, eight registered growth in total exports ahead of that experienced at EU level, while in seven the performance lagged behind the EU's performance. Again, the strongest relative growth was in the motor vehicles and parts and electrical engineering sectors, whose EU export market shares grew by 58% and 57% respectively, while the metal production sector recorded growth of 22%. The sectors registering the steepest relative decline were footwear and clothing (-11%), and leather and leather goods (-10%).

The progress of the electrical engineering sector, which saw strong growth in its RCA, specialization and export market share, was concurrent with the strongest sectoral real growth in value added, both absolute and relative to all manufacturing, and real labour productivity growth. However, the sector showed the steepest decline in the investment/value added ratio.

The motor vehicles and parts sector, having also performed well in terms of specialization and export market share, ranked poorly among sectors in terms of value added and labour productivity. It seems likely that, once again, these curious trends are the result of the activities of subsidiaries of multinationals, which have dominated both sectors over the period. With the ability to boost exports by way of concentrating established export activity more heavily in Ireland-based affiliates, such multinationals may be boosting Irish sectoral exports without proportionately altering the productive characteristics of these sectors. On the other hand, the sector manufacturing transport equipment other than motor vehicles depends much less on foreign-owned firms for exports, and in this sector the investment/value added ratio grew strongly over the period examined.

Factor flows – methodology

In so far as Ireland was treated as one region for the purpose of this study, we did not attempt to compare trends in international labour migration flows and those occurring within different regions within Ireland. To examine the trend in Irish–EU labour migration flows, we used data from the CSO, which offer official estimates of inward and outward migration broken down by source and destination. An important consideration in this regard was labour migration between Ireland and the UK, which remains the single largest destination for Irish outward labour migration. As no significant barriers to labour movement between Ireland and the UK needed to be removed as part of the SMP, we examined the trend in relation to all of the EU, and to the EU other than the UK. The period covered was 1987–94. We distinguished between trends in outward, inward and total labour migration.

In relation to FDI flows, we used data published by the OECD, based on the records of the IDA, the state agency responsible for industrial development. The data referred to direct fixed asset investment by foreign-owned firms that is eligible for grant assistance from the authority. We examined the absolute trend over the period of 1985–92 in such investment from other EU countries, as well as relative to the trend in investment from all countries.

Finally, we calculated the trend in the capital/labour ratio over the period 1985–93. Without data on the national stock of capital, we followed the methodology proposed, i.e. we took the capital stock in a year to amount to the sum of all capital investment over the previous 10 years, and the stock of labour in a year to amount to the average number of persons at work in the economy over the previous 10 years. Figures for national investment were total gross domestic fixed capital formation (valued at constant prices), the data for which came from the CSO National Income and Expenditure Accounts, while the CSO's annual Labour Force Survey supplied estimates of national employment over the period.

Factor flows – results

Table 4.1.4 indicates the trend in labour migration between Ireland and the whole of the EU, and between Ireland and EU countries other than the UK during the period 1987–94.

As can be seen from the table, total migration flows between Ireland and the EU relative to those between Ireland and all other countries grew strongly between 1987 and 1989, but the trend was largely downward thereafter until 1994. However, when the UK is not included, Irish migration flows with the EU relative to non-EU countries have grown and remained high. In 1994, total labour migration flows to EU countries beyond the UK accounted for twice the share of all flows than was the case in 1987.

Table 4.1.4.   Labour migration trends, 1987–94

Year	Outward		Inward		All	
	EU	EU less UK	EU	EU less UK	EU	EU less UK
1987	61.9	7.7	59.9	12.8	61.3	9.2
1988	70.4	4.6	65.1	13.5	69.1	6.7
1989	74.1	5.5	66.7	13.5	72.0	7.7
1990	72.6	9.1	67.9	15.0	70.9	11.3
1991	73.9	8.8	68.8	12.6	71.4	10.6
1992	72.0	22.1	71.6	16.1	71.8	19.0
1993	66.6	20.7	69.7	20.3	68.0	20.5
1994	59.0	16.1	69.5	20.6	63.6	18.1

Source: CSO Annual Population and Migration Estimates.

While the share of total migration flows is important, it is also revealing to examine the absolute trend. Over the period 1987–94, the total for annual migrants from Ireland who went to EU countries other than the UK grew from approximately 3,100 to 6,700, having reached a high of 8,500 in 1993. At the same time, the total for those entering Ireland from these states increased from 2,200 to 6,500, having reached 7,100 in 1993.

The evidence, therefore, is of strong growth in inward and outward labour migration flows between Ireland and EU countries other then the UK during the period, although 1994 saw a slight decline. While the SMP obviously cannot be regarded as the only force behind the trend in absolute numbers, the growing share of the EU in existing migration flows does support the premise of changing labour migration patterns in favour of EU Member Sates during the programme. Comparable data both pre-1987 and post-1994 will indicate the extent to which such a shift proves to be permanent.

Turning to FDI migration, while there is no data available on Irish outward FDI, it is expected to be negligible in comparison to that coming into Ireland. The trend in EU FDI into Ireland between 1985 and 1992 is summarized in Table 4.1.5.

The OECD data do not seem to confirm the proposition of growing FDI in Ireland from within the EU over the period examined. With the total value (measured at current prices) having fallen from Ir.£50 million to Ir.£27 million in the eight years up to 1992, EU FDI has fallen both absolutely and relative to that from elsewhere. While the data obviously do not reflect the true extent of FDI in Ireland, its success in attracting foreign, and particularly US-based multinationals to locate manufacturing activity in Ireland is likely to be a factor behind the drop in the total FDI share held by the EU countries. Indeed, a central attraction of FDI into Ireland has been its membership of the EU and the increasingly liberated markets therein. It is probably not therefore surprising to see EU FDI in Ireland falling, both in absolute and relative terms, over the period.

Finally, our analysis found little evidence of a growing capital/labour ratio in Ireland during the period of the SMP. By adding together the figures for capital over ten years to give a capital stock figure and dividing this by the average total employment figure for the same period, we calculated the capital per employed person to be Ir.£34,600 in 1985 and Ir.£33,900 in 1993, both measured in constant 1985 prices, with little significant fluctuation within the period. However, as has been suggested, increases in a country's capital/labour ratio stemming from higher levels of income, and subsequently investment, are more likely to be in the long rather than the short or medium term. While such upward trends are not yet apparent, there is little reason to expect that Ireland will be exceptional in that regard.

Table 4.1.5.   FDI flows, 1985–92

Year	Total FDI from EU countries (Ir. £ million)	EU FDI as % of total
1985	50	26.7
1986	68	36.2
1987	61	29.0
1988	32	20.4
1989	25	18.4
1990	26	21.5
1991	29	13.0
1992	27	12.6

Source: OECD International Direct Investment Yearbook, 1994.

4.1.4.   Main conclusions

We summarize below some of the main results that emerged from the indicator analysis of trade and factor flows between Ireland and the EU during the period of the implementation of the SMP.

As has been discussed, there are some unique features of the Irish economy and economic history that we regard as playing central roles in the degree to which such trade and factor flows may have changed over the period. Notably, the extent to which increases in the numbers of multinational companies operating in Ireland – and their effect on total and, more importantly, sectoral intra-EU trade – are expected to have influenced the outcome considerably, although the actual degree to which it has done so is uncertain. To the extent that increases in intra-EU trade reflect regional competitiveness, the multinational companies will have undoubtedly enhanced the outcome for Ireland. However, there is, of course, ambiguity as to the extent to which this regional competitiveness is a reflection of growing competitiveness among Irish firms resulting from the SMP.

Another unique feature is Ireland's close trade relations with the UK. While indigenous firms continue to rely heavily on the UK market for export earnings, free trade has been in place for much longer than that which is currently emerging under the SMP.

We carried out the analysis in the light of the data constraints as we have seen them. However, because of these problems, we advise caution when drawing substantive conclusions.

The data support the premise of trade creation occurring as a result of the SMP. While the evidence suggests that this is strongest in sectors characterized by a high level of activity on the part of multinationals, there are interesting exceptions. In relation to trade diversion, however, the evidence is somewhat mixed.

The analysis showed that IIT between Ireland and the EU declined in the period examined, but this seems likely to reflect increases in intra-industry specialization which has been characteristic of Irish manufacturing over the period. The data suggested that the trend of declining IIT in Ireland during the late 1980s, exposed by Brülhart and McAleese (1994) and earlier studies, generally continued up to 1992. These findings are expected to reflect a process of inter-industry specialization from traditional labour-intensive industry into high-tech capital-intensive activity continuing in Irish manufacturing. This process, driven strongly by direct investment in Ireland on the part of multinationals, has been (and continues to be) the central development within Irish manufacturing since the early 1980s, and the central reason for the findings being contrary to expectations in the Irish case.

As we would have expected, the data showed Ireland to have an increased RCA over the period for all manufacturing, but notably among high-tech sectors dominated by foreign-owned firms.

In relation to factor flows, the data showed increased levels of Ireland–EU labour migration during the period. This trend held true even when the UK was not included as part of the EU. A somewhat surprising finding given that the language and cultural differences that were expected to suppress such increased mobility remain in abundant evidence in Ireland. On FDI, the data did not confirm increases in intra-EU capital mobility, while the analysis did not apparently indicate significant change in the Irish capital/labour ratio over the period.

4.1.5. Appendix A1 to Section 4.1. Background tables for Ireland: trade and factor flows

Table A1.4.1.1.   Ireland: trade creation

NACE	Sector	Average values		Growth rate
Trade creation: intra-EU exports and production		1985–87	1988–92	
2200	Production and preliminary processing of metals	0.84	1.02	22.03
2400	Non-metallic mineral products	0.15	0.16	9.18
3100	Metal articles	0.51	0.50	-0.64
3200	Mechanical engineering	0.84	0.99	18.09
3300	Office and data processing machinery	0.88	0.88	0.21
3400	Electrical engineering	0.61	0.84	37.99
3500	Motor vehicles, parts and accessories	0.77	1.08	39.91
3600	Other means of transport	0.47	0.77	64.52
3700	Instrument engineering	0.40	0.38	-4.55
4300	Textiles	0.69	0.81	17.25
4400	Leather and leather goods	0.40	0.49	20.65
4500	Clothing and footwear	0.48	0.61	26.52
4600	Timber and wooden furniture	0.42	0.41	-1.82
4700	Paper and printing	0.20	0.21	2.32
4800	Rubber products, plastic processing	0.60	0.62	3.65
9001	Total manufacturing	0.48	0.53	10.32
Trade creation: intra-EU imports and consumption				
2200	Production and preliminary processing of metals	0.84	0.90	7.76
2400	Non-metallic mineral products	0.20	0.25	26.25
3100	Metal articles	0.59	0.59	-0.69
3200	Mechanical engineering	0.82	0.88	7.21
3300	Office and data processing machinery	0.56	0.55	-2.43
3400	Electrical engineering	0.54	0.75	37.54
3500	Motor vehicles, parts and accessories	0.65	0.73	11.70
3600	Other means of transport	0.54	0.42	-22.15
3700	Instrument engineering	0.32	0.31	-3.39
4300	Textiles	0.72	0.78	8.05
4400	Leather and leather goods	0.42	0.47	12.25
4500	Clothing and footwear	0.69	0.73	5.29
4600	Timber and wooden furniture	0.34	0.31	-9.80
4700	Paper and printing	0.35	0.35	-0.18
4800	Rubber products, plastic processing	0.65	0.64	-1.30
9001	Total manufacturing	0.47	0.48	2.54

Table A1.4.1.2.   Ireland: trade diversion

NACE	Sector	Average values		Growth rate
		1985-87	1988-92	
Trade diversion: extra-EU exports and production				
2200	Production and preliminary processing of metals	0.14	0.10	-24.89
2400	Non-metallic mineral products	0.10	0.10	-2.89
3100	Metal articles	0.12	0.09	-27.02
3200	Mechanical engineering	0.46	0.45	-1.34
3300	Office and data processing machinery	0.27	0.26	-3.83
3400	Electrical engineering	0.29	0.26	-10.80
3500	Motor vehicles, parts and accessories	0.03	0.04	26.80
3600	Other means of transport	0.49	0.42	14.25
3700	Instrument engineering	0.26	0.25	-2.22
4300	Textiles	0.15	0.13	-17.80
4400	Leather and leather goods	0.14	0.13	-2.06
4500	Clothing and footwear	0.13	0.09	-32.42
4600	Timber and wooden furniture	0.06	0.03	-47.13
4700	Paper and printing	0.02	0.02	-12.12
4800	Rubber products, plastic processing	0.14	0.11	-23.79
9001	Total manufacturing	0.19	0.18	-5.35
Trade diversion: extra-EU imports and consumption				
2200	Production and preliminary processing of metals	0.15	0.15	-4.37
2400	Non-metallic mineral products	0.04	0.03	-19.53
3100	Metal articles	0.10	0.09	-15.41
3200	Mechanical engineering	0.33	0.36	6.63
3300	Office and data processing machinery	0.83	0.87	5.06
3400	Electrical engineering	0.37	0.39	6.52
3500	Motor vehicles, parts and accessories	0.32	0.29	-9.54
3600	Other means of transport	0.44	0.65	46.39
3700	Instrument engineering	0.18	0.17	-3.64
4300	Textiles	0.16	0.18	7.91
4400	Leather and leather goods	0.19	0.18	-5.04
4500	Clothing and footwear	0.09	0.13	39.03
4600	Timber and wooden furniture	0.27	0.26	-3.10
4700	Paper and printing	0.15	0.15	-1.53
4800	Rubber products, plastic processing	0.12	0.12	1.41
9001	Total manufacturing	0.18	0.19	6.58

Table A1.4.1.3. Ireland: Grubel-Lloyd indicator

NACE	Sector	Average values		Growth rate
		1985-87	1988-92	
2200	Production and preliminary processing of metals	55.51	60.51	9.00
2400	Non-metallic mineral products	87.01	77.90	-10.47
3100	Metal articles	83.30	81.67	-1.95
3200	Mechanical engineering	67.95	73.83	8.65
3300	Office and data processing machinery	40.62	36.93	-9.10
3400	Electrical engineering	98.03	79.81	-18.58
3500	Motor vehicles, parts and accessories	28.76	35.80	24.48
3600	Other means of transport	61.29	79.12	29.10
3700	Instrument engineering	71.19	73.24	2.88
4300	Textiles	84.89	88.43	4.17
4400	Leather and leather goods	85.33	95.44	11.84
4500	Clothing and footwear	56.91	57.26	0.61
4600	Timber and wooden furniture	96.54	95.32	-1.18
4700	Paper and printing	54.25	55.75	2.76
4800	Rubber products, plastic processing	90.54	92.00	1.72
9001	Total manufacturing	94.41	87.73	-7.07

Table A1.4.1.4. Ireland: absolute IIT indicator

NACE	Sector	Average values		Growth rate
		1985-87	1988-92	
2200	Production and preliminary processing of metals	260	398	53
2400	Non-metallic mineral products	235	288	22
3100	Metal articles	440	595	35
3200	Mechanical engineering	676	1,027	52
3300	Office and data processing machinery	1,031	1,179	14
3400	Electrical engineering	1,357	2,277	68
3500	Motor vehicles, parts and accessories	112	232	106
3600	Other means of transport	81	213	164
3700	Instrument engineering	227	309	36
4300	Textiles	687	921	34
4400	Leather and leather goods	36	45	26
4500	Clothing and footwear	345	409	19
4600	Timber and wooden furniture	196	269	37
4700	Paper and printing	271	393	45
4800	Rubber products, plastic processing	566	863	53
9001	Total manufacturing	16,035	20,876	30

Table A1.4.1.5.   Ireland: scaled IIT indicator

NACE	Sector	Average values		Growth rate
		1985-87	1988-92	
2200	Production and preliminary processing of metals	1.67	2.04	22.03
2400	Non-metallic mineral products	0.29	0.32	9.18
3100	Metal articles	1.02	1.01	-0.64
3200	Mechanical engineering	1.68	1.99	18.09
3300	Office and data processing machinery	0.45	0.40	-10.48
3400	Electrical engineering	1.18	1.12	-5.22
3500	Motor vehicles, parts and accessories	1.54	2.16	39.91
3600	Other means of transport	0.94	1.52	62.19
3700	Instrument engineering	0.44	0.44	-1.35
4300	Textiles	1.39	1.63	17.25
4400	Leather and leather goods	0.75	0.93	23.54
4500	Clothing and footwear	0.97	1.22	26.52
4600	Timber and wooden furniture	0.83	0.76	-8.58
4700	Paper and printing	0.41	0.41	2.32
4800	Rubber products, plastic processing	1.20	1.24	3.65
9001	Total manufacturing	0.86	0.83	-3.50

Table A1.4.1.6.   Ireland: RCAs

NACE	Sector	Average values		Change
		1985-87	1988-92	
2200	Production and preliminary processing of metals	-44.5	-39.5	5.0
2400	Non-metallic mineral products	-13.0	-22.1	-9.1
3100	Metal articles	-16.7	-18.3	-1.6
3200	Mechanical engineering	-32.0	-26.2	5.9
3300	Office and data processing machinery	59.4	63.1	3.7
3400	Electrical engineering	1.4	20.2	18.8
3500	Motor vehicles, parts and accessories	-71.2	-64.2	7.0
3600	Other means of transport	-38.7	-19.9	18.8
3700	Instrument engineering	28.8	26.8	-2.1
4300	Textiles	-15.1	-11.6	3.5
4400	Leather and leather goods	-9.5	-0.7	8.8
4500	Clothing and footwear	-43.1	-42.7	0.3
4600	Timber and wooden furniture	-3.5	2.0	5.6
4700	Paper and printing	-45.8	-44.3	1.5
4800	Rubber products, plastic processing	-9.6	-8.0	1.6
9001	Total manufacturing	5.6	12.3	6.7

Table A1.4.1.7.　　**Ireland: specialization indicator**

NACE	Sector	Average values		Growth rate
		1985-87	1988-92	
2200	Production and preliminary processing of metals	17.1	19.1	11.3
2400	Non-metallic mineral products	74.3	59.8	-19.5
3100	Metal articles	65.0	56.7	-12.8
3200	Mechanical engineering	33.4	33.2	-0.5
3300	Office and data processing machinery	642.9	576.3	-10.4
3400	Electrical engineering	88.7	126.7	42.8
3500	Motor vehicles, parts and accessories	4.2	6.0	44.2
3600	Other means of transport	21.4	19.4	-9.6
3700	Instrument engineering	158.2	142.7	-9.8
4300	Textiles	71.8	67.2	-6.4
4400	Leather and leather goods	34.2	28.0	-18.1
4500	Clothing and footwear	52.9	42.9	-18.9
4600	Timber and wooden furniture	57.0	52.1	-8.5
4700	Paper and printing	42.9	40.6	-5.4
4800	Rubber products, plastic processing	88.6	81.7	-7.8
9001	Total manufacturing	100.0	100.0	0.0

Table A1.4.1.8.　　**Ireland: export market share indicator**

NACE	Sector	Average values		Growth rate
		1985-87	1988-92	
2200	Production and preliminary processing of metals	0.00286	0.00350	22.4
2400	Non-metallic mineral products	0.01238	0.01094	-11.6
3100	Metal articles	0.01083	0.01038	-4.2
3200	Mechanical engineering	0.00557	0.00608	9.1
3300	Office and data processing machinery	0.10726	0.10562	-1.5
3400	Electrical engineering	0.01480	0.02325	57.1
3500	Motor vehicles, parts and accessories	0.00070	0.00111	58.3
3600	Other means of transport	0.00357	0.00354	-0.8
3700	Instrument engineering	0.02637	0.02625	-0.5
4300	Textiles	0.01197	0.01232	2.9
4400	Leather and leather goods	0.00570	0.00515	-9.7
4500	Clothing and footwear	0.00882	0.00787	-10.8
4600	Timber and wooden furniture	0.00950	0.00956	0.5
4700	Paper and printing	0.00717	0.00745	3.8
4800	Rubber products, plastic processing	0.01478	0.01500	1.5
9001	Total manufacturing	0.01668	0.01836	10.0

Table A1.4.1.9.   Ireland: explanatory variables

NACE	Sector	Subperiod growth rates			
		Real value added	Investment/ value added (to 1990)	Real labour productivity	Specializ-ation
2200	Production and preliminary processing of metals	36.71	-14.00	25.34	3.33
2400	Non-metallic mineral products	13.18	72.15	19.07	-15.83
3100	Metal articles	12.93	50.61	11.99	-12.98
3200	Mechanical engineering	27.06	15.91	9.96	-4.38
3300	Office and data processing machinery	n/a	-16.11	n/a	-1.26
3400	Electrical engineering	76.06	-25.09	38.47	30.66
3500	Motor vehicles, parts and accessories	15.74	-4.93	18.39	-5.91
3600	Other means of transport	n/a	42.34	n/a	-7.66
3700	Instrument engineering	58.41	-1.16	18.27	9.98
4300	Textiles	2.72	57.48	8.11	-22.77
4400	Leather and leather goods	n/a	n/a	n/a	n/a
4500	Clothing and footwear	n/a	8.57	n/a	-33.50
4600	Timber and wooden furniture	37.00	23.22	12.81	11.20
4700	Paper and printing	n/a	65.20	n/a	-1.18
4800	Rubber products, plastic processing	n/a	25.19	n/a	-4.69
9001	Total manufacturing	31.03	8.58	18.98	0.00

Table A1.4.1.10.   Ireland: capital/labour ratio

Year	Investment[1] in year (Ir.£ million)	Investment – 10-year sum (Ir.£ million)	Workforce in year ('000)	Workforce – 10-year average ('000)	Capital/labour ratio[2] (Ir.£ '000)
1984	3,876.3	37,562.9	1,103	1,115.0	33.7
1985	3,549.7	38,595.9	1,079	1,115.6	34.6
1986	3,450.3	38,720.1	1,081	1,117.3	34.7
1987	3,258.6	38,507.1	1,090	1,118.0	34.4
1988	3,127.3	37,807.9	1,090	1,116.0	33.9
1989	3,812.4	37,165.4	1,088	1,110.3	33.5
1990	4,731.8	38,120.2	1,134	1,108.1	34.5
1991	4,394.5	38,393.6	1,134	1,106.9	34.7
1992	3,681.0	37,747.5	1,139	1,106.2	34.1
1993	3,656.5	37,538.4	1,146	1,108.4	33.9

[1] Gross domestic fixed capital formation (1990 constant prices).

[2] Sum of 10-year investment/average of 10-year workforce.

4.2. Italy

Paola Fasulo and Pierantonio Rosso, Greta Econometrics, Venice, Italy

4.2.1. Background

Italy emerged from World War Two with an economic problem that differed in both magnitude and kind from the ones of the other Western European countries. Indeed, Italy also needed to correct some major structural asymmetries that had been inherited from a much more distant past. The notion that the structure of the Italian economy was biased at quite an early stage of its industrial revolution was present in the minds of many Italian economists before World War One and since World War Two, all Italian governments have been conscious of the need for achieving economic unification and harmonization.

The main conclusion is that such marked dualism makes Italian problems of underdevelopment different from all other cases and it is best treated as a case *sui generis*. The *Rapporto 1993 sull'economia del Mezzogiorno* (1993 Report on the economy of the Mezzogiorno) (SVIMEZ, 1993) provides a clear and vast description of the real situation in Southern Italy.

Italy is currently characterized by a profound transformation process that involves both the institutional-political and the socio-economic assets. This process has a national dimension (visible in the change in the electoral system, the abolition by referendum of some ministries and of extraordinary measures for the Mezzogiorno, the reduction of public presence in the market, the improvement in public spending, judicial investigations of the political class) and an international one (since January 1993, the SMP has been working fully).

In 1992, strong signs of crisis began to be present in Southern Italy. The GDP, which had increased by 1.3% in the Northern regions, decreased in the Southern regions by 0.2% (each sector's performance was worse than its Northern equivalent); households' consumption slowed down and investment fell; the unemployment rate in Southern Italy was 16.3% against 6.2% in Northern Italy; and, finally, the improvement in the balance of payments was brought about almost entirely by Northern Italy.

During the first 20 years of the activities of the Cassa per il Mezzogiorno (1950–70), various interventions regarding drainage, irrigation and infrastructure were carried out to help the development of Southern Italy's regions. However, a worsening in the public actions and in crime came about in the early 1970s and persisted throughout the 1980s. In 1986, it was decided to end the extraordinary intervention in the South and this was the beginning of the repetitive use of special laws for specific events.

Since 1986, all interventions have been characterized by an evident lack of planning. The plurality of centres of decision, the sectoral characterization of abilities, the changes in progress of pluriannual financial plans, the relieving of responsibility and disqualification of administrative personnel, the absence of control over the outcome when action is taken are all factors that help explain why the recent interventions by the Mezzogiorno have failed. It is often also argued that the method of joint national and Community co-financing is another cause. Indeed, the Confindustria Report of 1993 on the progress in the Community programmes states that only 62% of the entire financial plan programmed in 1989–93 had been implemented and only 33% of the budget had been spent by the end of July 1993.

However, it is one of the goals of this study to quantify in which regions and sectors EU funds provided an economic benefit.

The convergence process in Italy

The theoretical framework of convergence was analysed in Chapter 2. As far as the Italian case is concerned, recent analyses have been carried out by Di Liberto (1994) and Goria and Ichino (1994), while the relationship between the labour force and convergence has been investigated by Sestito (1991) and Attanasio and Padoa Schioppa (1991).

Di Liberto examined the pattern of convergence among Italian regions using a data set over the period 1960–91 and both descriptive and regression analysis. These two methodologies yielded the same results. They both showed a different pattern of convergence across regions during the 1960s compared to the subsequent period. In particular, the results highlighted that the Italian regions, starting from a high level of inequality in 1960, seemed to have gone through a period of fast convergence in the standard of living until the end of the 1960s, but after this period, convergence seemed to be less and less effective.

Goria and Ichino provided evidence on the relationship between migration and per capita income convergence among Italian regions and took into account the human capital content of migration flows. Migration appeared to favour the process of regional convergence observed in Italy between 1962 and 1975. In fact, in this period, population movements seem to have been characterized in the main by flows of unskilled labour from Southern and North-Eastern regions towards North-Western and Central regions. After 1975, the intensity of migration flows decreased and the nature of these flows seemed to change. Descriptive evidence based on individual micro-data suggested that these more recent flows were mainly constituted by white-collar workers looking for public administration jobs in the hypertrophied Southern bureaucracy. These movements, far from being factors favouring convergence, may have contributed to generating the divergence of per capita income across regions that has actually been observed in Italy since 1975.

Among the determinants of economic development, Sestito identified the importance of human capital and he analysed the phenomenon statistically in Southern Italy. He recognized improvements in the productivity and efficiency of the labour force as very relevant in increasing the per capita income. The gap between the Northern and Southern situations persists, despite the fact that the number of employees with educational qualifications has increased in both regions. The inability to exploit the labour resources in the South, the differences in the investment of human capital and in the rates of participation in labour markets, the predominance of graduates with arts degrees, are all factors influencing the different composition of the labour force.

Attanasio and Padoa Schioppa focused on the role of labour mobility – within and between regions and macro-regions – as a way of levelling inter-regional inequalities in income levels. Mostly by means of descriptive analysis, they tried to identify some determinants of migration rates within Italy. In particular, they aimed to understand why, unlike during the 1960s, workers do not migrate from the South to the North–Centre of Italy, even in the presence of persisting regional imbalances and, at the same time, without any significant substituting movement of capital. The authors used the traditional model of migration developed by Harris and Todaro (1970) as their theoretical framework. Moreover, they adopted basic statistical instruments: some simple regressions that, as the authors say, should be interpreted as a measure of partial correlation coefficients, and tables showing disaggregation (by macro-region, age, sex, and professional status) for intra- and inter-regional migration flows. After the early 1970s, they registered a general decrease in inter-regional mobility (mainly from the South to the North–Centre) matched by a reduction in intra-regional mobility, with differences between regions and age groups. They explained that the decline in the spatial mobility of labour related to:

(a)   the corresponding increase in aggregate unemployment, given the unemployment differentials between regions;
(b)   the strong decrease in inter-regional net real wage differentials, coupled with an increase in the net real wage in the Southern–Western areas relative to the Northern ones;
(c)   a rise in government transfers, in various forms, to the Southern regions;
(d)   an increase in the fixed costs relating to the decision as to whether or not to move, typically the housing rental prices.

Expectations of the SMP

From the Treaty of Rome of 1957 to about 1987, European countries increased their internal trade exchanges, but their world trade volume declined (the USA has been the object of a similar decline, while Japan has quadrupled its volume of trade). Starting from this observation, the European Commission was aware of the problems related to market segmentation and chose to strengthen the European single market. In the Single European Act of July 1987, the political lines and the legal context were defined in order to complete integration by 1992. In particular, the proposed measures were: elimination of technical and physical barriers, liberalization of public tenders, the opening up of services markets, the liberalization of capital flows and the abolition of fiscal barriers.

Taiti (1987) examined the effects of the above interventions, both from a macro-economic viewpoint (increased competition level, scale economies, best resources allocation) and from a micro-sectoral one (reallocation of roles and weights). Estimating the effects of the measures one by one, he showed that the GDP of the EU would increase by 12–20% thanks to the opening up of trade. The effects on productive sectors and on enterprises would differ in relation to the specific characteristics of each sector. Taiti singles out the following industries:

(a)   global strategic sectors (telecommunications, electronics, aviation), where the market extension represents only the minimal base for such a development due to R&D investments and public demand;
(b)   mature industrial sectors (chemicals, industrial vehicles, motor vehicles and equipment, tyres, food, civil electronics), where reallocations and strategies of innovation are compatible only through scale economies, influenced overall by technical change;
(c)   sectors with high segmentation of product and/or market (small and medium-sized enterprises), for which *niche* effects are relevant both for products and markets;
(d)   traditional services (banks, finance, insurance, transport), for which high levels of specialization – high dimensional threshold, strong ability in organization, definite market segmentation – are foreseen.

As far as the Italian situation is concerned, a worsening of the economic balance had to be expected in all sectors: sectors already in deficit (agricultural products, chemicals products, food products, precision instruments, electrical materials), because of better foreign performance due to scale economies and strong specialization; sectors of traditionally good performance (industrial and agricultural machines, textiles, clothing, leather and footwear), because of the lower commercial ability of national enterprises; and traditional services sectors (banks, insurance, transport, commerce), because of the better performance of other EU firms in relation to penetration ability.

A quantitative analysis of trade performances of the EU Member States is provided by AA.VV (1989). Two types of indicators expanded on IMF data:

(a)   indices of introversion and orientation of the EU in the exchanges to measure the level of commercial integration among the Member States;

(b)   indices of introversion and orientation in the commercial imbalances to measure the level of financial integration.

The general conclusion was that, during the 1980s, the EU gave a strong impulse to Member States to work towards commercial integration, but this has not involved an abandonment of markets in the rest of the countries covered by the OECD (it has, in fact, led to *trade creation*). Intra-EU trade disequilibrium has increased, but the different positionings of the various Member States were attributed to their different structural situations and/or to insufficiently harmonized policies.

National and regional foreign trade structure

Let us focus on the effects on Italian regions. Cipolletta and de Nardis (1987) studied the level of geographic flexibility of Italy's exports in relation to its market shares for the years 1976–87. They pointed out that there were three phases: 1976–79, characterized by the weakness of the US dollar and the free fluctuation of the lira, which could move tactically and take advantage of market movements; 1980–85, which featured the second oil shock, the international recession, the formation of the single market and the revaluation of the US dollar; 1986–87, which was marked by the petrol countershock and the depreciation of the US dollar. The analysis of the geographic structure of Italy's exports in relation to the OECD highlights that, although there are structural geographic differences (the most important foreign market for Italian exports is Europe), the Italian economy is no different than those of other industrial countries in how it evolves, both in terms of time and direction. The traditional major geographic flexibility relates only to the US market and what happens is strongly dependent on events in the world market. As far as this is concerned, it is worth remembering how Italian international trade policies have always been characterized by a lack of strategies aimed at ensuring a continuous and stable presence in foreign markets. As regards market share, there seems to be no clear correlation with geographic flexibility. The principal factor that influences the success or otherwise of strategies of geographic orientation is the state of the competition in the area characterized by the major inertia of Italian exports, i.e. Europe.

Conti (1987) analysed Italy's trade structure, noting the contributions made by different regions, and tried to explain the joint presence of traditional sectors and more technologically advanced products. The main conclusions arrived at for the 1970s and early 1980s can be summarized as follows:

(a)   the national performance has been strictly tied up with regional developments in production;

(b)   the Italian sectoral specialization of exports has followed the model of the more dynamic regions (the North, the Centre and, in the South, Abruzzi and Puglia);

(c)   the evolution in production in some regions seems to be towards more technological products.

The author chose to analyse an ISTAT data set for the years 1985–86 as the monetary values of the Ufficio Italiano Cambi (UIC) – the only ones available for the years before 1985 – depict a biased scene, referring to legal more than operative sites of enterprises. The international position that emerged from the analysis showed the following characteristics.

A total of 86% of Italian exports come from the North and Centre of the country. The aggregate NEC (composed of Veneto, Friuli–Venezia Giulia, Emilia–Romagna, Toscana, Umbria and Marche) has reached a level of industrialization not far from that of traditionally more advanced regions (referring to the UIC data, in 1968 the NEC area accounted for 23% of total exports).

The commercial deficit is principally due to the Mezzogiorno (namely, the surplus to the NEC area and the deficit to insular Italy).

In terms of specialization, the North-West shows comparative advantages in chemicals and mechanics, the North-East in iron products, textile-clothing-footwear and wooden furniture, the Centre in minerals, non-metallic products and textile-clothing-footwear, the South in ferrous and non-ferrous minerals, agriculture and fishing, motor vehicles and engines, textile-clothing-footwear, the Isles in energy products, chemicals, agriculture and fishing. Within the macro-areas, further specializations are notable: wood and furniture in Friuli–Venezia Giulia, Veneto and Marche; minerals and non-metallic products in Emilia–Romagna and Toscana; electric materials in Lazio and Marche; motor vehicles and engines in Lazio, Abruzzi and Campania; chemicals and petrochemicals in Umbria).

As regards the foreign regional performances, a shift and share analysis of the UIC data was carried out. This suggested that a positive dynamic was operating in the Southern regions, even if it related more to the effects of growing competition than to structural change. It must also be noted that productive organizations and decisions made outside the area play a fundamental role. For example, Sicilia and Sardegna have performed positively in their capital-intensive sectors such as chemicals and rubber materials. The nature of the positive performance of Puglia is different, for the best sectors are textile-clothing-footwear, furniture, agricultural-industrial machines, electric materials.

Viesti (1991) has provided a model of the exports of the Southern Italian regions of Abruzzi, Molise, Campania, Basilicata, Puglia, Calabria, Sicilia and Sardegna by analysing what and how many manufactured goods they exported. He started with an analysis of the Italian foreign component of regional development.[19] Regional structures differ remarkably, as well as geographically, in the productive organization. Sectoral compositions are very different, too,

---

[19]   The statistical problems (as we saw earlier, ISTAT data series start from 1985) and the doubts regarding the real significance of regional exports/imports (for example, attributing the term 'export' to the region that commercializes and does not produce an item; the treatment of the importers problem – the import of a good does not imply that it is used in the same region) contribute to complicating the analysis process. A correct analysis would also need to include the inter-regional trade flows.

as the export potential for any one product varies widely according to several factors (relevance of transport costs, for building materials and some food products; policies regarding import substitution, for petrochemicals, for example; regulations, for the iron and steel industry). Hence, regional exports are mainly determined by the sectoral structure.

The economic development of the Southern regions lags behind that of the Northern regions for many reasons. This fact has important implications as the firms, trying either to start up or grow, have to face a very competitive national market, characterized by a variety of scales of static and dynamic economies. During the period 1989–91, the lowest transport costs, the progressive convergence of lifestyle and regional consumption habits towards a national model and the changed structure of distribution increasingly eliminated protected market areas where Southern regions could compete more efficiently by virtue of their geographic position or product specialization. The South of Italy still presents a low level of economic infrastructure (in terms of the sophistication of its transport, communications and energy systems) relative to the rest of the country, a low number of public and private research centres and a low diffusion of services to industries. Other things being equal, a Southern firm faces the disadvantages of higher costs of transport, of less contact and control of markets, and the fact that it simply takes longer to reach customers located elsewhere. All these reasons account for this region having the lowest figures for international trade.

As we have seen, the historical determinants and the sectoral characterization of the Southern regions are jointly responsible for their low participation in international trade. Within manufacturing, a series of characteristics should be pointed out:

(a)   the significant presence of base industries (such specialization is due to the policies adopted in the past);

(b)   a productive structure influenced by a policy of incentives, that has always preferred to allocate and subsidize the supposed scarce factor, the physical capital, in these regions;

(c)   a consistent presence of firms connected with external investors and which have directed their attention to national rather than foreign clients; a low presence of high-tech and R&D-intensive manufacturers.

Analysing Southern exports, they mainly come from two kinds of firms:

(a)   those created from local capital and means;

(b)   those which are branches of external groups.

This distinction has to be made to stress the different weight that the two types of investment/exports have on the real economic capacity of the Southern regions.

The main conclusions that can be drawn are these:

(a)   the export model of the South is a consequence of the policy measures adopted during the last 30 years;

(b)   during the second half of the 1980s, the base and some of the large industry sectors experienced a crisis, which entailed a worsening of exports from Southern regions;

(c)   despite the good performance of endogenous exports, the total performance is negative, not being compensated by the bad performance of some exogenous exporting centres.

The model of Italian international specialization

The indications coming from the most relevant works concerning the Italian international trade position, despite the variety of the econometric methodologies used (cross-sector analysis with OLS and panel data, cross-countries analysis with OLS and canonical analysis), can be summarized as follows.

During the 1970s and the early 1980s, the model of Italian international specialization was based on sectors and compartments with low R&D intensity, low capital per labour unit intensity and medium-high skilled labour intensity (this characteristic is marked in the sectors of traditional mechanics). The cross-countries analyses confirm that in the manufacturing sectors where a high surplus in the trade balance is present, competition from countries with abundant labour resources has increased, shifting the Italian comparative advantage towards high-intensity skilled labour compartments. It is also to be noted that in the sectors characterized by low Italian specialization, countries characterized by high R&D efforts and fixed capital equipment per inhabitant have relevant positions. Furthermore, Italy's low level of specialization persists in sectors with a high scientific basis, and increasing weakness is registered in the sectors dominated by scale economies, oligopolistic competition and mass production.

Onida (1987) studied Italy's international performance, paying particular attention to aspects of specialization. He carried out cross-section regressions on figures for the trade of manufacturing products, focusing with particular interest on technological intensity, computed specialization indices and found a negative correlation with respect to R&D and physical capital.

Regression analyses were performed on three periods (the averages for 1972–73, 1974–76, 1978–80) and 21 sectors, on dependent variables, such as specialization and RCA indices. Some of the findings were as follows:

(a)   capital intensity correlated negatively with specialization, but the relationship with respect to the RCA was unclear;

(b)   labour intensity correlated positively with specialization in all periods, whereas it correlated positively to the RCA only in the early 1970s;

(c)   technological intensity depended on the regressor used – for example, either the number of patents or an R&D indicator or factor intensities calculated on input-output matrixes (however, most of the correlations had negative signs);

(d)   the concentration indices of partial correlation were near to 0.

In general, the statistical performance was better when the endogenous variable in the regressions was specialization rather than the RCA.

The results of the cross-sector analyses indicated that the impact of physical capital and R&D intensity on Italian comparative advantages has been negative or neutral. On the other hand, a variable indicating the human capital intensity seems to have been a real positive driving factor for Italian exports. The role of technological variables was less clear. When the variables indicating the relative level of technological production (patents) were substituted with variables representing the relative level of technological inputs (R&D expenditures), the negative correlation with specialization became uncertain. The number of patents being a good proxy both of innovations obtained by incremental processes and product differentiation, the results are likely to reflect the existence of a meaningful portion of specialized export sectors. Positive regression coefficients for the R&D variable emerged where technological intensity was measured within an input–output scheme (in such a way that R&D flows were included in all intermediate inputs).

Helg (1989) extended cross-sector regression to a temporal dimension (using panel data analysis) in order to verify the conditions of the Heckscher–Ohlin theorem. The estimated equation considered the indicator of international performance as a dependent variable, and indicators of capital intensity, skilled labour intensity and innovation intensity as explanatory variables. Capital intensity was approximated by the ratio between the net value added of labour expenditures and the number of workers. Two alternative indicators were used for labour intensity, the ratio between skilled and unskilled workers, and the personnel expenditure per employee. Innovation intensity was measured by the ratio between R&D expenditure and the value of sales. The market structure was represented by the industrial concentration index of Hirschman–Herfindahl. The international performance was proxied by the specialization index. Each variable was calculated for 21 manufacturing sectors for the years 1972–80. The results seemed to show that Italian international performance was associated positively with skilled labour intensity and negatively with innovation intensity.

Coglio and Polimeni (1989), referring to Bowen (1983) where a modification to the cross-countries approach was introduced, selected and aggregated in two macro-sectors the sectors registering the greatest surplus/deficit. Hence, the analysis of the first group, where exports have more weight than imports, captured the comparative advantage, while the analysis of the second group outlined the comparative disadvantage, due to the prevalence of imports. Moreover, in order to evaluate the impact on the Italian comparative advantage structure of the international distribution of resources, a canonical correlation analysis was carried out on three macro-sectors, obtained by arranging in descending order the net exports of 115 manufacturing sectors for the two periods 1976-77 and 1982-83.

The resulting framework – obtained by looking both at the sectoral composition of commercial surplus/deficit and at the factors contributing to sustain international competition – seemed to present sharp differences between head and tail sectors. In the case of sectors in surplus, the set of industries belonging to the macro-sector had not changed in the two periods (with the traditional and electrical sectors firmly at the top of each list). Labour, especially unskilled, seemed to represent the characteristic more steadily associated with the best international country performances. It is confirmed that Italian specialization is mainly in the sectors where competition comes from countries characterized by a low tendency to undertake R&D.

The tail macro-sector appeared to be more affected by variability. In fact, there has been a substitution of industries and redistribution of positions within this macro-sector. The most important indication that emerged was that the Italian comparative disadvantage has been shifting in the latest years towards high-tech sectors highly dependent on scale economies. The central macro-sector has given complementary results with respect to the tail sector. It was the most sensitive to the propulsive action of technological variables and, within the aggregate, these variables mainly influenced the sectors with negative net balance. Once more, it confirmed the limited Italian competitive capacity in the sectors characterized by a more sophisticated technological profile.

The reorganization of production in the industrial countries during the 1970s and 1980s entailed a marked development of interdependence of production functions. This process led to forms of industrial specialization based on product differentiation and the exploitation of scale economies. In such a context, the development of IIT requires interpretative schemes of international exchanges that are different from the traditional ones, which assume an inverse relationship between grades of similarity of countries and volumes of exchanges. In fact, an increasing exchange among industrial countries with similar equipment emerged. The new theory of international trade (Helpman and Krugman, 1985) explained this phenomenon by relating the comparative advantage to the relaxation of the perfect competition hypothesis and by giving relevance to the existence of industries with increasing scale returns. These factors induce countries to exchange products, although there is no difference in the productive equipment and in technology. Furthermore, because of the economic growth and the increasing income per capita, consumers ask for wider varieties of goods, thus leading each country to specialize in only some of these goods and to import the other products.

De Nardis (1990) developed his empirical analysis while pointing out two kinds of problems:

(a)   that of defining industry, which is also tied up with the problem of the availability of statistical data;

(b)   measurement indices.

After choosing the Michaely index (which is equal to 1 in cases of perfect similarity of trade flows, and 0 in the opposite case), the author reported its values, calculated for the years 1980 and 1987 using SITC data for the 12 EU Member States, the USA and Japan. In all countries, the index increased for total manufacturing goods, both for the products for which the IIT component was relevant (where goods were differentiated to please the demand characteristics, such as motor vehicles and machine tools) and for some product categories that have been boosted by the widening of the market (namely high-scale production industries, such as iron and steel, and R&D-intensive industries, such as pharmaceutical products, office machines and precision instruments).

In 1987, three relatively homogeneous groups are distinguishable among the European countries studied, which accorded to decreasing values of the index. The first group, with index values of between 0.6 and 0.68, comprised Germany, France, the UK, the Netherlands, Belgium. The second group – Spain, Italy, Denmark and Ireland – had an index value of about 0.5. The third group's values ranged between 0.2 and 0.3 and consisted of Greece and Portugal. As far as Italy was concerned, the following results were reported: the total index increased by 6%, the higher indices were found in the chemicals sector, meaningful intra-industry specialization results in machinery and transport means a sensitive increase was registered in traditional manufactured goods, classified by the materials used (leather, metal, textiles etc.).

4.2.2. Data

The impact of the SMP was analysed at the NUTS 2 regional level and NACE two-digit sectoral level. As for the NUTS 2 disaggregation, Italy consists of 20 regions (Piemonte, Valle d'Aosta, Liguria, Lombardia, Trentino–Alto Adige, Veneto, Friuli–Venezia Giulia, Emilia–Romagna, Toscana, Umbria, Marche, Lazio, Abruzzi, Molise, Campania, Puglia, Basilicata, Calabria, Sicilia, Sardegna), but the less developed Italian regions (Objective 1) considered in this review number only eight: Abruzzi, Basilicata, Calabria, Campania, Molise, Puglia, Sardegna and Sicilia.

General data availability

For all the regions, it was possible to collect most of the data from the National Statistical Institute (ISTAT). The publications *Conti economici regionali* (Regional economic accounts) and *Statistica del commercio con l'estero* (External trade statistics) are the main sources of data that we used to build up a homogeneous data set.

The data series for national accounts (sectoral value added, GDP, sectoral gross fixed investment, sectoral total labour units, population) were collected from *Conti economici regionali* for the period 1980–92, while the data for international trade flows came from *Statistica del commercio con l'estero*, for the years 1985–92.

However, both sources use their own classification systems, as shown in Tables 4.2.1 and 4.2.2.

Table 4.2.1.   Regional economic accounts, ISTAT (1980–92) classifications

Sectors	NACE R44
Market goods and services	
Agriculture, forestry and fisheries	01
Industry	
Industry in the strict sense	
Energy products	03+05+07+11
Industrial processing products	
Ferrous and non-ferrous ores and metals, other than radioactive	13
Non-metallic minerals and mineral products	15
Chemical and pharmaceutical products	17
Metal products, machinery, equipment and electrical goods	19+21+23+25
Transport equipment	27+29
Food, beverages and tobacco	31+33+35+37 +39
Textiles and clothing, leather and footwear	41+43
Paper and printing products	47
Wood, rubber and other manufacturing products	45+49+51
Building and civil engineering works	53
Services	
Wholesale and retail trade and lodging and catering services	55+57+59
Transport and communications	61+63+65+67
Credit and insurance	69
Other market services	71+73+75+77+79
Non-market services	81+85+89+93

Table 4.2.2.   External trade statistics, ISTAT (1985–92) classifications

Sectors	NACE R44
Agriculture, forestry and fisheries	01
Energy products	03+05+07+11
Crude oil	
Ferrous and non-ferrous ores and metals, other than radioactive	13
Non-metallic minerals and mineral products	15
Chemical and pharmaceutical products	17
Petrochemical products	
Metal products, machinery, equipment and electrical goods	19+21+23+25
Metal products	19
Agricultural and industrial machinery	21
Office machines	23
Electrical goods	25
Transport equipment	27+29
Motor vehicles and engines	27
Food, beverages and tobacco	31+33+35+37+39
Meat and meat products	31
Textiles and clothing, leather and footwear	41+43
Textiles and clothing	41
Leather and footwear	43
Wood, paper, rubber and other manufacturing products	45+47+49+51
Wood and wooden furniture	45
Paper and printing products	47

After verifying the correspondence between the two classifications described above and the NACE R44, it was possible to merge them in order to obtain the adopted classification in 11 classes for the tradable sectors as shown in Table 4.2.3. This table also shows the sensitivity of the sectors to the SMP following Buigues *et al.* (1990). Account must be taken here of the conversion to the NACE 70 classification (see the explanatory note at the beginning of this chapter), and the incomparability, for Italy, between this and the Buigues *et al.* study (see comments on this under Section 4.2.3).

Data for the trade flow analysis

Given the general data availability, the main task faced in refining the data set for the purposes of the review was the construction of the import/export trade flows between each region and the EU. Hence new data sources had to be considered in order to obtain the series of 11 sectoral coefficients respectively for X^E/X^W and M^E/M^W for the period 1985–92. Recent data from both the UIC and the External Trade Inistitute (Istituto del Commercio con l'Estero

(ICE)) were used to calculate (after aggregating some of the classes) the sectoral regional coefficients.

Table 4.2.3.   Matched classifications and sector labels

Sector	NACE R44	Label	Sensitivity to the SMP
Agriculture, forestry and fisheries	01	AGR	
Energy products	03+05+07+11	ENP	
Ferrous and non-ferrous ores and metals, other than radioactive	13	MEM	NS
Non-metallic minerals and mineral products	15	NMM	MS
Chemical and pharmaceutical products	17	CHP	HS
Metal products, machinery, equipment and electrical goods	19+21+23+25	MEP	HS
Transport equipment	27+29	TRE	HS
Food, beverages and tobacco	31+33+35+37+39	FBT	NS
Textiles and clothing, leather and footwear	41+43	TEC	MS
Paper and printing products	47	PAP	NS
Wood, rubber and other products	45+49+51	WOR	MS

Data for the factor flow analysis

The regional factor flow analysis was mainly carried out at the aggregate regional level, because of the serious lack of data disaggregated along both the regional and sectoral dimensions.

As far as labour was concerned, the best we could obtain was the series on the number of persons enrolled/cancelled as residents from/to the EU and the rest of the world for the period 1980–92 in the Statistical Yearbook (*Annuario Statistico* (ISTAT)).

Concerning FDI, we were able to collect regional (but not sectoral) data, classified according to the origin/destination country (EU and the rest of the world), from the UIC and the Annual Report (*Relazione annuale*) of the Bank of Italy (1994). More specifically, data on FDI consisted of capital transactions excluding the estate investment.

Data for capital stocks

In order to obtain the sectoral and regional capital stocks series, we had to make assumptions about the depreciation rate and the level of capital stocks at the beginning of the period under analysis. We chose to use the estimates of aggregate regional capital stocks for 1985 computed by Picci (1995), and we then disaggregated them by sector using the available data on sectoral gross fixed investment for the period 1980–84. Moreover, we assumed for each sector the same series of the depreciation rate, obtained as the difference between the gross and net aggregated investment in each year.

Data for EU interventions

European Commission interventions considered in the analysis were of two kinds. The first type was the number and type of measures implemented during the period 1985–92, following the SMP, while the second type was the amount of the joint – national and EU – financial aids (FEOG, FSE) to the regions included in the Objective 1 area.

Both qualitative and quantitative information was collected on these topics. The sources of information were mainly the local Euro-info-centres, which provided copies of the necessary published EU statistics on the execution of Community funding, their Community support frameworks (QCS: Quadri Comunitari di Sostegno) and the national implementation of EU law.

Particular difficulties arose with the definition of 'year when a Community directive is received by the national authorities', because of the differences in the legal systems of each of the Member States. Sometimes the procedure of application/implementation was very hard to understand and disentangle. Nonetheless, homogeneous information was provided by the European Commission publication 'National implementing measures to give effect to the White Paper of the Commission on the completion of the internal market', updated at 31 October 1993.

As far as data on structural funds was concerned, we used data on actual expenditures rather than on allocations in order to capture the direct effects of used funds rather than the effects of the expectation of future expenditure.

Data for the regression analysis

Although the regression analysis mainly used the data and the elaboration of the data (indices) already described in the previous sections, it was necessary to work with two other variables:

(a)   the index of technological progress;
(b)   the index of education level.

As far as the index of technological progress was concerned, we considered the ratio between the 'new efficiency improving' and the 'old' capital stocks taken from the WARM model (see Chapter 3, Section 3.3.3 for a more detailed description). As a measure of the level of education, the ratio between the number of secondary school students (obtained from 'The Regions in Figures' (*Le regioni in cifre*), ISTAT) and the total population aged between 15 and 24 (Statistical Yearbook (*Annuario statistico*), ISTAT) was used.

4.2.3. Indicator analysis

Introduction

The first part of this country report presented some descriptive statistics that provided a first insight into the relationship between the implementation of the SMP and trade and factor flows in the eight less developed regions of Italy.

In order to capture the behaviour of trade and factor flows before and after the implementation of the SMP, we singled out a few indicators, as described in the general framework of this review. These trade and factor flow indicators were related to other economic indicators, designed to identify the main characteristics of each sector in each region. We wanted to present the main results that can be derived from the analysis of the relationship between these indicators and trade and factor flows.

The indicator analysis developed in this section is structured as follows. Next, the methodology used to summarize the large amount of information provided by the calculation of the proposed indicators for different regions, sectors and years is briefly described. Then, we briefly describe the main regional macro-economic indicators that help identify the characteristics of the different regions. Following that, some results at the regional and sectoral levels for both trade flow indicators and factor flow indicators are described. Lastly, we present a summary of our main results.

Methodology

The amount of information supplied by the analysis of the indicators was very large. In fact, for each indicator, we had 8 regions multiplied by 11 sectors multiplied by 8 years, giving 704 values to compute and analyse. Therefore, it was necessary to perform the indicator analysis using a methodology that helped us to summarize the relevant information produced by the available data.

We decided to proceed as follows:

(a)   We described the main characteristics of the eight regions we studied.
(b)   We then computed the value of the indicators described in Section 3.2.[20] For each indicator, we identified the best-performing sectors in each region, i.e. the sectors for which we observed the largest change from the value before and the value after the implementation of the SMP. More precisely, after computing the average value of each indicator in each region before and after 1987, we chose as the best-performing sectors the ones for which the change of the average indicator was the largest. Then, we showed some tables in which these sectors were coupled with a descriptive assessment of their main characteristics. For example, if in region i sector j was the best-performing with respect to indicator k, we described the characteristics of this sector in terms of growth in value added, accumulation rate (the investment/VA ratio), a specialization index (measured as VA_{ij}/VA_j over VA_i/VA), and labour productivity.
(c)   We focused on four indicators for trade flows and four indicators for factor flows. For trade flows these were the exports to EU countries/value added ratio for trade creation, the exports to non-EU countries/value added ratio for trade diversion, the deflated IIT as a measure of IIT, and the RCA index to measure RCA. For factor flows, we focused on employment and investment flows (Herfindahl indices), FDI, and migration as indicators of factor accumulation. For these eight indicators we computed the growth rate of the average indicator from the first subperiod (1985–87) to the second one (1988–92). Then, we analysed these growth rates against four variables meant to capture the main features

---

[20]   Note that, in practice, the Italian database did not enable us to compute all the indicators. For example, it is important to underline the fact that only one indicator among those suggested for trade creation and trade diversion could be computed, namely the export/production ratio. The import/consumption ratio could not be considered because of the complete lack of correspondence between the final household consumption and the import classification systems. The indices of export market shares were also not computed because of the lack of correspondence between different disaggregations.

of the sectors and regions considered in the review. These variables were the change from one subperiod to the other of:

(i)   the growth rate of VA in sector i of region j;

(ii)   the growth rate of the investment/VA ratio in sector i of region j;

(iii)   the growth rate of labour productivity in sector i of region j;

(iv)   the growth rate of a specialization index measured as VA_{ij}/VA_j over VA_i/VA (the specialization of region j in sector i with respect to the national ratio).

Note that statistics for migration and labour, investment and FDI flows were available at the aggregate regional level but not at sectoral level. Therefore, for factor flow indicators we analysed changes in variables that took into account the relative positions of the regions, rather than the sectors.

(d)   We considered another way to summarize the statistical information provided by our sample. We computed correlation indices between trade and factor flow indicators and our trade liberalization index (LI), the construction of which was described in Section 3.4. These correlation indices showed how the increasing adoption of policy measures targeted at implementing the SMP is correlated with trade and factor flow indicators. We could then analyse these correlation indices against the average level in the sample of the four variables that were assumed to capture the main characteristics of the different sectors. Hence, we could obtain correlation values in a way similar to the one described above. Note that for the four trade flow indicators, the relative positions of the sectors were considered in region-specific tables, whereas for the four factor flow indicators the relative positions of the regions were shown in a single table.

The analysis of all the tables was carried out according to the following logical path. First, we identified the main phenomena characterizing the implementation of the SMP and its impact on trade and factor flows for the aggregate macro-region (Southern Italy). This allowed us to single out a few main stylized facts concerning the impact of the SMP. Then, we verified whether or not each region showed a set of indicators the behaviour of which was consistent with the main stylized facts previously identified or if some relevant differences had to be underlined.

The next subsection is devoted to the analysis of some of the regional macro-economic indicators. Then, we move on to cover the analysis of trade flows and factor flows.

The main regional macro-economic indicators

Table A1.4.2.1 (in Appendix A1 to Section 4.2) shows the macro-economic performance of the eight regions considered in this review and of two macro-regions, Southern Italy (the aggregate of the eight regions) and Northern-Central Italy. Also reported are indicators for Italy as a whole.

The macro-economic variables for which the average values before and after 1987 are shown in the table are the following: per capita GDP, GDP growth rate, population growth rate, labour productivity in agriculture, industry and services, and the shares of GDP, investment, population, and valued added in agriculture, industry and services.

From this table, a few stylized facts can be emphasized:

(a)   The largest regions, in terms of size, are Campania, Sicilia and Puglia. However, only Campania and Puglia increased their share of GDP in the post-1987 subperiod. All the indicators showed a relative decline in Sicilia's economic performance.

(b)   A second group of fairly homogeneous regions could be observed, composed of Abruzzi, Calabria and Sardegna. However, Calabria and Sardegna show an economic decline similar to that of Sicilia.

(c)   There are two small, marginal regions – Molise and Basilicata – that were quite stable in the sample period, even if Basilicata was moving faster in terms of economic growth.

(d)   The regional differences were much smaller when we looked at per capita GDP. The highest value was achieved in Abruzzi. Molise, Campania, Puglia, Sicilia and Sardegna have about the same per capita GDP (Puglia and Molise have a slightly higher value), whereas Basilicata and Calabria were the poorest regions.

(e)   In all regions, the population growth was declining quickly. This phenomenon was particularly strong in Calabria, Basilicata and Sardegna.

(f)   In the best-performing regions (Campania, Puglia and Abruzzi), the share of agriculture increased after the implementation of the SMP. This suggested that agriculture may be a leading sector in the growth of Southern regions. Notice that regions of Southern Italy account for about 40% of total Italian agricultural production.

(g)   After the implementation of the SMP, we observed that, in all regions, there was an increase in labour productivity (in the agriculture, industry and services sectors) and in per capita GDP. However, the GDP growth rate increased only in Campania, Basilicata and Sardegna. Sardegna and Puglia showed an increase in their share of the services sector due to development of the tourism industry.

(h)   The share of investment increased after the implementation of the SMP in the regions in which GDP growth also increased, i.e. in Campania, Basilicata and Sardegna.

Trade flow indicators

As previously stated, we used the following three main approaches to the analysis of trade and factor flow indicators:

(a)   the analysis of the best-performing sectors in each region;
(b)   the correlation analysis between trade and factor flow indicators and some sectoral characteristics, such as the growth rate of value added, capital accumulation, specialization and labour productivity;
(c)   the correlation analysis between trade and factor flow indicators and the liberalization index defined in Chapter 3.

This indicator analysis provided a first insight (later deepened by means of a regression analysis) into the impact of the SMP on the main sectors of the Southern regions. A previous report of the European Commission (see Buigues *et al.*, 1990) suggested that completion of the SMP should change neither the sectoral specialization across regions nor the geographical structure of economic activities, even if some adjustments could take place in the medium run. The reason for this has to be found mainly in the fragmented economic structure of most Italian sectors, which are dominated by the presence of a large number of small firms. However, the Buigues *et al.* (1990) report focused on data for a large number of sectors for the whole country, whereas in this review, in order to achieve the required regional disaggregation, we had to reduce the number of sectors we studied. Most importantly, this review focused only on the regions of Southern Italy. Given the relevant structural differences between the North and South of Italy, this review can hardly be compared with the one by Buigues *et al.* (1990). Rather, it can be considered complementary to it. Nonetheless, at the end of this review we try to assess whether or not our empirical evidence is consistent with one of the scenarios outlined in Buigues *et al.* (1990) for the less developed regions of Italy.

As far as the analysis of best-performing sectors was concerned (summarized in Appendix A1 to Section 4.2, Tables A1.4.2.2 to A1.4.2.6 and A1.4.2.7 to A1.4.2.10), the sector characteristics – growth, accumulation, specialization and productivity – were measured by the 1985–92 average value of, respectively, the growth rate of value added, the level of the investment/value added ratio, the level of the specialization index, and the level of labour productivity. The labels 'bad', 'low', 'average', 'good' and 'high' were used to divide the range of variation of the sector characteristics with respect to the regional aggregate value as follows:

0.5	0.5–0.9	0.9–1.1	1.1–1.5	1.5
Bad	Low	Average	Good	High

Note that when the labels were used not to refer to sectors but to regions, the indices were compared to Italian values and the range was divided as follows:

0.75	0.75–0.95	0.95–1.05	1.05–1.25	1.25
Bad	Low	Average	Good	High

Let us now proceed to the analysis of the trade and factor flow indicators singled out and explained in Chapter 3. As already noted, the lack of correspondence between the final household consumption and the import classification systems prevented us from computing the import/consumption ratio as one possible proxy for trade creation. This latter indicator was therefore computed as the ratio between exports and production.

Trade creation

The best-performing sectors in terms of trade creation were the following:

(a)   agriculture (in Campania and Molise);
(b)   wood and rubber (in Abruzzi and Puglia);
(c)   textiles and clothing (in Sicilia and Sardegna);
(d)   metal minerals (in Calabria and Sardegna);
(e)   transport equipment (in Molise and Basilicata).

However, there was no common feature of these sectors in the sample period. For example, in some of them growth of value added was high, whereas in others it was low. This was also the case for the other indicators of sectoral characteristics.

A similarly fuzzy picture emerged when we looked at the table showing the relationship of the change in average trade creation after the implementation of the SMP and the change in the average indicators of sectoral characteristics (see Appendix A2 to Section 4.2, Table A2.4.2.1). For example, the cross-sector correlation between the change in trade creation and the change in sectoral value added was small, even if it was generally positive. The correlation with the change in the accumulation rate varied, with large or small, positive or negative changes (on average, it was slightly negative). The correlation with the change in labour productivity was generally small and negative, whereas correlation with the change of the specialization index was small (positive in some regions, negative in others).

The situation did not improve when we looked at the correlation between trade creation and the liberalization index (r_{tc}) and the indicators of sectoral characteristics (see Appendix A2 to Section 4.2, Table A1.4.2.2). The correlation between r_{tc} and growth in value added varied, with positive or negative, large or small changes (on average, it was negative and small). A similar variability emerged when we looked at the correlation between r_{tc} and the accumulation rate and between r_{tc} and labour productivity. Very small values were instead found for the correlation between r_{tc} and the specialization index.

Note that there was a positive correlation between trade creation and the liberalization index in only five sectors: wood and rubber, transport equipment, metal minerals, energy products and textiles and clothing. Among these five, only four sectors showed a positive change in trade creation between the two subperiods 1985–87 and 1988–92: wood and rubber, transport equipment, metal minerals and textiles and clothing. Note that these sectors were the ones identified by looking at the table of the best-performing sectors in each region.

We can therefore conclude that the implementation of the SMP had a minor effect on trade creation and that this effect can hardly be associated with some sectoral characteristics.

Trade diversion

An increase in this index captured an increase of exports to non-EU countries. The sectors in which this index increased most were:

(a)   agriculture (in Molise);
(b)   wood and rubber (in Abruzzi and Puglia);
(c)   non-metal minerals (in Abruzzi and Basilicata);
(d)   metal minerals (in Campania, Sicilia and Basilicata);
(e)   transport equipment (in Calabria and Basilicata);
(f)   food, beverages and tobacco (in Sardegna and Calabria).

With respect to trade diversion, we observed that textiles and clothing disappeared from the list of best-performing sectors, whereas food, beverages and tobacco and non-metal minerals remained on the list.

As in the case of trade creation, it was difficult to identify the economic factors that characterized the best-performing sectors in terms of trade diversion. All indicators showed a large variability across regions and sectors, as was also shown by the tables in Appendix A2 to Section 4.2.

Consider first the cross-sector correlation between the change in average trade diversion before and after 1987 and the economic indicators of sectoral characteristics. The correlation with growth in value added was small and took both positive and negative values. The variability was even greater when we looked at the correlation with the accumulation rate. The correlation rate with labour productivity was zero on average and there were small positive or negative values in the different regions. A similar conclusion held for the specialization index.

Consider now the correlation rate (r_{td}) between trade diversion and the liberalization index. Its correlation with growth in value added was small on average and characterized by a high level of variability (both positive and negative values occurred). The same result emerged when we looked at the cross-sector correlation between r_{td} and the accumulation rate, labour productivity, and the specialization index.

Note that the correlation rate r_{td} was positive in most sectors (the exceptions were agriculture, metal minerals, metal products and chemicals). However, the change in average trade diversion after 1987 was positive mainly in the wood and rubber, metal minerals, and food, beverages and tobacco sectors (also in transport equipment in Basilicata). Therefore, the positive correlation was not sufficient to induce a positive effect on the level of trade diversion after the implementation of the SMP.

We concluded that the indicators showed a small positive impact of the implementation of the SMP on trade diversion even if the two variables were positively correlated. The positive impact is limited mainly to the wood and rubber, metal minerals, and food, beverages and tobacco sectors. Note that wood and rubber and metal minerals were also the sectors where an increase of average trade creation occurred after 1987. By contrast, textiles and clothing was replaced by food, beverages and tobacco.

Let us look at these last two sectors. Both were characterized by a large increase in growth of value added rates after 1987. However, in the food, beverages and tobacco sector, we also observed a large increase in labour productivity, whereas in the textiles and clothing sector a large increase in the specialization index occurred after 1987.

This suggested the following conclusion. Even if a positive change of average trade diversion were observed in only a few sectors, we could argue that this positive change was more likely in those sectors in which labour productivity also increased, whereas an increase of trade creation was more likely to occur in those sectors where specialization increased. Then, we might argue that specialization leads to trade creation, whereas higher labour productivity leads to trade diversion.

However, this statement needed to be checked using more powerful analytical tools (such as the regression analysis of Section 4.2.4) before it could be confirmed. However, if it were true, it would also suggest that the change in trade creation and trade diversion was more likely to be related to these economic factors than to a direct effect of the implementation of the SMP. This latter variable must affect specialization and labour productivity in order to affect trade creation and trade diversion, respectively.

IIT

The tables in Appendix A2 to Section 4.2 show two indicators of IIT the benefits and costs of which were discussed in the General Report. Let us consider the IIT index rather than the Grubel-Lloyd index. We can see that the best-performing sectors were the following:

(a)   metal products (in Abruzzi and Basilicata);
(b)   transport equipment (in Molise and Basilicata);
(c)   food, beverages and tobacco (in Campania and Molise);
(d)   textiles and clothing (in Puglia, Sardegna and Sicilia);
(e)   non-metal minerals (in Basilicata);

(f)   energy products (in Calabria);

(g)   paper (in Puglia and Calabria).

In this case the picture was clearer and more precise. The average IIT index increased in most sectors after 1987. Moreover, the sectors in which the greatest changes occurred were generally characterized by good and high accumulation rates, low and bad specialization indices and low labour productivity. Therefore, the accumulation of physical capital seemed to be the channel through which an increase in IIT induced by the implementation of the SMP may have led to higher growth rates of per capita GDP.

This important result was also confirmed by the tables and correlation rates shown in Appendix A2 to Section 4.2. First, note that there was a positive correlation of IIT and the liberalization index in almost all sectors in most regions. Second, the average IIT index increased after 1987 in almost all sectors and regions. The few exceptions to the above results were the chemicals, metal minerals and metal products sectors. Therefore, there was some evidence that the implementation of the SMP stimulated IIT in the regions of Southern Italy.

Now, let us look at the cross-sector correlation between the change in the average IIT index and the change in the average sectoral indicators. Note that correlation with the growth in value added was small and highly variable. By contrast, correlation with the accumulation rate was not large, but positive in almost all regions. Correlation with labour productivity was negligible and very variable, whereas correlation with the specialization index looked positive in most regions.

Let us consider the correlation rate (r_{iit}) between the liberalization index and the IIT index. Its correlation with growth in value added was very variable, with changes from positive to negative values occurring when we moved from one region to another. A similar conclusion held when we looked at the cross-sector correlation between r_{iit} and the accumulation rate or labour productivity. The correlation of r_{iit} with the specialization index was generally positive, albeit only slightly.

Therefore, the clearest evidence came from the analysis of the best-performing sectors, i.e. those sectors which had experienced the highest increase in the IIT index in the different regions after 1987. As previously stated, in these sectors an increase in the IIT index was associated with an increase in the accumulation rate after 1987.

When we coupled this result with the one that showed that the implementation of the SMP had a positive impact on IIT in most regions and sectors, we concluded that the accumulation of physical capital was likely to be the main channel through which the SMP affected economic growth and convergence.

RCA

In terms of an increase in the RCA index, the best-performing sectors were:

(a)   wood and rubber (in Abruzzi and Sardegna);

(b)   textiles and clothing (in Molise);

(c)   transport equipment (in Campania, Puglia, Basilicata, Calabria, Sicilia);

(d)   wood and rubber (in Puglia, Sardegna and Basilicata);

(e)   agriculture (in Campania).

In most of these sectors, labour productivity was low, as well as the specialization index. By contrast, we observed a good accumulation rate and a generally high growth (with a few exceptions) in value added. Therefore, the increase in the RCA seemed to be associated with a positive swing in the business cycle above all.

Was this conclusion confirmed by the correlation shown in Appendix A2 to Section 4.2? First of all, note that a positive change in the RCA index occurred in a few sectors (mainly wood and rubber and transport equipment). Second, the correlation rate between the liberalization index and the RCA index (r_{rca}) was positive mainly in the wood and rubber and the transport equipment sectors again. These two sectors were also characterized by the highest average growth of value added and possessed the highest growth of value added in most regions.

This seems to confirm the idea that the implementation of the SMP may have had a positive impact on the RCA index in only a few sectors and only if the progressive liberalization of the European market produced an upswing in the business cycle.

Factor flow indicators

In this section we focus on four main indicators of factor flow movements:

(a)   foreign direct investment from EU countries;
(b)   investment flows;
(c)   employment flows;
(d)   migration.

For these variables no sectoral observation was available. We therefore restricted our analysis to regional indicators and to their cross-region variability (see Appendix A2 to Section 4.2, Tables A2.4.2.3 to A2.4.2.8).

Foreign direct investment

First of all, note that average FDI increased after 1987 only in Sardegna and Campania. These two regions were characterized by a large increase in labour productivity in the same period and, above all, by an increase in the specialization index (together with Molise, these were the only regions in which the specialization index increased). Therefore, the increase in FDI was likely to be associated with an increased specialization in these two regions.

At the same time, the correlation between FDI and the liberalization index was almost always negative (the exception was Sicilia). It is therefore difficult to argue in favour of a positive impact of the implementation of the SMP on FDI in the regions of Southern Italy.

Investment flows

Even more negative conclusions emerged when we looked at investment flows. A positive change in average investment flows after 1987 was observed only in Molise. Moreover, in no region was there a positive correlation between the liberalization index and investment flows.

Employment flows

A positive change of average employment flows after 1987 took place in Sicilia, Calabria and Puglia. Moreover, in Puglia and Sicilia there was also a positive correlation between the liberalization index and employment flows. Note that there was no distinguishing feature of these two regions in terms of changes from the pre-1987 to the post-1987 period. However, these two regions were characterized by high average levels of labour productivity and of the specialization index over the whole sample period.

Migration flows

Average migration flows from and towards EU countries increased in all regions after 1987. The net flow in the regions of Southern Italy was generally positive. However, its share of total population decreased in all regions in the subperiod after 1987. The largest increase took place in Basilicata, probably the most dynamic of Italy's Southern regions, but also in Campania and Calabria. Campania and Calabria are the regions in which the correlation between migration flows and the liberalization index was the highest. Note that this correlation rate was positive in most regions. However, given the recent history of migration flows in Italy, and the lower share of migrants over total population after 1987, we found it difficult to conclude that the increased migration flows were linked to the implementation of the SMP.

Conclusions

There are a few main results that the previous analysis singled out. Let us provide a brief summary of these:

(a)   The effect of the implementation of the SMP on trade diversion and trade creation was very small and limited to a few sectors. There was, however, evidence of an increase in IIT linked to the implementation of the SMP. The positive impact of the SMP on IIT occurred in most sectors and regions. It was, however, larger in those sectors in which the accumulation rate was greater.

(b)   As a consequence, it is likely that the accumulation of physical capital was the main transmission mechanism through which the implementation of the SMP could affect economic growth and convergence.

(c)   Among the regions of Southern Italy, the one in which we observed the largest increase of trade flow indicators in most sectors was Basilicata. In the others, the post-1987 change in trade flow indicators concerned only a few sectors.

(d)   The sectors in which the impact of the implementation of the SMP was stronger were textiles and clothing, transport equipment and food, beverages and tobacco.

(e)   No significant change in factor flows after 1987 were identified. As a consequence, we concluded that the implementation of the SMP was likely to have had a larger effect on trade flows than on factor flows.

4.2.4. Regression analysis

Introduction

The indicator analysis presented in the previous section was only suggestive of the main phenomena that characterized the economic performance of the regions of Southern Italy in the period during which the SMP was implemented.

A more precise assessment of the quantitative relationship among the economic variables that have to be considered in order to assess the effects of the implementation of the SMP on factor and trade flows and on growth was obtained using the regression approach described in Section 3.3.

Objectives and model specification

The regression analysis was designed to achieve four main goals:

(a) **To quantify the impact of the SMP on some trade indicators and factor flows.** This was done by analysing the value of ρ in the following regressions:

Equation 1 $XE_t/Y_t = b_0 + X_t \psi + \rho I_t + \varepsilon_{1t}$

Equation 2 $B_t = b_0 + X_t \psi + \rho I_t + \varepsilon_{2t}$

Equation 3 $RCA_t = b_0 + X_t \psi + \rho I_t + \varepsilon_{3t}$

Equation 4 $FDI_t = b_0 + X_t \psi + \rho I_t + \varepsilon_{4t}$

where trade creation (XE_t/Y_t), IIT (B_t), RCA (RCA_t) and EU FDI (FDI_t) are the main indicators of trade and factor flows that we selected. The vector of explanatory variables, X_t, contained proxies for cyclical and globalization effects (the growth rate of industrial production and world trade growth respectively). In the set of explanatory variables, X_t, we also included the other variables that were used in the indicator analysis, namely labour productivity, sectoral specialization and capital intensity (the capital/labour ratio). Finally, we also accounted for CSF support in all regions. These variables enabled us to disentangle the effect of the SMP (quantified by the parameter ρ) on trade and factor flows from the effects of cyclical and globalization variables and of variables capturing the specificity of each sector (capital intensity, labour productivity, and specialization). In particular, the basic question was this: was the new equilibrium resulting from the implementation of the SMP achieved because of factor or trade movements (or both)?

Note that the regression analysis that helped us answer this question was carried out for all regions and sectors.

(b) **To assess whether or not the SMP, by changing the pattern of trade and factor flows, also modified the accumulation of (physical and human) capital in the Italian regions considered in this review.** To achieve this goal we ran the following regressions:

Equation 5 $k_t = s_0 + s_1 Y_t + s_2 K_t + s_3 \Delta XE_t/Y_t + s_4 \Delta B_t + s_5 \Delta RCA_t + s_6 \Delta FDI_t + \varepsilon_{5t}$

Equation 6 $h_t = r_0 + r_1 Y_t + r_2 H_t + r_3 \Delta XE_t/Y_t + r_4 \Delta B_t + r_5 \Delta RCA_t + s_6 \Delta FDI_t + \varepsilon_{6t}$

where the dynamics of the growth rate of physical (k_t) and human (h_t) capital is explained stock (K_t) and flow (Y_t) characteristics of each region and sector (Baldwin and Venables, 1995) to look out for possible effects of trade creation (XE_t/Y_t), IIT (B_t), international competitiveness (RCA_t) and EU FDI (FDI_t). Note that all these variables were entered into Equations 5 and 6 as first differences (Δ) of the original variables endogenized by Equations 1-4. As explained in Baldwin and Venables (1995), the rationale of Equations 5 and 6 was that capital accumulation was likely to be pro cyclical (in the empirical specification we also used the rate of change of Y_t) and faster when capital was small, i.e. regions with low levels of capital stocks were likely to grow more rapidly. This argument implicitly embodied the assumption of a technology characterized by decreasing returns. As this may not have been the case in some sectors, we did not expect the coefficients r_2 and s_2 to be necessarily negative.

Note that, given the available data, Equation 5 was run for all regions and sectors, whereas Equation 6 was run for all regions only.

(c)   **To assess the impact of the SMP on the growth rates of the different sectors in all regions.** Therefore, the following regression was also run:

Equation 7 $y_t = a_t + \alpha k_t + \beta h_t - (1-\gamma)l_t + \varepsilon_{7t}$

where y_t is per capita GDP growth, a_t is the rate of growth of technical progress, k_t and h_t of physical and human capital respectively, and l_t is the growth rate of unskilled labour. This regression was done for all regions and sectors. However, data on technical progress were available only at country level, whereas for human capital we were able to use data at regional level.

(d)   **Finally, the ultimate goal of our analysis was to verify in which sectors the implementation of the SMP increased or reduced the speed of convergence between the regions considered in this review.** To do that we had to calculate the *antimonde* growth path of per capita value added (see Section 3.3) and then we ran the following regression:

Equation 8 $IM_{j,avg} = cost°_j + (\alpha - \alpha^*)INV_{j,avg} - (\beta - \beta^*)RGDP_{j,85}$
$+ (\gamma - \gamma^*)GPO_{j,avg} - (\delta - \delta^*)SEC_{j,85} + (\varphi - \varphi^*)TECH_{j,avg}$
$+ (\theta - \theta^*)DUMMIES_j + \alpha^*(INV_{j,avg} - INV^*_{j,avg}) + \eta_j$

where the dependent variable was defined as the difference between the actual average relative rate of growth of sectoral per capita value added and the average *antimonde* rate of growth determined as explained in Section 3.7.[21] In Equation 8, we also added the average amount of CSF for each region.

The null hypothesis here was that the coefficient $\pi_1 \equiv \beta - \beta^*$ (and/or $\pi_2 \equiv \delta - \delta^*$) was statistically significant and positive. This hypothesis was easily tested using standard inference technique for all sectors considered in this review. Therefore, we produced information on the impact of the SMP on the speed of convergence in all sectors.

The results of this last equation – which was run for all regions and sectors of Greece, Ireland, Italy and Portugal because it exploits the sectional dimension of the sample – are reported in Chapter 5.

Methodology

From a methodological viewpoint, Equations 1 to 7 were estimated using the techniques described in Section 3.3. In particular, in the estimation process we accounted for:

---

[21]   The starred parameters and variables in Equation 8 were generated within the *antimonde* analysis, that is, assuming the liberalization index was equal to 1 over the whole sample.

(a) **co-integration**, by using the two-step Engle and Granger estimator (the one-step estimator proposed by Davidson and McKinnon proved to be less efficient);

(b) **simultaneity**, by using instrumental variables for the endogenous variables appearing among the explanatory ones;

(c) **regional heterogeneity** in the panel of data used to estimate Equations 1-7 (regional heterogeneity was tested by introducing regional dummies among the regressors);

(d) **structural breaks** related to the implementation of the SMP, by using the liberalization index as the explanatory variable for the dynamics of the equation coefficients;

(e) **heteroscedasticity**, by using a White-consistent estimator;

(f) **technical progress**, by constructing an index of the structure of capital stock that reflects the dynamics of economic indicators such as R&D, relative prices, GDP growth, patents etc. (see Section 3.3);

(g) **structural funds**, by explaining regional differences, also through a measure of CSF in each region.

The actual specification of the model was achieved following the 'encompassing principle' approach. That is, we started from the most general model in which all available variables were included and then we reduced the number of variables of the regressions by performing a cascade of t and F tests. If the 'true' model is 'encompassed' by the initial general model, this method leads the specification process just described to identify the 'true' model. Of course, the small number of degrees of freedom do not guarantee this outcome, which holds asymptotically. Therefore, once we had identified the 'true' model, we tested its robustness by using Pagan and Hall's residual analysis, that is, we regressed the residuals on the excluded variables and tested for the non-significance of the related coefficients.

This procedure (encompassing approach plus residual analysis), designed to guarantee the robustness of the estimated model, was followed for both the explanatory variables included in each regression and the regional dummies, which capture the difference between the region-specific effects and the average effects in the panel of regions. Note that when we applied this procedure, we did not use a rigid criterion to define the significance level of the various tests. In particular, the constants, $C0$, $C1$ and $C2$ (see Appendix A3 to Section 4.2) and the lagged variable of the second stage of the Engle and Granger procedure were maintained in the regression even when they were statistically non-significant. A few explanatory variables also appeared with low t statistics. This was done because our main goals were the robustness and the theoretical consistency of the model. Therefore, given the small number of degrees of freedom, in the selection of the variables, priority was given to these two objectives rather than to the choice of a given (say, 10%) significance level.

Robustness was also an issue as far as cointegration and structural breaks were concerned. In the case of co-integration, the small number of data did not enable us to perform the usual Dickey and Fuller's tests. However, we used a graphical representation of the time series as evidence of the presence of a common trend. Moreover, we exploited the super-consistency properties of the estimates of the co-integration vector in the Engle and Granger two-stage procedure in order to exclude from the co-integration regression those variables whose coefficients were not statistically significant in the first stage. These variables were then tested to see if they would belong to the 'true' model as stationary non-co-integrated variables. When this hypothesis could be accepted, the variables were maintained in the regression (their first difference was not introduced in the second stage of the Engle and Granger procedure).

In the case of structural breaks, we tested the robustness of the model in two ways: by running t tests on the significance of the coefficients explaining their variability and by comparing the model in which structural variability was assumed with the model in which coefficients were assumed to be constant. The computed likelihood ratio always led us to accept the hypothesis that the correct specification was the one that assumed structural variability. The power of these tests was certainly limited by the small size of the sample. However, the panel approach and the non-significance of many regional dummies provided us with a sufficient number of degrees of freedom for the estimation and the robustness check of the final model.

Trade and factor flows

All four of the equations describing the behaviour of trade and factor flows were estimated using the approach described above. The notable exception in the case of Equations 1 to 4 was that only the constant term was assumed to be time-varying, that is, the liberalization index was introduced into Equations 1 to 4 in an additive way. A panel data approach was used in order to increase the efficiency of our estimates. Therefore, all equations were estimated sector by sector, by stacking regional data. Regional dummies (both on constant and slope parameters) were introduced when statistically significant. The regions considered in the equations were Abruzzi (A), Basilicata (B), Campania (C), Calabria (L), Puglia (P), Molise (M), Sicilia (I) and Sardegna (S).

Let us consider the first equation, which captured the dynamics of trade creation. The eight parameters presented in Appendix A3 to Section 4.2 show the impact on trade creation of the:

(a)   world trade index ($x1$);
(b)   specialization index ($x2$);
(c)   capital/labour ratio ($x3$);
(d)   labour productivity ($x4$);
(e)   GDP growth rate ($x5$);
(f)   liberalization index ($x6$);
(g)   FDI ($x7$);
(h)   CSFs ($x8$).

In order to understand the results reported in Appendix A3 to Section 4.2 (Tables A3.4.2.1 and A3.4.2.2), note that the set of regressors is divided into two parts: the first block contains the regressors that were shown to be co-integrated (their coefficients were estimated in the first step); the second block contains the regressors that were not co-integrated (the constants and some explanatory variables) and the lagged dependent variable, which had to be introduced into the second step (we did not show the coefficients related to the first differences of the co-integrated variables, because they were relevant only in order to perform a correct inference on the other parameters). Note that the second block of coefficients is shown after the constant CO and the coefficient of the lagged variable (RIT).

For a clear reading of the tables shown in Appendix A3 to Section 4.2, also note that xi, $I = 1$, $2, \ldots 8$, are the average panel coefficients, whereas xij, $I = 1, 2 \ldots 8$, and $j = A, B, C, L, P, M, I, S$ are the regional dummy coefficients. For example, $x1A$ denotes the differential impact of the world trade index in Abruzzi. When only the regional dummy appears, the differential impact is with respect to zero (the hypothesis that the average coefficient was zero could be accepted). The sector label appears after the coefficient one. For example, *x1AGR* denotes the average impact of the world trade index in the agricultural sector.

Let us focus now on the impact of the liberalization index (which captured the progressive implementation of the SMP) on trade creation. It was found that a positive and significant effect occurred in only a few sectors. These were the paper sector (with the exception of Sardegna), the wood and rubber sector (with the exception of Sardegna and Molise), the metal products sector (with the exception of Basilicata, Puglia and Sicilia), the food, beverages and tobacco sector (only for Molise and Basilicata), the transport equipment sector (only for Molise, Puglia and Sicilia), the metal minerals sector (only for Calabria and Sardegna) and the agricultural sector (only for Molise and Calabria). In all other cases, the liberalization index had either a negative or a non-significant impact on trade creation.

Therefore, these results confirmed what was suggested by the indicator analysis. The impact of the SMP on trade creation was not strong and it was limited to a few sectors (mainly, paper, wood and rubber, and metal products).

More favourable results were to be found when we focused on the IIT indicator (see Appendix A3 to Section 4.2). A positive impact of the liberalization index on IIT was found in almost all sectors and regions (the exception to this was agriculture). A positive and significant coefficient was found for transport equipment (all regions), wood and rubber (all regions), chemical products (with the exception of Campania), energy products (with the exception of Molise), paper (with the exception of Sicilia and Sardegna), food, beverages and tobacco (with the exception of Puglia and Sardegna), metal minerals (with the exception of Abruzzi, Campania and Basilicata), non-metal minerals (with the exception of Campania, Sicilia and Sardegna), metal products (with the exception of Puglia and Sicilia), textiles and clothing (with the exception of Abruzzi, Calabria, Campania and Sicilia), agriculture (only in Molise and Basilicata).

Therefore, the SMP seems to have had a generalized, positive impact on IIT, as we saw in Section 4.2.3, which was devoted to the indicator analysis.

Let us next consider the RCA indicator. Again the results seemed to confirm the outcome of the indicator analysis, which suggested a weak effect of liberalization on RCA. From Appendix A3 to Section 4.2, we can see that a positive impact of the liberalization index is found only for the paper sector (with the exception of Abruzzi), energy products (with the exception of Campania and Sicilia), the transport equipment sector (in Abruzzi and Sardegna), metal products (in Abruzzi, Calabria and Sicilia), non-metal minerals (in Abruzzi, Campania, Puglia and Sicilia). In all other cases, the impact was either negative or statistically insignificant.

Finally, the equation for FDI was estimated for all sectors because data were available at the regional, but not at the sectoral level. Therefore, one equation with regional dummies was used to capture the dynamics of FDI from EU countries (see Appendix A3 to Section 4.2). In this case, the results suggested that the SMP had a negative impact on FDI (a possible exception was Basilicata). Again, this result was found using the indicator analysis. This implied that the implementation of the SMP seemed to have had a larger impact on trade flows than on factor flows. More specifically, a generalized positive effect was found only for IIT.

As far as sectors and/or regions were concerned, positive effects of the implementation of the SMP were most frequently found for the paper sector and for the Molise region (in particular, for trade creation and IIT). The Abruzzi region was most frequently characterized by positive changes in its RCAs.

Factor accumulation

Equations 5 and 6 were designed to assess the impact of trade and factor flow changes on the accumulation of physical and human capital in the different regions and sectors. Capital accumulation (the growth rate of physical and human capital) was therefore explained by the standard stock flow law of motion and by the possible effects of changes in trade and factor flow indicators. In the estimation of these two equations, we accounted for heteroschedasticity due to regional variability, structural breaks induced by the implementation of the SMP (both on constants and slope parameters), regional dummies, co-integration (using the Engle and Granger two-step estimator) and simultaneity (by means of the available instrumental variables).

The estimation results for Equation 2 are shown in Appendix A3 to Section 4.2 (Table A3.4.2.1). The regressors were as follows:

(a)   regional value added ($x1$);
(b)   level of the physical capital stock ($x2$);
(c)   trade creation ($x3$);
(d)   FDI ($x4$);
(e)   IIT ($x5$);
(f)   RCA ($x6$).

Moreover, the coefficient C_0 accounted for regional differences due to the initial 1985 level of the capital stock, while C_2 accounted for regional differences due to CSF. The coefficient C_1 measured the break induced on the panel fixed effect by the increase in the liberalization index. Again, xij, $i = 1, 2, \ldots, 6$ and $j = A, B, C, L, P, M, I, S$ denotes a regional dummy.

Looking at the results, we note that an increase in regional value added had a positive impact on capital accumulation in all regions and sectors. Moreover, with a few exceptions, the parameter related to the level of the capital stock had the expected negative sign, thus showing that capital accumulation was faster when the level of the capital stock was lower.

As far as our objectives were concerned, the most interesting results were those that showed the impact of trade and factor flow indicators on capital accumulation. Consider, for example, the paper sector, in which we found a significant influence of the SMP on trade and factor flows. There the only indicator that showed a statistically significant impact on capital accumulation was B, the indicator for IIT. The impact was positive in all regions, with the exception of Campania and Puglia. As we found that the progressive implementation of the SMP had increased IIT in the paper sector (in almost all regions), we concluded that liberalization, because of its effects on IIT, also had a positive impact on the accumulation of physical capital (the last equation would tell us whether or not the increased capital accumulation also stimulated growth).

A similar conclusion could be reached for the wood and rubber sector, where, again, IIT was the only significant indicator, for the textile and clothing sector, where the coefficient was positive in all regions except Abruzzi, Campania and Sardegna, and for the food and beverages sector, where, however, the coefficient was positive only for Abruzzi, Campania, Puglia, and Sicilia.

Turning things around, the IIT indicator had a statistically non-significant impact on capital accumulation in the transport equipment sector, where a positive impact was found for the FDI indicator in all regions, and in the non-metal minerals sector, where the positive impact was achieved by the RCA indicator. A non-significant impact was also found in the metal products sector (with the exception of Puglia and Calabria, where the impact was positive) where no trade and factor flow indicator was statistically significant. A slightly different result was found in the metal minerals sector, where trade creation had a positive effect (albeit hardly significant) and IIT was statistically significant only in Sardegna, but this time with the negative sign.

In the case of the energy products sector, there was a positive impact on the capital accumulation of two indicators: IIT and RCA (the impact of FDI was positive but slightly non-significant). As we showed that in the energy products sector the implementation of the SMP had a positive impact on both IIT and RCA (with very few exceptions), we concluded that liberalization stimulated capital accumulation in this sector.

The situation was slightly more complicated in the agricultural and chemical products sectors. In the first, there was a positive impact on IIT only in Abruzzi and Campania (the other indicators were not significant, even if a change in FDI may have had a negative impact). In the chemical products sector, IIT had a negative effect in Abruzzi and Calabria, but a positive one in Puglia, whereas trade creation had a positive effect (almost statistically significant at the 5% level).

We can therefore conclude that, among trade and factor flow indicators, only the one capturing changes in IIT seems to have had a generalized positive effect on capital accumulation (with a few exceptions). This was also the indicator that showed a general positive reaction to the implementation of the SMP. Therefore, our regression analysis suggests that liberalization had a positive impact on capital accumulation due to an increase in IIT.

A couple of other remarks seem to be relevant:

(a)   The implementation of the SMP induced a generalized structural break on the model coefficients. In particular, in some sectors the constant term was increased by the SMP. The sectors in which this effect was statistically significant were energy products, food, beverages and tobacco, textiles and clothing, and paper. A negative impact was found only in the transport equipment sector. Therefore, a positive impact of the SMP on capital accumulation was also found as a result of the change in the economic structure.

(b)   Capital accumulation grew faster in those regions in which more CSFs were introduced. The coefficient of this variable was indeed positive and statistically significant in the following sectors: energy products, non-metal minerals, chemical products, transport equipment, food and beverages, and textiles and clothing. In all the other sectors, the effect was non-significant (albeit generally positive).

Let us now consider human capital. This variable was proxied by the number of students in secondary school, a variable that was obviously defined at the regional level (it would have been meaningless to disaggregate this variable for each sector). This proxy was the one most used in the literature on convergence (see Levine and Renelt, 1992, and Baldwin and Venables, 1995). The fact that only regional observations were used implied that only one regression was run, where regional data were considered as a panel. The results are shown in Appendix A2 to Section 4.2. Again, the growth rate of the stock of human capital was negatively related to its level, thus indicating that human capital increased faster when the level was low. The effect of growth in value added on growth in human capital was positive, as expected.

As far as trade and factor flow indicators were concerned, we found a positive impact on human capital of changes in the trade creation indicator, and a negative effect of changes in the RCA indicator. No effect was found for changes in FDI. The effect of changes in IIT was generally negative (the exception was Basilicata), but it was statistically less significant.

However, a strong effect of the implementation of the SMP was found on the constant term that indicated a structural break induced by market liberalization. Different growth rates in different regions were explained by the amounts of CSF and the initial level of human capital. CSF increased the growth rate of human capital; moreover, this growth rate was higher in the region in which the initial capital stock was lower.

Therefore, the impact of trade and factor flow indicators on the dynamics of human capital was different to the one found for the dynamics of physical capital. In the case of human capital, the SMP seems to have had either a non-significant or a negative impact as a result of trade indicators. The reason is that IIT and RCA, which are generally increased by liberalization, have a negative effect on the dynamics of human capital. Vice versa, changes in trade creation have a positive effect, but are slightly influenced by the implementation of the SMP. Finally, changes in FDI are not significant in this equation. However, the SMP had a strong, positive, direct effect on human capital accumulation because of a structural break on the fixed effect. This result was also consistent with our expectations.

Regional growth

The previous analysis suggested that the implementation of the SMP had a positive effect on the accumulation of physical capital because of a direct structural effect and an indirect effect via an increase in IIT. Did this lead to increased economic growth? The answer to this was provided by the last equation of our regression model, which linked the growth rate of per capita income to technical progress $(x1)$, the accumulation of physical $(x2)$ and human $(x3)$ capital, and to the growth rate of the labour force $(x4)$, which was assumed to be exogenous; xij, $i = 1, 2, \ldots, 4$ and $j = A, B, C, L, P, M, I, S$ denotes a regional dummy.

Let us move immediately to the crucial question. In which sector did the accumulation of physical capital have a positive effect on economic growth (as measured by the growth rate of per capita income)? The answer is again provided in Appendix A3 to Section 4.2. The growth rate equations showed that the coefficient of physical capital $(x2)$ was positive and statistically significant in the following sectors:

(a)   metal minerals (mainly for Molise, Campania and Sardegna);
(b)   chemical products (with the exception of Abruzzi);
(c)   metal products (all regions);
(d)   food, beverages and tobacco (all regions).

Therefore, only in 4 of the 11 sectors, did we observe a positive impact of the implementation of the SMP on per capita income growth (as a result of the effects of the SMP on the accumulation of physical capital). In all the other sectors, the accumulation of physical capital had a positive but non-significant impact on per capita income growth.

Let us now consider human capital. The dynamics of this variable had a positive influence on per capita income growth only in the wood and rubber sector (in all regions). In all other sectors, the impact was statistically non-significant. Therefore, the direct effect of the SMP on human capital accumulation is not transmitted into higher growth levels in the regions of Southern Italy (with the exception of the wood and rubber sector).

The economic growth of the regions of Southern Italy is explained in the main by technical progress (in agriculture and chemical products above all) and the dynamics of the labour force (in all sectors and regions). The implementation of the SMP did not have a positive impact on economic growth via changes in the economic structure. The structural break coefficient on the constant term was positive and statistically significant only for agriculture.

These results led us to the following conclusion. Even if the implementation of the SMP had a statistically significant effect on trade flows (mainly IIT) and, from this latter variable, on the accumulation of physical capital, the final impact on the growth of per capita income was quite limited and confined to four sectors – metal minerals, chemical products, metal products, food, beverages and tobacco. A direct structural effect was, however, found for agriculture, and an increase in growth via human capital accumulation was found for the wood and rubber sector. As a consequence, six sectors seem to have benefited from the implementation of the SMP (in terms of growth in per capita income).

One must be cautious when evaluating these conclusions. Even if the methodology used in the regression analysis is quite sophisticated, even if all equations were tested and modified according to the results of the specification search, the quality of the data and the shortness of the time series may have increased the variance of the estimates, thus leading us to consider statistically non-significant parameters that might capture actual relevant effects.

The estimation of the growth rate equations, shown in Appendix A3 to Section 4.2 provided other interesting results:

(a) The coefficient C_0, which related the growth rate of per capita income to the per capita income level, was generally statistically significant and negative. This implied that a convergence process was taking place among the eight regions of Southern Italy, i.e. the less developed regions were catching up with the other ones. A test of whether or not the implementation of the SMP increased the speed of convergence is shown in Chapter 5.

(b) The coefficient C_2, which explains regional differences in growth rates by taking into account the amount of CSF, was positive and statistically significant in the energy products, metal products, food, beverages and tobacco sectors. This implied that regions where CSFs were higher have experienced a higher growth rate of per capita value added in the above sectors.

Conclusions

There are a few conclusions that the regression analysis seems to support:

(a)   The implementation of the SMP had more of an effect on trade flows than on factor flows. In particular:

    (i)   the impact of the SMP on trade creation was not strong and limited to a few sectors (mainly, paper, wood and rubber, and metal products);

    (ii)   the SMP had a generalized positive impact on IIT;

    (iii)   a weak effect of the SMP on RCAs was found;

    (iv)   the SMP had a negative impact on FDI from EU countries.

(b)   Among trade and factor flow indicators, only the one capturing changes in IIT had a generalized positive effect on capital accumulation (with a few exceptions), and this is also the indicator that showed a general positive reaction to the implementation of the SMP, so our regression analysis suggested that liberalization had a positive impact on capital accumulation mainly through an increase in IIT.

(c)   A positive impact of the SMP on physical capital accumulation can also be found as a result of the change in the economic structure.

(d)   As far as the accumulation of human capital was concerned, the SMP had a positive impact because of the induced structural break, but not because of a change in trade and/or factor flows.

(e)   Only in 6 of the 11 sectors did we observe a positive impact of the implementation of the SMP on per capita income growth, and these were those sectors in which the SMP had affected the accumulation of physical capital (metal minerals, chemical products, metal products, food, beverages and tobacco), one in which it had brought about a direct structural break effect (agriculture), and those in which it had had a positive effect on the accumulation of human capital (the wood and rubber sectors).

(f)   The growth rate of per capita income seemed to depend more on the growth rate of the labour force and on technical progress than on the rate of accumulation of physical and human capital and, although there seems to be no structural break in the average level of the growth rate of per capita income, there is clear evidence that a convergence process is taking place among the studied regions, i.e. the less developed regions are catching up with the most developed ones.

4.2.5. General conclusions

The survey of the economic literature on the development of the regions of Southern Italy proposed in the first section of this country report highlighted a few important points:

(a)   In the regions of Southern Italy, economic growth is slowing down in most sectors, thus negatively affecting convergence both among these regions and between them and the rest of Italy. This also reduces the expectations that the SMP and other EU measures can positively affect economic growth and trade and factor flows in these regions. In particular, Taiti (1987) stressed the high probability that opening the European market may worsen the trade balance for the regions of Southern Italy in all sectors.

(b)   A positive stimulus to growth in Southern Italy may come mainly from an increase in human capital. There have been many public interventions to support the accumulation of physical capital that do not seem to have yielded relevant positive effects on growth. Both Onida (1987) and Sestito (1991) emphasized the positive role of increased human capital in those regions (mainly Puglia and Abruzzi) in which we can observe significant growth dynamics.

(c)   When looking at the performance of specific sectors, all studies emphasized a high degree of asymmetry among the different regions of Southern Italy. However, the type of sectoral specialization, the increased competitiveness of the domestic market, the lack of export penetration, and the quality of products suggested that niche effects were the most important for the development of Southern Italian regions. As a consequence, Iit has been found to be increasing in all regions of Southern Italy (de Nardis, 1990).

In many cases, our empirical analysis provided results that were consistent with the previous literature, even if the possibility of carrying out an extended regional and sectoral analysis, with both statistical and econometric tools, enabled us to provide not only a more complete and internally consistent picture of economic development in Southern Italy, but also some new results.

From the indicator analysis presented in Section 3.2, we obtained evidence that supported some of the above conclusions. In particular, in the sample period 1985–92, the increase in trade diversion and trade creation was very small and limited to a few sectors, but there was evidence of an increase in IIT. This increase seemed to be linked also to the implementation of the SMP. The positive impact of the SMP on IIT concerned most sectors and regions. It was, however, larger, in those sectors in which the accumulation rate was larger.

This was another important issue. In contrast with Onida's and Sestito's indications, the accumulation of physical capital was still the main engine bringing about economic growth in Southern Italy and this was also likely to be the main transmission mechanism via which the implementation of the SMP could affect economic growth and convergence. This conclusion was supported also by our regression analysis.

Among the regions of Southern Italy, the one in which we observed the largest increase of trade flow indicators in most sectors was Basilicata. In the other ones, the post-1987 change of trade flow indicators concerned only a few sectors. Still, the regions in which we observed the highest average economic performance were Puglia, Campania and Abruzzi. As far as sectors are concerned, post-1987 changes were relevant mainly in traditional sectors, in which niche effects could be singled out (textiles and clothing, transport equipment, food, beverages and tobacco).

These results were largely confirmed by the regression analysis described in Section 4.2. Both the indicator and the regression analysis led to one important conclusion. The implementation of the SMP affected trade flows more than factor flows. In particular, the SMP had a generalized positive impact on IIT, whereas the impact on trade creation was weak and limited to a few sectors (mainly, paper, wood and rubber, and metal products). A weak effect of the SMP on RCAs was also found; negative or statistically insignificant effects were instead found for factor flows.

Did this positive effect of the SMP on trade flows (mainly IIT) affect economic growth? If yes, through which channels? The answer was clearly provided by our regression analysis which showed that liberalization had a positive impact on capital accumulation (mainly via the increase in IIT). However, from capital accumulation, the impact of the SMP was transmitted to per capita income growth in only a few sectors (metal minerals, chemical products, metal products, food, beverages and tobacco).

The implementation of the SMP also introduced a widespread structural break in the economies of the regions of Southern Italy. This structural break concerned the accumulation of both physical and human capital, which increased. However, again, even the increase of human capital induced by this structural break was not translated into higher economic growth (with the exception of the wood and rubber sector).

As a consequence, only in 6 of the 11 sectors did we observe a positive impact of the implementation of the SMP on per capita income growth. These were metal minerals, chemical products, metal products, food, beverages and tobacco where the SMP had an effect on the accumulation of physical capital, agriculture, via a direct structural break effect, and in the wood and rubber sector, because of a positive effect on the accumulation of human capital.

These results were consistent with the expectations of Buigues *et al.* (1990). In this work, the analysis of the comparative advantages of Member States revealed as the most striking characteristic of Italy its strong position in labour-intensive sectors, while weak trade performances characterized capital-intensive sectors that displayed economies of scale. The strength of the Italian economy was credited to fragmented sectors dominated by small firms. Hence, the expectation in Buigues *et al.* (1990) was that the completion of the SMP should change neither the sectoral specialization across regions, nor the geographical structure of economic activities, even if some adjustments could take place in the medium run. A weak impact of the SMP on trade and factor flows in the regions of Southern Italy was also found in their study.

Moreover, two adjustment scenarios were postulated for the less developed regions in Buigues *et al.*'s report. The first was of an inter-industry nature where they increased the specialization in those sectors where they currently enjoyed comparative advantages; the second was an intra-industry scenario where the structure of industrial production converged towards that of the more developed countries. The results presented in their study partly supported the second scenario. Indeed, there was clear evidence of a development of IIT and of a convergence process among the regions of Southern Italy, i.e. less developed regions were catching up with the most developed ones. The issue of whether or not this convergence process was stimulated and increased by the implementation of the SMP will be addressed in Chapter 5.

4.2.6. Appendix A1 to Section 4.2.

Table A1.4.2.1. The main economic indicators

Indicator	1985–87	1988–92	1985–87	1988–92	1985–87	1988–92
	South**		North–Centre **		Italy	
GDP per capita	10.1	11.1	17.1	19.2	14.6	16.2
GDP growth	2.5	2.0	3.0	2.3	2.9	2.2
Population growth	6.1	3.8	-0.4	0.8	2.0	1.9
Agricultural labour productivity	14.0	15.2	17.4	21.3	15.7	18.3
Manufacturing labour productivity	34.3	38.2	42.0	48.1	40.3	45.9
Services labour productivity	37.1	40.7	45.2	48.1	42.9	46.0
GDP share	25.2	25.1	74.8	74.9		
Investment share	29.5	27.6	70.5	72.4		
Population share	36.3	36.6	63.7	63.4		
Agriculture share	42.1	40.6	57.9	59.4		
Manufacturing share	18.9	18.5	81.1	81.5		
Services share	25.0	25.3	75.0	74.7		
	Abruzzi*		Molise*		Campania*	
GDP per capita	12.6	14.1	10.5	11.7	9.9	10.9
GDP growth	2.7	2.6	3.0	2.1	2.1	2.3
Population growth	4.3	3.5	2.2	1.6	7.4	6.2
Agricultural labour productivity	12.7	14.1	11.0	13.2	10.5	12.2
Manufacturing labour productivity	39.3	42.6	34.5	38.3	33.1	37.6
Services labour productivity	39.0	43.3	39.4	44.2	36.6	40.7
GDP share	7.5	7.6	1.7	1.7	26.8	27.2
Investment share	7.5	7.7	2.5	2.1	26.3	26.4
Population share	6.0	6.0	1.6	1.6	27.3	27.6
Agriculture share	6.4	6.5	1.9	2.1	19.6	21.1
Manufacturing share	9.7	10.0	2.0	2.1	25.5	26.4
Services share	7.3	7.5	1.6	1.7	28.4	28.0

Table A1.4.2.1. (continued)   The main economic indicators

Indicator	1985–87	1988–92	1985–87	1988–92	1985–87	1988–92
	Puglia*		*Basilicata**		*Calabria**	
GDP per capita	10.4	11.7	8.9	9.7	8.6	9.1
GDP growth	3.2	2.2	-0.9	2.3	2.6	1.1
Population growth	6.0	3.4	2.7	1.3	5.6	0.8
Agricultural labour productivity	19.7	24.3	10.2	10.8	10.0	8.6
Manufacturing labour productivity	31.7	36.4	29.5	31.8	28.4	31.6
Services labour productivity	37.5	40.4	38.2	43.8	38.3	42.4
GDP share	19.8	20.3	2.6	2.6	8.8	8.3
Investment share	17.1	17.1	3.7	3.3	10.1	10.1
Population share	19.3	19.3	3.0	3.0	10.3	10.2
Agriculture share	23.8	24.8	3.4	3.1	10.7	9.1
Manufacturing share	19.6	20.3	2.9	2.8	7.1	6.4
Services share	19.5	20.1	2.5	2.6	8.9	8.6
	Sicilia*		*Sardegna**			
GDP per capita	10.1	10.8	10.8	11.9		
GDP growth	3.1	1.5	1.5	2.7		
Population growth	6.4	3.5	5.0	2.6		
Agricultural labour productivity	18.0	18.8	14.0	14.5		
Manufacturing labour productivity	37.0	40.9	41.2	42.3		
Services labour productivity	36.6	39.9	36.3	38.0		
GDP share	24.4	23.8	8.5	8.4		
Investment share	23.3	23.3	9.6	9.9		
Population share	24.6	24.5	7.9	7.9		
Agriculture share	27.7	26.8	6.6	6.6		
Manufacturing share	23.7	22.6	9.5	9.3		
Services share	24.1	23.7	7.7	7.8		

* Share (%) referred to the South. GDP growth (%).

** Share (%) referred to Italy. Population growth (%).

Table A1.4.2.2. Trade creation index: best-performing sectors

Region	Sector	Means		Sector characteristics			
		1985–87	1988–92	Growth	Accumulation	Specialization	Productivity
Abruzzi	WOR	39.83	73.15	High	Average	Low	Low
Molise	AGR	0.97	2.09	Bad	Low	Average	Good
	TRE	0.05	0.25	Good	High	High	Good
Campania	AGR	5.76	5.84	Bad	Bad	Low	Good
Puglia	WOR	11.42	25.28	High	Low	Low	Bad
Basilicata	NMM	0.56	5.10	Bad	High	Bad	Low
	CHP	28.63	61.56	Bad	High	Low	Low
	TRE	-	137.67	High	High	Bad	Bad
	FBT	3.74	8.36	High	High	Low	Low
	PAP	3.76	16.44	High	Good	Average	Bad
Calabria	MEM	-	49.54	Bad	High	Low	Bad
Sicilia	TEC	2.21	5.70	Low	Low	Low	Bad
Sardegna	MEM	18.52	39.85	Bad	Average	High	Bad
	TEC	16.66	53.99	Bad	Low	High	Bad
South	WOR	15.45	23.84	High	Average	Low	Bad

Table A1.4.2.3.   Trade diversion index: best-performing sectors

Region	Sector	Means		Sector characteristics			
		1985–87	1988–92	Growth	Accumulation	Specialization	Productivity
Abruzzi	NMM	1.73	4.65	Bad	Good	Average	Good
	WOR	13.11	29.91	High	Average	Low	Low
Molise	AGR	0.01	0.23	Bad	Low	Average	Good
	TEC	4.75	6.25	High	Average	Bad	Bad
Campania	MEM	7.27	19.74	Bad	High	Good	Low
Puglia	WOR	15.79	28.25	High	Low	Low	Bad
Basilicata	MEM	1.61	11.72	Bad	High	Good	Bad
	NMM	0.71	3.02	Bad	High	Bad	Low
	CHP	1.48	5.44	Bad	High	Low	Low
	TRE	16.89	122.16	High	High	Bad	Bad
	FBT	1.84	9.50	High	High	Low	Low
	TEC	0.21	2.57	High	Good	Bad	Bad
	PAP	2.56	8.16	High	Good	Average	Bad
Calabria	TRE	1.03	1.75	Bad	High	Low	Bad
	FBT	-	1.57	Average	High	Bad	Low
Sicilia	MEM	23.79	54.22	Bad	High	High	Bad
	CHP	44.83	83.57	Bad	High	Good	Bad
Sardegna	FBT	11.59	14.52	Good	Good	Bad	Low
South	WOR	13.51	19.28	High	Average	Low	Bad

Table A1.4.2.4. Grubel-Lloyd index: best-performing sectors

Region	Sector	Means		Sector characteristics			
		1985–87	1988–92	Growth	Accumulation	Specialization	Productivity
Abruzzi	NMM	17.88	21.65	Bad	Good	Average	Good
Molise	ENP	0.66	2.33	Low	High	High	Low
	MEM	19.85	44.48	High	High	Low	Low
	NMM	23.81	54.52	Average	High	Low	Low
	TRE	5.06	15.93	Good	High	High	Good
	PAP	7.70	38.76	Bad	High	Bad	Bad
Campania	TRE	45.92	60.05	High	High	Good	Good
	FBT	45.26	58.73	High	High	Low	Low
Puglia	PAP	15.17	26.22	Average	Average	Average	Bad
Basilicata	TRE	0.00	14.91	High	High	Bad	Bad
	PAP	28.04	50.88	High	Good	Average	Bad
Calabria	ENP	15.19	39.36	Low	High	High	Low
	MEM	0.00	13.75	Bad	High	Low	Bad
Sicilia	TRE	47.96	56.65	Low	Good	Low	Bad
	TEC	60.22	68.97	Low	Low	Low	Bad
Sardegna	ENP	30.90	39.13	High	High	Good	High
	MEM	17.48	22.56	Bad	Average	High	Bad
South	FBT	56.27	61.92	High	High	Low	Low

Table A1.4.2.5.   IIT index: best-performing sectors

Region	Sector	Means		Sector characteristics			
		1985–87	1988–92	Growth	Accumulation	Specialization	Productivity
Abruzzi	MEP	138,415	238,496	High	Good	Low	Low
	WOR	137,444	235,078	High	Average	Low	Low
Molise	TRE	125	759	Good	High	High	Good
	FBT	5,767	128,68	Bad	High	Bad	Good
	PAP	81	582	Bad	High	Bad	Bad
Campania	FBT	419,841	611,708	High	High	Low	Low
Puglia	TEC	166,263	304,317	High	Low	Low	Bad
	PAP	3,733	6,649	Average	Average	Average	Bad
Basilicata	NMM	1,235	10,266	Bad	High	Bad	Low
	CHP	18,536	70,677	Bad	High	Low	Low
	MEP	5,656	11,860	High	Good	Low	Bad
	TRE	-	3,095	High	High	Bad	Bad
	FBT	4,362	13,628	High	High	Low	Low
	TEC	4,754	18,769	High	Good	Bad	Bad
	PAP	986	6,282	High	Good	Average	Bad
Calabria	ENP	1,384	5,176	Low	High	High	Low
	MEM	0	14,270	Bad	High	Low	Bad
	PAP	318	689	Good	High	Average	Bad
Sicilia	TEC	16,984	38,342	Low	Low	Low	Bad
Sardegna	TEC	10,361	28,280	Bad	Low	High	Bad
South	WOR	678,007	1,157,000	High	Average	Low	Bad

Table A1.4.2.6.   RCA index: best-performing sectors

Region	Sector	Means		Sector characteristics			
		1985–87	1988–92	Growth	Accumulation	Specialization	Productivity
Abruzzi	WOR	-2.24	28.52	High	Average	Low	Low
Molise	TEC	-6.06	21.64	High	Average	Bad	Bad
Campania	AGR	-46.36	-35.01	Bad	Bad	Low	Good
	TRE	-54.08	-38.13	High	High	Good	Good
Puglia	TRE	-4.78	18.73	Low	good	Low	Bad
	WOR	-3.75	19.13	High	Low	Low	Bad
Basilicata	TRE	-100.00	44.86	High	High	Bad	Bad
	WOR	10.07	36.35	High	good	Low	Bad
Calabria	TRE	-29.25	-3.18	Bad	High	Low	Bad
Sicilia	TRE	-9.78	23.01	Low	good	Low	Bad
Sardegna	WOR	-61.40	-21.94	High	Low	Low	Bad
South	TRE	-18.31	1.33	High	High	Average	Low

Table A1.4.2.7.   Shares of FDI from the EU

% of total investment	Means		Sector characteristics			
	1985–87	1988–92	Growth	Accumulation	Specialization	Productivity
Abruzzi						
In	1.66	0.38				
Out	0.16	0.06				
Net	1.50	0.32	Good	Low	Good	Good
Molise						
In	0.14	0.03				
Out	0.12	0.06				
Net	0.02	-0.03	Good	Low	High	Good
Campania						
In	1.07	0.34				
Out	0.63	0.31				
Net	0.44	0.03	Low	Low	Good	Good
Puglia						
In	1.42	2.05				
Out	0.48	0.26				
Net	0.94	1.79	Average	Low	Average	Good
Basilicata						
In	0.23	0.12				
Out	0.16	0.16				
Net	0.07	-0.04	Bad	Bad	High	High
Calabria						
In	0.21	0.05				
Out	0.11	0.04				
Net	0.10	0.01	Bad	Bad	High	High
Sicilia						
In	1.45	1.18				
Out	1.04	0.58				
Net	0.41	0.60	Low	Low	Good	Good
Sardegna						
In	0.93	0.28				
Out	0.10	0.03				
Net	0.83	0.25	Low	Low	High	Good
South						
In	1.11	0.78				
Out	0.53	0.28				
Net	0.58	0.50	Low	Low	Good	Good

Table A1.4.2.8.   Shares of migration from and into the EU

% of total population	Means		Sector characteristics			
	1985–87	1988–92	Growth	Accumulation	Specialization	Productivity
Abruzzi						
In	0.98	0.62				
Out	0.32	0.39				
Net	0.66	0.23	Good	Low	Good	Good
Molise						
In	1.04	0.78				
Out	0.47	0.70				
Net	0.57	0.08	Good	Low	High	Good
Campania						
In	0.37	0.31				
Out	0.26	0.46				
Net	0.11	-0.14	Low	Low	Good	Good
Puglia						
In	0.92	0.62				
Out	0.77	0.92				
Net	0.15	-0.30	Average	Low	Average	Good
Basilicata						
In	0.64	0.41				
Out	0.37	0.75				
Net	0.26	-0.34	Bad	Bad	High	High
Calabria						
In	0.71	0.48				
Out	0.42	0.76				
Net	0.29	-0.28	Bad	Bad	High	High
Sicilia						
In	1.30	0.93				
Out	1.64	1.72				
Net	-0.34	-0.79	Low	Low	Good	Good
Sardegna						
In	0.81	0.60				
Out	0.53	0.61				
Net	0.28	0.00	Low	Low	High	Good
South						
In	0.83	0.59				
Out	0.75	0.91				
Net	0.08	-0.31	Low	Low	Good	Good

Table A1.4.2.9.   Regional employment flows (Herfindahl index)

Region	Means		Sector characteristics			
	1985–87	1988–92	Growth	Accumulation	Specialization	Productivity
Abruzzi	13.49	13.14	Good	Low	Good	Good
Molise	15.58	14.51	Good	Low	High	Good
Campania	14.69	14.67	Low	Low	Good	Good
Puglia	14.01	14.17	Average	Low	Average	Good
Basilicata	16.55	15.90	Bad	Bad	High	High
Calabria	17.46	17.63	Bad	Bad	High	High
Sicilia	15.30	15.56	Low	Low	Good	Good
Sardegna	15.61	15.64	Low	Low	High	Good
South	14.79	14.79	Low	Low	Good	Good

Table A1.4.2.10.   Regional investment flows (Herfindahl index)

Region	Means		Sector characteristics			
	1985–87	1988–92	Growth	Accumulation	Specialization	Productivity
Abruzzi	19.65	16.11	Good	Low	Good	Good
Molise	19.61	19.96	Good	Low	High	Good
Campania	23.47	19.86	Low	Low	Good	Good
Puglia	20.78	19.02	Average	Low	Average	Good
Basilicata	18.75	18.40	Bad	Bad	High	High
Calabria	23.91	19.63	Bad	Bad	High	High
Sicilia	23.97	22.70	Low	Low	Good	Good
Sardegna	18.27	15.38	Low	Low	High	Good
South	21.62	18.85	Low	Low	Good	Good

4.2.7. Appendix A2 to Section 4.2.

Table A.2.4.2.1. **Correlation between trade indicators and sectoral characteristics (1985–92)**

	Growth of VA	Productivity	Accumulation	Specialization
Abruzzi				
Correlation between change in TC and change in:	-0.24	-0.02	0.52	0.30
Correlation between change inTD and change in:	0.42	0.00	-0.24	0.11
Correlation between change in RCA-E and change in:	0.40	0.14	-0.34	0.21
Correlation between change in ITT-E and change in:	-0.14	0.50	0.23	0.46
Molise				
Correlation between change in TC and change in:	0.37	-0.31	-0.19	-0.11
Correlation between change in TD and change in:	-0.03	-0.63	-0.06	0.26
Correlation between change in RCA-E and change in:	0.28	-0.18	-0.22	0.52
Correlation between change in ITT-E and change in:	-0.20	-0.59	-0.49	-0.12
Campania				
Correlation between change in TC and change in:	0.37	-0.50	0.65	-0.11
Correlation between change in TD and change in:	-0.01	-0.22	-0.31	-0.65
Correlation between change in RCA-E and change in:	-0.08	-0.12	0.18	0.04
Correlation between change in ITT-E and change in:	0.43	-0.11	0.56	0.14
Puglia				
Correlation between change in TC and change in:	0.25	0.14	-0.25	-0.30
Correlation between change in TD and change in:	0.04	0.13	-0.13	-0.16
Correlation between change in RCA-E and change in:	0.05	0.23	-0.16	-0.28
Correlation between change in ITT-E and change in:	0.51	0.04	-0.51	0.11
Basilicata				
Correlation between change in TC and change in:	0.15	-0.17	0.11	-0.06
Correlation between change in TD and change in:	0.25	-0.21	0.00	0.04
Correlation between change in RCA-E and change in:	0.42	0.00	0.13	0.24
Correlation between change in ITT-E and change in:	-0.25	0.55	0.27	-0.32
Calabria				
Correlation between change in TC and change in:	0.23	-0.59	-0.25	-0.06
Correlation between change in TD and change in:	-0.29	0.55	0.24	0.07
Correlation between change in RCA-E and change in:	0.38	-0.27	-0.36	0.15
Correlation between change in ITT-E and change in:	-0.15	0.30	0.37	0.47

Table A.2.4.2.1. (continued) Correlation between trade indicators and sectoral characteristics (1985–92)

	Growth of VA	Productivity	Accumulation	Specialization
Sicilia				
Correlation between change in TC and change in:	-0.24	-0.60	0.76	0.11
Correlation between change in TD and change in:	-0.16	-0.06	0.48	0.16
Correlation between change in RCA-E and change in:	0.34	0.17	-0.06	0.36
Correlation between change in ITT-E and change in:	0.42	-0.26	0.25	0.03
Sardegna				
Correlation between change in TC and change in:	0.43	-0.03	0.52	-0.15
Correlation between change in TD and change in:	0.04	-0.16	0.08	0.00
Correlation between change in RCA-E and change in:	0.03	0.04	0.12	-0.13
Correlation between change in ITT-E and change in:	0.10	0.10	0.76	-0.12
Italy				
Correlation between change in TC and change in:	0.11	-0.08	-0.32	
Correlation between change in TD and change in:	0.02	-0.04	0.64	
Correlation between change in RCA-E and change in:	0.06	-0.27	-0.21	
Correlation between change in ITT-E and change in:	0.09	-0.65	-0.19	
South				
Correlation between change inTC and change in:	0.23	-0.11	-0.04	0.03
Correlation between change in TD and change in:	0.13	0.00	-0.35	-0.11
Correlation between change in RCA-E and change in:	-0.16	0.18	0.03	0.11
Correlation between change in ITT-E and change in:	0.39	-0.01	0.20	0.55
North-Centre				
Correlation between change in TC and change in:	0.18	0.00	-0.37	-0.08
Correlation between change in TD and change in:	-0.06	-0.14	0.61	0.13
Correlation between change in RCA-E and change in:	0.14	-0.28	-0.11	0.25
Correlation between change in ITT-E and change in:	0.07	-0.50	-0.21	0.17

Table A2.4.2.2.   **Correlation between trade indicators and the liberalization index and sectoral characteristics (1985–92)**

	Growth in VA	Productivity	Accumulation	Specialization
Abruzzi				
Correlation between r(TC,LI) and:	0.17	-0.39	-0.07	-0.10
Correlation between r(TD,LI) and:	0.08	-0.46	-0.34	-0.39
Correlation between r(RCA-E,LI) and:	0.52	0.05	-0.30	-0.32
Correlation between r(IIT-E,LI) and:	0.36	-0.65	-0.60	-0.31
Molise				
Correlation between r(TC,LI) and:	-0.52	-0.32	0.00	0.28
Correlation between r(TD,LI) and:	-0.25	-0.49	-0.42	-0.25
Correlation between r(RCA-E,LI) and:	0.05	0.23	0.33	-0.15
Correlation between r(IIT-E,LI) and:	-0.29	-0.52	-0.38	0.41
Campania				
Correlation between r(TC,LI) and:	0.04	-0.19	-0.10	-0.41
Correlation between r(TD,LI) and:	-0.56	-0.37	-0.26	-0.16
Correlation between r(RCA-E,LI) and:	-0.24	-0.22	-0.08	0.02
Correlation between r(IIT-E,LI) and:	0.02	-0.37	-0.34	-0.19
Puglia				
Correlation between r(TC,LI) and:	0.00	-0.15	-0.01	-0.19
Correlation between r(TD,LI) and:	-0.11	0.10	-0.08	0.04
Correlation between r(RCA-E,LI) and:	0.01	-0.04	-0.06	-0.17
Correlation between r(IIT-E,LI) and:	-0.01	-0.36	0.01	0.05
Basilicata				
Correlation between r(TC,LI) and:	0.04	0.14	-0.48	-0.25
Correlation between r(TD,LI) and:	-0.02	-0.32	-0.30	0.05
Correlation between r(RCA-E,LI) and:	0.51	0.06	-0.14	-0.55
Correlation between r(IIT-E,LI) and:	0.17	0.04	-0.52	-0.01
Calabria				
Correlation between r(TC,LI) and:	-0.11	-0.25	-0.08	-0.05
Correlation between r(TD,LI) and:	0.10	0.04	-0.23	-0.46
Correlation between r(RCA-E,LI) and:	-0.20	-0.05	-0.04	-0.74
Correlation between r(IIT-E,LI) and:	0.00	0.18	0.36	0.28

Table A2.4.2.2. (continued) Correlation between trade indicators and the liberalization index and sectoral characteristics (1985–92)

	Growth in VA	Productivity	Accumulation	Specialization
Sicilia				
Correlation between r(TC,LI) and:	-0.54	0.51	0.24	0.16
Correlation between r(TD,LI) and:	-0.45	0.43	0.19	0.05
Correlation between r(RCA-E,LI) and:	-0.08	-0.06	-0.32	-0.37
Correlation between r(IIT-E,LI) and:	-0.37	0.49	0.11	0.44
Sardegna				
Correlation between r(TC,LI) and:	-0.73	-0.08	0.38	0.06
Correlation between r(TD,LI) and:	-0.38	0.07	0.13	-0.24
Correlation between r(RCA-E,LI) and:	-0.28	0.11	0.07	0.32
Correlation between r(IIT-E,LI) and:	-0.66	0.22	0.51	0.27
Italy				
Correlation between r(TC,LI) and:	0.01	-0.14	0.32	
Correlation between r(TD,LI) and:	-0.10	0.12	-0.23	
Correlation between r(RCA-E,LI) and:	0.02	-0.25	0.24	
Correlation between r(IIT-E,LI) and:	-0.11	-0.21	-0.20	
South				
Correlation between r(TC,LI) and:	-0.10	0.28	0.51	-0.10
Correlation between r(TD,LI) and:	-0.22	0.22	0.24	-0.06
Correlation between r(RCA-E,LI) and:	0.23	-0.09	0.00	-0.29
Correlation between r(IIT-E,LI) and:	0.37	0.24	0.04	0.04
North-Centre				
Correlation between r(TC,LI) and:	0.03	-0.32	0.28	-0.64
Correlation between r(TD,LI) and:	-0.14	0.21	-0.25	0.53
Correlation between r(RCA-E,LI) and:	0.09	-0.33	0.28	-0.63
Correlation between r(IIT-E,LI) and:	-0.19	-0.61	-0.53	0.25

Table A2.4.2.3.   **Correlation between factor flow indicators and the liberalization index (1985–92)**

Region	r(Migration to EU,LI)	r(FDI from EU,LI)	r(Employment flows,LI)	r(Investment flows,LI)
Abruzzi	-0.10	-0.77	-0.93	-0.62
Molise	0.36	-0.86	-0.55	-0.58
Campania	0.70	-0.52	0.62	-0.64
Puglia	0.17	-0.16	0.96	-0.84
Basilicata	0.18	-0.15	-0.65	-0.59
Calabria	0.89	-0.75	-0.35	-0.63
Sicilia	0.01	0.03	0.74	-0.20
Sardegna	-0.06	-0.12	-0.01	-0.72
Italy	0.31	0.10	0.96	-0.45
South	0.29	-0.44	0.31	-0.74
North-Centre	0.34	0.10	0.98	0.07

Table A2.4.2.4   **Average of the percentage growth rate/level of the key economic indicators (1985–92)**

Region	Growth of VA	Productivity	Accumulation	Specialization
Abruzzi	-2.95	30.19	28.74	108.86
Molise	-3.27	24.26	45.24	132.90
Campania	-1.99	25.14	23.30	83.96
Puglia	-3.09	30.41	25.73	121.54
Basilicata	-0.84	19.74	40.74	123.53
Calabria	-4.32	15.88	37.62	115.75
Sicilia	-1.51	33.10	24.68	154.60
Sardegna	-1.89	31.42	42.27	136.13
Italy	-2.63	37.87	21.54	100.00
South	-2.11	27.40	28.05	104.92
North-Centre	-2.78	41.66	19.99	109.91

Table A2.4.2.5. **Difference of the percentage growth rate/level of the factor flow indicators (1987–92 minus 1985–87)**

Region	Migration to EU	FDI from EU	Employment flows	Investment flows
Abruzzi	47.48	-23.00	-0.35	-3.54
Molise	37.23	-700.00	-1.07	0.35
Campania	64.35	139.69	-0.01	-3.61
Puglia	34.57	-7.90	0.16	-1.76
Basilicata	195.33	-70.90	-0.66	-0.35
Calabria	65.72	-54.33	0.17	-4.28
Sicilia	43.59	6.45	0.26	-1.27
Sardegna	44.05	642.64	0.02	-2.89
Italy	32.07	13.10	0.16	-1.09
South	47.92	-5.14	0.00	-2.77
North-Centre	8.86	27.82	0.21	-0.40

Table A2.4.2.6. **Difference of the percentage growth rate/level of the key economic indicators (1987–92 minus 1985–87)**

Region	Growth in VA	Productivity	Accumulation	Specialization
Abruzzi	-0.57	3.45	4.51	-8.80
Molise	5.09	4.49	-14.36	2.41
Campania	-2.01	5.91	-0.81	5.87
Puglia	1.31	5.54	-2.22	-6.93
Basilicata	-4.65	2.75	-4.42	-15.92
Calabria	7.19	0.27	7.67	-19.08
Sicilia	2.06	2.81	-0.22	-11.07
Sardegna	-5.76	4.02	6.24	3.63
Italy	0.76	6.12	0.77	0.00
South	0.21	4.08	0.26	-3.64
North-Centre	0.86	6.81	0.93	-0.08

Table A2.4.2.7.   Correlation referred to in Tables A2.4.2.3 and A2.4.2.4 (1985–92)

	Growth in VA	Productivity	Accumulation	Specialization
Correlation between *r(Migration to EU, LI)* and average of:	-0.47	-0.46	-0.02	-0.49
Correlation between *r(FDI from EU, LI)* and average of:	0.50	0.67	-0.47	0.17
Correlation between *r(Employment flows, LI)* and average of:	0.08	0.64	-0.75	-0.15
Correlation between *r(Investment flows, LI)* and average of:	0.09	0.58	-0.43	0.15

Table A2.4.2.8.   Correlation referred to in Tables A2.4.2.5 and A2.4.2.6 (1985–92)

	Growth in VA	Productivity	Accumulation	Specialization
Correlation between change in *Migration to EU* and change in:	-0.39	-0.44	-0.14	-0.50
Correlation between change in FDI *Migration from EU* and change in:	-0.65	0.05	0.76	0.14
Correlation between change in *Employment flows* and change in:	0.02	0.11	0.71	-0.04
Correlation between change in *Investment flows* and change in:	0.01	0.38	-0.74	0.14

4.2.8. Appendix A3 to Section 4.2.

Explanatory note regarding the regression analysis

The regression parameters, X_{ijk}, have to be read as follows:

i is the index of the regressor (according to the three types of equations):

Trade and factor flows:

1 world trade index;
2 specialization index;
3 capital/labour ratio;
4 labour productivity;

5 GDP growth rate;
6 liberalization index;
7 FDI;
8 CSFs;

Human and physical capital:

1 regional value added;
2 level of the physical capital stock;
3 trade creation;

4 FDI;
5 IIT;
6 RCAs;

Economic growth:

1 technical progress;
2 accumulation of physical capital;

3 human capital;
4 growth rate of labour force;

j is the index of the region:

*A*bruzzi;
*C*ampania;
*B*asilicata;
S*i*cilia;

*M*olise;
*P*uglia;
Ca*L*abria;
*S*ardegna;

k is the index of the sector:

AGR
ENP
CHP
FBT
MEM
MEP

NMM
PAP
TEC
TOT
TRE
WOR.

Table A3.4.2.1. Sectoral regression parameters for Italy

Sector MEM

Growth equation

Variable	Param.	t student
X2MEM	0.520	1.157
X4MEM	-0.154	-0.467
X2MEM	0.937	1.859
X2CMEM	2.280	2.312
X2SMEM	1.500	2.602
X4MEM	-0.430	-1.944
X4MMEM	7.604	4.543
X4PMEM	0.785	3.216
X4BMEM	-0.303	-1.460
C0MEM	-0.432	-0.903
C1MEM	0.026	0.278
C2MEM	-2.519	-4.224
RITMEM	-0.132	-3.843
X3MEM	1.939	0.691
R-squared	0.751	

Physical capital equation

Variable	Param.	t student
X1MEM	11.464	2.681
X2MEM	-17.309	-2.507
X1CMEM	8.866	9.079
X1PMEM	-2.445	-4.291
X2SMEM	9.910	21.761
C0MEM	0.041	0.112
C1MEM	0.036	1.193
C2MEM	-0.041	-0.057
RITMEM	-0.048	-3.147
X3MEM	2.049	1.479
X5MEM	0.040	0.429
X5AMEM	0.754	1.231
X5SMEM	-0.666	-2.148
R-squared	0.275	

IIT-E equation

Variable	Param.	t student
X1MEM	48.027	0.826
X2MEM	65.991	5.930
X3MEM	-77.583	-3.159
X6MEM	40.935	0.696
X7MEM	11.765	3.522
X1MEM	46.372	2.183
X1AMEM	226.672	8.029
X1LMEM	314.419	9.744
X1IMEM	395.251	6.935
X6MEM	51.483	1.038
X6AMEM	-137.450	-1.689
X6CMEM	-476.821	-5.701
X6PMEM	104.923	2.267
X6BMEM	-718.925	-5.909
C0MEM	-415.485	-1.254
RITMEM	-0.725	-4.490
X5MEM	46.875	1.176
R-squared	0.752	

RCA-E equation

Variable	Param.	t student
X1MEM	141.946	4.050
X2MEM	-29.169	-3.125
X3MEM	40.539	3.737
X4MEM	1.342	4.928
X5MEM	18.976	2.326
X1AMM	262.414	5.082
X1PMM	-66.270	-2.278
C0MEM	537.458	0.806
RITMEM	-0.092	-1.816
X6MEM	-55.332	-1.441
R-squared	0.138	

TC equation

Variable	Param.	t student
X1MEM	268.929	1.745
X3MEM	36.463	3.048
X7MEM	31.000	-1.949
X8MEM	-1.577	-4.573
X1AMEM	-51.525	-6.220
X1MMEM	-184.266	2.188
X1PMEM	148.419	3.274
X1LMEM	797.707	
C0MEM	355.579	0.496
RITMEM	-0.736	-5.902
X6MEM	-76.566	-1.290
X6BMEM	-344.234	-2.944
X6LMEM	882.050	2.121
X6SMEM	806.097	4.150
R-squared	0.475	

Sector NMM

Growth equation

Variable	Param.	t student
X4NMM	-0.557	-2.969
X4ANMM	-0.799	-1.761
X4MNMM	2.345	2.499
X4CNMM	0.347	3.152
X4LNMM	-2.647	-4.414
X4INMM	-0.983	-2.260
C0NMM	-0.281	-1.552
C1NMM	-0.038	-1.190
C2NMM	0.456	0.986
RITNMM	-0.136	-5.006
X2NMM	0.763	1.275
X2SNMM	-0.544	-1.015
R-squared	0.628	

Physical capital equation

Variable	Param.	t student
X2NMM	-2.660	-2.467
X2ANMM	-7.865	-5.162
X2PNMM	-2.453	-2.618
X2BNMM	-2.637	-2.045
X2SNMM	-26.808	-18.734
C0NMM	-0.439	-1.589
C1NMM	-0.028	-0.926
C2NMM	0.582	2.777
RITNMM	-0.032	-5.309
X1NMM	0.092	1.142
X1LNMM	0.508	2.272
X5NMM	-0.044	-0.566
X5SNMM	-2.044	-1.882
X6NMM	5.115	4.171
R-squared	0.401	

IIT-E equation

Variable	Param.	t student
X1NMM	592.336	7.493
X5NMM	56.474	2.396
X6NMM	141.826	5.712
X8NMM	0.647	4.520
X1ANMM	239.094	2.413
X1BNMM	9014.050	2.338
X6ANMM	510.676	5.504
X6CNMM	-256.219	-4.108
X6BNMM	26390.800	4.706
X6INMM	-326.150	-2.852
X6SNMM	-441.647	-9.860
C0NMM	-224.174	-0.910
RITNMM	-0.711	-3.139
X1NMM		
R-squared	0.579	

RCA-E equation

Variable	Param.	t student
X2NMM	-40.224	-1.717
X4NMM	2.917	5.865
X6NMM	-242.890	-1.353
X7NMM	24.270	2.407
X6ANMM	390.206	3.580
X6MNMM	-780.649	-3.780
X6CNMM	5590.300	3.604
X6PNMM	1919.580	5.374
X6LNMM	230.499	11.127
X6INMM	283.439	3.310
X6SNMM	-3173.400	-5.683
C0NMM	-12015	-1.682
RITNMM	-0.321	-2.825
X1NMM	915.898	1.727
R-squared	0.290	

TC equation

Variable	Param.	t student
X1NMM	526.797	2.307
X2NMM	35.475	1.814
X1ANMM	86.042	2.114
X1MNMM	-702.527	-9.465
X1PNMM	-279.324	-2.790
X1BNMM	28869.600	4.990
X1INMM	-281.133	-2.589
X1SNMM	-475.553	-5.720
C0NMM	6505.810	2.048
RITNMM	-0.547	-3.487
X4NMM	-1.614	-1.973
X8NMM	-0.197	-1.947
R-squared	0.708	

Sector CHP

Growth equation

	Param.	t student
X1CHP	0.772	2.863
X4CHP	0.229	1.335
X4ACHP	0.445	10.480
X4MCHP	0.287	2.039
X4BCHP	-1.375	-10.892
X4LCHP	-0.601	-2.073
X4ICHP	-0.399	-1.352
X4SCHP	-0.641	-2.528
C0CHP	-0.695	-2.176
C1CHP	0.031	0.820
C2CHP	0.327	0.351
RITCHP	-0.118	-3.748
X2CHP	1.312	1.940
X2ACHP	-1.216	-1.760
X3CHP	1.770	1.373
X3SCHP	-1.493	-1.902
R-squared	0.611	

Physical capital equation

	Param.	t student
X1CHP	2.328	4.279
X2CHP	-7.274	-3.471
X1MCHP	5.701	2.087
X1SCHP	1.882	1.937
X2ICHP	1.342	4.857
C0CHP	0.124	0.541
C1CHP	-0.017	-0.550
C2CHP	0.949	2.376
RITCHP	-0.041	-2.731
X2CHP	-47.709	-2.370
X3CHP	3.952	1.748
X5CHP	0.014	0.707
X5ACHP	-5.483	-2.455
X5CCHP	-0.178	-1.621
X5PCHP	1.104	2.819
X5LCHP	-0.361	-2.406
X6CHP	-1.744	-1.440
R-squared	0.410	

IIT-E equation

	Param.	t student
X2CHP	42.674	3.324
X4CHP	0.507	1.780
X6CHP	89.513	2.520
X7CHP	6.025	2.853
X6ACHP	552.470	4.313
X6MCHP	489.564	3.014
X6CCHP	-190.864	-5.887
X6BCHP	2762.270	3.855
X6ICHP	298.698	3.228
X6SCHP	97.599	2.009
C0CHP	1487.800	2.407
RITCHP	-0.597	-5.293
X3CHP	-91.667	-2.593
X8CHP	-0.178	-2.261
R-squared	0.506	

RCA-E equation

	Param.	t student
X4CHP	1.274	3.928
X6CHP	-271.223	-2.499
X8CHP	3.407	1.279
X6ACHP	335.178	4.580
X6MCHP	-1030.400	-6.535
X6CCHP	-5321.130	-5.190
X6PCHP	21409.900	6.637
X6LCHP	815.836	1.705
C0CHP	2534.280	0.990
RITCHP	-0.587	-4.057
X2CHP	48.143	1.720
X3CHP	-300.646	-3.975
X5CHP	35.524	1.109
R-squared	0.456	

TC equation

	Param.	t student
X2CHP	-17.673	-1.322
X3CHP	177.377	4.583
X4CHP	0.435	2.243
X8CHP	0.222	1.812
C0CHP	-6054.720	-2.399
RITCHP	-0.069	-0.690
X1CHP	24.293	2.288
X6CHP	-87.278	-1.466
R-squared	0.441	

Sector MEP

Growth equation

	Param.	t student
X2MEP	0.832	3.634
X4MEP	0.122	2.458
X4AMEP	0.473	11.378
X4MMEP	0.049	1.241
X4CMEP	-1.461	-6.070
X4BMEP	-0.394	-10.394
X4LMEP	-1.018	-1.431
X4SMEP	-0.561	-4.090
C0MEP	-0.217	-0.839
C1MEP	-0.017	-0.490
C2MEP	0.996	2.620
RITMEP	-0.124	-4.702
R-squared	0.683	

Physical capital equation

	Param.	t student
X1MEP	0.587	1.365
X1AMEP	7.592	3.489
X1CMEP	-0.495	-2.701
C0MEP	0.378	1.583
C1MEP	-0.046	-1.477
C2MEP	0.203	1.566
RITMEP	-0.032	-2.199
X5MEP	-.39112E-	-0.234
X5PMEP	1.294	2.478
X5LMEP	0.251	1.831
X5IMEP	-0.444	-1.591
R-squared	0.634	

IIT-E equation

	Param.	t student
X2MEP	178.812	16.113
X3MEP	-65.101	-1.207
X6MEP	24.521	1.192
X7MEP	4.350	4.867
X6MEP	29.312	2.508
X6AMEP	518.791	6.376
X6MMEP	65.496	2.720
X6PMEP	-166.298	-6.842
X6LMEP	1092.660	13.405
X6IMEP	-136.513	-4.118
X6SMEP	283.832	15.184
C0MEP	95.796	0.417
RITMEP	-0.965	-7.750
R-squared	0.670	

RCA-E equation

	Param.	t student
X2MEP	-802.364	-5.155
X3MEP	419.646	2.749
X6MEP	10.183	6.076
X8MEP	140.445	1.393
X6MEP	-644.111	-2.239
X6AMEP	3488.620	4.185
X6MMEP	569.912	5.621
X6CMEP	-3723.150	-4.779
X6PMEP	-692.780	-4.168
X6BMEP	321.261	2.035
X6LMEP	1774.400	3.964
X6IMEP	75688.800	3.808
C0MEP	321.703	0.201
RITMEP	-0.149	-1.703
R-squared	0.153	

TC equation

	Param.	t student
X2MEP	105.386	2.656
X3MEP	163.791	1.654
X6MEP	-306.711	-3.922
X8MEP	0.319	2.445
X6AMEP	335.794	5.999
X6MMEP	354.514	7.849
X6CMEP	424.338	8.627
X6BMEP	575.845	4.218
X6LMEP	773.929	15.888
X6IMEP	152.985	4.318
X6SMEP	532.579	16.052
C0MEP	131.609	0.052
RITMEP	-0.366	-3.471
X4MEP	-0.384	-0.529
R-squared	0.489	

Sector	Growth equation	Param.	t student	Physical capital equation	Param.	t student	IIT-E equation	Param.	t student	RCA-E equation	Param.	t student	TC equation	Param.	t student
TRE	X2TRE	0.068	1.015	X2TRE	-5.113	-9.250	X6TRE	278.065	2.651	X2TRE	60.351	13.422	X3TRE	56.307	2.204
	X4TRE	0.541	9.135	X2ATRE	-203.449	-7.917	X8TRE	1.375	8.889	X6TRE	-355.201	-3.283	X4TRE	2.495	6.415
	X2ATRE	-0.036	-13.260	X2CTRE	-2.794	-1.762				X8TRE	1.759	2.426	X6TRE	-318.968	-3.239
	X2MTRE	1.163	3.091	X2PTRE	-259.803	-1.508	C0TRE	-941.195	-0.630	X6ATRE	479.703	8.402	X6MTRE	2151.630	4.657
	X4CTRE	-0.825	-8.748	X2BTRE	-562.607	-3.772	RITTRE	-0.551	-2.154	X6CTRE	209.469	3.570	X6CTRE	-449.408	-2.132
	X4PTRE	-0.644	-8.846	X2STRE	-12.280	-1.147	X3TRE	151.230	1.578	X6STRE	3892.160	3.028	X6PTRE	719.445	4.505
	X4STRE	0.062	1.322				X5TRE	166.551	1.653				X6ITRE	1138.970	7.889
	C0TRE	-0.334	-1.569	C0TRE	0.337	1.313				C0TRE	246.472	0.172	C0TRE	-2038.040	-0.912
	C1TRE	-0.417	-0.096	C1TRE	-0.058	-2.771				RITTRE	-0.779	-4.225	RITTRE	-0.725	-2.770
	C2TRE	-0.673	-3.031	C2TRE	1.313	2.541							X2TRE	33.108	1.370
	RITTRE	-0.139	-6.726	RITTRE	-0.102	-4.056									
	X3TRE	0.873	0.958	X4TRE	1.646	2.033									
	X3ATRE	1.642	2.212	X5TRE	-.81391E-	-0.385									
				X5MTRE	-21.496	-1.819									
	R-squared	0.757		R-squared	0.666		R-squared	0.409		R-squared	0.444		R-squared	0.524	
FBT	X2FBT	1.525	2.651	X1FBT	6.231	4.141	X1FBT	56.778	3.196	X2FBT	64.007	5.520	X3FBT	253.600	8.748
	X2LFBT	3.913	1.266	X2FBT	-39.235	-3.947	X2FBT	75.308	2.030	X7FBT	18.520	3.332	X4FBT	1.100	7.813
				X1AFBT	-0.194	-2.072	X4FBT	-2.093	-2.446				X6FBT	-208.880	-7.185
	C0FBT	-0.322	-1.152	X1SFBT	1.927	2.820	X6FBT	229.045	1.935	C0FBT	-300.804	-0.519	X7FBT	1.275	1.135
	C1FBT	-0.049	-0.903	X2CFBT	3.176	3.669	X7FBT	4.042	1.458	RITFBT	-0.365	-2.138	X6AFBT	79.930	2.450
	C2FBT	1.167	3.597				X11FBT	9.426	3.668				X6MFBT	228.896	7.061
	RITFBT	-0.088	-3.629	C0FBT	-0.294	-1.986	X6MFBT	523.874	3.113				X6BFBT	1539.750	4.932
	X3FBT	2.142	1.497	C1FBT	0.026	1.872	X6CFBT	516.566	4.510				X6LFBT	-128.775	-2.430
	X3SFBT	-1.839	-2.019	C2FBT	0.287	2.321	X6PFBT	-457.747	-17.797				X6IFBT	194.894	7.972
	X4FBT	-0.802	-2.188	RITFBT	-0.054	-4.516	X6SFBT	-306.490	-6.954				X6SFBT	137.544	4.552
	X4MFBT	-0.687	-0.871	X5FBT	-0.047	-0.958									
	X4CFBT	1.636	1.908	X5AFBT	0.145	1.206	C0FBT	-261.378	-0.475				C0FBT	-91.601	-0.360
	X4BFBT	1.051	2.281	X5CFBT	0.055	1.135	RITFBT	-1.314	-5.720				RITFBT	-0.572	-2.990
	X4LFBT	2.684	3.229	X5PFBT	0.158	2.848	X3FBT	-391.445	-2.140				X7FBT	2.552	1.885
				X5BFBT	-0.293	-2.638									
				X5IFBT	0.493	3.172									
				X5SFBT	-0.489	-2.225									
	R-squared	0.514		R-squared	0.371		R-squared	0.818		R-squared	0.226		R-squared	0.389	

Sector	Growth equation	Param.	t student	Physical capital equation	Param.	t student	IIT-E equation	Param.	t student	RCA-E equation	Param.	t student	TC equation	Param.	t student
TEC	X3TEC	1.119	1.376	X1TEC	0.482	2.107	X1TEC	33.903	3.711	X2TEC	82.577	4.643	X3TEC	129.770	3.362
	X4TEC	0.445	1.849	X1CTEC	0.509	2.222	X2TEC	234.728	4.115	X3TEC	35.037	1.777	X4TEC	3.537	9.264
	X4ATEC	2.995	11.133	X1PTEC	-0.229	-1.715	X3TEC	78.336	1.618	X4TEC	1.404	1.895	X7TEC	10.183	4.278
	X4CTEC	2.887	5.266	X1LTEC	35.975	2.940	X4TEC	-2.952	-2.155	X6TEC	-94.381	-1.472	X8TEC	-0.587	-4.557
	X4LTEC	2.938	1.841				X5TEC	47.164	1.155	X8TEC	0.536	3.745			
	X4ITEC	-0.993	-1.874	C0TEC	-0.433	-0.857	X8TEC	0.606	6.919	X6CTEC	-1996.340	-4.557	C0TEC	210.481	0.462
	X4STEC	-2.457	-4.565	C1TEC	0.790	1.943	X1MTEC	19.452	2.812	X6PTEC	63.092	2.600	RITTEC	-0.303	-2.530
				C2TEC	4.348	1.896	X1PTEC	28.835	4.030	X6LTEC	177.598	2.481			
	C0TEC	-0.078	-0.238	RITTEC	-0.046	-3.594	X1BTEC	263.015	5.801						
	C1TEC	0.004	0.149	X2TEC	-68.835	-1.877	X1LTEC	93.455	3.692	C0TEC	-243.496	-0.426			
	C2TEC	1.940	2.768	X2ATEC	-30.385	-1.525	X1ITEC	162.049	5.537	RITTEC	-0.370	-2.613			
	RITTEC	-0.154	-5.609	X2MTEC	-683.858	-1.945	X1STEC	49.264	4.680						
				X2CTEC	53.841	2.005	X6TEC	26.811	1.438						
				X5TEC	0.338	2.019	X6ATEC	-740.631	-3.066						
				X5ATEC	-1.170	-2.346	X6CTEC	-88.125	-3.598						
				X5CTEC	-0.545	-3.366	X6PTEC	328.676	2.604						
				X5BTEC	5.092	2.218	X6LTEC	-1283.960	-3.714						
				X5STEC	-3.695	-1.237	X6ITEC	-1586.980	-2.855						
							C0TEC	145.195	0.505						
							RITTEC	-0.740	-5.122						
	R-squared	0.722		R-squared	0.305		R-squared	0.878		R-squared	0.204		R-squared	0.275	
PAP	X4PAP	-0.531	-1.653	X1PAP	17.621	4.438	X2PAP	58.951	4.282	X3PAP	110.804	5.509	X3PAP	86.841	1.333
	X4APAP	2.696	2.635	X2PAP	-56.748	-4.521	X4PAP	0.985	3.689	X8PAP	3.571	7.300	X4PAP	0.805	1.888
	X4CPAP	1.203	3.595	X1APAP	-7.227	-2.622	X6PAP	131.979	4.009				X7PAP	5.302	2.225
	X4BPAP	-0.833	-1.541	X1BPAP	10.939	6.754	X7PAP	5.195	3.044	C0PAP	-1402.580	-1.057			
	X4LPAP	-0.338	-1.264	X2LPAP	10.602	3.531	X6MPAP	853.575	1.247	RITPAP	-0.489	-2.951	C0PAP	-808.354	-0.520
	X4IPAP	0.252	2.873	X2IPAP	4.945	1.978	X6CPAP	174.093	3.151	X6PAP	165.038	1.431	RITPAP	-0.901	-4.597
	X4SPAP	0.717	1.239				X6BPAP	3547.990	0.578	X6APAP	-658.139	-4.795	X2PAP	12.883	1.320
							X6LPAP	475.934	0.500				X6PAP	71.841	0.902
	C0PAP	-0.347	-1.265	C0PAP	-0.319	-2.771	X6IPAP	-382.580	-2.283				X6MPAP	378.276	3.624
	C1PAP	-0.050	-0.673	C1PAP	0.058	3.852	X6SPAP	-507.495	-3.485				X6PPAP	583.776	2.008
	C2PAP	0.749	1.923	C2PAP	0.134	0.272							X6BPAP	7436.740	2.024
	RITPAP	-0.124	-4.479	RITPAP	-0.110	-4.172	C0PAP	-669.686	-0.938				X6SPAP	-252.266	-2.892
	X3PAP	2.149	1.215	X5PAP	0.076	0.512	RITPAP	-0.835	-7.166						
	X3SPAP	-1.667	-1.627	X5CPAP	-0.852	-2.353	X1PAP	6.684	2.378						
				X5PPAP	-2.794	-2.084	X1PPAP	39.273	3.907						
				X5IPAP	11.925	5.622	X1BPAP	507.876	2.087						
							X1LPAP	61.968	2.309						
							X1IPAP	56.975	4.883						
	R-squared	0.660		R-squared	0.610		R-squared	0.725		R-squared	0.349		R-squared	0.594	

Sector	Growth equation			Physical capital equation			IIT-E equation			RCA-E equation			TC equation		
WOR		Param.	t student		Param.	t student		Param.	t student		Param.	t student		Param.	t student
	X3WOR	1.629	3.579	X1WOR	3.168	2.631	X1WOR	45.622	6.623	X2WOR	-267.105	-2.110	X2WOR	542.556	4.979
	X4WOR	1.825	3.651	X2WOR	-13.255	-2.188	X2WOR	165.727	2.879	X3WOR	137.022	2.528	X4WOR	-4.971	-2.409
	X4AWOR	1.308	1.817	X1PWOR	-0.959	-1.458	X4WOR	-4.436	-2.623	X4WOR	4.603	2.379	X8WOR	0.731	1.989
	X4CWOR	-1.079	-2.298	X1LWOR	12.616	1.647	X8WOR	0.563	3.491	X8WOR	0.994	1.752			
	X4PWOR	-0.693	-1.308	X1SWOR	139.236	3.115	X1AWOR	10.503	4.614	COWOR	-2098.110	-1.951	COWOR	845.589	0.641
	X4BWOR	-12.708	-3.924	X2AWOR	-250.899	-2.746	X1MWOR	-15.522	-2.852	RITWOR	-0.302	-2.949	RITWOR	-0.264	-2.283
	X4LWOR	-3.723	-6.220	X2MWOR	-140.626	-4.491	X1PWOR	-7.250	-5.534				X6WOR	76.021	0.756
	X4IWOR	-0.745	-1.577	X2BWOR	-8.654	-1.166	X1BWOR	48.803	3.729				X6AWOR	227.114	1.893
	X4SWOR	-5.037	-1.509	X2IWOR	-27.488	-2.912	X1SWOR	-23.617	-11.568				X6MWOR	-204.097	-1.098
	X3AWOR	1.460	1.632										X6SWOR	-322.055	-1.789
	COWOR	-0.177	-0.661	COWOR	-0.388	-0.820	COWOR	2859.750	2.448						
	C1WOR	-0.966	-0.312	C1WOR	-0.028	-0.273	RITWOR	-0.912	-7.744						
	C2WOR	1.968	3.003	C2WOR	0.197	1.244	X3WOR	-276.597	-2.874						
	RITWOR	-0.156	-5.679	RITWOR	-0.083	-4.297									
				X3WOR	10.094	1.837									
				X5WOR	0.030	0.369									
				X5MWOR	-1.942	-1.620									
	R-squared	0.680		R-squared	0.393		R-squared	0.771		R-squared	0.301		R-squared	0.269	

Note: A=Abruzzi; M=Molise; C=Campania; P=Puglia; B=Basilicata; L=Calabria; I=Sicilia; S=Sardegna.

Table A3.4.2.2. Non-sectoral regression parameters for Italy

Sector	FDI equation			Human capital equation		
		Param.	*t* student		Param.	*t* student
TOT						
	X2TOT	36.842	2.935	X1TOT	0.700	5.611
	X3TOT	-617.312	-2.706	X2TOT	-0.590	-5.582
	X4TOT	2.566	2.749	X2ATOT	0.552	5.603
	X6TOT	-256.783	-5.011	X2MTOT	0.585	5.626
	X7TOT	1.107	1.905	X2CTOT	0.433	5.660
	X6ATOT	-355.347	-2.589	X2PTOT	0.469	5.616
	X6BTOT	293.874	1.485	X2BTOT	0.578	5.601
				X2LTOT	0.545	5.598
	C0TOT	-4347	-2.122	X2ITOT	0.447	5.656
	RITTOT	-0.663	-3.507	X2STOT	0.549	5.629
	X1TOT	1.674	1.766			
	X1PTOT	1.733	3.116	C0TOT	-0.240	-3.148
	X8TOT	0.352	2.161	C1TOT	0.206	20.428
				C2TOT	15.464	2.591
				RITTOT	-0.054	-4.744
				X3TOT	9.158	9.886
				X5TOT	-0.001	-1.466
				X5MTOT	-0.126	-2.071
				X5CTOT	-0.020	-3.513
				X5PTOT	-0.009	-9.575
				X5BTOT	0.429	9.522
				X5ITOT	-0.004	-8.110
				X5STOT	0.043	5.296
				X6TOT	-1.795	-6.512
	R-squared	0.536		R-squared	0.784715	

Note: A=Abruzzi; M=Molise; C=Campania; P=Puglia; B=Basilicata; L=Calabria; I=Sicilia; S=Sardegna.

4.3. Greece

M. Antoninis, T. Papadopoulos, G. Papanikos, Centre for Economic Research and Environmental Strategy (CERES), Athens, Greece

4.3.1. Background

The published studies investigating the nature of factor and trade flows and the issue of convergence between Greece and the EU were limited. One of the latest analyses was that by Mardas (1993). He employed indicator analysis in an attempt to assess the impact of the SMP on the Greek export trade. In his study, industry data classified at the three-digit level according to the SITC were used, for the period 1981–88. The main findings suggested that the intensity of IIT in Greece was the lowest of all the Member States and was limited to the traditional export products (see also Table 4.3.1). This phenomenon was explained as being the result of the weakness of the Greek economy to create dynamic comparative advantages that were closely related to the investors' choices, the specialization profile and the complementarity of the Greek trade within the EU.

Earlier studies, such as that by Greenway and Hine (1991), showed a generally rising pattern of IIT for Greece until the 1980s, and constancy thereafter. The unadjusted Grubel-Lloyd index computed for Greece on the basis of three-digit SITC trade data suggested that, by 1985, 46.3% of the manufacturing trade of Greece was of the intra-industry type. Sarris *et al.* (1993), by using five-digit trade data, disputed the previous findings, suggesting that 'Greece is still a country where the bulk of external trade is of the inter-industry variety'. However, he argued that, despite the size of the IIT, the improvements that had been made were substantial. Furthermore, he indicated that the patterns of vertical IIT for Greece resembled those of a country that mainly exported low-quality products and imported high-quality ones.

Hassid and Katsos (1992) also devoted a part of their work on the IIT between Greece and the EU by concentrating their analysis on the two-digit sectoral level for the period 1970–88. They concluded that, despite marginal cases (the food industry, tobacco products and textiles), IIT between Greece and the EU was limited.

The most recent and probably most detailed study using trade indicators was carried out by Thomas (1993). He examined the performance of the Greek manufacturing industry by sector of activity at the three-digit level for the period 1985–92. He pointed out that the Greek competitive position relied on the local production of raw materials and on low labour costs in sectors facing weak international demand. Dealing with the IIT between Greece and the EU he indicated that Greece performed the lowest level of this form of trade within the EU, with Grubel-Lloyd coefficients equal to 0.29 in 1987 compared to 0.57–0.77 for the other 10 Member States. However, he pointed out that, overall, Greece increased the number of sectors it specialized in for intra-EU trade relative to its European partners. Specifically, 73 sectors, embodying 62.85% of exports, improved their specialization index and 35 industries covering 37% of exports found themselves worse off.

In addition, Thomas surveyed the competitive manufacturing sectors in 1991/92, indicating their relevance to the export performance of the country, and examined the development of each manufacturing sector and investigated the dynamics of sectoral competitiveness. According to his findings, Greek industry exhibited a strong competitive advantage

(100>RCA>0) in both world and EU trade in only 18 (see Table 4.3.1) out of 108 of its industrial sectors.

Table 4.3.1. Strong-performing Greek industries in terms of exports to the EU and the rest of the world

Number*	Sector (three-digit classification)
1	Electrical engineering
1	Manufacture of metal articles
4	Food, beverages and tobacco
1	Extraction and preparation of metallic minerals
1	Production and preliminary processing of metals
2	Extraction of minerals
3	Manufacture of non-metallic mineral products
2	Textiles
2	Footwear and clothing
1	Other manufacturing industries
18	Total

* Number of subsectors with strong RCA according to three-digit classification.

Furthermore, the manufacturing exports, both worldwide and to the EU, were highly concentrated and the majority of the strong sectors' products were in weak-demand growth sectors. Finally, the majority of exports to both the EU and the rest of the world were in labour-intensive sectors.

Dealing with the dynamics of sectoral competitiveness relative to the rest of the world, Thomas pointed out that the number of strong-performing sectors declined in the period 1985–92, while the majority of the industries suffered a deterioration in their competitive position for the same period. Concerning EU trade, on the other hand, the number of strong-performing sectors remained constant in the period 1985–92 and the majority of industries improved their competitive position during this same period.

The above results led to the conclusion that the restructuring and modernization of the traditional competitive sectors was indispensable in order for Greece to remain active in the world market. In addition, the development and diversification of other sectors in products facing above-moderate international demand growth were essential to achieving a healthier trade balance.

4.3.2. Data

All the studies mentioned in the brief survey above were based on the Objective 1 classification of regions and, as a result, adopted the *whole* of Greece as a single region. A significant innovation here is that we examine the impact of the SMP at *regional* level, specifically at NUTS 2 level, and NACE two-digit sectoral classification, by utilizing the most recently available data. This level of regional/sectoral disaggregation gave, for the case of Greece, 13 geographical regions and 20 sectors, as indicated in Tables 4.3.2 and 4.3.3.

Table 4.3.2. NACE 70 codes

NACE	Label
2200	Metals (production and preliminary processing)
2300	Non-metallifer. minerals, peat
2400	Non-metallic mineral products
2500	Chemical industry
2600	Man-made fibres industry
3100	Manufacture of metal articles
3200	Mechanical engineering
3300	Office and data processing machinery
3400	Electrical engineering
3500	Motor vehicles and parts
3600	Others means of transport
3700	Instrument engineering
4100	Food, beverages and tobacco industry
4200	Sugar manufacturing and refining
4300	Textile industry
4400	Leather and leather goods
4500	Footwear and clothing industry
4600	Timber and wooden furniture
4700	Paper, printing and publishing
4800	Processing of rubber and plastics
4900	Other manufacturing industries

Table 4.3.3. Greek regions at NUTS 2 level

RA11	Anatoliki Makedonia, Thraki
RA12	Kentriki Makedonia
RA13	Dytiki Makedonia
RA14	Thessalia
RA21	Ipeiros
RA22	Ionia Nisia
RA23	Dytiki Ellada
RA24	Sterea Ellada
RA25	Peloponnisos
RA3	Attiki
RA41	Voreio Aigaio
RA42	Notio Aigaio
RA43	Kriti

Data availability

Due to the lack of proper organization for data provision by the relevant authorities in Greece, most of the data were found in primary sources, where the national classification code differs from the one we needed to adopt here. The main sources of the data have been the National Statistical Service of Greece, the Ministry of National Economy, the Ministry of Industry, the Ministry of Labour and the Ministry of Trade.

The data available was classified in two broad categories: the aggregate national data, most of them contained in the VISA database, and the regional data, most of them obtained from Greek sources. Analytically, the aggregate data was presented as follows.

(a)   Trade flows (exports and imports) by three-digit NACE from/to the rest of the world, the EU and all of Europe (those in the EU plus other European countries in the OECD).
       Time series: 1980-93
(b)   Production (gross value added) data by three-digit NACE.
       Time series: 1980-94
(c)   Consumption data by three-digit NACE .
       Time series: 1980-93
(d)   Employment by three-digit NACE.
       Time series: 1980-94
(e)   Investment by three-digit NACE.
       Time series: 1987-92
(f)   GDP at market prices and GDP deflator.
       Time series: 1980-94
(g)   Price indices for each two-digit sector.
       Time series: 1980-94

Regional data

As mentioned earlier, an important problem with the data obtained from local sources concerned their correspondence with the classification codes. Although the review required the use of NACE codes, the National Statistical Service of Greece (NSSG) used its own classification coding. For this purpose the NSSG coding was converted to the NACE classification used here. However, this meant that we could not examine the following industries according to the NACE classifications.

(a)   Motor vehicles and parts (NACE code 3500) and other means of Transport (NACE code 3600). Both of these industries were therefore classified under motor vehicles and parts (NACE code 3500).
(b)   Instrument engineering (NACE code 3700) was included in other manufacturing industries (NACE code 4900).
(c)   The food, beverages and tobacco industry (NACE code 4100) and sugar manufacturing and refining (NACE code 4200). Both of the industries have been classified under the food, beverages and tobacco industry (NACE code 4100).
(d)   Finally, it was not possible to obtain data for the man-made fibres industry (NACE code 2600) or office and data processing machinery (NACE code 3300) at the required level.

Therefore, we ended up with revised NACE sectors, as shown in Table 4.3.4.

Table 4.3.4. NACE 70 codes revised according to Greek data availability

NACE	Label
2200	Metals (production and preliminary processing)
2300	Non-metallifer. minerals, peat
2400	Non-metallic mineral products
2500	Chemical industry and man-made fibres industry
3100	Manufacture of metal articles
3200	Mechanical engineering
3400	Electrical engineering
3500	Motor vehicles and parts and other means of transport
4100	Food, beverages and tobacco industry, and sugar manufacturing and refining
4300	Textile industry
4400	Leather and leather goods
4500	Footwear and clothing industry
4600	Timber and wooden furniture
4700	Paper, printing and publishing, and office and data processing machinery
4800	Processing of rubber and plastics
4900	Other manufacturing industries and instrument engineering

For the sectors shown in Table 4.3.4, the availability of regional data for Greece can be presented analytically as follows.

(a) Gross domestic product.
   Time series: 1980–92.
   At aggregate level by region. The dimensions available were GDP in million ECU.
   Source: National Accounts of Greece.

(b) Total production of the industries by region at two-digit classification.
   Time series: 1980–92.
   Source: National Accounts of Greece.

(c) Value added at factor cost for the industries at aggregate level by region.
   Time series: 1979–92.
   Source: National Accounts of Greece.

(d) Value added at factor cost for the industries at aggregate level by region at two-digit classification.
   Time series: 1979–92.
   Source: National Accounts of Greece.

(e) Total employment for all the industries at aggregate level in the regions and disaggregated at two-digit NACE.
   Time series: 1985–92.
   Source: National Accounts of Greece.

(f) FDI for all the industries at aggregate level by region and disaggregated at two-digit NACE.
   Time series: 1985–92.
   Source: Ministry of National Economy.

Data estimation

It is apparent from what we just mentioned that it was not possible to obtain all the data required for the indicator analysis in the case of Greece. Specifically, we had to estimate some trade and factor flow data, and our approach in this respect is described fully in Appendix A1 to Section 4.3.

Achieved coverage of trade and factor flow indicators

Even after using estimated regional data, it was not possible to calculate all the indicators mentioned in Chapter 2 for the case of Greece. Concerning trade flow indicators, more or less complete coverage was achieved. However, even then, the nature of data construction did not allow for the calculation of *alternative* forms of trade creation or trade diversion indicators, and we had to rely throughout on the share of exports in production.

Concerning factor flows, the situation was much worse. It was not possible to obtain any data on labour flows or on portfolio investment, so there is no analysis of these flows in the case of Greece.

Finally, it should be noted that the indicator analysis in the following two sections concentrated on the *regions* of Greece, given that the study by Thomas (1993), summarized in our introduction, included indicator analysis at three-digit manufacturing level for the whole country.

Nevertheless, under Introduction, below, we include trade indicators for the whole of Greece at two-digit level for comparison with other countries and with the regional indicator analysis for Greece.

To summarize, in the following sections, the indicators calculated and analysed are:

(a)   trade creation (*Exports to the EU/production*);
(b)   trade diversion (*Exports to non-EU countries/production*);
(c)   Grubel-Lloyd index;
(d)   IIT;
(e)   RCA;
(f)   export specialization;
(g)   capital/labour ratio;
(h)   Herfindahl indices of regional and sectoral employment concentration;
(i)   FDI.

4.3.3. Indicator analysis

Introduction

As mentioned in preceding sections, Greece has a weak manufacturing base, the size of which stagnated at around 15% of GDP throughout the 1980s. Further, production has generally concentrated in specific sectors and regions, a fact that one should not neglect in this review. We shall start here with some basic information concerning changes in the main trade indicators calculated at the two-digit level for the whole country.

National findings

Trade creation, trade diversion, Grubel-Lloyd and RCA indices were calculated for the period 1985–92 at national level. The data used for the calculations was extracted from the VISA database. The NACE sectors included in the calculation are those reported in Table 4.3.4. The necessary data adjustments were made in order to achieve correspondence with the sectors used in the regional analysis (as described in Section 4.3.2).

For each indicator, the average values of the periods 1985–87 and 1988–92 were calculated and then the growth rate of the indicator across the two periods was also calculated.

Table 4.3.5 reports the values of the trade creation and trade diversion indices for the whole of the country for each of the two periods and the change in the indicators that occurred between the periods.[22]

Table 4.3.5. Trade creation and trade diversion indices for national data

NACE	Trade creation indices			Trade diversion indices		
	1985–87 average	1988–92 average	% change	1985–87 average	1988–92 average	% change
2200	0.198	0.197	-0.51	0.165	0.109	-33.94
2300	0.163	0.255	56.44	0.117	0.172	47.01
2400	0.028	0.107	282.14	0.271	0.151	-44.28
2500	0.052	0.082	57.69	0.106	0.081	-23.58
3100	0.025	0.056	124.00	0.076	0.088	15.79
3200	0.121	0.198	63.64	0.147	0.377	156.46
3400	n.a.	0.110	-	n.a.	0.057	-
3500	0.024	0.028	16.67	0.052	0.034	-34.62
4100	0.120	0.100	-16.67	0.084	0.061	-27.38
4300	0.217	0.338	55.76	0.046	0.104	126.09
4400	0.072	0.152	111.11	0.161	0.144	-10.56
4500	0.838	0.600	-28.40	0.291	0.205	-29.55
4600	0.025	0.032	28.00	0.067	0.065	-2.99
4700	0.027	0.015	-44.44	0.054	0.039	-27.78
4800	0.069	0.090	30.43	0.078	0.067	-14.10
4900	0.117	2.342	1,901.71	0.255	1.130	343.14

---

[22] It was not possible to calculate the change in the value of the index of trade creation and trade diversion between the two periods for the electrical engineering sector (34) because there was no data available on production for the first period (1985-87).

The SMP had been expected to increase Greece's share of exports to the EU in production and decrease its share of exports to non-EU countries. Six sectors (non-metallic minerals, 24, chemical industry, 25, motor vehicles, 35, leather and leather goods, 44, timber and wooden furniture, 46, and processing of rubber and plastics, 48) showed the anticipated result: they increased their share of exports to the EU in terms of production while at the same time reducing their share of exports to non-EU countries in this regard.

Among the remaining sectors, four (metals, 22, food, beverages and tobacco, 41, footwear and clothing, 45, and paper and printing, 47) experienced a decrease in the values of both indices (trade creation and trade diversion) and five sectors (non-metallic minerals, 23, textile industry, 43, and other manufacturing industries, 49) exhibited increases in the values of both their trade creation and trade diversion indices.

These findings accorded with the findings of the regional analysis (presented in Tables 4.3.24 and 4.3.25). All sectors exhibited the same pattern of change at both the regional and national levels (except for the metals (22) sector, which presented an increase in the index of trade creation at regional level and a decrease at national level).[23] This also functioned as a useful check that our estimates of regional trade data were reasonably reliable.

The national Grubel-Lloyd and RCA indices (see Table 4.3.6 and Appendix A3 to Section 4.3), also presented a broadly similar picture to that shown by the regional analysis (Tables 4.3.26 and 4.3.27). There were, however, also some inconsistencies, especially with regard to the electrical engineering (34), motor vehicles and parts and other means of transport (35) and food, beverages and tobacco industry and sugar manufacturing and refining (41) sectors. The SMP was expected to increase IIT by increasing product differentiation due to an increase in market size and scale economies. Indeed, that was the case for the majority of sectors of the Greek economy. The largest change in the Grubel-Lloyd index (114.2%) took place in the non-metallic minerals (24) sector and the consistency of this change was supported by the regional analysis. Large, positive changes also took place in the leather and leather goods (44, 37%), chemical industries (25, 34.7%) and textile industry (43, 29.8%) sectors.

From the sectors presenting a negative change in both these indices it is worth mentioning that the index for the food industry (41) sector decreased by 4.5%, indicating a small decrease in IIT. This result seemed strange given that the products of this sector were easy to differentiate, so the SMP should have a positive impact, and given that the importance of the sector in Greek manufacturing grew between 1985 and 1992 (see also Table 4.3.7). However, given the nature of the products, this result may be indicative of the importance of 'distance' factors (see Chapter 2) operating negatively on Greek IIT.

---

[23]   It should be noted, however, that the indices of trade creation and trade diversion calculated for the other manufacturing (49) sector seemed to be unreliable. When examining the annual values of the indices (see Appendix A3 to Section 4.3), we observed that, for this sector, the values of both indices exceeded unity for most years. This meant that the exports of the sector to both the EU and to non-EU countries exceeded domestic production, which, clearly, was a very strange result. This result can occur in a sector only when there is a large difference between domestic and international prices. The latter, at least for the trade of Greece with the EU countries, was not the case. Another explanation is that this phenomenon can occur when a large part of a sector's exports are not of domestic origin (they are re-exports). The most probable explanation in this case, however, is that data for this sector encompassed industries that were not classified under all other sectors and, therefore, it is possible that the trade data for this sector included more unclassified industries than were included in the production data.

Table 4.3.6. RCA and Grubel-Lloyd indices for national data

NACE	RCA indices			Grubel-Lloyd indices		
	1985-87 average	1988-92 average	% change	1985-87 average	1988-92 average	% change
2200	-25.868	-14.048	45.69	74.132	85.952	15.94
2300	57.508	52.203	-9.22	42.492	47.797	12.48
2400	-69.401	-34.456	50.35	30.599	65.544	114.20
2500	-86.213	-81.434	5.54	13.787	18.566	34.66
3100	-81.721	-78.180	4.33	18.279	21.820	19.37
3200	-94.201	-93.338	0.92	5.799	6.662	14.88
3400	-76.092	-78.404	-3.04	23.908	21.596	-9.67
3500	-95.627	-96.605	-1.02	4.373	3.395	-22.36
4100	-44.082	-46.588	-5.68	55.918	53.412	-4.48
4300	55.437	42.148	-23.97	44.563	57.852	29.82
4400	-72.105	-61.769	14.33	27.895	38.231	37.05
4500	27.625	14.892	-46.09	72.375	85.108	17.59
4600	-65.597	-76.815	-17.10	34.403	23.185	-32.61
4700	-76.099	-86.214	-13.29	23.901	13.786	-42.32
4800	-70.960	-71.968	-1.42	29.040	28.032	-3.47
4900	-86.771	-29.723	65.75	13.229	70.277	431.23

The calculation of RCA indices at national level showed that comparative advantage was strengthened over the two periods in only five sectors (metals, 22, non-metallic mineral products, 24, chemical industry, 25, manufacture of metal articles, 31, mechanical engineering, 32, and other manufacturing industries, 49). Of importance was the increase in the RCA index for the non-metallic mineral products (24) sector by 50.4%, the largest achieved, which, as we saw above, was one of the three most important sectors of the Greek economy. This was, again, consistent with the very strong performance of this sector in regional trade (see Table 4.3.27).

In Tables 4.3.7 and 4.3.8, the shares of all sectors and regions in total manufacturing output at the beginning and the end of the periods in question (1985 and 1992) are presented.

Three sectors – namely food, textiles and mineral extraction – made up about half of all Greek manufacturing, indicating its low technological level and its specialization in activities characterized by low- and moderate- (in the case of food) demand growth and capital/labour intensity. These sectors draw their competitiveness from static comparative advantages created by the use of inputs such as cheap and low-skilled labour and raw materials. Note that mineral extraction and textiles shrank during these seven years, while the food sector flourished. Also note that the extraction of minerals sector is the only one that is classified as non-sensitive to the SMP according to Buigues *et al.* (1990).

Table 4.3.7.   Output by manufacturing sector for Greece in 1985 and 1992

Manufacturing sectors	1985	1992
22 Extraction and preparation of metallic minerals	7.7	7.9
23 Extraction of minerals	18.2	10.8
24 Non-metallic mineral products	5.2	5.6
25 Chemical products	8.0	8.4
31 Metal articles	4.8	4.3
32 Mechanical engineering	0.9	0.9
34 Electrical engineering	3.7	4.7
35 Motor vehicles, parts and accessories	3.5	4.5
41 Food, beverages and tobacco	22.8	28.1
43 Textile	13.3	9.4
44 Leather and leather goods	0.5	0.5
45 Footwear and clothing	3.4	4.6
46 Timber and wooden furniture	1.6	2.2
47 Paper, printing and publishing	3.4	4.7
48 Rubber and plastics	2.5	2.9
49 Other manufacturing industries	0.5	0.5

There is an overconcentration of manufacturing activity at regional level, too. Attiki, Kentriki Makedonia and Sterea Ellada accounted for more than three quarters of industrial production in 1992. On the other hand, there are 6 regions that have a share of around 1% or less. Both tables therefore suggested that not all regions and sectors are of equal importance and that some are of negligible importance. This should be born firmly in mind as we try to draw conclusions about the effects of the SMP.

Table 4.3.8.   Manufacturing output by region for Greece in 1985 and 1992

Regions	1985	1992
11 Anatoliki Makedonia and Thraki	3.8	4.4
12 Kentriki Makedonia	21.3	24.1
13 Dytiki Makedonia	0.6	0.4
14 Thessalia	5.7	5.8
21 Ipeiros	0.7	1.1
22 Ionia Nisia	0.2	0.2
23 Dytiki Ellada	4.3	4.3
24 Sterea Ellada	12.1	13.7
25 Peloponnisos	12.0	6.7
30 Attiki	37.4	37.7
41 Voreio Aigaio	0.3	0.2
42 Notio Aigaio	0.3	0.4
43 Kriti	1.2	1.1

Another factor to be taken into account was the structure of manufacturing within each region. Every region specialized in one or more activities. This aspect is examined in Table 4.3.9, with respect to years 1985 and 1992. Regions (11–43) are in the first row and the sectors (22–49) in the first column. The blank cells mean that there was no activity in the particular sector in that region. If it was found that a region produced a share of a sector's domestic output that was roughly equal to its total share in domestic manufacturing output (as happened in Table 4.3.8) the symbol '=' has been used.

Table 4.3.9. Regional specialization

Sectors	Regions												
	11	12	13	14	21	22	23	24	25	30	41	42	43
22	-	=		15				35		-			
	-	-		=				48		-			
23		=	-						28	51			
		=	-						33	58			
24	5	-	2	16		-	=	32	-	-	-	=	=
	6	-	1	16	-	-	8	26	-	-	-	1	2
25	8	=	4	-				=	-	53			-
	6	-	1	-	-			-	-	66			-
31	-	-	-	12	=		-	16	=	45	-		-
	-	-	-	8	=		6	22	9	=	=		2
32	-	26	=	=			-	-	=	47			=
	-	28	=	17			-	=	=	-			-
34	-	-	=	=			-	31	=	=			
	-	-	=	=			=	19	11	=			
35	-	-		10			-	=	-	61		4	
	-	-		17			-	=	-	47		3	-
41	6	27	-	=	2	=	6	-	=	-	=	=	4
	6	28	-	=	3	=	8	-	=	-	=	=	3
43	-	=		8	=		13	=	=	-	=	=	-
	=	38		13	2		=	-	-	-	=	=	-
44		-	13				21			=	27		
		-	25				20			=	1		
45	8	27	-	=	-		=	-	=	43		1	-
	10	38	-	=	-		=	-	-	=		1	-
46	6	25	-	=	2		6	24	=	-			-
	7	34	-	=	3		-	21	=	-			-
47	12	-		=			-	-	-	65			-
	9	-		-			-	-	-	70			-
48	=	=		=			8	17	-	=			2
	=	=		10			=	21	-	-			5
49	-	-		-		26	-	17	-	47			
	-	-		=		19	-	-	25	43		1	

If this share was below the region's average, the sign '-' has been put in the box, while in sectors with a share above the average, the exact number has been reported. To capture some of the dynamic processes that were underway each cell contains two figures: the upper one refers to the situation in 1985 and the lower one to that in 1992. For example, region 24 (Sterea Ellada) accounted in 1985 for 12.1% of total domestic manufacturing output. It produced about 35% of the metals output (sector 22, exact number is indicated), 10% of the chemical industry output (sector 25, = sign) and just 8% of the food output (sector 41, - sign).

Table 4.3.9 helped us choose the sectors on which to put special emphasis in the indicator analysis for each region. In fact, two aspects needed to be taken into account when we made this choice:

(a) **Static aspects** The analysis should shed light on sectors that traditionally have been important in Greek national and regional manufacturing. In other words, for each region the three dominant industrial sectors at national level should be analysed (food, textiles and minerals extraction) plus one to three sectors (depending on the size of the region) where the region has specialized.

(b) **Dynamic aspects** The analysis should also include any other sectors that had displayed changes over the seven-year period in two fundamental indicators, namely RCA and export specialization, provided that they were not of a negligible size, say, less than 5% of the region's production (in general, though, these sectors would have been covered already, as they happen to be important in static terms).

In Table 4.3.10, the selected sectors in every region produced by using these criteria are presented. The last row depicts the share the sum of those sectors have of each region's manufacturing output in 1992.

Table 4.3.10. Sectors to be studied in each of the 13 Greek regions

Sectors	Regions												
	11	12	13	14	21	22	23	24	25	30	41	42	43
22				+				+					
23		+	+						+	+			
24				+		+	+	+					+
25	+		+							+			
31							+	+	+				
32		+		+									
34								+	+				
35				+						+		+	
41	+	+	+	+	+	+	+	+	+	+	+	+	+
43	+	+		+	+		+	+	+	+	+	+	+
44			+								+		
45	+	+											
46		+			+								
47	+									+			
48													+
49					+				+				
Totals	82	68	72	88	96	100	82	70	91	75	94	73	94

Analysis of the main sectors in each region

We looked at all 13 Greek regions and analysed the effects on the trade and factor flow indicators for the main sectors of each region according to the selection shown in Table 4.3.10. For each region, a table shows the growth rates of the indicators in question. The numbers in the cells represent the growth rate of a specific indicator between its average value in subperiod 1985–87 and its average value in subperiod 1988–92 in order to capture any effects of the SMP.

You will see that each table has been split into two parts. The upper part describes the effects on six trade flow indicators plus the capital/labour ratio. The lower part shows the changes in three sectoral characteristics: output growth of the sector, labour productivity and production specialization of the region versus the national structure of manufacturing output. For these three characteristics two figures are given, which are the growth rates of their averages and the growth rates of their growth rates. In all the tables, after each sectoral code we have indicated the level of growth in demand (S stands for strong, M for moderate, W for weak) and whether the sector has been classified as highly sensitive (marked HS), moderately sensitive (MS) or non-sensitive (NS) to the SMP according to the methodology proposed by Buigues *et al.* (1990), and as applied to Greece by Mardas and Varsakelis (in Buigues *et al.*, 1990).

After each table, there is an analysis of its findings. Later in this section, under the heading 'Further analysis of the main trade flow indicators', the analysis moves from this disaggregated level to a more concise examination of each one of the main trade flow indicators, which allowed us to make inter-regional comparisons.

Table 4.3.11. Region 11: Anatoliki Makedonia and Thraki

Indicators	25 (S, HS) %	41 (M, MS) %	43 (W, MS) %	45 (W, HS) %	47 (M, MS) %
Trade creation	+105	-7	-14	-38	-8
Trade diversion	+11	-17	+40	-37	+4
Grubel-Lloyd	+98	+56	+28	-14	-50
Absolute IIT	+73	+9	+55	-16	-13
RCA	+2	+6	-14	-30	-2
Export specialization	+18	-25	+15	-16	-21
Capital/labour	+75	+34	+25	+10	+70
GDP growth (means)	-14.51	+15.56	+31.01	+31.20	-6.23
(growth rates)	-1.09	-1.54	-2.37	-1.00	-1.69
Labour productivity (means)	-1.98	-0.23	+5.34	-4.50	-0.50
(growth rates)	-0.08	-0.09	-0.03	-0.06	-0.11
Regional specialization (means)	-20.27	+0.50	+117.77	-4.15	-38.25
(growth rates)	-0.94	-1.02	-3.41	-1.31	1.24

With respect to the sectors presented in the table, the following are worth mentioning. The chemical industry (25) – one of the few manufacturing sectors that we found was very significant for Greece (see Table 4.3.7) and belongs to the strong-demand category – showed effects that would be expected after the completion of the SMP. Trade creation and IIT increased by a large magnitude – a fact that was supported by the increase in the export specialization index. However, the sector was declining in comparison with the national level and labour productivity fell as well. Besides, the trade diversion[24] indicator was higher than it was for any other region. The other sector with positive export specialization trends was the textile industry (43), probably a reflection of the fact that the sector grew relatively at regional level. However, the reported effects went against expectations: trade diversion increased and the RCA declined. It was the only region in which the trade creation indicator for the textiles industry fell.

Alarming, even if anticipated, were the effects in the 'highly sensitive' clothing (45) sector, despite the better prospects for this particular region, thanks to the strong incentives for investment and a pool of unskilled labour. The RCA fell by a spectacular 30%, trade activities almost halved (both to EU and non-EU countries) and IIT and the export specialization index reduced. A notable element of this was that the increase in the capital/labour ratio was very low and labour productivity actually fell by about 5%.

The paper and printing industry (47) was bolstered during the last decade thanks to the establishment of two paper mills, a fact revealed by the large increase in the capital/labour ratio (+70%). Among the trade indicators, the halving of the Grubel-Lloyd index was impressive and the reduction in the export specialization index worrying for the region that has been the second largest producer in the country. The food (41) sector's performance revealed some incompatible results. Export activity fell, but IIT rose and so did the RCA index.

Table 4.3.12. Region 12: Kentriki Makedonia

Indicators	23 (W,NS) %	32 (M,MS) %	41 (M,MS) %	43 (W,MS) %	45 (W, HS) %	46 (M,MS) %
Trade creation	+143	+65	-5	+6	-31	+42
Trade diversion	+123	+39	-15	+71	-29	+5
Grubel-Lloyd	-65	+55	+56	+28	-8	-51
Absolute IIT	+55	+81	+15	+67	+2	+107
RCA	+122	-	+2	-54	-6	-1
Export specialization	+135	+23	-20	+17	+1	+39
Capital/labour	+301	+59	+45	+60	+28	+33
GDP growth (means)	-27.4	+8.7	+18.8	+5.5	+43.4	+41.3
(growth rates)	-1.00	-1.29	-1.85	8.50	-0.68	-3.98
Labour productivity (means)		+11.3	+6.0	+4.9	+16.0	+16.2
(growth rates)	11.15	0.03	-0.01	0.02	0.13	0.10
Regional specialization (means)	+12.5	-0.8	-3.9	+73.1	+4.6	+1.2
(growth rates)	-3.97	-1.37	4.30	-0.19	-0.85	4.77

---

[24]   Remember that an increase in this indicator shows an increase in trade activity with countries outside the EU.

On the whole, the forces that have been dominant during the implementation of the SMP seem to have produced counteracting effects on the industrial structure of this region. This applied to the other regions as well, as will soon become clear. More general conclusions await the analysis of the individual indicators in the next section.

Kentriki Makedonia is particularly strong in the two major Greek industries, food (41) and textiles (43). The completion of the SMP does not seem to have favoured the food sector, which experienced a fall in trade towards EU countries and in export specialization. In general, a small decline in the relative importance of the sector in the region's manufacturing structure was observed. On the other hand, textiles, even though in the weak demand category and sensitive to the SMP, seemed to gain a dominant position (as revealed by the growth in the production specialization indicator). Trade was diverted towards non-EU countries. However, the most striking feature was that the RCA plummeted (only Voreio Aigaio had a slightly larger decline). Thus, the fact that the export specialization index managed to increase at a satisfactory pace was hard to explain.

Clothing (45) was a major contributor to the region's manufacturing output (in fact, together with the region of Anatoliki Makedonia and Thraki, it accounted for half of Greece's total production in this sector). Such production was often entirely for export and used under European brand names. However, as for Region 11, examined above, both trade indicators deteriorated significantly, and so did the RCA index. Export specialization stagnated, too, although other regions performed better in this field.

The minerals extraction (23) sector – the only non-sensitive important sector – experienced the highest increase in the RCA index at a national level for all sectors (+122%). This was reflected in the rapid increase in its trade flow indicators. The region specialized intensively in this activity at a time of accelerated recession at national level. Another striking aspect was the near tripling of the region's labour productivity index. The other sector shown in Table 4.3.12 is the wood (46) sector, where output growth was significant. The IIT indicators give conflicting pictures, but the increase in the trade creation index was noticeable (even though it was the lowest of all the regions).

Table 4.3.13. Region 13: Dytiki Makedonia

Indicators	23 (W,NS) %	25 (S,HS) %	41 (M,MS) %	44 (W,HS) %
Trade creation	+140	+184	-8	+75
Trade diversion	+122	+50	-18	-27
Grubel-Lloyd	-8	+64	+17	+94
Absolute IIT	+125	+61	-14	+121
RCA	-/+	+1	-	+3
Export specialization	+174	+11	-40	+23
Capital/labour	+302	+160	+44	+46
GDP growth (means)	-24.73	-31.80	-6.45	+19.82
(growth rates)	-1.22	-0.26	-2.49	-1.13
Labour productivity (means)	+237.65	-7.51	-19.66	+12.23
(growth rates)	11.46	-0.13	-0.21	0.16
Regional specialization (means)	+19.05	-35.42	-21.54	+40.30
(growth rates)	-9.92	-0.51	-0.50	-0.65

Note: The sign -/+ shows that the negative RCA index became positive.

This was one of the weakest regions in terms of manufacturing. It was characterized by the intense specialization in the (highly sensitive and weak-demand) leather (44) industry (more than a quarter of the national production, compared to its 0.4% share in the national total for manufacturing). Very interestingly, the sector exhibited a remarkable increase in trade with EU countries while trade with countries outside the EU fell by about 30%. The RCA improved slightly and so did the export specialization index. There was also an impressive doubling of the IIT indicators. In short, the sector seemed to behave according to expectations.

The most important sector in output value terms was the chemical (25) sector, but its share in regional production fell sharply in the last years (the fall in the regional production specialization index was -35%). Nevertheless, the trade creation indicator increased by almost three times and there had been a significant increase in IIT, which was confirmed by both indicators.

Table 4.3.14. Region 14: Thessalia

Indicators	24 (W,MS) %	32 (M,MS) %	35 (M,HS) %	41 (M,MS) %	43 (W,MS) %
Trade creation	+398	-31	+84	-2	+11
Trade diversion	-35	-48	-4	-12	+80
Grubel-Lloyd	+140	+91	+48	+55	+20
Absolute IIT	+424	+119	+158	+13	+65
RCA	-/+	-	-	+5	-10
Export specialization	-3	+74	+39	-21	+36
Capital/labour	+58	-28	+73	+44	+63
GDP growth (means)	+7	+154	+38	+14	+17
(growth rates)	-1.23	-0.67	-0.22	14.67	-1.55
Labour productivity (means)	+8	+36	+53	+5	+22
(growth rates)	0.05	0.25	0.72	0.06	0.25
Regional specialization (means)	-	+138	-15	-8	+90
(growth rates)	-1.23	-0.64	-0.79	-1.68	-0.56

Note: Sufficient data for the metals (22) sector do not exist.

A noteworthy change in the mineral extraction (23) sector was the reversal in the sign for the RCA index from negative to positive (the same occurred in the non-metallic mineral products (24) sector). This was accompanied by large increases in both the trade flow indicators, export specialization, capital/labour ratio and labour productivity. On the other hand, the food (41) sector appeared to be in decline, which could also be seen from the negative growth of its output at a time when the sector was undergoing a boom at national level.

Thessalia has specialized in heavy industry, i.e. in the metals, mechanical engineering and motor vehicles sectors. Non-metallic mineral products (24) – a sector on which Greece has traditionally based a large part of its export trade – was strongly represented in the region and, during the years of the implementation of the SMP three positive trends were reported. Trade with the EU countries increased five-fold, IIT relationships were intensified (the absolute IIT index increased by 424%) and the sector had a positive RCA in 1992 compared to a dominance of imports at the beginning of this period.

The region's specialization in mechanical engineering (32) – a sector that had been neglected in Greece – increased by 138%. In a generally stagnant environment, there had been positive developments with respect to IIT and growth in output. However, trade receded considerably (the largest reductions in both trade creation and trade diversion indicators were reported here). In another problematic industry, the motor vehicles and parts (35) sector, prospects of trade with the EU became more favourable (the figure reported showed that the trade creation indicator had almost doubled). Export specialization increased by 39% – the second highest recorded for all regions.

This also happened in the case of the textile industry (43), where the export specialization index increased by 36%, surpassed only by the Kriti region (the production specialization index also increased significantly). In general, though, the traditional industries (food, 41, and textiles, 43) did not show any deviation from the average record for the two sectors at national level.

Finally, a sector not mentioned in the table that seems to have gained in dynamic terms – the plastics and rubber industry (48). Its position improved relatively (the RCA index went up by 4%, the highest in the sector at a national level), while export specialization increased by about 60%.

Table 4.3.15. Region 21: Ipeiros

Indicators	41 (M,MS) %	43 (W,MS) %	46 (M,MS) %
Trade creation	-2	+16	+147
Trade diversion	-12	+86	+92
Grubel-Lloyd	+72	+33	-
Absolute IIT	+35	+65	+279
RCA	+18	-6	-
Export specialization	-7	+22	+177
Capital/labour	+45	+71	+125
GDP growth (means)	+35.42	+1.03	+57.02
(growth rates)	-5.45	-1.16	-0.55
Labour productivity (means)	+24.93	+9.57	+122.39
(growth rates)	0.22	0.18	2.15
Regional specialization (means)	+8.77	+64.99	+11.98
(growth rates)	-1.06	-5.83	-1.08

The mountainous region of Ipeiros has a constrained manufacturing base and has specialized in timber (46), food (41) and the textile industry (43). With respect to the former, trading opportunities have been exploited and the sector has experienced one of the highest growth rates of all the regions in its export specialization and trade creation indicators. In both cases, the increase was by far the largest of all regions for wood. Its RCA remained the same, while in most other regions it fell slightly. Its IIT indicators are very positive, especially if we keep in mind that in all other regions they deteriorated substantially. A relatively unexpected result was the large increase in trade diversion.

The food sector managed to raise its competitive position (the RCA index increased by 18%, the highest for food, increases occurring also in the Ionia Nisia and Voreio Aigaio regions) and strengthened its IIT relationships. Finally, textiles displayed increased specialization at the regional level (+65%) and managed the lowest decline in its RCA index of all the regions (-6%).

Table 4.3.16. Region 22: Ionia Nisia

Indicators	24 (W,MS) %	41 (M,MS) %	49 (W,MS) %
Trade creation	+24	+11	+133
Trade diversion	-56	-	+267
Grubel-Lloyd	+403	+56	-48
Absolute IIT	+704	+20	+63
RCA	+31	+18	-5%
Export specialization	+113	-13	+90
Capital/labour	-66	+67	+229
GDP growth (means)	+271.89	+12.31	-38.22
(growth rates)	-0.96	-1.10	-1.09
Labour productivity (means)	+125.09	+17.01	+38.43
(growth rates)	3.46	0.42	0.29
Regional specialization (means)	+237.61	-15.71	-34.86
(growth rates)	-0.99	-1.09	-1.15

The island region of Ionia Nisia has the thinnest manufacturing base of the country and few comments can be made about any effects of the 1992 programme. In general, in small regions the whole activity has been based in isolated production units, which do not form a critical mass for any effects to be transmitted, as linkages between them and the rest of the country are practically non-existent.

The non-metallic mineral products (24) sector had apparently more than tripled its production and its IIT ties. It achieved its highest increase in its export specialization index. This was also the sector with the highest increase in its regional specialization index in the country. The other two sectors, namely food (41) and other manufacturing industries (49) declined relatively. In the latter, trade expanded, with large quantities of products being exported to both EU and non-EU countries.

Table 4.3.17. Region 23: Dytiki Ellada

Indicators	24 (W,MS) %	31 (M,MS) %	41 (M,MS) %	43 (W,MS) %
Trade creation	+342	+106	+24	+46
Trade diversion	-38	+1	+12	+131
Grubel-Lloyd	+306	+180	+107	+99
Absolute IIT	+503	+412	+58	+70
RCA	-	+2	+10	-28
Export specialization	+21	+181	+9	-22
Capital/labour	+194	+213	+279	+110
GDP growth (means)	+40.90	+150.26	+25.57	-44.91
(growth rates)	-0.55	-0.55	1.95	0.18
Labour productivity (means)	+23.46	+127.56	+46.85	-31.99
(growth rates)	0.26	1.54	0.52	-0.38
Regional specialization (means)	+30.10	+186.57	+0.90	-10.58
(growth rates)	-0.15	-0.55	1.33	-0.39

The Dytiki Ellada region was characterized by large increases in its Grubel-Lloyd IIT indicator in all its four important sectors. Most striking was the increase in the non-metallic mineral products (24) sector, which also showed a more than four-fold increase in its trade creation indicator (still one of the lowest). On the other hand, trade diverted less to non-EU countries after the implementation of the SMP was completed. The growth rate in the regional specialization index was 30%, but the RCA index remained stagnant.

More positive was the increase in the regional specialization index for the metal articles (31) sector (+187%), which also boasted a slight increase in the RCA indicator. Labour productivity increased significantly. The sector also had the highest growth rate in the export specialization indicator (+181%) and displayed a large increase in output, whereas the sector had generally been in decline at national level.

As far as the traditional sectors were concerned, they followed the patterns of changes also observed at national level. The RCA was negative but improving for food (41) and positive but deteriorating for the textile industry (43). Trade opportunities seem to have been utilized by textiles more than by the food sector, but, in reality, regional activity in textiles shrank and the export specialization index deteriorated by 23%. On the other hand, the food sector retained a constant share in regional output.

Sterea Ellada was clearly established as the third largest manufacturing region of the country in this period, though much of this output should be regarded as an extension of the industrial activity in the neighbouring Attiki region. Sterea Ellada was particularly strong in the metals (22) sector (it was responsible for about half the country's production). The RCA and the export specialization index increased for this sector by more than it did for any other region (+21% and +77% respectively). It easily followed that the region had chosen to specialize further in this manufacturing activity (+92%).

Table 4.3.18. Region 24: Sterea Ellada

Indicators	22 (W,MS) %	24 (W,MS) %	31 (M,MS) %	34 (S,HS) %	41 (M,MS) %	43 (W,MS) %
Trade creation	+36	+641	+155	+98	+18	+49
Trade diversion	-12	-7	+26	+49	+7	+135
Grubel-Lloyd	+108	+228	+104	+18	+86	+39
Absolute IIT	+112	+607	+263	+81	+39	+65
RCA	+21	+70	+3	-	+9	-18
Export specialization	+77	+18	+97	+33	-3	+14
Capital/labour	+61	+126	+77	+113	+71	+115
GDP growth (means)	+53	+41	+46	-9	+14	-22
(growth rates)	-1.69	-0.98	-1.55	-1.04	-1.80	0.72
Labour productivity (means)	+62	+33	+62	+23	+30	+2
(growth rates)	0.59	0.23	0.52	0.14	0.32	-
Regional specialization (means)	+92	-13	+74	-24	-8	+27
(growth rates)	1.19	-0.20	-0.60	0.38	-1.69	-3.35

There was a more than seven-fold increase in the volume of trade with the EU countries in the non-metallic mineral products (24) sector. Of almost equal magnitude were the increases in IIT. Nevertheless, the sector's share of production in the region fell, although it still accounts for one quarter of national production. The RCA index rose by 70%, the highest growth achieved for the sector (which generally improved its position at national level) and one of the highest of all.

The traditional sectors were underrepresented in the region. Both food (41) and the textile industry (43) had a relatively low share of regional output and, in fact, their fate here shared many of the characteristics observed in the other regions. IIT expanded, trade opportunities were mostly utilized in the case of the textiles industry (where the trade diversion indicator increased markedly more than the trade creation one).

Finally, a few words about two less developed manufacturing sectors, in which the region seemed to specialize. Metal articles' (31) competitive position improved and both its specialization indices (export and regional) increased substantially. The electrical engineering (34) sector was rather more stagnant and its exports were diverted to non-EU countries (the indicator increased by about 50%).

In the southern region of Peloponnisos, the share of manufacturing production was cut by half in the short period of seven years preceding 1992. Specialization was high in the mineral extraction (23) sector (one third of domestic production), although the export specialization indicator declined dramatically. The same happened with the trade creation and trade diversion indices (-25% and -38%, respectively, were the largest reported reductions in the country). As a consequence, the RCA indicator fell by 5% – a development that could also be attributed to the decline in labour productivity of 17% and the loss of competitiveness.

Table 4.3.19. Region 25: Peloponnisos

Indicators	23 (W,NS) %	31 (M,MS) %	34 (H,HS) %	41 (M,MS) %	43 (W,MS) %	49 (W,MS) %
Trade creation	-23	+333	+77	+81	+229	-62
Trade diversion	-35	+136	+39	+72	+401	-33
Grubel-Lloyd	+96	+142	+59	+62	+50	-42
Absolute IIT	+57	+324	+146	+22	+69	+66
RCA	-5	+6	+3	+7	-22	-
Export specialization	-36	+143	+90	-14	+3	+91
Capital/labour	+39	+183	+87	+156	+791	-49
GDP growth (means)	-9	-11	+34	-42	-81	+232
(growth rates)	-1.10	-1.11	-1.49	-0.96	-0.78	-0.78
Labour productivity (means)	-17	+89	+74	+15	-6	+45
(growth rates)	-0.25	1.61	1.01	0.12	0.01	0.61
Regional specialization (means)	+42	+8	+12	-52	-68	+229
(growth rates)	-0.97	-0.91	-0.80	-0.40	-0.71	-0.94

Better prospects in trade seemed to open up for the metal articles (31) sector as the trade creation indicator rose by 333% (the largest increase in the country), but the trade diversion indicator increased significantly as well. Equally impressive were the figures reported for the volume of IIT. As a result, Peloponnisos recorded the best figure for the RCA index for the sector. The electrical engineering (34) sector had similar characteristics but to a more moderate degree. Labour productivity grew by 74%.

With respect to the traditional sectors, the same comments that were made for the previous regions apply to Peloponnisos as well, even though they were not as dominant here. The region had a declining RCA and increasing export specialization index in the textile industry (43) as opposed to an increasing RCA and diminishing export specialization in the food (41) sector. As usual, there was expansion in the trade diversion indicator in the textiles industry, only it was even more accentuated in this region (+401%). The trade creation indicator had its largest increase in this region, too (+229%). It was interesting that the same deviating characteristics were confirmed for the food sector as well (namely, high growth rates in both the trade creation and trade diversion indicators).

Other manufacturing industries (49) had been growing in the period under question, rendering the region the second largest producer. Nevertheless, the worst export trade indicators were reported as both trade creation and trade diversion indices plunged: they had been growing in all other regions.

Table 4.3.20. Region 30: Attiki

Indicators	23 (W,NS) %	25 (S,HS) %	35 (M,HS) %	41 (M,MS) %	43 (W,MS) %	47 (M,MS) %
Trade creation	-25	+67	+85	+5	+62	-17
Trade diversion	-38	-9	-10	-5	+159	-1
Grubel-Lloyd	+75	+105	+45	+86	-24	-41
Absolute IIT	+56	+98	+148	+38	+10	+10
RCA	-70	-	-	+1	-106	-
Export specialization	-49	+34	+10	-4	+14	+8
Capital/labour	+38	+47	+64	+56	+140	+57
GDP growth (means)	-23	+18	+22	+29	-29	+34
(growth rates)	-1.10	-1.94	-1.28	-5.98	0.21	-5.68
Labour productivity (means)	-33	+11	+25	+28	+2	+33
(growth rates)	-0.42	0.08	0.15	0.28	-0.03	0.37
Regional specialization (means)	+24	+9	-22	+4	+23	-12
(growth rates)	-1.25	-0.75	-0.41	-0.81	-3.10	4.25

Attiki is the principal manufacturing region of Greece and it is difficult to mention a sector in which it is not important at a national level. Activity seemed to be concentrated in some sectors that were underrepresented outside Athens. Production for two of them in Attiki accounted for almost 70% of total domestic output. Paper and printing (47) retained a constant RCA. Labour productivity increased by 33%. However, trade effects were not very favourable, even though the fall in the trade creation indicator was less than the average for other regions. A better picture applied to the chemicals (25) sector. The sector had achieved positive growth in trade creation (though this was less than for other regions) and IIT and the export specialization index rose by 34%.

An interesting feature of the textile industry (43) in Attiki was the fact that it already had a negative RCA index, in contrast to the other regions. Also, the index dropped significantly during these seven years. Trade diversion increased, as was the case in other regions, while there was an increased devotion of resources to the sector, which strengthened its position within the region. Food (41) exhibited the usual aspects of development and achieved high growth rates in volume of IIT. The sector's main characteristics (export and regional specialization, trade creation and diversion, RCA) remained constant.

Mineral extraction's (23) share of regional production increased relatively. However, all other indicators deteriorated. Trade with both EU and non-EU countries dropped, a fact most vividly expressed in the decline of the RCA indicator by a huge 70%. Labour productivity fell by

33%. Motor vehicles and parts (35) performed better. The trade creation indicator almost doubled and export specialization increased by 10%. However, the share in the region's production fell by 22%.

Table 4.3.21. Region 41: Voreio Aigaio

Indicators	41 (M,MS) %	43 (W,MS) %
Trade creation	+23	+68
Trade diversion	+11	+167
Grubel-Lloyd	+56	+18
Absolute IIT	+29	+67
RCA	+18	-56
Export specialization	-13	+30
Capital/labour	+82	+170
GDP growth (means)	+0.12	-23.66
(growth rates)	-1.44	-0.46
Labour productivity (means)	-0.96	+26.66
(growth rates)	-	0.26
Regional specialization (means)	-17.50	+25.90
(growth rates)	0.31	6.98

Note: Sufficient data for the leather (44) sector did not exist.

The leather (44) sector, for which sufficient data did not exist, was providing more than a quarter of the national production in 1985, but was reduced to a negligible size in just seven years. From the few existing data, it was shown that output fell by an amazing 77%.

With respect to the traditional sectors, food (41) improved its relative position (its RCA rose by 18%), but labour productivity slightly receded. The textile industry (43) had the second highest increase in the export specialization index and production specialization increased by 26%.

Notio Aigaio is another island region with a constrained industrial base. For the motor vehicles and parts (35) sector, it is important to understand that its shipbuilding industry (normally included in sector 36, but subsumed in this study under sector 35) was hit (right after the end of the period in question) by the closing down of the largest shipyard in the region. Until then, the sector had been performing according to expectations accompanying the implementation of the SMP in terms of trade creation, the fall in the trade diversion indicator and the increase in IIT.

The RCA indicator for the textile industry (43) turned negative, even though exports to both EU and non-EU countries increased. IIT declined according to the Grubel-Lloyd indicator and the export specialization index rose by less than it did in all other regions (except Peloponnisos). The performance of the food (41) sector was average.

Table 4.3.22. Region 42: Notio Aigaio

Indicators	35 (M,HS) %	41 (M,MS) %	43 (W,MS) %
Trade creation	+57	+21	98
Trade diversion	-17	+9	+216
Grubel-Lloyd	+38	+69	-21
Absolute IIT	+125	+34	+10
RCA	-	+9	+/-
Export specialization	+6	-7	+8
Capital/labour	+90	+91	+431
GDP growth (means)	+24.01	+10.72	-45.27
(growth rates)	-1.38	-1.69	0.05
Labour productivity (means)	+42.03	+24.56	+55.61
(growth rates)	0.35	0.17	0.54
Regional　　　specialization (means)	-19.54	-10.15	-7.55
(growth rates)	-0.88	-4.98	2.08

Note: The sign +/- implies that the positive RCA index became negative.

The region's comparative specialization in plastics and rubber (48) was rather attributed to the existence of one large productive unit located in the capital of the region, Heraklion. The fall in the trade diversion indicator was distinct, but the trade creation index failed to increase. In general, there was a 70% increase in the region's plastics output and a faint improvement of the RCA index.

In non-metallic mineral products (24), the regional characteristics largely followed those of other regions that specialized in this activity. However, the export specialization and RCA grew less than they did in those regions. The food (41) sector lost some of its dynamism (there was negative output growth between the two subperiods) and export specialization declined significantly. On the other hand, the textile industry (43) performed better than any other region in the export specialization index. Note, though, that its RCA index was negative throughout the period.

Further analysis of the main trade flow indicators

In this section, five trade flow indicators are examined on a comparative basis to help us draw conclusions about the performance of different sectors (first column) and regions (first row). The analysis of each indicator is preceded by a table reporting growth rates between the 1988–92 and 1985–87 subperiod averages in percentage terms. The aim is to have a full picture across regions irrespective of whether or not a particular sector was important for a specific region.

The establishment of the single market was expected to lead to trade creation (measured here by exports over production) in, at least, those industries in which Greece would choose to specialize. In general, common trends for particular sectors should be observed across different regions. A peculiar pattern was observed in the food (41) sector. Regions in northern Greece (11-21) failed to raise their levels of exports to EU countries, whereas the southern and island regions (22-43) unilaterally increased them. This development was probably related to the particular market niche in which each part of the country specialized.

Table 4.3.23. Region 43: Kriti

Indicators	24 (W,MS) %	41 (M,MS) %	43 (W,MS) %	48 (M,MS) %
Trade creation	+280	+5	+46	+4
Trade diversion	-52	-5	+135	-34
Grubel-Lloyd	+264	+28	-11	+43
Absolute IIT	+447	-4	+44	+75
RCA	+7	+5	-17	+2
Export specialization	+3	-32	+48	+21
Capital/labour	+24	+60	+121	+2
GDP growth (means)	+48.42	-9.38	-0.81	+69.73
(growth rates)	-0.55	-1.01	-0.86	-0.38
Labour productivity (means)	+14.01	-10.38	+33.44	+8.36
(growth rates)	0.17	-0.17	0.26	0.11
Regional specialization (means)	+36.91	+53.50	+69.62	+41.52
(growth rates)	-0.72	-0.57	-11.96	-0.70

The exact opposite of this observation applied in the case of mineral extraction (23). The two provinces in Makedonia raised their exports to the EU following the change in the policy regime, while the two southern provinces, which accounted for most of the output, experienced a fall in their trade creation indicator.

With respect to uniform effects during the 1985-92 period, it was observed that the textile industry (43) almost invariably increased its share of exports to the EU (with the exception of Anatoliki Makedonia and Thraki). Non-metallic mineral products (24) had an outstanding performance (growth rates ranged between 257% and 642%). Very positive developments took place in the metal articles (31) sector. In brief, there have also been positive effects for all regions with regard to metals (22), chemicals (25), electrical engineering (34), motor vehicles (35), leather (44), timber (46) and plastics (48).

The only sectors to undergo negative developments, contrary to the expected outcome, were the paper (47) and, surprisingly, the clothing (45) sectors in all the main regions producing these items (Anatoliki Makedonia and Thraki, Kentriki Makedonia, Thessalia and Attiki – particularly in the first two regions).

Following the establishment of a single market, an expected effect would be for trade with countries outside the integrated zone to subside. This, however, was not the conclusion that could be drawn after examining Table 4.3.25. When we compared the trade diversion with the trade creation data, interesting proportionalities occurred.

Table 4.3.24. Trade creation indicator

Sectors	Regions												
	11	12	13	14	21	22	23	24	25	30	41	42	43
22	+30	+32						+36		+41			
23		+143	+140						-23	-25			
24	+257	+375	+480	+398		+24	+343	+642	+51-	+466	+367		+280
25	+106	+87	+184	+29				+147	+235	+67			+177
31	+124	+123		+246	+36		+106	+155	+333	+198			+106
32	+121	+65	-6	-32			+65	-29	+258	+162			+114
34	+161	+102	+87	+47			+59	+99	+77	+56			
35	+19	+69		+84			+76	+69	+151	+86		+57	
41	-7	-5	-8	-2	-2	+11	+24	+17	+81	+5	+23	+21	+5
43	-13	+6		+11	+16		+46	+49	+229	+63	+68	+98	+46
44		+11	+75				+120			+92			
45	-38	-31	+4	-11	+31		-	-25	+50	-11		-28	-17
46	+52	+42	+58	+92	+147		+94	+83	+117	+67		+85	+144
47	-8	-33		-7			-32	-33	+51	-17			-39
48	+103	+39		+34				+69	+255	+99			+4
49	+139	+26		-		+133	+31	+46	-63	+35			

For example, in the food (41) sector the same export trade pattern continued. The northern regions experienced falling exports, while the southern and island regions increased their volume of trade with non-EU countries – a fact that can hardly be directly attributed to measures used to build up the single market. Note, though, that in Attiki and Kriti, the indicator fell as well (but by only 5%, which was much less than in Northern Greece). For the mineral extraction (23) sector, the same thing happened in the trade diversion as in the trade creation indicator: there was an increase in the two Makedonia regions and a significant fall (exceeding 35%) in the Attiki and Peloponnisos regions.

In the textile industry (43), the very large increase in the trade diversion indicator (ranging from 40% in Anatoliki Makedonia and Thraki to 400% in Peloponnisos) was beyond any expectation. However, it was not the only sector with positive trade diversion growth rates. In the metal articles (31), mechanical (32) and electrical engineering (34) and timber (46) sectors, the index increased. In chemicals (25), in most regions, trade diversion occurred, but in the largest producing region, Attiki, it declined by 9%.

A mixed picture was the outcome for plastics and rubber (48) as the indicator declined in the three regions that accounted for 40% of the national output (Kentriki Makedonia, Thessalia and Kriti), but increased in the other regions producing these outputs. In the paper (47) industry, the indicator remained stagnant in the two main producing regions and oscillated above and below zero in the others.

Table 4.3.25. Trade diversion indicator*

Sectors	Regions												
	11	12	13	14	21	22	23	24	25	30	41	42	43
22	-18	-17						-12		-9			
23		+123	+122						-35	-38			
24	-54	-39	-30	-35		-56	-38	-8	+7	-23	-41		-52
25	+106	+2	+50	-29				+32	+8	-9			+44
31	+125	+12		+81	-35		+1	+27	+136	+50			+2
32	+121	+39	-23	-47			+44	-33	+274	+133			+90
34	+161	+54	+41	+8			+18	+49	+39	+15			
35	+19	-18		-4			-15	-16	+104	-10		-17	
41	-17	-15	-18	-12	+12	-	+12	+7	+72	-5	+10	+9	-5
43	+40	+71		+80	+86		+131	+135	+401	+159	+167	+216	+135
44		-49	-27				-8			-20			
45	-37	-29	+6	-9	+26		+2	-24	+54	-10		-25	-17
46	+12	+5	+17	+45	+92		+44	+34	+81	+25		+40	+73
47	+4	-24		+12			-24	-25	+116	-1			-28
48	+27	-12		-13				+13	+194	+33			-34
49	+296	+104		+61		+267	+104	+128	-33	+116			

* Remember that an increase in this indicator shows an increase in trade activity with countries outside the EU.

In the clothing industry (45), the trend was strongly negative (especially in the main regions of production). The only sectors where the indicator was clearly negative for all regions were the metals (22), non-metallic mineral products (24), motor vehicles (35) and leather (44). These four sectors – which in 1992 made up just 18.5% of manufacturing output – seemed to have been the only ones to conform with what would be anticipated in view of a single market, regarding both trade creation and trade diversion.

Integration into the single market was predicted to lead to a general intensification of IIT relationships between Member States. Greece – as the country with the lowest volume of IIT by far – was a unique case and so two alternative scenarios for how it could fare appeared. Either the country would move towards further specialization in its traditional industries (an inter-industry scenario) or it would differentiate its manufacture to resemble the trade pattern of its partners. Table 4.3.27 offers the opportunity for a quick assessment of the situation as it cross-references all sectors and regions for one of the most often used IIT indicators. It should be noted, though, that the following conclusions may change, but only very slightly, for other types of indicators, such as the absolute IIT indicator.

Table 4.3.26. The Grubel-Lloyd indicator

Sectors	Regions												
	11	12	13	14	21	22	23	24	25	30	41	42	43
22	+78	+35						+108		+94			
23		-65	-8						+96	+75			
24	+101	+279	+137	+140		+403	+306	+228	+134	+305	+77		+264
25	+98	+62	+64	+105				+180	+95	+105			+117
31	+30	+27		+59	+16		+180	+104	+142	+15			+36
32	+69	+55	-10	+91			+81	-8	+163	+78			+42
34	+33	+137	+49	+58			+41	+18	+59	+9			
35	+93	+59		+48			+27	+53	+40	+45		+38	
41	+56	+56	+17	+56	+72	+56	+107	+86	+62	+86	+56	+69	+28
43	+28	+28		+20	+33		+99	+39	+50	-24	+18	-21	-11
44		+137	+94				+80			+74			
45	-14	-8	-6	-2	+25		-4	+59	+3	-10		-15	-38
46	-48	-51	-59	-41	-		-56	-48	-38	-52		-53	-22
47	-50	-10		-60			-53	-51	-35	-41			-24
48	+105	+50		+99				+94	-23	+59			+43
49	-25	-58		-44		-48	-59	-70	-42	-58			

Without doubt, the single market supported the increase in IIT. The indicators increased in most sectors. In the following ones, the positive developments applied invariably to all regions: metals (22), chemicals (25), metal articles (31), electrical engineering (34), motor vehicles (35), food (41), leather (44) and non-metallic minerals (24). In this last sector, the growth rates were the largest reported. Generally, increasing trends characterized the mechanical engineering (32) and plastics (48) industries. IIT in the textile industry (43) declined in Attiki (by 24%) and in two island regions, but it flourished in the main areas producing textiles.

In contrast, in the clothing (45) sector, the volume of IIT declined by about 10% in the main producing regions. Two other sectors had negative growth of the Grubel-Lloyd indicator. IIT in paper (47) and wood (46) subsided by about 50%. If we add to this the other manufacturing industries (49), then these four sectors with declining IIT had just 12% of manufacturing output in 1992 – a rather small share of domestic production.

A general characteristic of Table 4.3.27 is the limited number of cases in which there was a change on the RCA indicator. All of them were concentrated in the mineral extraction (23) and textile (43) industries (and, even then, not in all regions), plus, for two regions, non-metallic mineral products (24). It should be stressed from the beginning that the two-digit classification was not very illuminating, as it hid important strongholds of Greek manufacturing, that could only be revealed through three-digit analysis. In this way, as the study by Thomas (1993) showed, positive RCA indicators existed for the metal articles (forging), electrical engineering (wires), food (processed fruit and vegetables, grain milling, soft drinks, tobacco products) and clothing (ready-made clothing, furs) sectors. These were suppressed here as a result of the sectoral aggregation process.

Table 4.3.27. The RCA indicator

Sectors	Regions												
	11	12	13	14	21	22	23	24	25	30	41	42	43
22	+14	+5						+21		+3			
23		+122	-/+						-5	-70			
24	+57	+30	-/+	-/+		+31	+1	+70	+46	+9	+1		+7
25	+2	+1	+1	+1				+4	+1	0			-
31	+1	-		+1	-		+2	+3	+6	0			+1
32	-	-	-	-			-	-	+1	0			-
34	+1	+1	+7	+2			+1	+1	+3	0			
35	-	-		-			-	-	-	0		-	
41	+6	+2	-	+5	+18	+18	+10	+9	+7	+1	+18	+9	+5
43	-14	-54		-10	-6		-28	-18	-22	-106	-56	+/-	-17
44		+2	+3				+4			0			
45	-30	-6	-	-	+6		-15	+4	+1	-4		-6	-4
46	-2	-1	-2	-1	-		-	-1	-2	0		-2	-
47	-2	-		-2			-2	-2	-1	0			-
48	+3	+1		+4				+3	-1	0			+2
49	-	-		-		-5	-	-1	-	0			

Key:
-/+ means that the negative indicator turned positive
+/- means that the positive indicator turned negative
Bold numbers indicate that, in 1992, the RCA indicator was positive

Note: The plus and minus numbers in the cells indicate that the RCA indicator has, respectively, improved or worsened (numbers are in percentage terms). Thus, -106% means that the RCA index for the textile industry in Attiki dropped from an average of -18.61 in 1985–87 to an average of -38.45 in 1988–92.

With respect to the textile industry, it was obvious that the situation deteriorated, with reduction rates ranging from -6 to -56%. Indeed, the small region of Notio Aigaio experienced a shift in signs. Other sectors performed better, especially non-metallic mineral products, which achieved change from negative to positive in the regions of Dytiki Makedonia and Thessalia. Other regions experienced significant increases in their RCA index figures. The balance for the food (41) sector was also on the plus side as Greek firms made their way towards achieving positive trade with other EU countries. Hopeful messages also came from the metals (22) sector, which, notably, has been concentrated in only four regions. Growth was highest in the most specialized region, Sterea Ellada.

With respect to the other sectors, there was not much to comment on. Some – plastics (48), metal articles (31), electrical engineering (34), chemicals (25) – had a slightly positive development, while others – paper (47), wood (46), other manufacturing industries (49) – had a slightly negative one. Such numbers did not really matter, though, as most of these sectors were stuck in the lowest values of the indicator (i.e. close to -100) and marginal changes did not affect the real picture of Greek manufacturing. Most alarming was the deterioration in the RCA indicator for the clothing industry (45) in those regions of northern Greece that have mostly specialized in this activity (Kentriki Makedonia -6%, Anatoliki Makedonia and Thraki -30%). The split pattern in the minerals extraction (23) sector that we saw earlier was visible in the RCA indicator as well, with the two northern regions performing impressively well and the two southern regions worsening their positions (especially Attiki).

Table 4.3.28. The export specialization indicator

Sectors	Regions												
	11	12	13	14	21	22	23	24	25	30	41	42	43
22	+36	+8						+77		+57			
23		+135	+174						-36	-49			
24	-32	+15	-10	-3		+113	+21	+18	-30	+19	-47		+3
25	+18	+6	+11	+29				+77	+25	+34			+38
31	+17	+23		+47	+10		+181	+97	+143	+12			+30
32	+38	+39	-16	+74			+62	-14	+148	+68			+27
34	+43	+168	+80	+79			+64	+33	+90	+27			
35	+55	+31		+39			+7	+17	+5	+10		+6	
41	-25	-20	-40	-21	-7	-13	+9	-3	-14	-4	-13	-7	-32
43	+15	+17	+23	+36	+22		-23	+14	+3	+14	+30	+8	+48
44		+51					+20			+14			
45	-16	+1	+5	+9	+41		+6	+80	+15	+2		-2	-30
46	+34	+39	+15	+66	+177		+13	+46	+62	+37		+33	+11-
47	-21	+56		-30			-20	-17	+24	+8			+41
48	+59	+23		+64				+57	-38	+33			+21
49	+134	+42		+88		+90	+44	+9	+91	+50			

The figures for the export specialization indicator showed a general increase in almost all sectors and regions for the period of the implementation of the SMP. The only big exception to this rule was the food (41) sector. Apart from the Dytiki Ellada region, all Greek regions' food exports declined relatively to the exports of EU countries. This result cannot be easily explained by the available data, that is, given the fact that this particular sector raised its share in manufacturing output from 23 to 28% in a period of just seven years. The fall applied to both specialized and less specialized regions and fluctuated between -3% for Sterea Ellada and -40% for Dytiki Makedonia.

Another striking example of the relative diminution of export specialization was the mineral extraction (23) sector. The two regions responsible for 80% of national output – namely Peloponnisos and Attiki – saw their indices fall by 36% and 49% respectively. The implications are quite interesting if we consider that food and mineral extraction have been Greece's two biggest manufacturing industries (even if the latter is not a purely manufacturing sector and despite its being in a declining phase).

Two sectors presented a mixed picture. In the paper and printing industry (47), exports fell relative to those of other members of the EU in many regions. The shares fell for Anatoliki Makedonia and Thraki (a region specializing in this industry, by 21%), for Dytiki Makedonia, Dytiki Ellada and Sterea Ellada. They increased in the other four producing regions, among which was Attiki (+8%), which accounted for two-thirds of the sector's output. A similar picture applied in the case of non-metallic mineral products (24), where the export specialization index fell in three regions specializing in such production work (Anatoliki Makedonia and Thraki, Thessalia and Dytiki Makedonia) and in two other regions (Peloponnisos and Voreio Aigaio). However, it increased in the two largest producers, Sterea Ellada and Attiki, which together accounted for about 45% of total production.

Some notable examples of a rather unexpected decline in the index for regions specializing in particular sectors included the textile industry (43) in Dytiki Ellada (-23%) and the clothing industry (45) in Anatoliki Makedonia and Thraki (-10%). Note that in the clothing sector – which is considered to be a traditional industry – the two other major producers – Kentriki Makedonia and Attiki – have stayed at practically the same level of specialization that they were at before the implementation of the SMP (+1% and +2% respectively).

Results for other sectors showed uniformly positive changes in the indicator for the chemical industry (25), metals (22) and metal articles (31), motor vehicles (35) and electrical engineering (34), which speaks up for an intra-industry scenario put forward as a prediction of what the situation will be in the aftermath of the SMP rather than for further specialization in traditional industries.

Further analysis of the main factor flow indicators

Few comments can be made about the state of factor flows to and from Greek regions following the establishment of the single market because the available data was considered to be rather unreliable or was simply non-existent. Of what was available, a marked tendency for large increases in the capital/labour ratios in 95% of the cases across all sectors and regions (see Tables 4.3.11-4.3.23) can be interpreted tentatively as a sign of adjustment of domestic producers to the requirements of competition.

Another class of indicators that was of some interest in our analysis and is based on reliable data is the set of indices called the Herfindahl indices of employment concentration in sectors and regions that attempt to measure 'location effects'. An increase in the value of the regional index means that production has tended to concentrate in fewer manufacturing sectors or in larger productive units. An increase in the value of the sectoral index may imply that, over time, fewer regions have been engaged in a specific activity as it has paid some of them to specialize and others to abandon production or that larger productive units have been used. In

Table 4.3.29, the growth rates of the Herfindahl indices for regions and sectors between the 1985–87 and the 1988–92 subperiod averages are presented.

The results show that in four regions there was an increase in the concentration of employment across sectors during the 1985–92 period. These regions were Anatoliki Makedonia and Thraki, Kentriki Makedonia, Thessalia and Ipeiros. In all other regions, the concentration of 'employment' decreased but there were no dramatic changes. The largest absolute decrease occurred in Ionia Nisia, where employment concentration dropped from 0.23 in 1985 to 0.14 in 1992. There were, however, large differences between regions. The lowest concentration of employment in 1992 was reported in Kentriki Makedonia (0.02) and the largest in Ionia Nisia (0.14).

Table 4.3.29. The Herfindahl indices of employment concentration

Region	%	Sector	%
Anatoliki Makedonia and Thraki	+32.86	Metals	+5.85
Kentriki Makedonia	+24.49	Mineral extraction	-1.69
Dytiki Makedonia	-18.13	Non-metallic minerals	-13.99
Thessalia	+6.66	Chemicals	+10.89
Ipeiros	+6.46	Metal articles	-6.29
Ionia Nisia	-34.11	Mechanical engineering	-21.34
Dytiki Ellada	-14.10	Electrical engineering	+10.72
Sterea Ellada	-6.10	Motor vehicles	+5.37
Peloponnisos	-13.30	Food	+9.49
Attiki	+0.60	Textiles	+1.17
Voreio Aigaio	-24.92	Leather	-0.66
Notio Aigaio	-18.92	Clothing	+8.18
Kriti	-8.69	Timber	+7.10
		Paper and printing	+1.22
		Plastics and rubber	-4.56
		Other industries	-13.50

In terms of the sectoral Herfindahl indices, there were significant differences in employment concentrations across regions. In seven sectors, employment concentration decreased – mineral extraction (23), non-metallic minerals (24), metal articles (31), mechanical engineering (32), electrical engineering (34), rubber and plastics (48), other manufacturing industries (49). Concentration ranged from a minimum value of 0.16 in non-metallic minerals to a maximum of 0.59 in the chemical industry. The largest changes during the 1985-92 period occurred in other manufacturing industries (from 0.48 in 1985 to 0.37 in 1992), in mechanical engineering (from 0.34 to 0.23), in chemicals (from 0.5 to 0.59) and in electrical engineering (from 0.31 to 0.38).

In conclusion, the effect of the SMP on regional and sectoral employment concentration appears to have been very small during this period (1985–92).

The lack of available data prevented a complete analysis of FDI. Some data disaggregated by region and by sector existed for the 1988–92 period, and these are shown in Table 4.3.28.

The amount of FDI increased significantly, but it still remains at inadequate level. Moreover, as long as there is no reliable information as to its direction, no very useful conclusions can be drawn. A striking element, however, was the overwhelming concentration of such investment in the Attiki region. This underlined the fact that there was no satisfactory infrastructure elsewhere to facilitate the establishment of foreign firms. The acquisition of the Heraklis cement company can be understood only in the context of global competition, as Greek cement producers are strong exporters. In this sense, it should not necessarily be attributed to any effects of the SMP.

Table 4.3.30. Total FDI by region, 1988–92 (US$ million)

Regions	1988	1989	1990	1991	1992
Anatoliki Makedonia and Thraki	-	-	1.9	-	-
Kentriki Makedonia	12.4	10.2	26.7	10.1	5.5
Dytiki Makedonia	-	-	-	-	-
Thessalia	1.9	0.5	3.8	0.1	-
Ipeiros	0.1	-	-	-	-
Ionia Nisia	2.1	20.3	2.0	0.1	0.4
Dytiki Ellada	4.5	1.0	9.1	0.5	23.1
Sterea Ellada	6.5	26.7	53.6	38.4	11.8
Peloponnisos	2.0	1.1	0.3	1.4	0.3
Attiki	68.3	97.5	210.6	227.7	460.0
Voreio Aigaio	-	-	-	-	0.3
Notio Aigaio	2.4	0.9	3.4	0.6	0.1
Kriti	1.4	1.9	1.7	3.7	-
Others	-	15.8	12.0	0.3	334.4
Total	101.6	175.9	325.1	282.9	835.9

Note: 'Others' stands for investments spanning two or more regions. The outlier figure of 1992 can be explained by the takeover of a very large cement company (Heraklis) by an Italian competitor, which cost about US$ 317 million.
Source: Ministry of National Economy.

4.3.4. Main conclusions from the indicator analysis

The purpose of this section has been to provide a descriptive account of the trade and factor flow indicators for the Greek regions at the two-digit level of sectoral disagregation, throughout the period of the implementation of the SMP (1985-92). This account needed to be qualified by the regression results presented in the next section, though on the whole the pictures that emerged were broadly consistent with what we have just seen.

The disaggregated analysis presented above was not always useful as the manufacturing bases of many of the Greek regions were too narrow for the effects to be of any significant order. It can be said that Greek regions, except in a few cases, lacked any particular characteristics of regional specialization of the type one comes across in other parts of the EU. Linkages between different activities were poor and this was probably the outcome of an emphasis on activities with low value added and technological content.

However, some interesting changes have apparently occurred with respect to various manufacturing sectors (although we should take great care not to make the fallacy of aggregation). The food, beverages and tobacco sector dominated Greek manufacturing and has been characterized by differing performances between the northern and the southern regions. The first displayed declining trade activities (both to the EU and to non-EU countries), while the others increased their volume of export trade. For both types of regions, though, the signs concerning RCA across most sectors did not seem to be particularly encouraging.

A similarly split pattern, with a gap between the northern and the southern regions, took place in the mineral extraction sector – the second most important sector of Greek manufacturing (although not a manufacturing activity in the strict sense). In this case the north performed better than the south in trade creation, trade diversion (something that was contrary to the expectations of the SMP), RCA and export specialization, but worse in IIT.

The last example of erratic behaviour of the north in traditional industries was the footwear and clothing sector (responsible for 5% of output in 1992), as the regions of Anatoliki Makedonia and Thraki and of Kentriki Makedonia suffered more from a diminution of their export trade and relative competitive position compared to Attiki and Dytiki Ellada, which were located in the south.

The SMP seems to have benefited especially the non-metallic minerals sector, where Greece has traditionally based a large part of its external trade. Two regions even managed to turn the negative sign of their RCA indicator into positive figures. The other major Greek industry, textiles, experienced hard times during this period as its competitive position has been eroded. The volume of exports increased, though mainly to third countries rather than the EU.

Concluding, it may be said that the SMP led to beneficiary, though not substantial, trade creation in the majority of manufacturing activities and contributed significantly to the increase in IIT relationships. However, no important specialization trends seem to have taken place. The sectors based on more complicated technology remained stagnant and insignificant. Despite some isolated signs, the impression given is that Greek manufacturing will keep concentrating on activities deriving their competitiveness from static factors.

As explained towards the end of Section 4.3.3, not much can be said about the effects, if any, of the SMP on factor flows. This result was confirmed by the regression analysis presented in the next section. The increase in the capital/labour ratio for the vast majority of sectors and regions may be attributed to a modernizing stimulus in Greek manufacturing in response to the competitive pressures that grew with the single market. Its consequences have yet to be seen. The employment concentration indices did not reveal any significant regional or sectoral re-orderings. That was also the conclusion stemming from an analysis of the FDI data.

4.3.5. Regression analysis

Introduction

In the case of Greece, the regression analysis could not be performed for all the regions and sectors covered in the indicator analysis. The reason is that, in some regions, the data for many sectors were missing or very incomplete. This is why we decided to aggregate regions by constructing a few 'macro-regions', which were much more homogeneous in terms of economic structure and dynamics. In the sequel, eight 'macro-regions' will be considered. Their relationship with the original regions was as follows:

Region 1 = 12+13+21
Region 2 = 23+24
Region 3 = 22+41+42
Region 4 = 11
Region 5 = 14
Region 6 = 25
Region 7 = 3
Region 8 = 43

For these regions, statistical observations for the whole sample size (1985-92) and all sectors were available, with the exception of one important variable. The figure for FDI had to be an aggregated one, that is, we used the total amount of FDI in all regions and sectors, but not their distribution over time.

Objectives and model specification

The regression analysis was designed to achieve four main goals.

(a)   **To quantify the impact of the SMP on some trade indicators and factor flows.** This can be done by analysing the value of ρ in the following regressions:

Equation 1 $XE_t/Y_t = b_0 + X_t\psi + \rho I_t + \varepsilon_{1t}$
Equation 2 $B_t = b_0 + X_t\psi + \rho I_t + \varepsilon_{2t}$
Equation 3 $RCA_t = b_0 + X_t\psi + \rho I_t + \varepsilon_{3t}$
Equation 4 $FDI_t = b_0 + X_t\psi + \rho I_t + \varepsilon_{4t}$

where trade creation (XE_t/Y_t), IIT (B_t), RCA (RCA_t) and EU FDI (FDI_t) were the main indicators of trade and factor flows that we selected. The vector of explanatory variables, X_t contained proxies for cyclical and globalization effects (the growth rate of industrial production and world trade growth, respectively). In the set of explanatory variables, X_t, we also included the other variables that were used in the indicator analysis (labour productivity, sectoral specialization and capital intensity – the capital/labour ratio). Finally, we also accounted for CSF support in all regions. These variables enabled us to disentangle the effect of the SMP (quantified by the parameter ρ) on trade and factor flows, from the effects of cyclical and globalization variables and of variables capturing the specificity of each sector (capital intensity, labour productivity, and specialization). Note, however, that we did not know the distribution over time of FDI in all regions and sectors. This prevented us from estimating Equation 4 because the time series for the dependent variable was missing and the cross-section dimension was not large enough to provide significant estimates of the parameters. Therefore, we focused our analysis on the effects of the implementation of the SMP on factor flow indicators.

(b)   **To assess whether or not the SMP, by changing the pattern of trade flows, also modified the accumulation of (physical and human) capital in the Greek regions considered in this review.** To achieve this goal we ran the following regressions:

Equation 5 $k_t = s_0 + s_1 Y_t + s_2 K_t + s_3 \Delta XE_t/Y_t + s_4 \Delta B_t + s_5 \Delta RCA_t + s_6 \Delta FDI_t + \varepsilon_{5t}$

Equation 6 $h_t = r_0 + r_1 Y_t + r_2 H_t + r_3 \Delta XE_t/Y_t + r_4 \Delta B_t + r_5 \Delta RCA_t + s_6 \Delta FDI_t + \varepsilon_{6t}$

where the dynamics of the growth rate of physical (k_t) and human (h_t) capital explained stock (K_t) and flow (Y_t) characteristics of each region and sector (Baldwin and Venables, 1995) and for possible effects of trade creation (XE_t/Y_t), IIT (B_t), international competitiveness (RCA_t) and EU FDI (FDI_t). Note that all these variables entered into Equations 5 and 6 as first differences (Δ) of the original variables endogenized by Equations 1 to 4. As explained by Baldwin and Venables (1995), the rationale of Equations 5 and 6 is that capital accumulation is likely to be pro cyclical (in the empirical specification we also used the rate of change of Y_t) and faster when capital is small, i.e. regions with a low level of capital stocks are likely to grow more rapidly. This argument implicitly embodied the assumption of a technology characterized by decreasing returns. As this may not have been the case in some sectors, we did not expect the coefficients r_2 and s_2 to be necessarily negative.

Note that, given the available data, Equation 5 was run for all regions and sectors, whereas Equation 6 was run for all regions only. Moreover, remember that only the figure for the *total* amount of FDI was available for each region and sector. Therefore, in Equations 5 and 6, we introduced the level of this variable (rather than the change). The cross-section dimension of FDI helped us identify region-specific effects.

(c)   **To assess the impact of the SMP on the growth rates of per capita sectoral value added in the different sectors in all regions.** Therefore, the following regression was also run:

Equation 7 $y_t = a_t + \alpha k_t + \beta h_t - (1-\gamma)l_t + \varepsilon_{7t}$

where y_t is per capita GDP growth, a_t the rate of growth of technical progress, k_t and h_t physical and human capital respectively, and l_t the growth rate of unskilled labour. This regression was done for all regions and sectors. However, data on technical progress were available only at country level, whereas for physical capital we used data at regional level.

(d)   **Finally, the ultimate goal of our analysis was to verify in which sectors the implementation of the SMP increased or reduced the speed of convergence between the regions considered in this review.** To do that we had to calculate the *antimonde* growth path of sectoral per capita value added (see Section 3.3) and then run the following regression:

Equation 8 $IM_{j,avg} = cost°_j + (\alpha-\alpha^*)INV_{j,avg} - (\beta-\beta^*)RGDP_{j,85}$
$+ (\gamma-\gamma^*)GPO_{j,avg} (\delta-\delta^*)SEC_{j,85} + (\varphi-\varphi^*)TECH_{j,avg}$
$+ (\theta-\theta^*)DUMMIES_j + \alpha^*(INV_{j,avg} -INV^*_{j,avg}) + \eta_j$

where the dependent variable was defined as the difference between the actual average relative rate of growth of sectoral per capita value added and the average *antimonde* rate of growth determined as explained in Section 3.7. In Equation 8, we also added the average amount of CSF in each region.

The null hypothesis was that the coefficient $\pi_1 \equiv \beta-\beta^*$ (and/or $\pi_2 \equiv \delta-\delta^*$) was statistically significant and positive. This hypothesis was easily tested using standard inference technique. Note that the above tests were performed for all sectors considered in this study. Therefore, we produced information on the impact of the SMP on the speed of convergence in all sectors.

The results concerning this last equation – which was run for all regions and sectors of Greece, Ireland, Italy and Portugal because it exploited the sectional dimension of the sample – are reported in Chapter 5.

Methodology

From a methodological viewpoint, all the equations (1-7) were estimated using the techniques described in Chapter 3.[25] In particular, in the estimation process we accounted for:

(a) **co-integration**, by using the two-step Engle and Granger estimator (the one-step estimator proposed by Davidson and McKinnon proved to be less efficient);

(b) **simultaneity**, by using instrumental variables for the endogenous variables appearing among the explanatory ones;

(c) **regional heterogeneity** in the panel of data used to estimate Equations 1-7; regional heterogeneity was tested by introducing regional dummies among the regressors;

(d) **structural breaks** related to the implementation of the SMP by using the liberalization index as the explanatory variable for the dynamics of the equation coefficients;

(e) **heteroscedasticity**, by using a White-consistent estimator;

(f) **technical progress**, by constructing an index that reflected the dynamics of economic indicators such as R&D, relative prices, GDP growth, patents, etc.;

(g) **structural funds**, explaining regional differences by means of a measure of CSFs in each region.

The actual specification of the model was achieved by following the 'encompassing principle' approach. That is, we started from the most general model, in which all available variables were included, and then reduced the number of variables in the regressions by performing a cascade of t and F tests. If the 'true' model is 'encompassed' by the initial general model, this method leads the specification process just described to identify the 'true' model. Of course, the small number of degrees of freedom does not guarantee this outcome, which holds asymptotically. Therefore, once we had identified the 'true' model, we tested its robustness by using Pagan and Hall's residual analysis, that is, we regressed the residuals on the excluded coefficients.

This procedure – encompassing approach plus residual analysis – designed to guarantee the robustness of the estimated model, was followed for both the explanatory variables included in

---

[25] The starred parameters and variables in Equation 8 were generated within the *antimonde* analysis, that is, assuming that the liberalization index was equal to 1 over the whole sample.

each regression and the regional dummies, which captured the differences between the region-specific effects and the average effects in the panel of regions. Note that when we applied this procedure, we did not use a rigid criterion to define the significance level of the various tests. In particular, the constants CO, $C1$ and $C2$ (see Appendix A2 to Section 4.3) and the lagged variable of the second stage of the Engle and Granger procedure were maintained in the regression even when they were statistically non-significant. A few explanatory variables also appeared with low t statistics. This was done because our main goals were the robustness and the theoretical consistency of the model. Therefore, given the small number of degrees of freedom, in the selection of the variables, priority was given to these two objectives rather than to the choice of a given (say, 10%) significance level.

Robustness was also an issue as far as co-integration and structural breaks were concerned. In the case of co-integration, the small number of data did not enable us to perform the usual Dickey and Fuller's tests. However, we used a graphical representation of the time series as evidence of the presence of a common trend. Moreover, we exploited the super-consistency properties of the estimates of the co-integration vector in the Engle and Granger two-stage procedure in order to exclude from the co-integration regression those variables the coefficients of which were not statistically significant in the first stage. These variables were then tested to see if they belonged to the 'true' model as stationary non-co-integrated variables. When this hypothesis could be accepted, the variables were maintained in the regression (their first difference was not introduced in the second stage of the Engle and Granger procedure).

In the case of structural breaks, we tested the robustness of the model in two ways: by running t tests on the significance of the coefficients, explaining the variability of the coefficients, and by comparing the model in which structural variability was assumed with the model in which coefficients were assumed to be constant. The computed likelihood ratio always led us to accept the hypothesis that the correct specification was the one which assumes structural variability. The power of these tests is certainly limited by the small size of the sample. However, the panel approach and the non-significance of many of the regional dummies provided us with a sufficient number of degrees of freedom for the estimation and the robustness check of the final model.

Trade and factor flows

The three equations describing the dynamics of trade flows were estimated using the methodology described above. The notable exception in the case of Equations 1–3 was that only the constant term was assumed to be time-varying. That is, the liberalization index was introduced into Equations 1 to 3 in an additive way. A panel data approach was used in order to increase the efficiency of our estimates. Therefore, all equations were estimated sector by sector by stacking regional data. Regional dummies (both on constant and slope parameters) were introduced when they were statistically significant. Equation 4 was not estimated because of lack of sectoral time series data for FDI in Greece.

Let us consider the first equation, which captured the dynamics of trade creation. The eight parameters presented in Appendix A2 to Section 4.3 were the impact on trade creation of the following:

(a)   world trade index $(x1)$;

(b)   specialization index $(x2)$;
(c)   capital/labour ratio $(x3)$;
(d)   labour productivity $(x4)$;
(e)   GDP growth rate $(x5)$;
(f)   liberalization index $(x6)$;
(g)   FDI $(x7)$;
(h)   CSFs $(x8)$.

In order to understand the results reported in Appendix A2 to Section 4.3, note that the set of regressors is divided into two parts: the first block contains the regressors that were shown to be co-integrated (their coefficients were estimated in the first step); the second block contains the regressors that were not co-integrated (the constants and some explanatory variables) and the lagged dependent variable, which must be introduced into the second step (we do not show the coefficients related to the first differences of the co-integrated variables because they were relevant only to perform a correct inference on the other parameters). Note that the second block of coefficients is shown after the constant CO and the coefficient of the lagged variable (RIT).

For a clear reading of the tables shown in Appendix 2 to Section 4.3, also note that xi, $i = 1, 2, \ldots, 8$, are the average panel coefficients, whereas xij, $i = 1, 2, \ldots, 8$ and $j = 1, 2, \ldots, 8$ are the regional dummy coefficients. For example, $x12$ denotes the differential impact of the world trade index in region 2 of Greece. When only the regional dummy appears, the differential impact is with respect to zero (the hypothesis that the average coefficient was zero could be accepted). The sector label appears after the coefficient one. For example, $x1AGR$ denotes the average impact of the world trade index for the agricultural sector.

Let us focus on the impact of the liberalization index – which captured the progressive implementation of the SMP – on trade creation. A positive and significant effects was found only for the metal minerals sector and only for regions 3, 5 and 6. In all other sectors, either the effect was not statistically significant or was negative. By increasing the significance level, a mild, positive effect was also found for the transport equipment and the textile and clothing industries. By contrast, a statistically significant positive effect on trade creation was provided by an increase in the specialization index for most sectors (the exception was the non-metal minerals sector).

Let us now move to our indicator of IIT. There, the liberalization index had a positive impact on IIT in the following sectors and regions:

(a)   transport equipment (regions 3, 6 and 7);
(b)   food, beverages and tobacco (regions 3, 5 and 6);
(c)   chemical products (region 2);
(d)   paper (region 4);
(e)   metal products (regions 1, 2 and 7).

In all other cases, either the effect was negative or it was statistically non-significant. By contrast, the specialization index and labour productivity were generally positively correlated with IIT.

Was there a significant positive effect of the implementation of the SMP on the RCA indicator? The answer was in the negative for almost all sectors. The few exceptions were:

(a)   the textile and clothing industries (all regions);
(b)   non-metal minerals (region 7);
(c)   food, beverages and tobacco (region 6).

However, the correlation between the liberalization index and the RCA indicator identified was generally negative and statistically significant.

We therefore concluded – in agreement with the descriptive indicator analysis presented in the previous section – that the implementation of the SMP in Greece did not seem to have had a generalized positive effect on trade flow indicators. Only in a few sectors and regions did we identify a positive impact, particularly on IIT. By contrast, for many regions and sectors the impact of the implementation of the SMP on most other trade flow indicators seemed to have been a negative one.

Factor accumulation

Equations 5 and 6 were designed to assess the impact of trade and factor flow changes on the accumulation of physical and human capital in the different regions and sectors. Capital accumulation (the growth rate of physical and human capital) was therefore explained by the standard stock flow law of motion and by the possible effects of changes in trade and factor flow indicators. In the estimation of these two equations, we accounted for heteroscedasticity due to regional variability, structural breaks induced by the implementation of the SMP (both on constants and slope parameters), regional dummies, co-integration (using the Engle and Granger two-step estimator) and simultaneity (by means of the available instrumental variables). As previously said, the aggregate level of FDI for each region and sector was used to identify region-specific effects in the sectoral equations.

The estimation results of Equation 2 are shown in Appendix A2 to Section 4.3. The regressors were as follows:

(a)   regional value added ($x1$);
(b)   level of the physical capital stock ($x2$);
(c)   trade creation ($x3$);
(d)   FDI ($x4$);
(e)   IIT ($x5$);
(f)   RCA ($x6$).

Moreover, the coefficient C_0 accounted for regional differences due to the initial 1985 level of the capital stock, whereas C_2 accounted for regional differences due to CSF. The coefficient C_1 measured the break induced on the panel fixed effect by the increase in the liberalization index.

Looking at the results (see Appendix A2 to Section 4.3), note that an increase in regional value added had a positive impact on capital accumulation for all regions and sectors. Moreover, with the exception of the paper sector, the parameter related to the level of the capital stock had the expected negative sign, thus showing that capital accumulation was faster when the level of capital stock was lower.

As far as the impact of factor flows on physical capital accumulation was concerned, note the positive and statistically significant coefficient of trade creation in the metal minerals and chemical products sectors. IIT had a positive impact on physical capital in the non-metal minerals and food, beverages and tobacco sectors. The RCA had either a non-significant or negative impact on physical capital accumulation. Therefore, there was only mild evidence that changes in trade flow indicators had a positive effect on physical capital accumulation. Indeed, in most cases, the effect was statistically non-significant.

Finally, let us consider FDI. Even if this variable only captured cross-sectional variability, a few effects were identified. Regions with a larger amount of FDI were characterized by a larger rate of accumulation of physical capital in the transport equipment sector. Vice versa in the metal products sector. In all other cases, FDI did not show a statistically significant effect.

A similar conclusion held for CSFs. The estimated parameters showed that regions receiving larger amounts of CSFs were characterized by a larger accumulation rate in the textile and clothing industries than regions receiving less. Vice versa in the chemical products, wood and rubber, and paper sectors. In all other sectors, the coefficient C_2 was not statistically significant.

Therefore, no robust conclusion regarding the role of FDI and/or CSFs can be derived from the regression analysis.

Was there a convergence effect that explained the accumulation of human capital? Even in this case, the answer was not satisfactory. The coefficient C_0 was positive and statistically significant for most sectors (non-metal minerals, chemical products, metal products, transport equipment, the textile and clothing industries, wood and rubber, paper, and food, beverages and tobacco). This suggested that divergence rather than convergence in capital accumulation occurred in Greece.

A final result looked slightly more encouraging. There was evidence that the implementation of the SMP induced a positive structural break in the accumulation rate of physical capital in the metal minerals, wood and rubber, and paper sectors.

Let us next move on to human capital. This variable was proxied by the number of students in secondary school, a variable that was obviously defined at the regional level (it would have been meaningless to disaggregate this variable for each sector). This proxy was the one most used in the literature on convergence (see Levine and Renelt, 1992, and Baldwin and Venables, 1995). The fact that only regional observations were used implied that only one regression was run, where regional data were considered as a panel (the results are shown in Appendix A2 to Section 4.3). Again, the growth rate in the stock of human capital was negatively related to its level, thus indicating that human capital increased faster when the level was low. The effect of value added growth on human capital growth was positive, as expected.

As far as trade and factor flow indicators were concerned, we found a positive impact on human capital of changes in the RCA indicator, and a negative effect of changes in the IIT indicator. A positive, albeit slightly significant effect was found for FDI. The effect of changes in trade creation was not statistically significant.

The conclusions were therefore the reverse of those found for physical capital. That is, changes in IIT had a mild, positive effect, whereas changes in the RCA had a negative effect.

Moreover, no statistically significant effect on the accumulation of human capital was produced by different CSF values in different regions. There was also no evidence of an SMP-induced structural break, nor of convergence among regions.

The conclusions were therefore as follows. Trade and factor flow indicators did not seem to have had a generalized significant effect on capital accumulation. When the effects were statistically significant, they may have had opposite signs in different sectors. If we were to couple this conclusion with the previous one, that the SMP had little effect on trade flows, we could argue that our data did not provide evidence in favour of a positive impact of the implementation of the SMP on capital accumulation.

Regional growth

The previous analysis did not provide any behavioural link between the implementation of the SMP and economic growth. However, we thought it might be worth looking for the existence of a structural link. That is, if there was an increase in economic growth induced by the SMP via a structural change in the coefficients in the growth equation. We considered, therefore, the last equation of our regression model, which linked the growth rate of per capita sectoral value added to technical progress ($x1$), the accumulation of physical ($x2$) and human ($x3$) capital, and to the growth rate of the labour force ($x4$), which was assumed to be exogenous.

We then moved immediately to the crucial question: in which sector was there a positive structural break induced by the implementation of the SMP? Looking at the results shown in Appendix A2 to Section 4.3, a positive and statistically significant break occurred only in the paper sector. In all other sectors, the coefficient C_1 was either statistically non-significant or negative.

The growth equation provided other interesting information. There was mild evidence of convergence in economic growth in most sectors (particularly in transport equipment, wood and rubber, and paper). The coefficient C_0 was indeed always negative. Moreover, what explained economic growth in Greek regions was mainly the dynamics of the labour force (in all sectors and regions). Positive effects on growth were also related to human capital (in food, beverages and tobacco, and metal minerals), technical progress (in chemical products, transport equipment, the textile and clothing industries, wood and rubber), physical capital (only in the textile and clothing industries). No positive effect was found for CSFs.

However, the most striking result was the lack of an impact of the implementation of the SMP on economic growth. There was almost no effect as a result of capital accumulation and no effects arising from structural breaks (with the exception of the paper sector).

Conclusions from the regression analysis

There were a few conclusions that the regression analysis seemed to support:

(a) The implementation of the SMP had little effect on trade flows. Some positive effects could be identified in IIT. By contrast, the impact on the RCA was generally negative. These results were consistent with those emerging from the qualitative indicator analysis presented in Section 4.3.3.

(b) As far as human capital was concerned, we found a positive effect on its accumulation rate of changes in the RCA, and a negative effect of changes in the IIT indicator. A positive, albeit only slightly significant, effect was found for FDI. The effect of changes in trade creation was not statistically significant.

The reverse of these conclusions were arrived at when we considered physical capital, for which changes in the IIT indicator had only a mildly positive effect on its accumulation rate, whereas changes in the RCA had a negative effect.

(c)   No significant effect on the accumulation of physical and human capital was produced by different CSF values for different regions. There was evidence of an SMP-induced structural break, but only for physical capital and just for a few sectors.

(d)   By coupling the above results, we concluded that the regression analysis for the Greek regions suggested that almost no positive impact of the implementation of the SMP on capital accumulation was likely to have occurred.

(e)   Nonetheless, there was mild evidence of convergence in economic growth for most sectors (particularly transport equipment, wood and rubber, and paper). No positive effect on growth was found for CSFs.

(f)   The most striking result was the lack of impact of the implementation of the SMP on economic growth. There were almost no effects via capital accumulation, and no effects via structural breaks (with the exception of the paper sector).

4.3.6. Appendix A1 to Section 4.3.

The methodology used for data estimation

The regional final consumption, intermediate consumption and investment figures for the 20 sectors were calculated by means of the aggregate functions for each sector.

Specifically, the regional final consumption figure was obtained as follows:

The country final consumption figure for the good i was estimated by means of ordinary least squares. Annual data was utilized for the period 1979-93. The standard theory on consumption postulates that it depends on a scale variable and therefore the long-run consumption takes the form:

$$CFCi = a + bGDP + u_t$$

Then the estimated equation (which was tested to check that it satisfied the conditions for BLU estimators) was used to obtain the regional, r, final consumption for the good i by substituting the regional GDP, *GDPr*, for *GDP*. Therefore:

$$FCir = \hat{a} + \hat{b} \, GDPr$$

To satisfy the adding up conditions, the divergences between actual and estimated values, which in general were small, were distributed in the two largest regions of Greece.

For the estimation of the intermediate consumption we proceeded as follows:

The methodology described above was slightly modified in order to estimate the regional intermediate consumption. The data for the total regional intermediate consumption were calculated using the formula:

$$CIr = Xr - Yr$$

where CI_r is the total intermediate consumption for the region, r, X_r is the value of total production in region r, and Y_r is the value added for the region, r. Also, it was supposed that the home intermediate consumption for the good i (CIi) would be given by the formula:

$$CIi = \gamma + \delta Xi + \varepsilon t$$

Then the estimated equation, which was tested to check that it satisfied the conditions for BLU estimators, was used to calculate CI_{ir}, according to the formula:

$$CIir = \hat{\gamma} + \hat{\delta} \, Xr$$

To satisfy the adding up conditions, the divergences between actual and estimated values, which in general were small, were distributed in the two largest regions of Greece.

In the case of investment, the procedure described above was followed, taking into consideration the following:

We assumed that investment in industry, i (Ii), depended on the value of total production, X, that is:

$$Ii = c + f\ X + e$$

Then, by substituting regional production, Xr, in the estimated equation (which was tested to ensure that it satisfied the conditions for BLU estimators) for the investment in each industry, i, the regional investment for each industry was obtained, that is:

$$Iir = \hat{c} + \hat{f}\ Xr$$

Once more, to satisfy the adding up conditions, the divergences between actual and estimated values, which in general were small, were distributed in the two largest regions of Greece.

Coming to the calculation of trade flows, for regional imports the calculations were carried out using the following procedure:

Using the standard theory assumptions, total imports in industry, i, depend on the value of total production, X, and the value of the exchange rate, ER, which is the parity of national currency with the ECU. Thus, the formula took the form:

$$IMi = g + h\ X - mER + u$$

The estimating function was used to obtain the regional imports, thus:

$$IMir = \hat{g} + \hat{h}\ Xir - \hat{m}\ ER$$

The exports in industry, i, of the region to the rest of Europe, excluding Greece, were regarded as a function of the productivity of labour in the specific industry and region. Then it was assumed that the above exports to the EU followed the share of the country's total exports to the EU.

4.3.7. Appendix A2 to Section 4.3.

Explanatory note regarding the regression analysis

The regression parameters, *Xijk*, have to be read as follows:

(a)   *i* is the index of the regressor (according to the three types of equation) for:
    (i)   trade and factor flows:
        world trade index;
        specialization index;
        capital/labour ratio;
        labour productivity;
        GDP growth rate;
        liberalization index;
        FDI;
        CSFs;
    (ii)   human and physical capital:
        1 regional value added;
        2 level of the physical capital stock;
        3 trade creation;
        4 FDI;
        5 IIT;
        6 RCAs;
    (iii)   economic growth:
        1 technical progress;
        2 accumulation of physical capital;
        3 accumulation of human capital;
        4 growth rate of labour force;
(b)   *j* is the index of the region:
    1 Kentriki Makedonia and Dytiki Makedonia and Ipeiros;
    2 Dytiki Ellada and Sterea Ellada;
    3 Ionia Nisia and Voreio Aigaio and Notio Aigaio;
    4 Anatoliki Makedonia;
    5 Thessalia;
    6 Peloponnisos;
    7 Attiki;
    8 Kriti;
(c)   *k* is the index of the sector:
    AGR;   NMM;
    CHP;   PAP;
    ENP;   TEC;
    FBT;   TOT;
    MEM;   TRE;
    MEP;   WOR.

Table A2.4.3.1. Sectoral regression parameters for Greece

MEM

Sector	Growth equation			Physical capital equation			IIT-E equation			RCA-E equation			TC equation		
		Param	t.Student		Param	t.Student		Param	t.Student		Param	t.Student		Param	t.Student
	X3MEM	0.55	2.35	X1MEM	5.49	6.63	X1MEM	394.10	6.69	X1MEM	304.65	13.99	X1MEM	476.52	7.45
	X34MEM	2.85	1.07	X11MEM	55.75	6.83	X11MEM	81.09	2.61	X2MEM	5.26	1.09	X11MEM	294.92	6.01
	X4MEM	-0.09	-1.16	X14MEM	1346.47	4.85	X12MEM	-160.46	-12.40	X6MEM	-122.74	-2.45	X2MEM	402.78	9.28
	X41MEM	0.54	1.09	X17MEM	11.06	5.84	X2MEM	77.04	3.84	X61MEM	55.92	2.29	X3MEM	33.14	1.05
	C0MEM	-0.48	-0.73	C0MEM	0.09	0.73	X4MEM	-1.67	-3.05	X7MEM	1.89	1.81	X4MEM	-7128.07	-6.32
	C1MEM	-0.41	-1.04	C1MEM	0.07	2.85	X6MEM	-105.15	-2.21	C0MEM	65.10	0.47	C0MEM	-1765.70	-1.32
	C2MEM	-1.15E-08	-1.29	C2MEM	4.07E-08	1.08	C0MEM	-707.15	-1.67	RITMEM	-0.06	-1.18	RITMEM	-0.37	-2.48
	RITMEM	-0.13	-5.48	RITMEM	-0.03	-1.82	RITMEM	-0.64	-2.24				X6MEM	4694.06	3.59
	X1MEM	1.48	1.10	X2MEM	-1.67	-3.04	X5MEM	97.18	1.17				X61MEM	-3342.85	-3.52
	X2MEM	5.61	1.03	X3MEM	0.26	2.06							X62MEM	-4629.30	-3.99
				X5MEM	-0.01	-1.78							X64MEM	-4063.55	-3.79
				X6MEM	-1.05	-3.88							X67MEM	-3661.74	-3.54
	R-squared	0.61		R-squared	0.31		R-squared	0.76		R-squared	0.45		R-squared	1.00	

NMM

Sector	Growth equation			Physical capital equation			IIT-E equation			RCA-E equation			TC equation		
		Param	t.Student		Param	t.Student		Param	t.Student		Param	t.Student		Param	t.Student
	X1NMM	0.25	1.35	X1NMM	2.90	3.67	X2NMM	80.82	9.11	X1NMM	297.61	1.89	X1NMM	2048.03	15.29
	X4NMM	0.65	1.33	X11NMM	6.54	3.30	X3NMM	0.14	2.23	X14NMM	166.45	3.58	X11NMM	3563.07	6.40
	X42NMM	-0.95	-5.52	X12NMM	5.82	5.67	X4NMM	0.91	4.16	X15NMM	-134.05	-5.72	X13NMM	5147.90	6.14
	X45NMM	0.50	2.61	X13NMM	220.90	4.62	C0NMM	-745.68	-2.03	X17NMM	2415.84	21.17	X14NMM	1353.93	5.74
	X46NMM	67.51	2.12	X14NMM	161.23	9.88	RITNMM	-0.09	-0.87	X2NMM	57.63	3.33	X2NMM	-94.42	-6.61
	X47NMM	-0.27	-1.83	X15NMM	21.95	26.70	X6NMM	22.36	0.66	X3NMM	105.58	2.58	X4NMM	-3056.46	-10.82
	C0NMM	-0.20	-0.61	X16NMM	18.19	7.24	X7NMM	2.32	2.99	X6NMM	-114.29	-1.63	X8NMM	0.01	3.05
	C1NMM	-0.01	-0.75	X17NMM	2.07	2.09				X62NMM	107.75	9.67	C0NMM	6613.92	4.57
	C2NMM	-2.04E-08	-2.00	C0NMM	0.37	4.28				X67NMM	407.62	4.15	RITNMM	-0.72	-2.19
	RITNMM	-0.09	-4.87	C1NMM	-4.06E-03	-0.75				X7NMM	7.58	2.64	X3NMM	-1004.04	-2.51
	X3NMM	0.52	1.21	C2NMM	8.14E-09	0.14				C0NMM	-823.10	-1.77	X6NMM	-342.87	-3.95
				RITNMM	-0.02	-3.21				RITNMM	-0.23	-1.29	X7NMM	11.29	2.39
				X3NMM	0.02	1.84									
	R-squared	0.61		R-squared	0.22		R-squared	0.66		R-squared	0.18		R-squared	0.87	

Sector CHP

Growth equation

Variable	Param	t.Student
X1CHP	0.30	2.38
X4CHP	-0.17	-0.79
X44CHP	0.77	3.12
X47CHP	1.55	1.69
COCHP	-0.52	-1.73
C1CHP	0.02	0.80
C2CHP	4.90E-10	0.19
RITCHP	-0.12	-8.16
R-squared	0.68	

Physical capital equation

Variable	Param	t.Student
X1CHP	2.90	6.30
X11CHP	15.50	6.35
X12CHP	15.88	4.70
X14CHP	106.67	9.74
X15CHP	82.19	5.55
X16CHP	2906.48	8.89
X18CHP	4964.12	9.10
X2CHP	-0.62	-1.86
COCHP	0.29	2.41
C1CHP	1.09E-03	0.14
C2CHP	-2.61E-08	-2.05
RITCHP	-0.02	-1.54
X3CHP	5.61	7.12
X31CHP	-3.47	-2.91
X33CHP	-4.94	-6.79
X35CHP	-4.71	-6.22
X36CHP	-5.53	-7.06
X38CHP	-5.68	-6.80
R-squared	0.36	

IIT-E equation

Variable	Param	t.Student
X2CHP	36.10	3.86
X3CHP	0.13	4.88
X4CHP	2.58	5.86
X6CHP	-187.19	-3.28
X62CHP	315.84	4.63
X65CHP	185.45	3.62
X8CHP	4.25	2.74
COCHP	-830.04	-2.16
RITCHP	-0.31	-1.95
X7CHP	5.41	1.43
R-squared	0.50	

RCA-E equation

Variable	Param	t.Student
X1CHP	49.62	29.22
X2CHP	3.49	1.32
X6CHP	-357.67	-11.00
COCHP	-297.98	-2.32
RITCHP	-0.07	-1.08
R-squared	0.15	

TC equation

Variable	Param	t.Student
X3CHP	153.11	9.91
X4CHP	1974.10	4.22
X5CHP	29.70	0.99
COCHP	-6243.20	-4.03
RITCHP	-0.64	-2.06
X1CHP	284.61	4.04
X2CHP	62.35	2.65
X6CHP	-1983.50	-4.05
R-squared	0.94	

Sector MEP

Growth equation

Variable	Param	t.Student
X4MEP	2.19	2.96
X42MEP	-2.67	-3.58
X44MEP	-4.46	-4.00
X45MEP	-2.41	-3.05
X47MEP	-1.77	-2.32
X48MEP	-4.72	-6.22
COMEP	-0.55	-1.76
C1MEP	0.03	1.24
C2MEP	1.03E-09	0.27
RITMEP	-0.11	-6.38

Physical capital equation

Variable	Param	t.Student
X1MEP	3.44	4.38
X11MEP	9.41	5.63
X12MEP	6.24	4.82
X14MEP	689.13	4.68
X15MEP	27.09	5.91
X16MEP	37.84	6.18
X17MEP	2.52	3.91
X18MEP	1371.55	6.65
X2MEP	-0.98	-3.25
COMEP	0.35	3.16
C1MEP	-0.01	-0.65

IIT-E equation

Variable	Param	t.Student
X1MEP	25.05	6.78
X12MEP	-9.72	-6.26
X15MEP	-5.59	-5.10
X16MEP	-4.89	-3.08
X2MEP	35.54	3.41
X6MEP	-126.95	-1.91
X61MEP	275.72	4.32
X62MEP	205.64	4.42
X64MEP	77.99	3.87
X67MEP	167.81	9.21
X7MEP	2.48	1.37

RCA-E equation

Variable	Param	t.Student
X1MEP	31.50	24.74
X4MEP	312.83	1.55
X6MEP	-282.94	-8.58
COMEP	-0.11	0.00
RITMEP	0.00	0.15
X2MEP	-1.94	-4.06
X7MEP	0.08	1.63

TC equation

Variable	Param	t.Student
X1MEP	108.89	5.53
X12MEP	-59.49	-6.04
X17MEP	-46.73	-6.12
X2MEP	240.96	3.69
X4MEP	-16201.70	-3.15
COMEP	482.09	0.16
RITMEP	-0.81	-2.55

TRE

Variable	Coef	t-stat
R-squared	**0.66**	
X4TRE	-0.62	-10.36
X43TRE	0.49	1.13
X44TRE	-0.04	-1.87
X45TRE	0.80	4.10
C0TRE	-2.72	-2.85
C1TRE	-0.46	-1.92
C2TRE	1.30E-08	1.17
RITTRE	-0.07	-4.37
X1TRE	4.50	2.32
X2TRE	3.54	1.39
X3TRE	0.19	1.27

Variable	Coef	t-stat
R-squared	**0.64**	
C2MEP	2.26E-08	
RITMEP	-1.00E-02	-1.09
X4MEP	-8.56E-05	-3.13
R-squared	**0.63**	
X1TRE	5.89	4.95
X11TRE	14.93	2.52
X12TRE	10.56	3.56
X13TRE	39.05	3.50
X15TRE	36.93	7.35
X17TRE	-1.11	-2.45
X2TRE	-14.37	-2.14
C0TRE	0.32	2.87
C1TRE	-0.01	-1.82
C2TRE	-4.53E-08	-0.79
RITTRE	1.42E-03	0.32
X4TRE	6.16E-05	2.16

Variable	Coef	t-stat
COMEP	6843.85	3.17
RITMEP	-0.25	-1.72
X3MEP	-2.01	-2.71
X4MEP	-2.76	-2.49
R-squared	**0.72**	
X1TRE	-0.18	-1.21
X4TRE	6.58	35.98
C0TRE	-457.06	-0.45
RITTRE	-0.59	-3.55
X6TRE	-110.96	-1.06
X63TRE	258.45	2.21
X66TRE	209.28	1.45
X67TRE	146.63	2.14
X7TRE	3.32	1.25

Variable	Coef	t-stat
R-squared	**0.33**	
X1TRE	14.86	33.20
X6TRE	-387.13	-11.05
C0TRE	-7.99	-0.34
RITTRE	2.18E-03	0.15
X3TRE	2.97	1.09

Variable	Coef	t-stat
R-squared	**0.71**	
X1TRE	42.20	5.52
X12TRE	18.22	2.14
X13TRE	13.37	1.88
X4TRE	6606.23	1.58
C0TRE	-14780.60	-0.70
RITTRE	-1.29	-5.84
X3TRE	-2148.20	-1.56
X6TRE	1062.73	1.54

FBT

Variable	Coef	t-stat
R-squared	**0.90**	
X3FBT	0.021	0.208
X34FBT	0.74	4.09
X35FBT	0.57	3.24
X36FBT	2.75	4.76
X4FBT	-0.23	-2.53
X42FBT	0.39	5.41
X44FBT	1.31	6.13
X45FBT	0.99	3.48
X46FBT	-2.58	-9.36
C0FBT	-0.21	-0.57
C1FBT	4.74E-03	0.17
C2FBT	-5.75E-09	-2.83
RITFBT	-0.09	-3.62

Variable	Coef	t-stat
R-squared	**0.36**	
X1FBT	1.356	3.783
X11FBT	1.40	2.33
X12FBT	3.35	3.83
X13FBT	63.72	3.76
X14FBT	45.58	5.36
X15FBT	17.48	7.31
X16FBT	27.41	14.20
X17FBT	0.97	2.35
X18FBT	41.42	4.60
C0FBT	0.25	2.05
C1FBT	-	-0.13
C2FBT	-	0.79
RITFBT	-0.02	-1.36

Variable	Coef	t-stat
R-squared	**0.75**	
X2FBT	48.664	9.737
X3FBT	-6.02	-13.04
X4FBT	10.05	17.35
X6FBT	-631.66	-15.83
X63FBT	9524.11	4.15
X64FBT	572.16	2.78
X65FBT	1051.84	21.70
X66FBT	1351.16	7.13
X8FBT	4.23	4.61
C0FBT	582.86	1.50
RITFBT	-0.39	-2.10
X7FBT	2.13	1.59

Variable	Coef	t-stat
R-squared	**4.31E-03**	
X1FBT	68.882	35.645
X3FBT	-598.17	-6.22
X6FBT	-458.14	-10.36
X64FBT	485.83	8.07
X66FBT	478.86	21.85
C0FBT	-390.58	-1.13
RITFBT	-0.07	-0.93
X2FBT	-49.07	-1.21
X5FBT	23.57	1.78

Variable	Coef	t-stat
R-squared	**0.80**	
X1FBT	7.914	1.752
X12FBT	20.68	5.84
X15FBT	6.94	5.47
X17FBT	7.52	3.93
X2FBT	75.91	6.34
X3FBT	-158.04	-2.27
C0FBT	1738.82	1.45
RITFBT	-0.68	-3.15
X7FBT	11.11	1.51

Growth equation

Sector	Variable	Param	t.Student
TEC	R-squared	0.71	
	X2TEC	4.99	1.44
	X21TEC	5.30	2.19
	X4TEC	1.52	1.07
	X41TEC	6.44	6.76
	X42TEC	-1.62	-7.27
	X44TEC	2.61	2.92
	X46TEC	3.59	2.21
	X47TEC	1.31	14.95
	X48TEC	4.85	2.31
	C0TEC	-8.50	-1.64
	C1TEC	-0.93	-1.85
	C2TEC	-8.02E-09	-4.55
	RITTEC	-0.06	-4.36
	X1TEC	13.62	1.83
PAP	R-squared	0.68	
	X3PAP	0.30	0.77
	X4PAP	-0.33	-1.20
	X41PAP	-1.49	-1.79
	X42PAP	1.23	3.47
	X44PAP	0.51	6.05
	C0PAP	-0.91	-1.89
	C1PAP	0.07	2.27
	C2PAP	-1.67E-09	-0.58

Physical capital equation

Sector	Variable	Param	t.Student
	X2FBT	-0.38	-1.20
	X5FBT	0.01	4.54
	X6FBT	-0.10	-2.48
TEC	R-squared	0.24	
	X1TEC	1.85	4.59
	X12TEC	8.53	9.67
	X13TEC	148.41	10.24
	X14TEC	48.10	7.20
	X15TEC	10.15	5.32
	X16TEC	64.22	8.77
	X17TEC	1.99	4.60
	X18TEC	350.88	8.31
	X2TEC	-0.39	-2.28
	C0TEC	0.33	4.25
	C1TEC	4.15E-03	0.36
	C2TEC	1.44E-07	2.69
	RITTEC	-0.02	-2.00
PAP	R-squared	0.27	
	X2PAP	14.05	4.78
	X21PAP	27.28	4.12
	X22PAP	50.63	6.02
	X24PAP	446.70	10.70
	X26PAP	191.47	7.66
	X27PAP	9.14	2.96
	C0PAP	0.18	3.62
	C1PAP	0.04	5.63

IIT-E equation

Sector	Variable	Param	t.Student
TEC	R-squared	0.97	
	X1TEC	30.30	6.04
	X11TEC	-5.17	-5.69
	X12TEC	9.78	5.32
	X18TEC	-24.78	-4.18
	X2TEC	23.48	2.34
	X3TEC	0.42	3.03
	X4TEC	3.26	3.42
	X8TEC	1.87E-03	2.68
	C0TEC	539.62	3.49
	RITTEC	-0.69	-5.96
	X5TEC	40.47	1.16
	X6TEC	35.85	1.25
PAP	R-squared	0.95	
	X1PAP	32.74	1.71
	X16PAP	13.63	4.82
	X2PAP	31.97	2.20
	X3PAP	2.34	2.52
	X6PAP	-333.24	-2.91
	X62PAP	-159.52	-3.09
	X64PAP	448.73	7.02
	X7PAP	12.27	2.07

RCA-E equation

Sector	Variable	Param	t.Student
TEC	R-squared	0.47	
	X3TEC	231.55	2.67
	X6TEC	298.39	3.16
	X7TEC	15.15	1.91
	C0TEC	-141.01	-0.20
	RITTEC	-0.12	-2.00
PAP	R-squared	0.15	
	X1PAP	30.60	6.09
	X2PAP	10.48	4.52
	X3PAP	331.12	2.62
	X4PAP	1571.19	4.93
	X6PAP	-249.66	-6.60
	X61PAP	52.62	3.69
	X8PAP	3.63E-03	2.68
	C0PAP	-2.86	-0.22

TC equation

Sector	Variable	Param	t.Student
TEC	R-squared	0.59	
	X1TEC	12.86	1.96
	X11TEC	-5.77	-6.57
	X17TEC	12.31	4.47
	X3TEC	421.21	4.60
	X4TEC	4670.90	5.62
	C0TEC	-2129.05	-2.07
	RITTEC	-0.18	-0.70
	X6TEC	125.37	1.41
PAP	R-squared	0.57	
	X3PAP	644.20	2.50
	X4PAP	2155.89	4.86
	C0PAP	1260.08	1.14
	RITPAP	-0.48	-2.51
	X6PAP	-152.27	-1.69

WOR

	RITPAP	-0.06	-6.91
R-squared	0.59		
X4WOR	-3.18	-2.86	
X42WOR	-2.98	-1.73	
X45WOR	18.03	1.94	
X46WOR	10.45	2.93	
X47WOR	2.04	1.78	
COWOR	-12.40	-2.67	
C1WOR	-1.18	-2.29	
C2WOR	4.00E-09	1.30	
RITWOR	-0.07	-9.98	
X1WOR	19.32	2.54	
X3WOR	1.45	1.44	
R-squared	0.79		

	C2PAP	-4.78E-07	-9.31
	RITPAP	-0.11	-8.84
	X1PAP	0.43	2.27
	X14PAP	72.39	3.94
	X16PAP	33.80	3.01
R-squared	0.80		
X1WOR	5.93	4.10	
X11WOR	6.45	2.57	
X12WOR	9.13	5.59	
X14WOR	268.83	9.14	
X15WOR	41.52	5.21	
X16WOR	97.21	5.88	
X17WOR	7.01	3.64	
X2WOR	-1.48	-2.31	
COWOR	0.19	1.93	
C1WOR	0.02	2.19	
C2WOR	-9.44E-08	-3.03	
RITWOR	-0.04	-3.26	
X3WOR	2.74	1.23	
X6WOR	-1.72	-4.23	
R-squared	0.34		

	COPAP	-3718.03	-1.16
	RITPAP	-0.59	-7.04
	X4PAP	3.79	2.12
	X8PAP	1.31E-03	1.31
R-squared	0.92		
X1WOR	37.28	8.87	
X14WOR	-19.81	-6.66	
X15WOR	7.13	2.23	
X16WOR	-18.48	-12.78	
X17WOR	-2.82	-2.03	
X3WOR	1.37	3.79	
COWOR	2895.24	3.00	
RITWOR	-0.68	-13.62	
X2WOR	22.05	2.09	
X4WOR	-0.70	-1.11	
X5WOR	22.66	1.81	
X6WOR	-154.69	-9.27	
R-squared	0.99		

	RITPAP	-0.08	-4.35
R-squared	0.71		
X1WOR	6.78	2.36	
X11WOR	-3.00	-2.16	
X12WOR	-3.74	-3.72	
X2WOR	47.07	7.49	
X3WOR	766.91	6.05	
X4WOR	733.47	2.83	
X6WOR	-199.83	-6.52	
X61WOR	105.69	2.64	
X62WOR	140.07	4.54	
X7WOR	2.41	2.94	
COWOR	8.03	0.26	
RITWOR	-2.76E-03	-0.09	
R-squared	0.24		

	R-squared	0.54	
X1WOR	9.97	1.90	
X15WOR	7.27	2.68	
X17WOR	21.05	5.48	
X2WOR	147.38	9.95	
X4WOR	-2456.89	-4.24	
X8WOR	0.01	1.02	
COWOR	551.50	0.64	
RITWOR	-0.70	-3.61	
X6WOR	-99.74	-1.74	
R-squared	0.76		

Note:

1=Kentriki Makedonia + Dytiki Makedonia + Ipeiros;

2=Dytiki Ellada + Sterea Ellada;

3=Ionia Nisia + Voreio Aigaio + Notio Aigaio;

4=Anatoliki Makedonia; 5=Thessalia; 6=Peloponnisos

7=Attiki; 8=Kriti.

Table A2.4.3.2.   **Non-sectoral regression parameters for Greece**

Sector		Human capital equation	
		Param	*t Student*
TOT			
	X1TOT	3.62	3.74
	X11TOT	9.41	2.17
	X12TOT	14.99	3.76
	X14TOT	63.68	3.74
	X15TOT	318.28	3.88
	X2TOT	-13.56	-3.78
	X23TOT	13.40	3.68
	X25TOT	-55.94	-3.10
	X26TOT	12.90	3.76
	X27TOT	8.66	3.75
	X28TOT	13.38	3.75
	C0TOT	0.35	0.80
	C1TOT	-0.03	-0.68
	C2TOT	-0.43	-0.86
	RITTOT	-0.17	-5.17
	X4TOT	0.36	1.69
	X5TOT	-0.02	-4.58
	X6TOT	1.42	2.41
	R-squared	0.83	

Note:

1=Kentriki Makedonia + Dytiki Macedonia + Ipeiros;

2=Dytiki Ellada + Sterea Ellada;

3=Ionia Nisia + Voreio Aigaio + Notio Aigaio;

4=Anatoliki Makedonia; 5=Thessalia; 6=Peloponnisos;

7=Attiki; 8=Kriti.

4.3.8. Appendix A3 to Section 4.3.

Table A3.4.3.1. Trade creation indices for national data

NACE	1985	1986	1987	1988	1989	1990	1991	1992
2200	0.148	------	0.248	0.152	0.206	0.183	0.212	0.232
2300	0.000	------	0.325	0.262	0.260	0.246	0.250	0.256
2400	0.014	------	0.042	0.067	0.092	0.108	0.125	0.142
2500	0.054	------	0.050	0.048	0.093	0.085	0.093	0.092
3100	0.022	------	0.027	0.051	0.057	0.051	0.054	0.067
3200	0.139	------	0.102	0.113	0.165	0.219	0.269	0.222
3400	0.000	------	0.000	0.084	0.109	0.118	0.103	0.137
3500	0.005	------	0.043	0.018	0.016	0.031	0.037	0.039
4100	0.109	------	0.130	0.084	0.107	0.103	0.099	0.109
4300	0.167	------	0.266	0.221	0.288	0.323	0.366	0.492
4400	0.066	------	0.077	0.066	0.128	0.166	0.177	0.221
4500	0.757	------	0.919	0.638	0.610	0.519	0.608	0.626
4600	0.021	------	0.029	0.027	0.023	0.035	0.034	0.043
4700	0.023	------	0.030	0.017	0.016	0.017	0.013	0.014
4800	0.051	------	0.086	0.077	0.082	0.085	0.091	0.113
4900	0.094	------	0.140	1.635	3.042	2.266	2.532	2.234

Table A3.4.3.2. Trade diversion indices for national data

NACE	1985	1986	1987	1988	1989	1990	1991	1992
2200	0.206	------	0.124	0.110	0.108	0.098	0.099	0.132
2300	0.000	------	0.233	0.176	0.210	0.173	0.146	0.156
2400	0.304	------	0.237	0.146	0.176	0.143	0.133	0.158
2500	0.108	------	0.104	0.073	0.088	0.074	0.083	0.086
3100	0.083	------	0.068	0.057	0.091	0.080	0.113	0.100
3200	0.167	------	0.126	0.180	0.294	0.366	0.523	0.524
3400	0.000	------	0.000	0.044	0.050	0.058	0.054	0.078
3500	0.061	------	0.042	0.026	0.025	0.031	0.038	0.052
4100	0.094	------	0.073	0.043	0.066	0.058	0.058	0.078
4300	0.032	------	0.060	0.066	0.103	0.114	0.109	0.126
4400	0.134	------	0.187	0.139	0.141	0.162	0.151	0.125
4500	0.282	------	0.300	0.182	0.284	0.193	0.188	0.178
4600	0.074	------	0.059	0.058	0.061	0.056	0.078	0.074
4700	0.060	------	0.047	0.027	0.064	0.030	0.038	0.037
4800	0.081	------	0.074	0.054	0.058	0.059	0.069	0.097
4900	0.295	------	0.215	1.508	1.031	0.937	0.842	1.334

Table A3.4.3.3. Grubel-Lloyd indices for national data

NACE	1985	1986	1987	1988	1989	1990	1991	1992
2200	67.722	73.467	81.207	85.804	85.002	80.150	83.413	95.389
2300	40.806	39.752	46.917	35.812	46.693	52.976	55.436	48.070
2400	21.180	26.187	44.431	61.064	60.768	63.826	70.566	71.498
2500	16.665	12.772	11.925	13.298	21.734	19.473	19.611	18.715
3100	18.329	19.343	17.166	27.985	24.428	16.022	17.787	22.878
3200	6.409	6.319	4.669	5.479	6.249	7.177	8.239	6.168
3400	22.291	23.268	26.166	21.295	22.417	20.640	19.261	24.369
3500	1.109	3.987	8.023	3.857	2.457	3.717	3.863	3.079
4100	58.148	54.731	54.874	47.446	54.141	55.347	56.316	53.810
4300	48.364	43.111	42.214	50.616	58.748	63.027	62.052	54.819
4400	33.780	25.496	24.409	27.518	33.494	38.168	41.367	50.607
4500	78.195	68.578	70.351	75.953	88.164	87.961	85.912	87.549
4600	32.641	36.216	34.353	32.538	19.274	20.525	19.718	23.868
4700	23.748	19.889	28.066	17.694	13.683	14.767	10.778	12.009
4800	26.667	28.586	31.866	30.192	27.068	26.670	26.193	30.036
4900	13.554	14.809	11.325	64.128	81.888	67.611	72.534	65.223

Table A3.4.3.4. RCA indices for national data

NACE	1985	1986	1987	1988	1989	1990	1991	1992
2200	-32.278	-26.533	-18.793	-14.196	-14.998	-19.850	-16.587	-4.611
2300	59.194	60.248	53.083	64.188	53.307	47.024	44.564	51.930
2400	-78.820	-73.813	-55.569	-38.936	-39.232	-36.174	-29.434	-28.502
2500	-83.335	-87.228	-88.075	-86.702	-78.266	-80.527	-80.389	-81.285
3100	-81.671	-80.657	-82.834	-72.015	-75.572	-83.978	-82.213	-77.122
3200	-93.591	-93.681	-95.331	-94.521	-93.751	-92.823	-91.761	-93.832
3400	-77.709	-76.732	-73.834	-78.705	-77.583	-79.360	-80.739	-75.631
3500	-98.891	-96.013	-91.977	-96.143	-97.543	-96.283	-96.137	-96.921
4100	-41.852	-45.269	-45.126	-52.554	-45.859	-44.653	-43.684	-46.190
4300	51.636	56.889	57.786	49.384	41.252	36.973	37.948	45.181
4400	-66.220	-74.504	-75.591	-72.482	-66.506	-61.832	-58.633	-49.393
4500	21.805	31.422	29.649	24.047	11.836	12.039	14.088	12.451
4600	-67.359	-63.784	-65.647	-67.462	-80.726	-79.475	-80.282	-76.132
4700	-76.252	-80.111	-71.934	-82.306	-86.317	-85.233	-89.222	-87.991
4800	-73.333	-71.414	-68.134	-69.808	-72.932	-73.330	-73.807	-69.964
4900	-86.446	-85.191	-88.675	-35.872	-18.112	-32.389	-27.466	-34.777

4.4. Portugal

J. Confraria, Universidade Católica Portuguesa, Portugal

4.4.1. Background

Real convergence, defined as the decrease of the income gap between Portugal and the developed countries of Western Europe, is an issue that has often been present in the domestic literature, even if it has not always been based on a coherent model of domestic economic activity. For many years, Dias (1946) has been a landmark of this type of work, providing tentative estimates of the gap on the basis of international comparisons of the values of production and consumption in selected industries, as well as proposing a policy based on fostering (import substitution) industrialization and structural change to decrease the gap. Looking for the historical sources of Portuguese backwardness, Reis (1994) suggested that the income gap between Portugal and the developed West European countries increased in the second half of the nineteenth century and in the beginning of the twentieth century, and tried to discuss, using a simple counterfactual approach, if a substantially different outcome might have been achieved by pursuing different economic policies. An export-promoting strategy based on the development of wine production might have been the most promising strategy. However, it is not clear that this might have been a viable strategy, both in the sense that Portuguese producers might have found it impossible to increase external market shares and given the domestic political and social barriers to the success of a political coalition promoting such objectives.

The increasing availability of national accounting data has led to the possibility of analysing convergence processes in the long run, mainly from the late 1950s to the early 1990s. Barros and Garoupa (1993) used the Ben-David model (1993) for different sets of international data and found that 1951-73 and 1986-92 were periods of convergence with the EU. According to OECD data, Portuguese per capita GDP increased from 32% of the EU countries' average in 1960 to 40% in 1974; by 1985 it was around 31%, increasing to 48% in 1992 (current dollar values). At the same time, available data at the regional level, suggested that from 1970 to 1981 there was a trend for domestic convergence of income levels among different regions of the country, with the single exception of the Central region, but it did not seem possible to accept the hypothesis of convergence among the same regions for the periods 1980-86 and 1986-90 (see Tables 4.4.1, 4.4.2 and 4.4.3).

Table 4.4.1.   Regional gross value added per capita (% mainland value added per capita)

NUTS 2	1970	1981	1986	1990
Norte	73	85	87	87
Centro	93	75	77	77
Lisboa e Vale do Tejo	144	134	127	125
Alentejo	77	79	91	96
Algarve	63	88	99	105
Mainland	100	100	100	100

Sources: Instituto Nacional de Estatística and Direcção Geral do Desenvolvimento Regional.

Table 4.4.2.   Regional convergence for the period 1980–86

Region	φ *	t value	Critical value	Number of observations
Norte	0.103	0.763	2.447	7
Centro	-0.026	-0.746	2.447	7
Lisboa e Vale do Tejo	0.009	0.852	2.447	7
Alentejo	0.015	0.237	2.447	7
Algarve	0.034	0.431	2.447	7

* Estimated parameter. If positive, the convergence hypothesis could be accepted.

Table 4.4.3.   Regional convergence for the period 1986–90

Region	φ*	t value	Critical value	Number of observations
Norte	0.194	0.571	2.776	5
Centro	0.044	1.209	2.776	5
Lisboa e Vale do Tejo	0.007	0.173	2.776	5
Alentejo	0.067	2.084	2.776	5
Algarve	0.16	0.365	2.776	5

* Estimated parameter. If positive, the convergence hypothesis could be accepted.

More recently, convergence issues have been implicitly addressed in the context of the domestic effects of the Community Support Framework. The problem is knowing whether or not the convergence process observed for the period 1986–92 was the result of transfers from the EU.

Using a dynamic general equilibrium model, Gaspar and Pereira (1995), suggested that EU transfers might have led to an increase in annual GDP of around 0.4% in the short run and 0.5% in the long run. These estimates were similar to those produced by an optimal growth model based on endogenous growth literature (1992, quoted by Gaspar and Leite, 1995) and to simple computations based on growth accounting and on Solow's growth model (Gaspar and Leite, 1995). Government estimates for the period 1989–93, based on an open input-output model, included a distinction between direct effects of EU transfers, increasing GDP by around 0.7% a year, and total (direct and indirect) effects, leading to an annual increase in GDP of around 1,5% (SEPDR, 1993). Using a macro-economic model, Modesto and Neves (1995) suggested that the total accumulated increase in GDP that had resulted from the Second Community Support Framework (1994–99) would be, by 1999, around 8% – a value that would be similar, in annual terms, to the total effects from the First Community Support Framework.

According to these results, the Community Support Framework made a contribution to convergence, but did not explain the total decrease in the income gap between Portugal and the EU average. Moreover, Portuguese growth rates were higher in 1986–90, when EU transfers were at a relatively low level. Growth has decreased since then, but net transfers from the EU increased (see Tables 4.4.4 and 4.4.5). It might be suggested that these transfers helped to avoid increasing divergence between Portugal and the EU. If this was the case, the problem would be knowing what were the sources of potentially divergent trends.

Table 4.4.4.   Annual growth rates for GDP (%)

	1986	1987	1988	1989	1990	1991	1992	1993	1994
Portugal	4.1	5.3	3.9	5.2	4.4	2.1	1.1	-1.2	1.1
EU	2.9	2.9	4.3	3.5	3.0	1.5	1.0	-0.5	1.5

January-August.
Sources: Eurostat, OECD.

Table 4.4.5.   Net financial flows between Portugal and the EU (in billions of escudos)

	1986	1987	1988	1989	1990	1991	1992	1993	1994
Portugal	4.1	5.3	3.9	5.2	4.4	2.1	1.1	-1.2	1.1
EU	2.9	2.9	4.3	3.5	3.0	1.5	1.0	-0.5	1.5

January-August.
Sources: Eurostat, OECD.

Difficulties of adjustment to trade liberalization in industrial goods, following EU membership seem to be part of the answer. As shown below, after EU membership and until 1990, both the import penetration ratio and the exports/production ratio increased in most industries, but the effects of membership were more obvious on the import side than on exports. Moreover, between 1990 and 1993, import penetration went on increasing but there was no similar trend in the exports/production ratio. On average, it seems clear that the RCA did not improve in Portuguese manufacturing during the period 1985-93, although there was improvement in the RCAs for services until the late 1980s.[26]

Concerning intra-industry specialization, the distribution of the Grubel-Lloyd index for total trade shifted during the 1980s and early 1990s. In the case of industrial products, there was an increase in the number of industries, with index values in the middle ranges of the distribution (0.4, 0.6) and also above 0.9. In the case of services, there was an increase in the number of industries with index values in the lower and higher ranges. At least for industrial products, it seems possible that, for an increasing number of Portuguese industries, it has been difficult to develop patterns of intra-industry specialization since 1990 (in many cases since 1985) (for average values[27] and standards of deviation at different levels of classification, see Tables A1.4.4.1 and A1.4.4.2 in Appendix A1 to Section 4.4).

Actually, increasing integration may well have led to increasing divergence in the economic structure as processes of inter-industrial specialization may have arisen (Krugman and

---

[26]   During the early 1990s, substantial changes in monetary policy occurred, starting to privilege prices level and exchange rate stability. This is suggestive of some strictness in domestic prices, which may have influenced these results.

[27]   Throughout this country report, 'average' values of a given indicator means the average of that indicator computed for all agricultural and industrial sectors.

Venables, 1990, Krugman, 1991). This had been the case for most manufacturing industries (defined at the three-digit SITC level) in the EU Member States (Confraria, 1995). This suggests that the success of a monetary union may well depend on increasing labour mobility among the Member States, as the other 'necessary' condition for a successful monetary union – similarity among the economic structures of different areas in the Union – has not been met, at least in manufacturing. It also happens that Portugal and Greece have been the countries with greater divergence from other EU partners, and France, Germany, Italy and the United Kingdom the group of countries with greater convergence. In this sense, the manufacturing structures of the latter group of countries are better adapted to a monetary union than manufacturing in Portugal and Greece (Confraria, 1995).

Notwithstanding trade creation/specialization effects, the rationale for the creation of the EU was based on the dynamic effects resulting from investment decisions of domestic and foreign firms. In the long run, these effects may lead to pressures for industrial reallocation towards the larger economies. Actually, there are considerable ambiguities about the effects on the location of investments in the single market and increasing monetary integration.

Probably, the Portuguese economy was ill prepared to adjust to this type of effect. The increase in EU transfers happened at the same time as another important source of external funds (immigrants' transfers) was declining. Having peaked in 1979–80 at around 11% of GDP, immigrants' transfers were, in 1986/87, around 9% of GDP and, in 1992/93, less than 7%. Although the processes of domestic allocation of private and public transfers are different, total net transfers from abroad did not increase very much.

On the other hand, inward investment flows were traditionally based either on domestic market opportunities or on export possibilities dependant on specific domestic factors, such as relatively low pay and few raw materials. Attracting these types of investments has been increasingly difficult, given competition from countries in Eastern Europe. The economic structure of Portugal was not well prepared to attract other types of investment. It could be argued that even export oriented domestic industries were not based on regional clusters, and that could well be at the seat of the country's competitive disadvantages as firms could not profit from positive externalities traditionally attributed to cluster dynamics. Several policies tried to address this problem, the most obvious of them related to the auto industry. The government managed to attract several large foreign investments in this area and has been trying to develop component production around these large projects.

Inward investment increased dramatically in the period 1986–91. However, it remains to be seen if the values attained are sustainable. Investment in industrial exporting projects also increased, but most of the investment, which took place in 1986–92, has gone to the (protected) services industries – wholesale and retail trade, banking, insurance and real estate. Meanwhile, inward investment has been falling, from US$ 2.3 billion in 1991 to US$ 1.9 and US$ 1.5 billion in 1992 and 1993, respectively (Confraria, 1995, and Simões, 1994). Emigration levels also suggested some difficulties in the domestic economy. The total number of emigrants declined from around 25,000 in 1980 to 18,000 in 1988, but by 1992 it stood at 36,000; most of the increase since 1988 was accounted for by permanent emigrants (they made up around 60% of the total in 1992). Actually, total numbers could be much higher if temporary migration flows have been underestimated, which seems likely.

4.4.2. Data

General issues

The construction of the data set was the most demanding part of the work for the Portugal country report. Two basic problems have been addressed. In some cases, relating mainly to EU funds, foreign investment, trade and investment data at the regional level, the Portuguese statistical agency, Instituto Nacional de Estatística (INE), often did not have estimates available. On the other hand, regional and even national INE estimates of variables related to employment and value added were not always arrived at according to the same methodologies; those estimates did not always allow for the construction of consistent time and cross-section series.

Concerning the first type of problem, we tried, initially, to produce estimates of the missing variables using mainly INE estimates of the same variables for mainland Portugal and regional data from other government agencies. The assumptions taken are explained below, for each relevant case. Both INE estimates and our own estimates were consistent with the following national/regional accounting restriction for each NACE 2 sector and NUTS 2 regional level:

$$Q_{ir} + M_{i}r = CI_{ir} + PC_{ir} + SI_{ir} + G_{ir} + X_{ir}$$

where $_{ir}$ refers to sector, i, region, r, and the variables are as follows:

Q = production;
M = imports;
CI = sales to intermediate consumption;
PC = sales to private consumption;
SI = sales to investment;
X = exports.

Variables were measured in producer market prices, i.e. including indirect taxes and subsidies, except value added tax, and excluding trade margins. The latter were measured separately as they were included in outputs of sector 58. Standard national accounting assumptions concerning the output of some non-tradables, mainly construction (sector 53) and non-market private and public services (sector 86), were also followed. This method allowed for the internal consistency of the complete set of estimates, given current national accounting frameworks. Moreover, total values at sector and mainland levels were made consistent with the total levels available from the INE.

One remaining shortcoming related to the INE's trade data for mainland Portugal. Methodological changes in 1991 implied that rates of change in exports and imports observed from 1990 to 1991 were not necessarily related to real economic change, being just the result of statistical errors and methodological reviews. It is likely that import and export values for sector 36 were particularly sensitive to these problems.

Finally, even accepting what sometimes were probably strong assumptions, we did not present estimates for intra-EU trade in services and labour flows among Portuguese regions, nor for capital stock. Moreover, specialization and export market share indicators were computed only for the mainland, using the NACE 2 level in the VISA database, as it was not possible to find regional data consistent with data for EU trade.

Taking into account these exceptions, the indicators were computed for each NACE 2 sector and for total industry;[28] for mainland Portugal and for the five NUTS 2 mainland regions of Norte, Centro, Lisboa e Vale do Tejo, Alentejo and Algarve.

Variables and indicators: sources and estimation assumptions

The general framework for the estimation of regional income, consumption, investment and trade flows: The general case

Portuguese regional accounts included only estimates for value added of good i in region r, denoted by Y_{ir}, and for families' gross disposable income (RDF_r) for the period 1985-90. Value added values for 1991 and 1992 were obtained from earnings data available for all firms (see below).

Assuming that there were no meaningful differences in the technology of production between each region and the national average, the value of production in each region was obtained by means of the equation:

$$Q_{ir} = Y_{ir} / (Y_i/Q_i)$$

where Y_i and Q_i are the national value added and production values for good i.

Final consumption could then be estimated as follows:

$$C_{ir} = \Phi_i\, RDR_r$$

where

$$\Phi_i = \Phi_i\, C_i/RDF$$

$$\Sigma_r\, RDF_r = RDF;\ \Sigma_r\, C_{ir} = C_i$$

For I_{ir} and CI_{ir} a plausible assumption was to consider that they depended on the general level of economic activity in the region r on the share of investment and intermediate consumption in the total demand for good i at the national level and, eventually, on policy variables that may have led to increases in investment in less favoured regions:

$$I_{ir} = \theta_i\, Q_r$$

where $\theta_i = I_i/Q$ and Q and I_i are the national values of total production and the value of the supply of good i allocated for investment.

$$CI_{ir} = \psi_i\, Q_r$$

where $\psi_i = CI_i/Q$, and CI_i is the value of the supply of i allocated for intermediate consumption.

---

[28]   At NACE 2 level it is impossible to isolate the manufacturing industry.

Again, adding up the conditions that had to be satisfied:

$$\Sigma_r I_{ir} = I_i$$

$$\Sigma_r CI_{ir} = C_{ii}$$

Accepting these assumptions, net trade flows at the sector level were obtained for each region (some minor additional work was necessary to input value added tax and tariffs, as in Portuguese accounts production is valued at market prices and consumption at current prices). The net sectoral trade balance for each can be disagreement between the trade balance with foreign countries and the trade balance with the other regions. For each sector, it was assumed that regional exports/production and imports/consumption were the same as the national average. By definition, the total net trade for each product at the regional level was zero.

Two further comments about the basic accounting framework should be made. First, estimates were based on current prices due to a lack of data sources recording constant prices that might allow for the construction of consistent time series. Second, the use of proportionality assumptions imposed serious restrictions on the interpretation of several regional indicators. Essentially, it allowed us to discuss what happened if 'average' regional firms had the same behaviour as the 'average' national firm. For instance, indicators related to trade creation and trade diversion had, for each region, the same value as the mainland ones; differences in regional trade performance appeared to be a result of the location of industries. However, we think that this was the approach best suited to the current lack of data as it allowed us to define exactly the limits of the exercise we undertook.

Particular cases

Some particular cases resulted from current national accounting conventions:

(a)   government services were used only as final consumption;
(b)   tourism receipts were not considered to be an export of services – they were included as part of the total revenues of trade, restaurants and hotels and consumed inside a region;
(c)   the output of the construction industry was mainly categorized as investment and, for a minor part, as consumption.

Estimates and sources

Concerning the set of variables selected for indicator and regression analysis, the sources and the steps taken in estimating them were as follows.

L_j - employed persons

The sources of data were the INE's regional accounts. As the sum of total employment for every region given in regional accounts was different from total mainland employment given by INE employment surveys, an adjustment was made to make the sum of total employment in regions consistent with these total values for mainland Portugal.

Y_j - value added

Y_j - value added

Q_{ij} - production

Q_{ij} - production

Data for the period 1985-90 were gathered from the INE's regional accounts. For 1991-93 estimates were based on earnings data supplied by the Ministério do Emprego e Equipamento Social, using the following equation:

$$Q_{ij} = a + b \ (earnings \ ij) + \varepsilon \ ^{29}$$

Parameter estimates were used to compute the share of value added of each sector in value added. The shares were then multiplied by the totals of value added resulting from the INE quarterly national accounts.

Production levels were obtained using sector ratios of value added to production available from the INE national accounts.

M_{ij} - imports

M_{eij} - imports from EU countries

X_{ij} - exports

X_{eij} - exports to EU countries

For each non-services sector in each region, it was assumed that the share of total and EU trade was the same as the national share, as given in the INE's national accounts and external trade statistics. For services sectors for the period 1991-93, it was not possible to have estimates of trade flows, even accepting these assumptions, because of lack of national accounting data or other data for trade in services.

EU exports and EU imports

The sources used were the VISA database and two-digit NACE figures.

CSF_i - CSFs

Data for the regional distribution of CSFs, given as total cumulative values, for the period 1988-92, were available from the Direcção Geral do Desenvolvimento Regional. This data was used to estimate regional shares that were then multiplied by total annual values, available from the national accounts and the OECD's economic surveys of Portugal.

---

29   As in the other cases considered below, the objective of the regressions was seen as being to discover a statistically strong relationship between explained and explanatory variables and not to estimate earnings or, as below, investment functions. Functions and variables were chosen after experiments with several other functions and variables. In almost every case, estimates of branch and regional data were based on final regressions with a coefficient of determination above 0.95.

I_{ij} - investment

There was no available investment data at the regional level. A two-step procedure was followed (except for the non-market services (86) sector). First, national data was used to estimate the relationship:

$$I = a + bY + \varepsilon$$

Parameter estimates were used to estimate investment in each sector and region according to value added of the same sector and region. These estimates were used to compute shares of investment, of each sector in each region, in total estimated investment. These shares were then multiplied by the values of mainland investment available from the INE and national accounts data.

Investment by non-market services (86) sector organizations was mainly public investment. In this case, public investment was divided into two parts. The first was public investment supported by EU funds; the regional distribution of CSFs has been used to provide estimates at the regional level. The remaining investment values were allocated to regions according to the share of the regional population in the total population.

FDI_{ij} - FDI

For the period 1990-93, sector and regional data were supplied by the Instituto do Comércio Externo de Portugal (ICEP) for investments not subject to a contractual relationship with the government. Mainland estimates for 1985-89 at the sector level were available from ICEP. Regional estimates were constructed according to the following process:

(a) first, it was assumed that, for each sector, the share each region had of FDI would be the same as the share that same region had in 1990;
(b) then, these estimates were corrected according to the regional distribution of the largest investments, obtained from the Ministério do Comércio e Turismo.

Consultational reports were also used to increase the accuracy of some of the estimates resulting from the initial set of assumptions.

FDI values related to foreign equity and so were not necessarily linked to the amount of investment in a given project. In the case of large projects, where the investment took place over several years, the value of the equity was distributed evenly over the lifetime of that investment.

P_i - population

Population values at national and regional levels were available from the INE's statistical regional and population data.

SEC_i - secondary enrolled students

For the period 1985-90, the INE's population statistics were used. For 1991-93, the INE's population statistics and the Ministério da Educação provided the data.

Sectoral coverage

The indicator analysis of the Portuguese country report used the NACE-CLIO RR17 industrial classification. The sectors included in this are shown in Table A1.4.4.3, Appendix A1 to Section 4.4, which also indicates the terminology used in the text to describe these sectors. Finally, this table shows the sensitivity of the Portuguese industrial sectors to the SMP according to the Buigues *et al.* (1990) methodology (the correspondence here was not completely accurate because in Buigues, the NACE 70 classification was used).

4.4.3. Indicator analysis

Import penetration, export growth, trade creation and trade diversion

For mainland Portugal, European import penetration ratios and the proportion of exports to the EU to production have increased for every sector, with import ratios increasing faster than export ratios. Not surprisingly, increases in both indicators were higher for trade with the EU than they were for trade with the rest of the world (see Tables 4.4.6 and 4.4.7). Assuming that trade creation (diversion) is related mainly to positive growth in trade with the EU and positive (negative) growth of trade with the rest of the world, EU membership and the SMP were related to trade creation in some (traditional) industries that accounted for most of manufacturing output and exports, and to trade diversion in agriculture and fishing, mining, transport equipment and other manufacturing (see Table 4.4.8).

Agriculture and fishing, food and beverages, the textile, clothing and footwear industries, pulp and paper, as well as other manufacturing, were the sectors most affected by increasing import penetration by the EU (see Table 4.4.6). Excluding the food and beverages sector, the values for which may have been affected by changes in statistical sources, there was a positive relationship between growth in import penetration and growth in labour productivity, but not with value added growth, suggesting that productivity increases may be related to the exit of inefficient producers. Moreover, in some cases, there was an 'investment' response of survivors to the new competitive environment, as in agriculture and textiles, sectors with high levels of import penetration, and of increases in investment rates (see Table 4.4.9).

Productivity growth did not always follow this pattern of adaptive response to increased imports. In some sectors – such as metallic minerals and products of non-metallic minerals – high growth rates in labour productivity were simultaneous with relatively low rates of import penetration, suggesting that, since the beginning of trade liberalization, productivity growth increased domestic competitiveness versus imports. This also contributes to explaining the negative correlation between labour productivity and import penetration from non-EU countries, although trade diversion may also have played a role, as it did in agriculture and transport equipment.

Increases in exports to the EU were also positively related to labour productivity growth (again excluding food and beverages; see Table 4.4.9). However, there was no common pattern for the most successful exporters. Products of non-metallic minerals and transport equipment displayed high growth in value added and labour productivity but slower growth in investment rates. The textile, clothing and footwear industries showed growth in their export ratios and value added, and labour productivity was close to the average. The negative correlation between export ratios to non-EU countries and value added and labour productivity growth could probably be explained by trade diversion and also by the possibility that some domestic producers, badly affected by EU competition, may have found some export outlets in less competitive third countries, improving, for some time, their chances of survival.

At the regional level, as expected, we found differences between the regions that, given the assumptions accepted in the preparation of the data, were strongly influenced by regional differences in the structure of economic activity (see Tables 4.4.10 and 4.4.11). Differences between the correlation coefficients of trade indicators with labour productivity growth indices highlighted differences in labour productivity changes in the same industries in different regions. For instance, textiles, agriculture and paper showed higher productivity growth in Norte, Lisboa e Vale do Tejo and Alentejo than they did in Centro, which accounted for most of the differences between the correlation coefficients of import growth with labour productivity growth. Actually, this might indicate either that, other things being equal, in regions with higher productivity (Norte and Lisboa e Vale do Tejo), the increase in import penetration would be lower than the average or that, in the same regions, import penetration might lead to above average growth in productivity because of the exit of firms with low productivity. All this aside, value added growth, changes in regional specialization and productivity growth, seem to be positively related, suggesting that in many sectors exit of inefficient producers was at least partly offset by the growth of firms with higher productivity. Similar reasoning applies to exports. There, it applies to transport equipment, products of non-metallic minerals and agriculture. Regions with higher value added and productivity growth in the relevant sectors – Centro and Lisboa e Vale do Tejo – might have higher than average growth in their export/production ratios.

Table 4.4.6. Increase in trade with the EU: sectors with higher growth (in decreasing order of growth rates)

Share of imports from the EU in apparent consumption (range of growth rates: 80–400%)	Share of exports to the EU in production (range of growth rates: 40–120%)
Food and beverages	Food and beverages
Textile, clothing and footwear industries	Transport equipment
Agriculture and fishing	Non-metallic mineral products
Other manufacturing	Agriculture and fishing
Paper	Metallic minerals
Industry average 0.79	**Industry average 0.48**

Table 4.4.7. Increase in trade with non-EU countries: sectors with non-negative growth (in decreasing order of growth rates)

Share of imports in apparent consumption (range of growth rates: 0–100%)	Share of exports in production (range of growth rates: 0–55%)
Food and beverages	Food and beverages
Paper	Energy products
Textile, clothing and footwear industries	Chemicals
Energy	Metal products and engineering
Chemicals	Non-metallic mineral products
	Textile, clothing and footwear industires
	Industry average 0.09

Table 4.4.8.   Sectors showing trade creation and trade diversion on the mainland

Trade creation	Trade diversion
Textile, clothing and footwear industries	Agriculture and fishing
Food and beverages	Metallic minerals
Energy	Transport equipment
Chemicals	Other manufacturing

Table 4.4.9.   Correlation between external trade growth and product, investment and productivity growth on the mainland

Imports/apparent consumption		Export/production	
$r\,(ME_j/C_j, Y_j)$	+0.00	$r\,(XE_j/Q_j, Y_j)$	+0.12
$r\,(ME_j/C_j, I_j/Y_j)$	-0.06	$r\,(XE_j/Q_j, I_j/Y_j)$	+0.05
$r\,(ME_j/C_j, Y_j/L_j)$	+0.24	$r\,(XE_j/Q_j, Y_j/L_j)$	+0.26
$r\,(MO_j/C_j, Y_j)$	+0.78	$r\,(XO_j/Q_j, Y_j)$	-0.44
$r\,(MO_j/C_j, I_j/Y_j)$	-0.62	$r\,(XO_j/Q_j, I_j/Y_j)$	+0.63
$r\,(MO_j/C_j, Y_j/L_j)$	-0.29	$r\,(XO_j/Q_j, Y_j/L_j)$	-0.54

Table 4.4.10.   Regions

Region	$r\,(ME_{ij}/C_{ij}, Y_{ij})$	$r\,(ME_{ij}/C_{ij}, Y_j/L_j)$	$r\,(ME_{ij}/C_{ij}, Y_{ij}/Y_j/Y_i/Y)$
Norte	+0.05	+0.43	-0.03
Centro	-0.63	-0.37	-0.4
Lisboa e Vale do Tejo	+0.4	+0.48	+0.6
Alentejo	+0.01	+0.36	+0.05
Algarve	-0.39	-0.65	-0.4

Table 4.4.11.   Regions

Region	$r\,(XE_{ij}/Q_{ij}, Y_{ij})$	$r\,(XE_{ij}/Q_{ij}, Y_j/L_j)$	$r\,(XE_{ij}/Q_{ij}, Y_{ij}/Y_j/Y_i/Y)$
Norte	-0.31	-0.32	-0.51
Centro	+0.04	+0.29	+0.11
Lisboa e Vale do Tejo	+0.19	+0.40	+0.3
Alentejo	-0.18	+0.27	-0.23
Algarve	+0.03	-0.17	+0.13

European IIT

As might be expected, there was, in mainland Portugal, a general increase in the value of European IIT at current prices (IIT_j) and in IIT as a percentage of production (IIT_j/Q_j). At the same time, in most agricultural and industrial sectors, as well as in industry as a whole, there was a decrease in the 'degree' of intra-industry specialization, as measured by the Grubel-Lloyd index (B_j). Traditional sectors – such as textiles, clothing and footwear and paper as well as other manufacturing and, to a smaller extent, energy products – were the only ones where IIT's share of total trade increased after EU membership and the introduction of the SMP (see Table 4.4.12). These sectors and transport equipment also recorded the strongest increases in the value of IIT and in IIT as a percentage of production.

The evolution of IIT's shares in production had a weak correlation with value added and labour productivity growth (see Table 4.4.13). This suggested – bearing in mind the previous evidence about import and export ratios – that trade growth was not always closely related to growth in IIT. As seen below, this led to shifts in patterns of RCAs – positive or negative RCAs became weaker or stronger, respectively.

Table 4.4.12. European intra-industry specialization (B_j)

Region	Sectors with increases in European intra-industry specialization (in decreasing order of growth rates)	Sectors with positive correlation between European intra-industry specialization and trade liberalization index
Mainland	Textile, clothing and footwear industries Other manufacturing Pulp and paper Energy products	Transport equipment Textile, clothing and footwear industries Pulp and paper Other manufacturing
Norte	Other manufacturing Textile, clothing and footwear industries Pulp and paper Energy products Non-metallic mineral products	Non-metallic mineral products Chemicals Transport equipment Textile, clothing and footwear industries Pulp and paper Other manufacturing
Centro	Textile, clothing and footwear industries Other manufacturing Pulp and paper Energy products Metallic minerals Metal products and engineering	Metal products and engineering Textile, clothing and footwear industries Pulp and paper Other manufacturing
Lisboa e Vale do Tejo	Pulp and paper	Transport equipment Pulp and paper
Alentejo	Minerals (metallic and non-metallic) Energy products Other manufacturing	Energy products Non-metallic mineral products Chemicals
Algarve	Energy products Metal products and engineering Transport equipment Pulp and paper Non-metallic mineral products	Metal products and engineering Transport equipment Pulp and paper

At the regional level, the pattern of intra-industry specialization in the regions of Norte and Centro was probably reinforced as in these regions there has long been a strong concentration of paper, textile, clothing and footwear industries. According to the estimates presented, minerals – metallic and non-metallic[30] – accounted for some additional intra-industry specialization in Alentejo. However, these results may well have been influenced by the assumptions made to obtain estimates for regional exports and imports. Probably, these assumptions led to overestimates of the imports of these products made by firms in Alentejo. If so, it is likely that intra-industry specialization played an important role in the increase in the external trade of minerals in Alentejo; estimated values probably lent too much weight to the role of IIT in regional specialization (see Table 4.4.12).

Table 4.4.13. Correlation between IIT growth and value added, investment and productivity growth for the mainland

Value of IIT		IIT/production	
$r\ (IIT_j, Y_j)$	+0.61	$r\ (IIT_j/Q_j,\ Y_j)$	+0.06
$r\ (IIT_j, I_j/Y_j)$	+0.38	$r\ (IIT_j/Q_j,\ I_j/Y_j)$	+0.22
$r\ (IIT_j, Y_j/L_j)$	+0.46	$r\ (IIT_j/Q_j,\ Y_j/L_j)$	-0.06

Relative competitiveness and specialization

Some care was needed when it came to interpreting the changes that occurred in the RCA index. The positive values accompanying the growth rate between the two periods were consistent with the two different situations, i.e. RCAs increased in industries where the country held comparative advantage in both periods and they decreased in sectors where the country held comparative disadvantage in both periods. By the same token, the negative values in the index resulted from either a shift from a situation of comparative disadvantage to a situation of comparative advantage or, in the opposite case, where comparative advantages in a given sector deteriorated fast enough to create a shift from a position of trade surplus to a position of trade deficit.

EU membership and the SMP seemed to be related to decreasing comparative advantages in almost every sector in the Portuguese economy, described at the NACE 2 level of disaggregation.

For most agricultural and industrial sectors, as well as for the whole of industry, on mainland Portugal, initial positions of comparative disadvantage ($RCA_j<0$) were reinforced (see Tables 4.4.14 and 4.4.15). The comparative advantages enjoyed by some traditional industries, which held a position of relatively strong RCAs in the mid-1980s, such as the textile, clothing and footwear industries, and pulp and paper, became increasingly weak. This could be a consequence of the process of intra-industry specialization, highlighted in the previous section. Actually, the same happened with tourism (see Table 4.4.16). In only one case – non-metallic mineral products – was there an increase in the value of the RCA index and in another – energy products – decreasing competitive disadvantages.

---

[30]   And, to a smaller extent, energy products and other manufacturing.

This evolution bore no clear relationship with product and productivity growth, nor with the accumulation process. The non-metallic mineral products sector had one of the highest growth rates of product and productivity growth, but relatively low growth of the investment rate. Sectors with declining comparative advantages, such as the textile, clothing and footwear industries and pulp and paper – had growth rates of value added and productivity that were close to the average, but growth of investment rates were much higher for the textile, clothing and footwear industries. Agriculture and fishing, transport equipment and metallic minerals were among the sectors with larger increases in labour productivity, despite increasing comparative disadvantages. This, as suggested above, may well have resulted from the exit from the market of inefficient producers. The strong increase in investment rates in agriculture, fishing, food and beverages, also suggested a dynamic response on the part of surviving producers.

On the other hand, the overall negative changes in patterns of comparative advantage were mainly due to an increase in imports, as it had been simultaneous with an improvement in Portugal's share of EU exports, both in sectors with declining comparative advantages and in sectors, such as engineering and motor vehicles, where comparative disadvantages prevailed. In these cases, the evolution in the domestic share of EU exports was positively correlated with trade liberalization (see Table 4.4.17) but there was no strong correlation with value added growth (see Table 4.4.19). Portugal's share of the export market declined in only a few of the sectors for which data was available – sugar manufacturing and refining, metals and the manufacture of metal articles, and other manufacturing.

The almost general increase in the share of the export market was not always related to increased specialization of production. Specialization patterns evolved within traditional industries (such as clothing and footwear, and man-made fibres, but not in the textile industry), resource-dependent industries (such as non-metallic mineral products, and timber and furniture) and more high-tech industries (such as electrical engineering, and motor vehicles and parts; see Table 4.4.18). Possibly, firms in these industries responded in different ways to increasing European integration. Motor vehicles and clothing and footwear may well provide two examples of this. The development of motor vehicles and parts and, to a lesser degree, electrical engineering, was closely related to the country's capabilities to attract inward investment and to play some role in the location decisions of multinational firms. Small- and medium-sized national firms have prevailed in the clothing, footwear, timber and furniture sectors. For many of them (notwithstanding some interesting exceptions), dislocation of production was not likely to be an issue and so their survival and growth were closely related to the development of domestic production and export capabilities.

In almost every region, initial positions of comparative disadvantage in agriculture and industry were reinforced after 1988 (meanwhile, industry in Norte and agriculture in Alentejo shifted from a position of trade surplus to one of trade deficit).

Comparative advantages in regions Lisboa e Vale do Tejo, Alentejo and Algarve seemed to be concentrated in non-metallic mineral products (in the case of Algarve, the value of the RCA index may well have been influenced by some upward bias in the estimates of regional exports). In Centro and Norte, there seemed to be a slightly richer mix of sectors with positive RCAs, as well as some potential positive effects of trade liberalization on patterns of comparative advantage in chemicals and transport equipment (see Table 4.4.15). Possibly the same might be said of Lisboa e Vale do Tejo concerning the evolution of transport equipment during the 1990s as, since 1990/92, there have been some large investments in vehicle and component plants.

Table 4.4.14. Changes in comparative advantage and disadvantage for the mainland

Sectors with increasing comparative disadvantage	Sectors with decreasing comparative disadvantage	Sectors with increasing comparative advantage	Sectors with decreasing comparative advantage
Agriculture and fishing Metallic minerals Chemicals Metal products and machinery Transport equipment Food and beverages	Energy products	Non-metallic mineral products	Textile, clothing and footwear industries Pulp and paper Other manufacturing

Table 4.4.15. Comparative advantage

Region	Sectors with comparative advantage ($RCA_j > 0$) (average for 1988-92)
Mainland	Non-metallic mineral products Textile, clothing and footwear industries Pulp and paper Other manufacturing
Norte	Textile, clothing and footwear industries Pulp and paper Other manufacturing
Centro	Non-metallic mineral products Textile, clothing and footwear industries Pulp and paper Other manufacturing
Lisboa e Vale do Tejo	Non-metallic mineral products Pulp and paper
Alentejo	Non-metallic mineral products
Algarve	Non-metallic mineral products

Table 4.4.16. Competitiveness of the Portuguese tourism industry* relative to EU and non-EU countries

Measures	Average for 1986–88	Average for 1989–91
RCA index	65.3	60.6
Grubel-Lloyd index	34.7	39.4
Portugal's share of EU exports	3.0%	3.5%
Portugal's share of EU imports	0.7%	0.9%

Note: 'Exports' defined as consumption by non-residents of the country and 'imports' as consumption by residents abroad.
Source: OECD, *Statistics on International Transactions*, 1993.

Table 4.4.17. The mainland's shares of the export market

Sectors showing increases in XMS_i for the mainland	Sectors showing a positive correlation between XMS_i and trade liberalization
Non-metallic mineral products	Metals
Chemicals	Non-metallic mineral products
Man-made fibres	Motor vehicles and parts
Electrical and instrument engineering	Instrument engineering
Motor vehicles and parts	Sugar and refining
Food, beverages and tobacco products	Textile industry
Textile industry	Leather and leather goods
Leather and leather goods	Clothing and footwear industry
Clothing and footwear industries	Timber and wood
Timber and furniture	Rubber and plastic products
Paper, printing and publishing	
Rubber and plastics products	

Table 4.4.18. The specialization process on the mainland

Sectors showing increases in the specialization index (SI_i)	Sectors showing a positive correlation between the specialization index and trade liberalization
Non-metallic mineral products	Non-metallic mineral products
Man-made fibres	Man-made fibres
Metal products	Metal products
Electrical engineering	Mechanical, electrical and instrument engineering
Motor vehicles and parts	Motor vehicles and parts
Clothing and footwear industries	Sugar and refining
Timber and furniture	Textile industry
Rubber and plastics products	Clothing and footwear industries
	Timber and furniture
	Rubber and plastic products

Table 4.4.19. Correlation between growth in share of the export market and specialization and value added growth

$r\ (XMS_i,\ Y_i)$	+0.0358
$r\ (SI_i,\ Y_i)$	+0.0877

FDI

In every sector, inward flows of FDI increased after 1985 and were positively correlated with the trade liberalization index. FDI flows were also positively correlated with product and labour productivity growth, as well as with growth in the rates of investment (see Table 4.4.20). As suggested below, different causality relationships may have been the source of these correlations.

On the mainland, as well as in most of the regions, the largest increases were concentrated in the non-tradable sectors, such as construction and public works, banking and insurance, and market services. Non-tradable sectors – including financial services, trade, real estate and tourism-related activities – also accounted for the largest inflows in 1990-92 (see Table 4.4.21). Taking advantage of domestic market opportunities was certainly one of the main reasons for inward investment in sectors such as construction and public works, wholesale trade, and real estate. Possibly the same applied to inward investment in financial sectors and other market services, even if, in these cases, it may also have been related to potential increases in EU trade in services that were expected to result from the completion of the SMP. In these cases, the positive correlation between FDI and product, labour productivity and rates of investment growth – as shown in Table 4.4.20 – might well have resulted from the attractiveness of growth sectors to foreign firms.

Food and beverages, metal products, engineering, transport equipment, energy products, chemicals, and agriculture accounted for most of the increase in industrial and agricultural investment. In each case, different rationales may be suggested. For instance, investments in energy products followed the lifting of some restrictions previously imposed on private energy production and distribution, as well as the initial development of the natural gas project. As seen before, comparative disadvantages of domestic producers were reinforced in agriculture, fishing, food and beverages, and inward investment played a role in the restructuring of domestic production. Government policies, aimed at the development of large investment projects, played an important role in fostering the domestic production of vehicles and components as well as in some engineering industries. In these cases, inward investment might well have been an important source of product and productivity growth, contributing to the positive relationships shown in Table 4.4.20.

Overall, these cases cast some doubts on the view that the Portuguese economy might build on its position as a low-pay country in the EU to attract large inflows of export-oriented FDI. Again, there were some differences among the regions. In Norte, Centro and Alentejo, FDI was less concentrated in construction and services, while the opposite was happening in Lisboa e Vale do Tejo.

Table 4.4.20. Correlation between FDI growth and product and productivity growth for the mainland

$r\ (FDI_j, Y_j)$	+0.29
$r\ (FDI_j, I_j/Y_j)$	+0.12
$r\ (FDI_j/C_j, Y_j/L_j)$	+0.45

Table 4.4.21. Inward FDI

Region	Sectors with above regional average growth	Sectors with above regional average inflows of FDI (1990-93)
Mainland	Construction/public works Banking and insurance Market services	Trade and tourism Market services Banking and insurance
Norte	Construction/public works Market services Banking and insurance Food and beverages	Textile, clothing and footwear industries Other manufacturing Trade and tourism Banking and insurance Market services
Centro	Transport/communications Construction and public works Market services	Non-metallic mineral products Metal products and machinery Food and beverages Pulp and paper Other manufacturing Trade and tourism Banking and insurance
Lisboa e Vale do Tejo	Construction/public works Banking and insurance Market services	Trade and tourism Market services Banking and insurance
Alentejo	Textile, clothing and footwear industries Food and beverages Chemicals	Agriculture and fishing Non-metallic mineral products Chemicals Metal products and machinery Trade and tourism Transport/communications
Algarve	Non-metallic mineral products Metal products and machinery Transport equipment	Agriculture and fishing Construction and public works Trade and tourism Market services

Inter-regional and inter-industry employment and investment flows

In general, trade liberalization was negatively correlated with the evolution of the concentration of employment (measured using the Herfindahl index), the exception being the Algarve region. However, strong increases in employment concentration in Lisboa e Vale do Tejo and the Algarve, accounted for a general increase in concentration for mainland Portugal (see Table 4.4.22).

Table 4.4.22. Herfindhal index for employment

Herfindhal index (employment)		Correlation between Herfindhal index (employment) and trade liberalization index	
Increases	**Decreases**	**Positive correlation**	**Negative correlation**
Mainland	Norte	Algarve	Mainland
Lisboa e Vale do Tejo	Centro		Norte
Algarve	Alentejo		Centro
			Lisboa e Vale do Tejo
			Alentejo

These changes were deeply influenced by a trend common to all regions: the shift in employment patterns to the services sectors. In the case of Lisboa, public administration, financial services and real estate, trade and tourism and other market services already had a relatively high share of regional employment and this concentration increased further. The same situation applied in the Algarve, where there was already some concentration of employment in trade and tourism, real estate and public administration. The shift to services sectors and also to mining and quarrying, combined with a decline in agricultural employment, accounted for a decline in concentration of employment in Alentejo. In Norte and Centro, a similar process happened – slow growth in employment combined with growth in services.

As a result, there were increasing similarities between the economic structure of Alentejo and the other regions, with the exception of the Centro region. At the same time, the region of the Algarve was involved in a process of structural divergence, which was related to the high and increasing expansion of the tourism, real estate and construction sectors of employment.

Increasing concentration in employment was strongly correlated with product and productivity growth as well as with regional specialization, suggesting that location factors played an important role both in regional specialization and growth (see Table 4.4.24).

In general, similar conclusions followed from the strong positive correlation between concentration of investment and trade liberalization (see Table 4.4.23). However, the process of concentration of investment did not seem to follow closely the process of concentration of employment. Actually, concentration of investment had a strong *negative* correlation with the rate of investment growth, *but* a very weak correlation with product and productivity growth (see Table 4.4.24).

Bias in estimates of regional and sectoral investment might have accounted for some of these differences. However, other explanations, other than errors in estimates, could be considered.

For example, it is likely that the increasing specialization of investment in some sectors at the regional level was not enough to compensate for lower investment rates in low-growth or declining sectors; this was probably the case for the Algarve. On the other hand, it is possible that, in almost every region, some of the (agricultural and industrial) firms badly affected by EU membership and by the SMP tried to maintain relatively high levels of investment, as a percentage of their output, and pursued labour-saving restructuring processes.

Table 4.4.23. Herfindahl index for investment

Herfindhal index (investment)	Correlation between Herfindhal index (investment) and trade liberalization index
Increases	Positive correlation
Mainland	Mainland
Norte	Norte
Centro	Centro
Lisboa e Vale do Tejo	Lisboa e Vale do Tejo
Alentejo	Alentejo
Algarve	Algarve

Table 4.4.24. Correlation between changes in the Herfindahl index and product and productivity growth

Herfindahl index for employment		Herfindahl index for investment	
$r (H_j, Y_j)$	+0.882	$r (H_j, Y_j)$	+0.076
$r (H_j, I/Y_j)$	-0.355	$r (H_j, I/Y_j)$	-0.979
$r (H_j, Y/L_j)$	+0.88	$r (H_j, Y/L_j)$	-0.185
$r (H_j, Y/Y)$	+0.86	$r (H_j, Y/Y)$	-0.094

4.4.4. Main conclusions from the indicator analysis

For the period 1986-92, import penetration growth rates were higher than export/production growth, this trend being more obvious after 1990. Several factors contributed to this: EU membership, implying both trade liberalization with partner countries and lower degrees of protection from third countries' imports, the SMP, and adjustments following the progressive reversal of exchange rate policies, aiming at greater exchange rate stability in the early 1990s.

In general, this process led to decreasing comparative advantages for domestic firms. This may have been related to the role of IIT. In sectors such as paper and the textile, clothing and footwear and tourism industries, increasing IIT led to decreasing positive comparative advantages. In agriculture and in most of the other industrial sectors, starting from their initial positions of negative comparative advantages, decreasing shares of IIT reinforced the comparative disadvantages of the domestic firms. Products of non-metallic minerals and energy were the exceptions to this last general trend. Thus, in the first case, positive comparative advantages were reinforced and, in the second, comparative disadvantages weakened.

At the same time, domestic firms increased their share of many EU exports. This was related to a process of specialization centred on the textile, clothing and footwear industries, non-metallic mineral products, timber and furniture, electrical engineering, and motor vehicles. Although EU data for tourism was not available, it is likely that tourism activities may also be included in this group. Foreign investment seems to have played a role in the development of this specialization pattern, mainly with regard to electrical engineering, motor vehicles and components and tourism. However, in the case of motor vehicles and parts, several large, foreign projects benefited from government support, and it remains to be seen if that was enough to build a sustainable motor industry at the domestic level.

There were important differences in labour productivity changes among the regions. In Norte, Centro and Lisboa e Vale do Tejo, growth in trade seemed to be positively related to growth in value added and labour productivity. The regions of Norte and Centro seem to have had a greater variety of industries with positive comparative advantages, although this conclusion was sensitive to assumptions made in the processing of the trade data. It seemed clear that the same regions had a greater number of industries with positive changes in regional specialization patterns. In Lisboa and the Algarve, concentration of economic activity in terms of employment increased, which was explained by the growth in the services sectors. Moreover, this increased concentration seemed to be closely related to increasing labour productivity, suggesting a fast concentration of resources in higher productivity non-tradable activities. On the other hand, this was positively related to value added growth. The concentration of investment flows may well have reinforced this pattern, having increased everywhere, although this may be sensitive to assumptions made in our processing of the investment data.

4.4.5. Regression analysis for Portugal and Ireland

Introduction

It is important to stress that it was not possible to carry out the regression analysis for Ireland alone. There was no regional disaggregation and data for some sectors were also missing. Therefore, the number of available statistical observations was not sufficient to perform robust and convincing regression analysis. For this reason we decided to stack Irish data with the Portuguese ones. This choice was made because of the similarity in the economic structures of the two countries and because, for Portugal, we had a smaller number of regions than for Italy, Greece and Spain. However, we always tested whether or not the structural coefficients and the fixed effects for Ireland coincided with the ones for Portugal. As the null hypothesis of homogeneity could be accepted in many cases, we were able to derive interesting conclusions for Ireland by exploiting both the available data for the country and their cross-correlations with the Portuguese data.

Objectives and model specification

The regression analysis was designed to achieve four main goals.

(a)   **To quantify the impact of the SMP on some trade indicators and factor flows.** This was done by analysing the value of ρ in the following regressions:

Equation 1 $XE_t/Y_t = b_0 + X_t\psi + \rho I_t + \varepsilon_{1t}$

Equation 2 $B_t = b_0 + X_t\psi + \rho I_t + \varepsilon_{2t}$

Equation 3 $RCA_t = b_0 + X_t\psi + \rho I_t + \varepsilon_{3t}$

Equation 4 $FDI_t = b_0 + X_t\psi + \rho I_t + \varepsilon_{4t}$

where trade creation (XE_t/Y_t), IIT (B_t), RCA (RCA_t) and EU FDI (FDI_t) are the main indicators of trade and factor flows that we selected. The vector of explanatory variables, X_t, contained proxies for cyclical and globalization effects (the growth rate of industrial production and world trade growth respectively) and dummies for accession effects. In the set of explanatory variables, X_t, we also included the other variables that were used in the indicator analysis, namely labour productivity, sectoral specialization and capital intensity (the capital/labour ratio). Finally, we also accounted for CSF support in all regions. These variables enabled us to disentangle the effect of the SMP (quantified by the parameter ρ) on trade and factor flows from the effects of cyclical and globalization variables and of variables capturing the specificity of each sector (capital intensity, labour productivity and specialization). In particular, the basic question was this: was the new equilibrium resulting from the implementation of the SMP achieved because of factor or trade movements (or both)?

Note that the regression analysis that helped us answer this question was carried out for almost all regions and sectors (only in the trade creation equation is the energy products sector missing).

(b)   **To assess whether or not the SMP, by changing the pattern of trade and factor flows, also modified the accumulation of (physical and human) capital in the Portuguese regions considered in this review and in Ireland.** To achieve this goal we ran the following regressions:

Equation 5 $k_t = s_0 + s_1 Y_t + s_2 K_t + s_3 \Delta XE_t/Y_t + s_4 \Delta B_t + s_5 \Delta RCA_t + s_6 \Delta FDI_t + \varepsilon_{5t}$

Equation 6 $h_t = r_0 + r_1 Y_t + r_2 H_t + r_3 \Delta XE_t/Y_t + r_4 \Delta B_t + r_5 \Delta RCA_t + s_6 \Delta FDI_t + \varepsilon_{6t}$

where the dynamics of the growth rate of physical (k_t) and human (h_t) capital explained stock (K_t) and flow (Y_t) characteristics of each region and sector (Baldwin and Venables, 1995) for possible effects of trade creation (XE_t/Y_t), IIT (B_t), international competitiveness (RCA_t) and EU FDI (FDI_t). Note that all these variables were entered into Equations 5 and 6 as first differences (Δ) of the original variables endogenized by Equations 1 to 4. As explained in Baldwin and Venables (1995), the rationale of Equations 5 and 6 was that capital accumulation was likely to be pro cyclical (in the empirical specification we also used the rate of change of Y_t) and faster when capital was small, i.e. regions with low levels of capital stocks were likely to grow more rapidly. This argument implicitly embodied the assumption of a technology characterized by decreasing returns. As this may not have been the case in some sectors, we did not expect the coefficients r_2 and s_2 to be necessarily negative.

Note that, given the available data, Equation 5 could not be run by considering all regions. In the chemical products sector, data for the Algarve and Ireland was missing;

in the agriculture, food, beverages and tobacco, and energy products sectors, data for Ireland was missing; in the metal minerals, and textile and clothing industries sectors, data for the Algarve was missing. As far as Equation 6 was concerned, all regions were considered (including Ireland), but no sectoral data were available.

(c)   **To assess the impact of the SMP on the growth rates of sectoral per capita value added in the different sectors in all regions.** Therefore, the following regression was also run:

Equation 7 $y_t = a_t + \alpha k_t + \beta h_t - (1-\gamma)l_t + \varepsilon_{7t}$

where y_t is per capita GDP growth, a_t is the rate of growth of technical progress, k_t and h_t of physical and human capital respectively, and l_t is the growth rate of unskilled labour. This regression was done for almost all regions and sectors (data was missing for the Algarve for the metal minerals sector and for the Algarve and Ireland for the chemical products sector). Note that data on technical progress was available only at country level, whereas for human capital we used data at the regional level.

(d)   **Finally, the ultimate goal of our analysis was to verify in which sectors the implementation of the SMP increased or reduced the speed of convergence between the regions considered in this review.** To do that we had to calculate the *antimonde* growth path of sectoral per capita value added (see Section 3.3) and then we ran the following regression:

Equation 8 $IM_{j,avg} = cost°_j + (\alpha-\alpha^*)INV_{j,avg} - (\beta-\beta^*)RGDP_{j,85}$

$$+ (\gamma-\gamma^*)GPO_{j,avg} - (\delta-\delta^*)SEC_{j,85} + (\varphi-\varphi^*)TECH_{j,avg}$$

$$+ (\theta-\theta^*)DUMMIES_j + \alpha^*(INV_{j,avg} - INV^*_{j,avg}) + \eta_j$$

where the dependent variable was defined as the difference between the actual average relative rate of growth of sectoral per capita value added and the average *antimonde* rate of growth determined as explained in Section 3.7.[31] In Equation 8, we also added the average amount of CSFs for each region.

The null hypothesis here was that the coefficient $\pi_1 \equiv \beta-\beta^*$ (and/or $\pi_2 \equiv \delta-\delta^*$) was statistically significant and positive. This hypothesis was easily tested using standard inference technique for all sectors considered in this review. Therefore, we had information on the impact of the SMP on the speed of convergence in all sectors.

The results of this last equation – which was run for all regions and sectors of Greece, Ireland, Italy and Portugal because it exploits the sectoral dimension of the sample – are reported in Chapter 5.

---

[31]   The starred parameters and variables in Equation 8 are those that were generated within the *antimonde* analysis, that is, assuming the liberalization index was equal to 1 over the whole sample.

Methodology

From a methodological viewpoint, Equations 1 to 7 were estimated using the techniques described in Section 3.3. In particular, in the estimation process we accounted for:

(a) **co-integration**, by using the two-step Engle and Granger estimator (the one-step estimator proposed by Davidson and McKinnon proved to be less efficient);

(b) **simultaneity**, by using instrumental variables for the endogenous variables appearing among the explanatory ones;

(c) **regional heterogeneity** in the panel of data used to estimate Equations 1-7 (regional heterogeneity was tested by introducing regional dummies among the regressors);

(d) **structural breaks related to the implementation of the SMP**, by using the liberalization index as the explanatory variable for the dynamics of the equation coefficients;

(e) **heteroscedasticity**, by using a White-consistent estimator;

(f) **technical progress**, by constructing an index that reflects the dynamics of economic indicators such as R&D, relative prices, GDP growth, patents, etc. (see Section 3.3);

(g) **structural funds**, by explaining regional differences, also through a measure of CSFs in each region.

The actual specification of the model was achieved following the 'encompassing principle' approach. That is, we started from the most general model in which all available variables were included and then we reduced the number of variables of the regressions by performing a cascade of t and F tests. If the 'true' model is 'encompassed' by the initial general model, this method leads the specification process just described to identify the 'true' model. Of course the small number of degrees of freedom does not guarantee this outcome, which holds asymptotically. Therefore, once the 'true' model was identified, we tested its robustness by using Pagan and Hall's residual analysis. That is, we regressed the residuals on the excluded coefficients.

This procedure (encompassing approach plus residual analysis), designed to guarantee the robustness of the estimated model, was followed for both the explanatory variables included in each regression and the regional dummies, which capture the difference between the region-specific effects and the average effects in the panel of regions. Note that when we applied this procedure, we did not use a rigid criterion to define the significance level of the various tests. In particular, the constants, CO, $C1$ and $C2$ (see Appendix A2 to Section 4.4) and the lagged variable of the second stage of the Engle and Granger procedure were maintained in the regression even when they were statistically non-significant. A few explanatory variables also appeared with low t statistics. This was done because our main goals were the robustness and the theoretical consistency of the model. Therefore, given the small number of degrees of freedom, in the selection of the variables, priority was given to these two objectives rather than to the choice of a given (say, 10%) significance level.

Robustness was also an issue as far as co-integration and structural breaks were concerned. In the case of co-integration, the small number of data did not enable us to perform the usual Dickey and Fuller's tests. However, we used a graphical representation of the time series as evidence of the presence of a common trend. Moreover, we exploited the super-consistent properties of the estimates of the co-integration vector in the Engle and Granger two-stage procedure in order to exclude from the co-integration regression those variables whose coefficients were not statistically significant in the first stage. These variables were then tested to see if they would belong to the 'true' model as stationary non-co-integrated variables. When this hypothesis could be accepted, the variables were maintained in the regression (their first difference was not introduced in the second stage of the Engle and Granger procedure).

In the case of structural breaks, we tested the robustness of the model in two ways: by running t tests on the significance of the coefficients explaining their variability and by comparing the model in which structural variability was assumed with the model in which coefficients were assumed to be constant. The computed likelihood ratio always led us to accept the hypothesis that the correct specification was the one that assumed structural variability. The power of these tests was certainly limited by the small size of the sample. However, the panel approach and the non-significance of many regional dummies provided us with a sufficient number of degrees of freedom for the estimation and the robustness check of the final model.

Trade and factor flows

All four of the equations describing the behaviour of trade and factor flows were estimated using the methodology described above. The notable exception in the case of Equations 1-4 was that only the constant term was assumed to be time-varying, that is, the liberalization index was introduced into Equations 1-4 in an additive way. A panel data approach was used in order to increase the efficiency of our estimates. Therefore, all equations were estimated sector by sector, by stacking regional data. Regional dummies (both on constant and slope parameters) were introduced when statistically significant. The regions considered in the equations were Northern Portugal (N), Central Portugal (C), Lisbon (L), Alentejo (J), the Algarve (A), and Ireland (E).

Let us consider the first equation, which captured the dynamics of trade creation. The eight parameters presented in Appendix A2 to Section 4.4 show the impact on trade creation of the following:

(a)   world trade index ($x1$);
(b)   specialization index ($x2$);
(c)   capital/labour ratio ($x3$);
(d)   labour productivity ($x4$);
(e)   GDP growth rate ($x5$);
(f)   liberalization index ($x6$);
(g)   FDI ($x7$);
(h)   CSFs ($x8$).

In order to understand the results reported in Appendix A2 to Section 4.4, note that the set of regressors is divided into two parts: the first block contains the regressors that were shown to be co-integrated (their coefficients were estimated in the first step); the second block contains the regressors that were not co-integrated (the constants and some explanatory variables) and the lagged dependent variable, which had to be introduced into the second step (we did not show the coefficients related to the first differences of the co-integrated variables because they were relevant only in order to perform a correct inference on the other parameters). Note that the second block of coefficients is shown after the constant CO and the coefficient of the lagged variable (RIT).

As far as trade creation was concerned, the impact of the liberalization index (which captured the progressive implementation of the SMP) was positive and statistically significant for only a few sectors. These were the chemical products sector, and the metal minerals sector. In the other sectors, the impact was generally negative.

Similar results were found when we focused on the IIT indicator (see Appendix A2 to Section 4.4). The impact of the liberalization index on IIT was generally negative, with a few exceptions. Indeed, a positive impact was found only for the non-metal minerals and energy products sectors (with the exception of Portugal's Central region), and for the food, beverages and tobacco sector (all regions).

The impact of the SMP on the RCA indicator also seemed to have been negative. Again, there are two exceptions, where the effect was positive: the non-metal minerals sector (with the exception of Northern Portugal) and the metal minerals sector (with the exception of Ireland).

Therefore, the empirical evidence suggested that the implementation of the SMP had a positive and beneficial impact, mainly on FDI from EU countries, particularly for Northern Portugal and the Lisbon region. A positive impact was found for metal minerals, food, beverages and tobacco, paper, chemical products, and energy products. In the case of Northern Portugal and the Lisbon region, a positive effect occurred also in the non-metal minerals sector. The positive effect was particularly strong for the Lisbon region and for Ireland in the energy products sector. A negative effect was found only for the transport equipment sector.

This led us to conclude that the implementation of the SMP seemed to have had a larger impact on factor flows rather than on trade flows. More specifically, a generalized positive effect was found only for FDI from EU countries.

Factor accumulation

Equations 5 and 6 were designed to assess the impact of trade and factor flow changes on the accumulation of physical and human capital in the different regions and sectors. Capital accumulation (the growth rate of physical and human capital) was therefore explained by the standard stock flow law of motion and by the possible effects of changes in trade and factor flow indicators. In the estimation of these two equations, we accounted for heteroscedasticity due to regional variability, structural breaks induced by the implementation of the SMP (both on constants and slope parameters), regional dummies, co-integration (using the Engle and Granger two-step estimator) and simultaneity (by means of the available instrumental variables).

The estimation results for Equation 2 are shown in Appendix A2 to Section 4.4. The regressors were as follows:

(a)   regional value added ($x1$);
(b)   level of the physical capital stock ($x2$);
(c)   trade creation ($x3$);
(d)   FDI ($x4$);
(e)   IIT ($x5$);
(f)   RCAs ($x6$).

Moreover, the coefficient C_0 accounted for regional differences due to the initial 1985 level of the capital stock, while C_2 accounted for regional differences due to CSF. The coefficient C_1

measured the break induced on the panel fixed effect by the increase in the liberalization index.

Looking at the results, we noticed that an increase in regional value added had a positive impact on capital accumulation in all regions and sectors. The coefficient was positive and strongly significant, particularly for Northern Portugal and the Lisbon region. Moreover, with a few exceptions, the parameter related to the level of the capital stock had the expected negative sign, thus showing that capital accumulation was faster when the level of the capital stock was lower.

Let us now consider the impact of trade and factor flow indicators on capital accumulation. In particular, let us focus on the impact of FDI because this was the only indicator that was shown to react significantly to the implementation of the SMP. This impact was positive and statistically significant for the following sectors:

(a)   chemical products;
(b)   paper;
(c)   energy products;
(d)   non-metal minerals;
(e)   wood and rubber.

For all the other sectors, the impact was not significant, with the exception of the food, beverages and tobacco sector where the effect was negative. Again, note that the regional dummies signalled a stronger effect for Northern Portugal and the Lisbon region.

Therefore, we concluded that the SMP had a positive impact by increasing the level of FDI in the above five sectors in all regions considered in the review.

Finally, note that the impact of CSFs on physical capital accumulation was positive and statistically significant only for the non-metal minerals, and wood and rubber sectors. For all the other sectors, the effect was non-significant, with the exception of agriculture.

Let us now consider human capital. This variable was proxied by the number of students in secondary schools, a variable that was obviously defined at the regional level (it would have been meaningless to disaggregate this variable for each sector). This proxy was the most-used one in the literature on convergence (see Levine and Renelt, 1992, and Baldwin and Venables, 1995). The fact that only regional observations were used implied that only one regression was run, where regional data were considered as a panel. Again, the growth rate of the stock of human capital was negatively related to its level, thus indicating that human capital increased faster when the level was low. The effect of growth in value added on growth in human capital was positive as expected (it was stronger in Ireland).

Note that the change in FDI had a positive impact on human capital accumulation in all regions. A stronger positive effect was produced by IIT.

Note also that the SMP did not seem to have induced a positive structural break (the coefficient C_1 was not statistically significant in the equation describing human capital accumulation). However, accumulation was faster in the regions where the initial level was lower (the coefficient C_0 was negative), thus again showing a tendency for convergence in the area of human capital accumulation. Finally, CSFs did not seem to have had a statistically significant impact on human capital accumulation.

Summing up, the implementation of the SMP had a positive impact on capital accumulation, mainly as a result of the fact that it led to an increased level of FDI. A positive stimulus to physical capital accumulation was also provided by CSFs (at least in some sectors) and, for both types of capital, by the long-run trend towards convergence.

Regional growth

Previous results suggested that the implementation of the SMP had a positive effect on the accumulation of physical and human capital mainly because it led to an increase in FDI from EU countries. Did this lead to increased economic growth? The answer to this question was provided by the last equation of our regression model, which linked the growth rate of sectoral per capita value added to technical progress ($x1$), the accumulation of physical ($x2$) and human ($x3$) capital, and to the growth rate of the labour force ($x4$), which was assumed to be exogenous.

Let us move immediately to the crucial question. In which sector did the accumulation of physical and human capital have a positive effect on economic growth (as measured by the growth rate of sectoral per capita value added)? The answer is again provided in Appendix A2 to Section 4.4. The growth rate equations showed that the coefficient of physical capital ($x2$) was positive and statistically significant in the following sectors:

(a)   paper;
(b)   non-metal minerals (only in Northern Portugal and the Lisbon region);
(c)   wood and rubber
(d)   metal products;
(e)   food, beverages and tobacco;
(f)   agriculture.

In all the other sectors, the accumulation of physical capital had a positive but non-significant impact on sectoral per capita value added growth.

The coefficient of human capital ($x3$) was slightly statistically significant only in the metal products sector, and had a positive sign. In all other sectors, the impact was statistically non-significant. What explained the economic growth in the Portuguese regions and in Ireland was mainly the accumulation of physical capital (particularly in the sectors indicated above), technical progress (in the paper and energy products sectors above all) and the dynamics of the labour force (in all sectors and regions).

Did the implementation of the SMP induce a structural break in the growth equations? By looking at the coefficient C_l in these equations (see Appendix A2 to Section 4.4), we concluded that a positive and statistically significant break was found in the non-metal minerals, wood and rubber, metal minerals, energy products and food, beverages and tobacco sectors. In all the other sectors, the coefficient was generally positive (the exception was chemical products), even if it was non-significant. Therefore, the SMP had a positive direct impact on economic growth in most sectors.

These results led us to the following conclusion: that the implementation of the SMP had a statistically significant effect mainly on FDI and, as a result of this, on the accumulation of physical and human capital. However, only physical capital seemed to have had a positive impact on economic growth in some sectors (paper, non-metal minerals, wood and rubber, metal products, food, beverages and tobacco, and agriculture). However, in many sectors there was also a direct impact of the SMP via a structural change in the growth equations, which seemed to have increased the growth rate of Portuguese regions and of Ireland.

The estimation of the growth rate equations shown in Appendix A2 to Section 4.4 provided other interesting results:

(a)   The coefficient C_0, which related the growth rate of sectoral per capita value added to the sectoral per capita value added level, was generally statistically significant and negative. This implied that a convergence process was taking place in the regions of Portugal and Ireland, i.e. less developed regions were catching up with others. A test of whether or not the implementation of the SMP had *increased* the speed of convergence is shown in Chapter 5.

(b)   The coefficient C_2, which explained regional differences of growth in terms of the amount of CSFs received, was generally statistically non-significant. The exceptions were the wood and rubber, and the food, beverages and tobacco sectors, where the coefficient was positive. This implied that, only in these two sectors, regions where CSFs were higher experienced a higher growth rate of sectoral per capita value added.

Main conclusions from the regression analysis

There are a few conclusions that the regression analysis seemed to support:

(a)   The implementation of the SMP had a larger impact on factor flows than it did on trade flows. More specifically, a generalized positive effect was found only on FDI from EU countries.

(b)   The change in FDI had a generalized positive effect on both physical and human capital accumulation. Therefore, our regression analysis suggested that liberalization had a positive impact on capital accumulation via its effect of increasing FDI. A positive stimulus to physical capital accumulation was also provided by CSFs (at least in some sectors).

(c)   The convergence process of the regions was an important effect that explains the dynamics of both physical and human capital.

(d)   Only physical capital seems to have had a positive impact on economic growth in some sectors (paper, non-metal minerals, wood and rubber, metal products, food, beverages and tobacco, and agriculture). Therefore, in these sectors, the implementation of the SMP, via its effects on FDI, had a positive impact also on economic growth. In many sectors, there was a further direct effect of the SMP by means of a structural change in the growth equations that seemed to increase the growth rate of Portuguese regions and of Ireland.

(e)   There was clear evidence that a convergence process was occurring in the studied regions, i.e. less developed regions were catching up with the most developed ones.

4.4.6. Appendix A1 to Section 4.4.

Table A1.4.4.1. Grubel-Lloyd coefficient (GL_i), NCN 4

Sectors	1980	1981	1982	1983	1984	1985	1986	1987	1988	1989
Agriculture										
Number of products	12	12	12	12	12	12	12	12	12	12
Average	0.27	0.20	0.20	0.25	0.25	0.26	0.30	0.30	0.30	0.43
Standard deviation	0.26	0.17	0.25	0.26	0.26	0.25	0.25	0.36	0.36	0.37
Coefficient variation	0.98	0.88	1.26	1.07	1.03	0.96	0.84	0.21	1.21	0.86
Industry										
Number of products	190	190	190	190	190	190	190	190	190	190
Average	0.39	0.40	0.4	0.38	0.40	0.41	0.42	0.42	0.43	0.43
Standard deviation	0.32	0.32	0.31	0.31	0.31	0.30	0.32	0.31	0.30	0.29
Coefficient variation	0.82	0.79	0.75	0.81	0.77	0.75	0.75	0.73	0.70	0.68

Source: Instituto Nacional de Estatística (INE).

Table A1.4.4.2. **Grubel-Lloyd coefficient (GL_i), NACE 2**

Sectors	1985	1986	1987	1988	1989	1990	1991	1992	1993
Agriculture									
Average	15	21	20	19	22	22	21	16	12
Industry									
Number of products	10	10	10	10	10	10	10	10	10
Average	62	62	57	57	61	63	53	53	54
Standard deviation	20.14	19.00	21.13	21.67	17.91	17.76	23.02	22.31	24.27
Coefficient variation	0.322	0.309	0.369	0.377	0.293	0.281	0.435	0.425	0.446
Services									
Number of products	4	4	4	4	4	4	4	4	4
Average	31	31	42	43	31	33	40	25	37
Standard deviation	18.04	18.87	27.35	24.87	18.66	18.32	30.78	27.52	38.53
Coefficient variation	0.579	0.613	0.644	0.574	0.607	0.556	0.767	1.092	1.035

Source: Instituto Nacional de Estatistica (INE).

Table A1.4.4.3. NACE-CLIO RR17

Branches	Label	Term used in text	Sensitivity to SMP*
01	Agriculture, forestry and fishing	Agriculture and fishing	
06	Energy products	Energy products	
13	Metallic minerals	Metallic minerals Mining	NS
15	Non-metallic mineral products	Non-metallic mineral products	HS
17	Chemicals	Chemicals	HS
24	Metal products and engineering	Metal products and engineering Metal products and machinery	 HS
28	Transport equipment	Transport equipment	HS
36	Food, beverages and tobacco	Food and beverages	HS
42	Textiles, clothing, leather and footwear industries	Textile, clothing, and footwear industries Textiles	 HS
47	Paper, products of paper, publishing	Paper	NS
50	Other manufacturing	Other manufacturing	
53	Construction and public works	Construction and public works	
58	Repair, trade and tourism	Trade and tourism	
60	Transport and communications	Transport and communications	
69	Banking and insurance	Banking and insurance	
74	Other market services	Market services	
86	Non-market services		

Note: HS = highly sensitive; NS = not sensitive.

* According to Buigues *et al.* (1990) methodology. See in particular the study by P. M. Conçalves in the Buigues report.

4.4.7. Appendix A2 to Section 4.4.

Explanatory note regarding the regression analysis

The regression parameters, X_{ijk}, have to be read as follows:

(a) i is the index of the regressor (according to the three types of equation) for:
   (i)   trade and factor flows:
         1 world trade index;
         2 specialization index;
         3 capital/labour ratio;
         4 labour productivity;
         5 GDP growth rate;
         6 liberalization index;
         7 FDI;
         8 CSFs;
   (ii)   human and physical capital:
         1 regional value added;
         2 level of the physical capital stock;
         3 trade creation;
         4 FDI;
         5 IIT;
         6 RCAs;
   (iii)   economic growth:
         1 technical progress;
         2 accumulation of physical capital;
         3 accumulation of human capital;
         4 growth rate of labour force;
(b) j is the index of the region:
      *A*lgarve;
      *C*entral Portugal;
      Ir*E*land;
      Alente*J*o;
      *L*isbon;
      *N*orthern Portugal;
(c) k is the index of the sector:
      AGR   NMM
      CHP   PAP
      ENP   TEC
      FBT   TOT
      MEM   TRE
      MEP   WOR.

Table A2.4.4.1.   Sectoral regression parameters for Portugal and Ireland

Sector	Growth equation			Physical capital equation			IIT-E equation			RCA-E equation			TC equation			FDI equation		
		Param	t Student		Param	t Student		Param	t Student		Param	t Student		Param	t Student		Param	t Student
AGR	X1AGR	0.26	1.42	X1AGR	2.65	3.05	X1AGR	724.74	4.36	X1AGR	46.56	15.92	X1AGR	50.47	40.37	X1AGR	5.79	2.37
	X2AGR	1.79	1.76	X1LAGR	2.12	3.52	X1NAGR	312.41	2.28	X3AGR	-4.99	-4.23	X3AGR	-30.75	-2.50	X3AGR	36.89	1.22
	X2CAGR	2.94	2.93	X1AAGR	5.87	3.83	X1LAGR	374.72	1.61	X2AGR	-4.85	-8.05	X6AGR	-30.15	-5.03	X5AGR	11.77	2.62
	X4AGR	0.45	2.69	X2AGR	-1.28	-2.90	X2AGR	53.20	1.18	X6AGR	-108.32	-3.55	X7AGR	13.49	4.21	C0AGR	83.83	1.83
	X4LAGR	-0.57	-1.80	X2NAGR	0.91	3.64	X4AGR	-26790.10	-1.88	X6NAGR	68.07	4.95	C0AGR	212.80	3.62	RITAGR	-1.66	-5.51
	X4JAGR	-0.52	-3.06	X2CAGR	0.90	2.40	X6AGR	-1337.02	-3.00	X6CAGR	489.14	5.34	RITAGR	-0.97	-8.93			
	X4AAGR	-0.98	-4.09				X6LAGR	1712.53	2.43	X8AGR	2.20	6.77	X4AGR	-156.67	-2.01			
	C0AGR	-0.19	-1.09	C0AGR	0.24	1.95	X6AAGR	4246.09	2.82	C0AGR	94.43	1.38						
	C1AGR	0.02	0.55	C1AGR	-0.05	-2.04	X7AGR	272.89	2.23	RITAGR	-0.10	-1.12						
	C2AGR	-5.93E-06	-1.47	C2AGR	-1.93E-04	-6.76	X8AGR	19.04	3.28									
	RITAGR	-0.23	-4.60	RITAGR	-0.14	-7.45	C0AGR	3241.57	5.15									
				X6AGR	-0.54	-4.60	RITAGR	-0.55	-2.00									
	R-squared	0.67		R-squared	0.80		R-squared	0.92		R-squared	0.14		R-squared	0.84		R-squared	0.77	
ENP	X1ENP	0.25	2.47	X1ENP	1.53	4.05	X2ENP	41.76	3.11	X1ENP	1.64	3.28				X1ENP	0.93	3.40
	X4ENP	-0.01	-1.61	X1CENP	6.60	2.49	X4ENP	234.88	1.57	X1CENP	-0.47	-1.62				X1LENP	-0.18	-2.17
	X4NENP	0.88	2.31	X2ENP	-0.85	-3.62	X6ENP	18.34	0.37	X1LENP	1.43	2.61				X1JENP	1.41	3.10
	C0ENP	-0.62	-1.80	X2LENP	0.53	2.51	X6CENP	-266.69	-3.24	X2ENP	4.79	3.05				X2ENP	-2.95	-2.91
	C1ENP	0.12	1.81	C0ENP	0.53	2.65	X6LENP	243.51	2.61	X3ENP	-46.75	-2.57				X3ENP	29.68	1.47
	C2ENP	1.39E-05	1.01	C1ENP	-0.10	-3.37	X6AENP	219.17	1.32	X4ENP	6.63	3.28				X6ENP	13.29	10.93
	RITENP	-0.06	-2.07	C2ENP	-1.29E-04	-1.31	C0ENP	-801.23	-4.08	X7ENP	11.90	2.16				X6LENP	18.50	3.75
	X2ENP	1.05	0.65	RITENP	-0.09	-3.99	RITENP	-0.70	-4.02	C0ENP	179.00	2.19				C0ENP	-7.92	-0.81
				X4ENP	2.20E-03	2.58				RITENP	-0.47	-3.28				RITENP	-1.37	-8.70
				X5ENP	-6.02E-02	-3.81				X6ENP	-28.85	-1.45						
										X8ENP	0.32	1.61						
	R-squared	0.42		R-squared	0.45		R-squared	0.86		R-squared	0.61					R-squared	0.84	

Sector: MEM

Growth equation	Param	t Student	Physical capital equation	Param	t Student	IIT-E equation	Param	t Student	RCA-E equation	Param	t Student	TC equation	Param	t Student	FDI equation	Param	t Student
X1MEM	0.11	1.51	X1MEM	3.71	3.02	X1MEM	353.74	45.09	X4MEM	136.61	4.39	X1MEM	31.50	13.20	X2MEM	1.06	3.01
X4MEM	0.13	3.11	X1EMEM	-2.92	-2.55	X1NMEM	58.69	3.70	X6MEM	14.71	1.51	X2MEM	2.91	4.00	X4MEM	25.93	2.77
X4CMEM	-1.33	-6.40	X2MEM	-1.20	-2.63	X1CMEM	-48.06	-3.94	X6NME	191.40	4.32	X3MEM	-3.44	-2.64	X8MEM	0.04	1.34
X4EMEM	-1.86	-4.14				X3MEM	91.75	1.95	X6CMEM	74.11	3.64	X4MEM	-29.74	-6.11	C0MEM	-457.82	-3.64
			C0MEM	0.07	0.60	X6MEM	-97.72	-7.09	X6LMEM	122.63	6.10	X7MEM	15.68	1.96	RITMEM	-0.66	-4.07
C0MEM	-0.23	-1.56	C1MEM	0.01	0.77	X7MEM	34.48	1.43	X6JMEM	74.19	4.50	X8MEM	0.20	3.30	X1MEM	12.12	3.02
C1MEM	0.04	1.95	C2MEM	-7.66E-05	-1.02	X6CMEM	-268.21	-2.92	X6EMEM	-69.51	-2.66	C0MEM	-87.75	-2.02	X3MEM	1.71	1.85
C2MEM	-9.32E-06	-1.58	RITMEM	-0.08	-5.89	X6LMEM	233.06	4.54	X7MEM	51.74	2.79	RITMEM	-0.43	-2.55	X6MEM	2.03	1.39
RITMEM	-0.16	-3.32	X5MEM	0.04	1.38	C0MEM	-273.52	-2.60	C0MEM	292.75	4.95	X5MEM	2.02	2.92			
						RITMEM	-0.79	-3.56	RITMEM	-0.18	-2.08	X6MEM	5.83	3.22			
									X2MEM	-2.57	-5.11						
R-squared	0.84		R-squared	0.64		R-squared	0.93		R-squared	0.67		R-squared	0.75		R-squared	0.88	

Sector: NMM

Growth equation	Param	t Student	Physical capital equation	Param	t Student	IIT-E equation	Param	t Student	RCA-E equation	Param	t Student	TC equation	Param	t Student	FDI equation	Param	t Student
X2NMM	0.85	0.97	X1NMM	1.20	2.20	X1NMM	1031.54	15.77	X2NMM	3.23	15.30	X1NMM	167.87	33.05	X3NMM	213.27	2.89
X2NNMM	4.14	1.92	X1NNMM	11.63	2.90	X1NNMM	383.68	5.57	X3NMM	17.60	3.04	X2NMM	-0.70	-1.53	X6NMM	-46.31	-3.58
X2LNMM	5.33	1.63	X1CNMM	4.76	4.72	X1ANMM	179.36	1.40	X6NMM	46.33	4.31	X3NMM	-13.35	-3.57	X6NNMM	780.36	2.85
X4NMM	-0.06	-0.21	X1LNMM	5.74	15.52	X3NMM	411.01	1.92	X6NNMM	-82.17	-2.39	X4NMM	-85.65	-9.22	X6LNMM	799.97	6.50
X4LNMM	0.73	1.24	X2NMM	-0.55	-1.23	X4NMM	-244.51	-2.87	X6LNMM	84.77	2.25	C0NMM	183.64	4.54	X8NMM	1.45	3.79
X4ANMM	-0.99	-2.13	X2ANMM	-1.59	-2.54	X6NMM	48.54	1.58	X6ANMM	-20.99	-5.48	RITNMM	-0.25	-3.11	C0NMM	-1702.42	-1.44
X4ENMM	0.87	1.34	C0NMM	0.02	0.39	X6CNMM	-324.89	-4.18	C0NMM	7.46	0.22	X6NMM	-8.90	-1.93	RITNMM	-0.66	-2.96
C0NMM	-0.43	-1.95	C1NMM	3.50E-03	0.39	X6ANMM	1187.64	4.60	RITNMM	-0.46	-3.95				X2NMM	9.96	1.53
C1NMM	9.60E-02	2.40	C2NMM	2.45E-04	7.56	C0NMM	612.48	1.68	X5NMM	7.01	1.48				X4NMM	-127.11	-1.86
C2NMM	7.86E-07	0.25	RITNMM	-0.03	-7.84	RITNMM	-0.54	-3.35							X5NMM	19.10	1.75
RITNMM	-0.10	-2.25	X4NMM	2.31E-03	3.62												
			X4LNMM	0.01	10.01												
			X5NMM	-0.19	-11.38												
			X6NMM	0.20	4.13												
R-squared	0.57		R-squared	0.90		R-squared	0.76		R-squared	0.63		R-squared	0.41		R-squared	0.65	

Sector: CHP

Growth equation

Variable	Param	t Student
X1CHP	0.28	1.42
X4CHP	0.36	4.39
X4CCHP	1.25	3.11
X4LCHP	-1.57	-1.43
C0CHP	0.08	0.26
C1CHP	-0.15	-1.41
C2CHP	-1.58E-05	-0.93
RITCHP	-0.21	-6.24
R-squared	0.85	

Physical capital equation

Variable	Param	t Student
X1CHP	1.47	3.93
X2CHP	-0.64	-3.42
C0CHP	0.03	0.25
C1CHP	-0.04	-1.76
C2CHP	-1.04E-04	-0.70
RITCHP	-0.02	-0.76
X4CHP	2.77E-03	2.32
X4NCHP	0.01	4.51
X5CHP	0.02	1.30
X6CHP	-0.04	-1.53
R-squared	0.52	

IIT-E equation

Variable	Param	t Student
X1CHP	29.34	6.68
X1NCHP	18.62	8.84
X1CCHP	-4.35	-3.38
X3CHP	178.14	1.84
X4CHP	950.72	4.74
X6CHP	-447.46	-3.28
X6NCHP	-933.77	-6.51
X6LCHP	-93.00	-2.42
X8CHP	3.00	2.42
C0CHP	354.79	1.26
RITCHP	-0.74	-4.79
R-squared	0.98	

RCA-E equation

Variable	Param	t Student
X1CHP	6.12	5.42
X1NCHP	-1.23	-4.94
X1CCHP	2.83	7.39
X2CHP	-10.96	-2.77
X3CHP	191.73	3.37
X8CHP	1.91	2.52
C0CHP	483.85	2.82
RITCHP	-0.06	-0.54
R-squared	0.80	

TC equation

Variable	Param	t Student
X1CHP	2.37	5.64
X3CHP	4.73	1.99
X4CHP	53.54	2.84
X6CHP	36.46	2.73
C0CHP	-369.44	-4.15
RITCHP	-0.95	-1.31
X5CHP	3.56	3.14
R-squared	0.79	

FDI equation

Variable	Param	t Student
X3CHP	58.35	5.89
X4CHP	-28.23	-4.54
X6CHP	19.43	8.92
C0CHP	-5.21	-0.29
RITCHP	-1.52	-5.89
R-squared	0.80	

Sector: MEP

Growth equation

Variable	Param	t Student
X2MEP	8.04	1.61
X4MEP	0.54	1.26
X4NMEP	-1.00	-9.78
X4AMEP	0.96	2.72
C0MEP	-0.17	-0.30
C1MEP	-0.18	-1.47
C2MEP	1.45E-06	0.27
RITMEP	-0.22	-3.59
X3MEP	0.74	1.36
R-squared	0.78	

Physical capital equation

Variable	Param	t Student
X1MEP	0.63	3.74
X1NMEP	3.35	5.72
X1LMEP	1.73	3.46
X2MEP	-0.90	-3.37
X2LMEP	0.74	2.45
X2EMEP	-0.80	-3.35
C0MEP	0.01	0.07
C1MEP	-0.02	-1.41
C2MEP	-3.22E-05	-0.95
RITMEP	-0.05	-2.79
R-squared	0.43	

IIT-E equation

Variable	Param	t Student
X1MEP	38.18	27.51
X1NMEP	12.05	7.79
X1CMEP	-3.28	-2.88
X1LMEP	8.13	5.66
X3MEP	429.91	1.71
X4MEP	-228.18	-4.92
X6MEP	-71.34	-2.86
X6LMEP	335.51	4.38
X6AMEP	3389.30	8.53
C0MEP	-1680.44	-2.20
RITMEP	-0.64	-5.81
X5MEP	52.72	3.60
X7MEP	5.65	1.92
R-squared	0.87	

RCA-E equation

Variable	Param	t Student
X1MEP	3.62	21.10
X1JMEP	-0.35	-1.55
X6MEP	-74.58	-5.36
X6NMEP	304.86	4.51
X6CMEP	-43.24	-4.48
X6LMEP	157.88	6.49
X6JMEP	36.56	2.18
X8MEP	2.43	4.50
C0MEP	44.66	0.37
RITMEP	-0.17	-1.65
X3MEP	-1.96	-1.52
X4MEP	17.71	2.61
R-squared	0.44	

TC equation

Variable	Param	t Student
X1MEP	1.74	8.94
X1NMEP	1.94	9.16
X1CMEP	2.06	9.35
X1LMEP	2.15	9.70
X1JMEP	2.12	8.54
X1AMEP	2.39	9.51
X2MEP	2.11	9.55
X3MEP	-2.71	-2.14
X4MEP	-35.62	-7.25
X5MEP	0.92	1.74
C0MEP	10.01	0.27
RITMEP	-1.29	-3.90
R-squared	0.34	

FDI equation

Variable	Param	t Student
X1MEP	1.68	4.96
X2MEP	2.53	8.16
X3MEP	-225.07	-1.92
X4MEP	-54.28	-5.66
C0MEP	177.82	3.57
RITMEP	-0.49	-2.16
R-squared	0.65	

Sector: TRE

Growth equation			Physical capital equation			IIT-E equation			RCA-E equation			TC equation			FDI equation		
	Param	t Student		Param	t Student		Param	t Student		Param	t Student		Param	t Student		Param	t Student
X1TRE	1.41	1.42	X1TRE	4.35	4.06	X1TRE	26.66	14.73	X1TRE	1.35	15.09	X2TRE	18.63	8.92	X1TRE	4.75	3.67
X4TRE	-0.40	-2.55	X1CTRE	11.26	5.10	X1LTRE	5.60	2.94	X1ETRE	-0.36	-2.15	X3TRE	-7.61	-2.72	X2TRE	-11.00	-1.94
X4NTRE	1.95	2.30	X1LTRE	2.34	2.33	X1ATRE	7.75	4.46	X2TRE	-1.47	-1.49	X4TRE	-60.13	-2.17	X4TRE	-161.99	-3.35
X4CTRE	-7.41	-6.18	X1ETRE	1.96	1.22	X4TRE	-778.26	-4.67	X6TRE	-56.02	-3.29	X5TRE	1.95	1.88	X6TRE	-98.12	-2.65
X4ATRE	0.76	4.61	X2TRE	-2.00	-3.44	X5TRE	37.64	2.01	X6CTRE	58.97	2.04	C0TRE	-1144.32	-1.02	C0TRE	465.95	0.30
X4ETRE	-1.77	-3.00	X2TTRE	-2.07	-2.93	X6TRE	-515.30	-5.69	X6LTRE	103.47	4.32	RITTRE	-0.41	-2.36	RITTRE	-0.92	-8.32
C0TRE	-0.88	-1.27	C0TRE	0.08	0.43	X7TRE	96.22	2.57	X6ETRE	24.31	2.35	X1TRE	1.96	1.38			
C1TRE	-0.13	-0.52	C1TRE	-2.53E-03	-0.09	C0TRE	-1429.24	-0.93	X8TRE	0.33	2.02	X6TRE	-44.88	-2.02			
C2TRE	-2.32E-06	-0.11	C2TRE	1.04E-06	0.01	RITTRE	-0.56	-2.18	C0TRE	32.82	0.30						
RITTRE	-0.32	-6.62	RITTRE	-0.01	-1.84				RITTRE	-0.71	-3.14						
									X4TRE	34.52	3.05						
									X7TRE	9.84	1.78						
R-squared	0.92		R-squared	0.35		R-squared	0.67		R-squared	0.59		R-squared	0.30		R-squared	0.52	

Sector: FBT

Growth equation			Physical capital equation			IIT-E equation			RCA-E equation			TC equation			FDI equation		
	Param	t Student		Param	t Student		Param	t Student		Param	t Student		Param	t Student		Param	t Student
X2FBT	2.51	1.81	X1FBT	1.13	4.44	X1FBT	26.30	1.26	X1FBT	60.57	4.66	X1FBT	8.13	36.89	X3FBT	741.06	4.22
X2CFBT	22.35	1.74	X2FBT	-0.81	-3.73	X1NFBT	9.75	1.46	X1NFBT	6.72	1.31	X5FBT	5.65	2.91	X6FBT	93.22	4.44
X4FBT	-0.13	-1.07	C0FBT	0.25	2.27	X2FBT	147.91	1.57	X2FBT	-84.46	-3.77	X6FBT	-189.69	-10.38	X6CFBT	192.26	1.12
X4LFBT	0.17	1.74	C1FBT	-0.08	-4.34	X4FBT	-3500.06	-1.51	X3FBT	-884.35	-3.10	X6NFBT	-30.63	-2.51	X6JFBT	3479.17	1.18
X4AFBT	-0.42	-4.47	C2FBT	-9.74E-06	-0.22	X6FBT	1387.24	9.59	X6FBT	-794.88	-2.40	X6LFBT	-40.05	-2.63	X6AFBT	2690.08	1.24
C0FBT	-0.54	-1.67	RITFBT	-0.07	-4.48	X6NFBT	1155.47	3.53	X6LFBT	-476.94	-2.32	X8FBT	1.25	5.86	C0FBT	-6338.13	-2.36
C1FBT	0.11	2.11	X3FBT	9.25	1.90	X6CFBT	1040.91	2.86	X6AFBT	-616.35	-3.07	C0FBT	-394.65	-2.37	RITFBT	-0.98	-2.98
C2FBT	2.19E-05	3.27	X4FBT	-8.58E-04	-2.04	X6LFBT	2027.58	4.63	C0FBT	995.16	1.12	RITFBT	-0.82	-3.59	X2FBT	139.97	2.73
RITFBT	-0.18	-3.88	X5FBT	-0.03	-2.18	X6JFBT	648.26	1.91	RITFBT	-0.26	-1.55	X2FBT	-3.02	-2.09	X4FBT	-2404.02	-2.20
			X6FBT	-0.45	-2.16	X6AFBT	2172.71	5.08				X4FBT	156.25	3.24	X5FBT	43.37	1.79
						C0FBT	359.09	0.14									
						RITFBT	-0.84	-1.92									
						X8FBT	9.19	1.75									
R-squared	0.70		R-squared	0.61		R-squared	0.90		R-squared	0.15		R-squared	0.85		R-squared	0.72	

Sector: TEC

Growth equation

	Param	t.Student
X1TEC	0.11	1.00
X4TEC	1.05	13.24
X4NTEC	-0.83	-7.58
X4CTEC	-0.94	-6.06
X4LTEC	-1.37	-1.44
X4JTEC	-1.08	-13.41
C0TEC	-0.67	-1.49
C1TEC	0.24	1.32
C2TEC	-3.60E-05	-1.06
RITTEC	-0.96	-2.43
X2TEC	4.80	1.40
R-squared	0.63	

Physical capital equation

	Param	t.Student
X1TEC	1.04	2.79
X1NTEC	1.72	3.69
X1LTEC	1.09	6.03
X1ETEC	-0.28	-2.22
X2TEC	-0.85	-2.32
X2CTEC	-0.68	-2.57
C0TEC	0.21	0.59
C1TEC	2.30E-03	0.04
C2TEC	3.82E-05	0.30
RITTEC	-0.05	-2.20
X5TEC	-0.03	-2.27
X6TEC	0.24	1.38
R-squared	0.62	

IIT-E equation

	Param	t.Student
X1TEC	40.71	4.56
X1NTEC	68.59	8.47
X1CTEC	129.10	13.84
X1LTEC	81.61	8.11
X1JTEC	24.37	1.29
X2TEC	13.73	1.21
X3TEC	1079.30	2.90
X6TEC	-183.50	-2.47
X6TEC	2245.19	2.15
X8TEC	2.56	3.89
C0TEC	1434.46	3.35
RITTEC	-0.40	-1.91
X4TEC	-377.73	-3.17
R-squared	0.78	

RCA-E equation

	Param	t.Student
X1TEC	2.98	8.76
X1CTEC	-0.36	-1.79
X3TEC	25.45	5.97
X4TEC	145.06	2.70
X6TEC	-30.41	-3.13
X6JTEC	116.74	5.81
C0TEC	-2.19	-0.04
RITTEC	-0.60	-1.18
R-squared	0.30	

TC equation

	Param	t.Student
X1TEC	6.59	24.35
X1NTEC	-0.54	-2.76
X2TEC	1.12	2.66
X6TEC	-22.61	-7.10
X1ETEC	-0.61	-1.51
X6ETEC	7.35	2.36
C0TEC	227.73	11.04
RITTEC	-0.14	-2.42
X4TEC	-54.96	-5.96
X8TEC	0.15	2.57
R-squared	0.77	

FDI equation

	Param	t.Student
X1TEC	0.72	1.98
X1NTEC	3.46	1.87
X1CTEC	5.36	2.24
X1LTEC	8.95	3.45
X2TEC	5.81	6.60
X3TEC	-59.15	-1.60
X5TEC	0.93	1.29
C0TEC	-47.63	-2.61
RITTEC	-0.74	-5.41
R-squared	0.70	

Sector: PAP

Growth equation

	Param	t.Student
X2PAP	0.27	1.74
X2JPAP	3.60	2.01
X4PAP	0.09	0.60
X4NPAP	-0.61	-2.70
X4CPAP	0.39	4.19
X4EPAP	0.87	1.48
C0PAP	-0.69	-1.89
C1PAP	0.05	0.98
C2PAP	-9.56E-07	-0.54
RITPAP	-0.19	-8.55
X1PAP	0.42	2.51
R-squared	0.53	

Physical capital equation

	Param	t.Student
X1PAP	2.47	4.88
X1LPAP	4.27	4.59
X2PAP	-1.53	-3.55
X2APAP	-1.09	-1.44
C0PAP	0.35	2.11
C1PAP	-0.06	-1.70
C2PAP	3.16E-04	1.53
RITPAP	-0.02	-1.10
X4PAP	0.00	1.65
X5PAP	-0.10	-1.26
R-squared	0.35	

IIT-E equation

	Param	t.Student
X1PAP	37.54	4.70
X1NPAP	37.59	10.44
X1LPAP	30.20	11.72
X1JPAP	-19.61	-3.70
X2PAP	32.81	3.43
X3PAP	415.85	1.56
X4PAP	-700.58	-3.47
X6PAP	-103.79	-2.24
X6CPAP	964.48	10.36
X6JPAP	3716.75	9.79
X6APAP	4309.69	3.46
C0PAP	-419.58	-1.65
RITPAP	-0.16	-3.10
X7PAP	21.72	4.61
X8PAP	0.34	1.89
R-squared	0.89	

RCA-E equation

	Param	t.Student
X1PAP	2.34	5.56
X1EPAP	-1.42	-3.94
X3PAP	-6.35	-2.50
X4PAP	106.91	3.71
X6PAP	-32.25	-3.00
X6NPAP	-44.73	-2.75
X6CPAP	-48.82	-11.25
X6LPAP	24.20	3.18
X6APAP	35.92	4.33
X6EPAP	20.33	4.46
C0PAP	-34.80	-0.84
RITPAP	-0.36	-3.10
R-squared	0.46	

TC equation

	Param	t.Student
X1PAP	6.48	30.76
X3PAP	2.91	1.81
C0PAP	272.33	4.90
RITPAP	-0.65	-4.17
X6PAP	-31.65	-3.90
R-squared	0.29	

FDI equation

	Param	t.Student
X3PAP	10.90	2.56
X4PAP	38.59	3.17
X6PAP	10.39	1.76
C0PAP	-479.56	-3.31
RITPAP	-0.98	-6.70
X2PAP	3.60	3.09
R-squared	0.64	

Sector	Growth equation			Physical capital equation			IIT-E equation			RCA-E equation			TC equation			FDI equation		
		Param	t.Student		Param	t.Student		Param	t.Student		Param	t.Student		Param	t.Student		Param	t.Student
WOR	X2WOR	1.25	2.49	X1WOR	1.37	7.91	X1WOR	41.77	7.57	X2WOR	4.25	18.18	X1WOR	1.78	12.97	X1WOR	3.70	5.31
	X2NWOR	7.94	1.43	X1NWOR	3.38	4.61	X1NWOR	91.94	17.19	X3WOR	-5.84	-3.94	X1NWOR	0.44	3.95	X4WOR	-126.86	-3.13
	X2CWOR	6.82	1.83	X1CWOR	4.89	2.12	X1LWOR	48.55	10.22	X5WOR	1.43	2.10	X1CWOR	0.57	5.75	X8WOR	0.32	1.19
	X2JWOR	38.30	2.56	X1LWOR	4.17	7.13	X4WOR	-766.24	-2.54	X6WOR	-67.15	-11.59	X1LWOR	1.31	10.47	C0WOR	213.04	1.19
	X2EWOR	1.91	3.95	X2WOR	-0.84	-6.23	X7WOR	43.19	1.79	X6LWOR	-51.35	-3.22	X1JWOR	1.51	6.99	RITWOR	-0.91	-3.94
	X4WOR	0.30	2.36	X2JWOR	-1.58	-1.86	X6WOR	-6.65	-0.41	X6IWOR	-248.01	-5.28	X1AWOR	1.58	9.59			
	X4CWOR	1.09	2.69	X2AWOR	-2.56	-3.98	X6LWOR	4443.02	9.13	X6AWOR	-181.78	-7.81	X1EWOR	-1.26	-15.67			
	X4JWOR	-3.58	-3.77							X6EWOR	42.27	7.65	X2WOR	3.81	11.63			
	X4EWOR	3.32	2.54	C0WOR	-0.07	-0.72	C0WOR	734.50	3.04	C0WOR	-119.47	-3.42	X4WOR	-9.64	-2.33			
	C0WOR	-1.31	-3.13	C1WOR	-1.16E-03	-0.06	RITWOR	-0.39	-3.89	RITWOR	-0.87	-2.73	X8WOR	0.04	1.70			
	C1WOR	0.27	4.14	C2WOR	1.19E-04	2.61							C0WOR	46.38	2.61			
	C2WOR	7.97E-06	2.86	RITWOR	-0.04	-1.66							RITWOR	-0.19	-1.49			
	RITWOR	-0.23	-2.47	X4WOR	3.10E-04	2.18												
				X5WOR	-0.02	-1.59												
	R-squared	0.89		R-squared	0.60		R-squared	0.86		R-squared	0.76		R-squared	0.19		R-squared	0.56	

Note: N = Northern Portugal; C = Central Portugal; L = Lisbon; J = Alentejo; A = Algarve; E = Ireland.

Table A2.4.4.2. Non-sectoral regression parameters for Portugal and Ireland

Sector		Human capital equation	
		Parameter	*t* student
TOT			
	X2TOT	-0.032	-3.164
	C0TOT	-1.740	-3.972
	C1TOT	-0.373	-1.636
	C2TOT	0.000	-0.867
	RITTOT	-0.698	-3.834
	X1TOT	0.079	1.793
	X1NTOT	0.321	2.021
	X1CTOT	1.051	2.148
	X1LTOT	0.154	1.807
	X1JTOT	4.438	2.108
	X1ATOT	4.747	1.819
	X1ETOT	1.141	1.679
	X4TOT	0.000	1.851
	X5TOT	0.012	2.002
	X6TOT	-0.511	-2.917
	R-squared	0.859	

Note: N = Northern Portugal; C = Central Portugal; L = Lisbon; J = Alentejo; A = Algarve; E = Ireland

4.5. Spain

J. Castillo and A. Roca, Instituto Valenciano d'Investigaciones Económicas (IVIE), Spain

4.5.1. Background

The basic structural equation of β convergence (see also Section 3.3.8) has been estimated using Spanish regional data in at least two studies: Dolado *et al.* (1994), and Raymond *et al.* (1994). The main conclusions from these were that:

(a)   a significant reduction in regional inequality had taken place in Spanish regions since the 1950s;

(b)   however, this regional convergence process was showing signs of stagnation in the last two decades.

The results regarding β convergence in Spanish regions are shown in the first column of Table 4.5.1. The figure for the unconditional convergence rate is at a remarkably similar level (although it indicated that the process has been somewhat faster) to that found in other data sets.

The core of these contributions was recently put into jeopardy in a paper by Canova and Marcet (1995). They claimed that β convergence estimates obtained were subject to the kind of bias that is typical in panel data when individual-specific intercepts are not included.

Canova and Marcet allowed for a more flexible specification. They introduced a country-specific intercept, which let the data show whether or not countries might have different steady states.[32] Their results indicated that:

(a)   countries do converge to a steady state, at a rate much faster than that found by BS (about 20%) per year;

(b)   the steady states are markedly different for different countries.

Canova and Marcet obtained these results both in a database panel of developed countries and OECD regions. A similar study was conducted with Spanish data (de la Fuente, 1995) that reproduced the same main conclusions. They found that the convergence rate was fast (12.7%), and about half of the regional dummy variables were significant (meaning that regions' steady state level of per capita income was estimated to be different). These results are shown in the second column of Table 4.5.1. Moreover, the Spanish regions (at NUTS 2 level) were found to be close to their steady states.

Some authors have focused on specific micro-economic mechanisms of regional convergence,[33] such as factor flows and, in particular, migrations. Regarding Spain, Bentolila and Jimeno (1995) measured the degree of regional wage and unemployment persistence in Spain. They found that 'the responses of the migration rates and participation rates to labour

---

[32]   They used a Bayesian procedure that makes it possible to estimate fixed effects.

[33]   A case in point of this type of model is that described by Parente and Prescott (1994), where, in a neoclassical framework with exogenous technological change, firms face a (country-specific) fixed cost of updating their technology.

demand shocks seem to be significantly lower than in US states and EU regions'. Although they did not point to explanations of reported pay and participation persistence, it became clear that a not well understood[34] barrier to migration might well be working and that this would explain the persistent regional differences in growth levels.

A different avenue of research has been the sectoral composition of regions. Marimon and Zilibotti (1995) pointed out that different sectors have different productivity levels. Therefore relative sector participation in the regional economy might account for heterogeneous steady states. They estimated that about half of the observed income convergence in Spanish regions was a consequence of the generalized reduction in the participation of agriculture in regional economies, which had, until recently, played a larger role in poorer regions since the 1950s. In this respect, de la Fuente (1995) showed (see Table 4.5.2) that productivity in Spanish sectors varied widely (both within and between regions) and, in particular, that agricultural productivity did not show signs of convergence across regions. Again, although these results were merely descriptive, they were very suggestive of the importance of focusing on multisector models.

A possible explanation of heterogeneous steady states is the potential influence on regional growth of regional policies such as public investments in infrastructure. This point has been examined in a number of recent papers by de la Fuente and Vives (1995), who also claimed that the long-run effect of public input on regional growth was important. Given certain assumptions, they claimed that almost 50% of the regional variation in income in Spain was due to differences in human capital and public infrastructures. Yet other studies (Garcia-Mila and Marimon (1995)) have argued that public infrastructures have little effect beyond their direct effect on the productivity of the public and construction sectors, at least in the least-developed regions. Other growth policies, such as the SMP or the Community Support Framework have not, to our knowledge, been evaluated at the regional level.

A simple and potentially useful exercise would be to repeat the estimation procedure Canova and Marcet used, but allow for structural change after, say, 1986. That is, to estimate using Spanish data regional steady states that could change before and after 1986. This would require some restrictions in order to limit the number of parameters we would need to estimate. A possibility would be to sophisticate further Canova and Marcet's Bayesian procedure using information on regions' distance (i.e. a conditional heterodastik extension). More interesting would be to introduce sectoral information. That is, to study the convergence (or lack of it) of productivity levels in sectors and regions, allowing, similarly, for structural changes after 1986.

A more ambitious project would be the structural estimation or calibration of a 'complete' (dynamic, general equilibrium) multisector model of regional growth. A number of theoretical contributions should be most helpful in this. Shioji (1995) provided a very tractable and parsimonious multisector model of regional growth. The model pointed to explicit costs (high land rents) and benefits (Lucas-type externalities) of agglomeration. Although the model was dynamic and considered general equilibrium, steady states and comparative dynamics were easily characterized.

---

[34]   A potential explanation of this barrier to factor flows might be found in the structure of collective pay bargaining.

Table 4.5.1. *ß* **convergence in Spanish CCAA (1991–95)**

	Coefficient	t	Coefficient	t
Convergence coefficient	0.0295	(4.78)	0.1273	(6.23)
Andalucia			-0.0938	(2.16)
Aragon			0.0500	(1.15)
Asturias			-0.0404	(0.92)
Baleares			0.2344	(5.36)
Canarias			0.0343	(0.77)
Cantabria			-0.0210	(0.48)
Castilla–La Mancha			-0.1554	3.54)
Castilla y Leon			-0.1067	(2.47)
Catalonia			0.1930	(4.34)
Extremadura			-0.2834	(6.44)
Galicia			-0.4036	(9.24)
Madrid			0.2985	(6.84)
Murcia			-0.0766	(1.77)
Navarra			0.1056	(2.44)
País Vasco			0.1701	(3.69)
Rioja			0.0289	(0.67)
Valencia			0.0344	(0.80)
R^2	0.758		0.1924	
s.e. regression	0.0219		0.0211	
standard deviation y_i^*			0.1753	
standard deviation y_i in 1991			0.1558	

Note: Panel data estimation. 17 observations per region.

Table 4.5.2. β convergence in product/employment

	Region		Industry		Services		Construction		Agriculture	
	Coefficient	(r)	Coefficient	(r)	Coefficient	(r)	Coefficient	(r)	Coefficient	(t)
Unconditioned										
β	0.0347	(5.29)	0.0825	(6.43)	0.0428	(4.06)	0.1952		0.0586	(3.86)
y^*	0.0000		0.1171	(4.05)	-0.0191	(0.26)	-0.1792	(11.1)	-0.6325	(7.12)
R^2	0.1128		0.1373		0.0569		0.2182		0.0527	
s.e. regression	0.0190		0.1364		0.0245		0.0478		0.0830	
Conditioned										
β	0.1252	(6.04)	0.1313	(7.38)	0.0892	(5.28)	0.2539	(8.22)	0.1800	(6.70)
Andalucia	-0.0930	(2.39)	-0.0248	(0.36)	-0.0748	(1.02)	-0.0355	(0.67)	0.0108	(0.09)
Aragon	0.486	(1.25)	0.0507	(0.72)	0.0124	(0.17)	0.0509	(0.97)	0.1355	(1.14)
Asturias	-0.0081	(0.21)	0.2332	(3.34)	-0.0217	(0.28)	-0.1191	(2.26)	-0.6179	(5.16)
Baleares	0.0958	(2.46)	-0.2052	(2.90)	0.0916	(1.20)	0.0320	(0.61)	0.0756	(0.64)
Canarias	0.0263	(0.66)	0.0622	(0.89)	-0.0182	(0.24)	0.0553	(1.05)	-0.0533	(0.45)
Cantabria	0.0208	(0.53)	0.1046	(1.47)	0.0653	(0.90)	-0.0449	(0.85)	-0.2107	(1.77)
Catalonia	0.1844	(4.60)	0.0484	(0.69)	0.1240	(1.64)	0.0269	(0.51)	0.2350	(1.98)
Castilla–La Mancha	-0.1243	(3.12)	-0.0761	(1.09)	-0.1382	(1.91)	-0.0579	(1.10)	0.1470	(1.23)
Castilla y Leon	-0.0960	(2.46)	0.0981	(1.41)	-0.867	(1.19)	-0.0295	(0.56)	-0.0729	(0.61)
Extremadura	-0.2490	(6.18)	0.0430	(0.58)	-0.2120	(2.81)	-0.0987	(1.88)	-0.1678	(1.41)
Galicia	-0.3396	(8.49)	-0.0067	(0.10)	-0.0945	(1.30)	0.0113	(2.15)	-0.6535	(5.49)
Madrid	0.2617	(6.64)	0.0936	(1.34)	0.1705	(2.27)	0.0504	(0.96)	0.0355	(0.30)
Murcia	-0.0532	(1.36)	-0.0972	(1.38)	-0.0783	(1.04)	0.0632	(1.20)	0.0714	(0.60)
Navarra	0.0909	(2.34)	-0.0439	(0.62)	0.0561	(0.78)	0.0485	(0.92)	0.4167	(3.50)
Pais Vasco	0.2022	(4.89)	0.1326	(1.86)	0.1032	(1.37)	0.0151	(0.29)	0.3195	(2.69)
Rioja	-0.002	(0.01)	-0.2590	(3.56)	0.580	(0.80)	0.0810	(1.54)	0.4168	(3.50)
Valencia	0.0327	(0.08)	-0.1536	(2.17)	0.0433	(0.58)	0.0754	(1.43)	0.0633	(0.53)
R^2	0.1975		0.2468		0.1100		0.2749		0.1800	
s.e. regression	0.0186		0.0350		0.0245		0.0474		0.0795	
standard deviation y_i^*	0.0000		0.1407		0.1191		-0.1784		-0.6904	
s.e. y_i^*	0.1493		0.1243		0.0998		0.0655		0.2921	

4.5.2. Data

FDI

The data used was that for FDI in Spanish NUTS 2 regions for the period 1988–94. The units of observation are acts of investment. The characteristics noted were the following:

(a)   nominal size of the investment in Spanish currency;
(b)   country of origin of the FDI;
(c)   sector, at NACE 3 level;
(d)   destination of the FDI at NUTS 2 level.

Also available was data on Spanish FDI abroad, which was analysed in the same way as above.

Migration

A number of statistical sources were combined (Encuesta de Población Activa – the EPA active population survey – and the Encuesta Socio-Demografica – socio-demographic survey) to best measure the flow of workers from region to region and over time. Data in the EPA active survey contained 'directed' information, i.e. they recorded the regional source and origin of the migrants. Moreover, they allowed for the separate study of migration flows for different levels of human capital of the migrants as the unit of observation was the individual included in the survey. Unfortunately, this data, with information on characteristics of migrants by level of human capital and NACE activity, was not available to us at the time we carried out our review.

Capital/labour ratio and the concentration indices

For the construction of the capital/labour ratios and the Herfindahl indices of investment and employment concentration, the main types of data sources used were as follows.

(a)   The source used to obtain the values of regional and sector stock of capital was the study by the Valencian Institute of Economic Research (IVIE, 1995), 'The stock of capital in Spain and its regions'. This study supplied historical series of the net stock of private capital by region for 1964–92, classified by branches of activity and disaggregated into 13 sectors. This disaggregation corresponded closely to the NACE 2 level of classification. The values were supplied already deflated, in millions of constant pesetas at 1990 values.
       The methodology used for the estimation of these series of stock of capital followed the permanent inventory method. This involved deriving the stock of capital from the investment series and is the method adopted by all the countries of the OECD that and of the deflators and statistical sources used for its construction, see Volume 1 of this series (European Commission, 1997).
(b)   The industrial survey drawn up by the National Statistical Institute was the source of both investment and employment series.
       For the employment series – used to find the denominator for the capital/labour ratio and as the basic input for the Herfindahl indices – the industrial survey supplied annual data for 1978–92. The Institute classified the data according to its own system and disaggregated data for industry into 89 sectors. In order to use the data, we converted

this information using the NACE 2 level of classification so as to construct the Herfindahl indices and into the 13–sector classification system used by the IVIE for the stock of capital so as to construct the capital/labour ratios.

This source was also used to construct the investment series (FBKF), necessary for the Herfindahl indices of investment concentration, and so it was also necessary to convert the data in the 89–sector classification using the NACE 2 level of classification.

Data sources for trade indicators

Regional trade data was very hard to obtain. The only source was a Customs register, compiled by the Directorate-General of Customs (DGA), which had been exploited only by a few Spanish regional governments. The main problem was that the regions, although they publish their own commercial statistics more and more, have followed *ad hoc* classifications based on NIMEXE/TARIC, as this is the classification used by the DGA, which is the primary source of information for all the regions, and, in general no regional data is included in the NACE classification.

Given these problems, we gathered only the information directly from those regions (Catalonia, the Basque country and Madrid) that compiled foreign trade statistics separately in the CNAE classification, the traditional Spanish version of the NACE system, which can be easily converted to it.[35]

The lack of CNAE-NACE data for other regions compelled us to limit the study of trade indicators to the four regions of Catalonia, the Basque country and Madrid (which contain a very high percentage of Spain's industrial production) and the aggregate 'all other regions' data was obtained from the difference between the data for these three regions and the national total (the national trade data was already classified according to the NACE system and was supplied by Eurostat).

Further, data for the above-mentioned regions was only available for the period 1988–92, although Catalonia and Madrid provided information until 1994. Madrid was a special case: its series covered the period 1990–94, so it was necessary to estimate the trade data for the period 1988–89, applying the average cumulative annual rate obtained for the interval 1990–94. This estimation may possibly have introduced some small distortion in the trade data for the aggregate 'all other regions' figure for the years 1988 and 1989. However, the main factor that may have distorted the trade data obtained for the set 'all other regions' lay in the heterogeneity of the sources used to construct the series: the national data was correctly converted from the TARIC to the NACE system by Eurostat, but the data from each of the three regions was converted to CNAE separately as each region followed its own conversion procedures.

The data for industrial production, which was necessary in order to calculate the indicators of trade creation and trade diversion, was also obtained from the industrial survey. However, when checked against other sources, it was seen to be unreliable in very few sectors, especially in NACE sector 35, automobiles, because, for reasons of statistical confidentiality, accurate information at regional level had to be witheld, given the dominance of a small number of multinationals in the output of this sector. For this reason, in the tables we have not supplied

---

[35]   The CNAE-NACE conversion was done by us, on the basis of the conversion table published by J. Gual (1993).

the regional values for these indicators but have taken as points of reference the values of the national sector indicators.

4.5.3. Indicator analysis

Spain has a productive structure with a high level of sectoral diversification. However, the regions have acquired a degree of specialization (see Table 4.5.3) and the type of specialization predominant in each of them was observed by using the stock of capital as the criterion. Also, using the percentage of capital absorbed by the four principal sectors in each region, we could get an indication of the industrial diversification of the regions: Aragon, Catalonia, Valencia, Madrid and Navarra were the most diversified and Asturias and Cantabria the least diversified, followed by Andalusia, Castilla y Leon and the Basque country.

Table 4.5.3. Regional specialization from capital stock

	Agriculture	Industry	Services
Agriculture	Castilla–La Mancha Castilla y Leon Extremadura Galicia	Aragon Cantabria La Rioja Navarra	Murcia Andalucia
Industry		Asturias País Vasco	Catalonia Valencia
Services			Baleares Canarias Madrid

When the degree of diversification was related to the trends in demand, according to the OECD classification, the results were as follows:

(a)   Catalonia, Madrid, Aragon and Navarra showed a sufficiently diversified industrial fabric, oriented towards sectors with strong or medium demand, the exception being Valencia, which showed an orientation towards sectors with weak demand.

(b)   The excessively specialized regions were Asturias and the Basque country, with an inclination towards sectors of weak demand, and Cantabria, Castilla y Leon and Andalusia inclined towards sectors of medium demand, bringing about a trend towards industrial decline in the first case rather than better chances of growth for the second group of regions.

Altogether, using a varied set of indicators to position the regions according to the type of demand for their products, their technological intensity and the productivity of the labour employed, the following features were identified:

(a)   Aragon, Catalonia, Madrid and Navarra were the regions that benefited from the type of demand for their industrial production, from the degree of technological intensity and from their comparatively high levels of labour productivity.

(b)   Rioja and Valencia were oriented towards medium- and/or weak-demand sectors, with low technological intensity and medium-high levels of labour productivity.

(c)   Castilla–La Mancha's industry had low diversification but was highly specialized in sectors of strong demand and had high technological intensity and medium-high labour productivity.

(d)   Andalusia and Murcia had little in the way of industrial specialization, but were orientated towards sectors that did not have weak demand and productivity was high.

(e)   Asturias, Cantabria and the Basque country did not show sufficient diversification, were oriented towards sectors of weak demand and had high pay costs.

(f)   Extremadura, Castilla y Leon and Galicia were regions with insufficient diversification and had the following features: there was hardly any industrial fabric, they were oriented towards sectors that did not have weak demand and productivity was high, which enabled them to absorb high pay costs, and Galicia specialized in labour-intensive industries based on using local natural resources.

(g)   The Balearic and Canary Islands had sparse industrial fabric linked to tourism and construction.

Last, it must be emphasized that the Spanish economy in general and the regions in particular have, since the 1980s, developed a notable process of structural change in their sectors, as can be observed from the evolution of the flow of factors towards the various sectors and regions. This process has not been evenly distributed and the incorporation of the Spanish economy into the EU has made it advisable to study such effects with the aim of knowing the depth of regional disparities through a more profound study of the flows of factors and various trade indicators. We found that we could underline the relative decline of regions such as Asturias, Cantabria and the Basque country, and the vitality of others such as Rioja, Navarra and Castilla–La Mancha, and even Valencia.

The SMP and factor flows: FDI and migration

FDI analysis

FDI is one of the most important mechanisms in the transmission of blueprints and know-how from foreign countries into Spain, as well as being an important engine of economic growth. It was therefore important to understand the determinants of the spatial location of FDI. In particular, for our purposes, we were interested in relating the share of FDI that a region receives to its level of development. As we were interested in capturing the effect of unobserved regional characteristics that might affect how much FDI was attracted, we measured that relationship introducing regional (and possibly also sectoral) dummy variables in a regression of the log FDI sunk in a region and NACE 2 sector in a given year over the log of total employment in that regional sector and year. The endogenous variable log of FDI was separated into two categories: FDI from the EU into a Spanish region and sector, on the one hand, and total FDI from non-EU countries into a Spanish region and sector, on the other. A dummy variable was included in the right-hand side that took the value of 1 for the EU's FDI and the value of 0 for non-EU FDI. More precisely our FDI regression was:

$$E(f_{ij}) = \sum_{i=1}^{17} \alpha_i d_i + \sum_{j=1}^{9} \beta_j s_j + \gamma x_{ij} + \delta E_{ij}$$

where f_{ij} is FDI flow in region i (there are 18 autonomous communities) and sector j.[36] d_i are regional dummies, s_j are NACE 1 level sectoral dummies, x_{ij} is the log of total employment in i and j, and E_{ij} is a dummy indicating if the origin of f_{ij} is the EU. The regional index $i = 1, \ldots$,18 corresponds to the following index of autonomous communities:

$\quad$ 1 = Andalucia
$\quad$ 2 = Aragon
$\quad$ 3 = Asturias
$\quad$ 4 = Baleares
$\quad$ 5 = Canarias
$\quad$ 6 = Cantabria
$\quad$ 7 = Castilla y Leon
$\quad$ 8 = Castilla–La Mancha
$\quad$ 9 = Catalonia
$\quad$ 10 = Valencia
$\quad$ 11 = Extremadura
$\quad$ 12 = Galicia
$\quad$ 13 = Madrid
$\quad$ 14 = Murcia
$\quad$ 15 = Navarra
$\quad$ 16 = País Vasco
$\quad$ 17 = Rioja
$\quad$ 18 = Ceuta and Melilla

A high value coefficient in a regional dummy was interpreted as a productivity premium on FDI specific to that region. The coefficients were region-specific elasticities of FDI with respect to employment, averaged over a sample of industrial sectors. Moreover, we performed this regression for two years, 1988 and 1994.

We were interested in a number of (descriptive) issues regarding this regression.

(a)$\quad$ Was there a large dispersion of regional fixed effects?

(b)$\quad$ How did the regional fixed effect relate to the development level of the region. In particular, were poorer regions more or less attractive to foreign investors? As FDI is an engine of growth, if the answer to this last question were in the affirmative, the evidence would be that FDI was working in the direction of convergence achievement, otherwise it would be working in the direction of divergence.

(c)$\quad$ What was the trend relating these regional fixed effects; were they converging themselves?

(d)$\quad$ Did FDI that originated from EU countries behave differently to FDI from non-EU countries?

The results were as follows. We observed a significant degree of heterogeneity: 5 out of 18 of the regions showed different degrees of elasticity of their FDI to total employment.

---

[36]$\quad$ To be precise, f_{ij} refers to FDI inflows in region i and sector at NACE 3 level, but dummies were defined at NACE 1 level. We intended to control partially for sectoral characteristics, but doing it at a higher level of dissagregation would cost too much in terms of degrees of freedom.

Interestingly, a region's employment had less explanatory power than did the regional dummies, although it was significant at the 5% level. FDI originating from the EU had a higher elasticity in the average region. Results with the robust procedure were qualitatively similar to (1) except that the β coefficients were restricted to be zero. Results were similar but then only two (three in the robust procedure) were significant. That is, fixed effects seemed to be more concentrated and therefore our measure of regional attractiveness showed greater homogeneity across regions.

The pattern that emerged was consistent with convergence: less attractive regions were becoming more attractive to foreign investors. However, a non-linear relationship appeared. Regions that were attracting FDI at higher rates than the rest (Madrid and Catalonia) had growth rates in fixed effects similar to those regions attracting more modest levels of investment in 1988. In summary, the great bulk of the regions showed convergence in the share of FDI they attracted, except the richest regions, which did not show signs of being caught up by the others.

For 1994, the regression results indicated, interestingly, that the average region received more FDI per employee in the specific region and sector, both from EU or non-EU countries. Moreover, only four of the regions had an elasticity that was statistically more significant than the rest of the regions. Interestingly, the coefficient on log of sectoral employment in the region was not significant at this point, i.e. regional characteristics became relatively more important in explaining which would be the recipients of FDI than this factor.

Migration analysis

An examination of the net inflow of migration into each of the 18 regions indicated that, contrary to what is often argued, Spain had registered a sizeable amount of internal migration, with an average of 160,000 individuals per year changing the region in which they resided in the period 1979–93. Interestingly, 1986 appeared in most of these graphs as a shift in the migration trend. Indeed, after 1986 it seemed that the average of the series of total migration increased markedly.

In general, the pattern for the individual regions followed what might have been expected. Poorer communities tended to have negative net inflows and vice versa. País Vasco was an exception (it expelled workers), but that was most likely due to the political climate in the region. A case in point was Navarra, which, since 1986, had been attracting a steadily growing number of migrants. In 1990, both Madrid and Catalonia showed a reversal of such a trend, when they started to move towards a negative net inflow position. The large negative net inflow values of 1993 for both of these communities was striking, and the whole shift in the trend required explanation on its own. A symmetric puzzling pattern appeared in Andalucia and Castilla–La Mancha, poorer regions that, since 1990, have registered a trend reversion towards net migrant reception.

Capital/labour ratio

Private industrial capital was highly concentrated in six regions: Catalonia, the Basque country and Valencia constituted the greatest concentrations of industry, followed by Andalusia, Castilla y Leon and Madrid. These six regions accounted for more than two thirds of Spain's industrial capital. In general, the relative shares each region had of the stock of private capital remained constant throughout the period analysed in Table 4.5.4. Nevertheless, Castilla–La Mancha, Castilla y Leon, Valencia and, above all, Extremadura showed strong growth in their industrial capital, thus increasing their share of total national private capital.

Table 4.5.4.   Regional shares of private capital stock (%)

Region	1965–75	1976–85	1986–89	1965–89
Andalucia	9.44	8.83	8.58	8.98
Aragon	3.82	3.56	3.51	3.64
Asturias	5.45	5.20	5.53	5.35
Baleares	0.85	0.91	0.87	0.88
Canarias	1.71	1.57	1.50	1.61
Cantabria	2.62	2.13	1.99	2.27
Castilla–La Mancha	3.77	4.59	5.03	4.40
Castilla y Leon	7.52	8.19	8.34	8.00
Catalunia	21.81	22.34	22.51	22.20
Extremadura	2.13	3.25	3.57	2.94
Galicia	4.90	4.8	4.81	4.85
Rioja	0.71	0.68	0.66	0.69
Madrid	8.72	8.41	8.03	8.44
Murcia	1.94	1.4	1.33	1.60
Navarra	2.02	1.99	1.92	1.98
País Vasco	13.81	12.60	12.42	12.97
Valencia	8.76	9.41	9.36	9.18

Source: IVIE.

Table 4.5.5 presents the summary of the evolution of the capital/labour ratios by region, measured in millions of constant pesetas at 1990 values, as well as the ranking from highest to lowest capital/labour values. The analysis that follows was based on the comparison of the average values of the ratio between 1978–85 and 1986–92.

All the Spanish regions, without exception, increased their capital/labour ratio values during the period 1986–92 over the average for the period 1978–85, but the following differences in the scale of the increase were notable.

(a)   In many of them, this growth was moderate, being merely a continuation of the behaviour that was already being observed in the years prior to the SMP and Spain's integration into the EU. Therefore, in the absence of a more precise econometric study, we included in this group a number of regions that did not seem to have witnessed much of an improvement in their capital/labour ratio: Aragon, Galicia, Andalusia and Castilla–La Mancha.

(b)   At the other extreme, a number of regions experienced intense growth in the values of the ratio, reflecting the notable effort of capitalization in the last years of the previous decade and the first years of the 1990s: Canarias (60%), though it continued to be the region with the lowest capital/labour ratio, Asturias (39%), Extremadura (23.5%) and Madrid (22%).

(c)   The remaining regions were in an intermediate position – the increments in the capital/labour ratio varied between Cantabria's 11% and Castilla y Leon's 16.8%. These regional differences in the evolution of the capital/labour ratio were not intense enough to modify the relative positions of the regions substantially in terms of the intensity of their capitalization. In this regional classification, four groups were distinguished:

(i) The three regions of the north coast continued to be those of greatest intensity of capitalization, due to the type of industrial specialization, which centred on heavy industry. Of the three, Asturias stood out as having the greatest increase in the capital/labour ratio, taking the first place nationwide from Cantabria.

(ii) A second group contained the regions with intermediate intensity of capitalization (with capital/labour ratio values of between 5 and 6): Andalusia, Castilla y Leon, and Navarra. Of the three, Castilla y Leon showed the most dynamic growth in its capital/labour ratio.

(iii) Most of the regions had very similar ratios, in a narrow band between 4.3 and 4.9. Among them, Madrid was the most outstanding, with a notable growth in the average value of the ratio that took it from tenth to eighth place. Notable increases were also shown by Extremadura and Rioja. Catalonia kept its previous position, with a moderate growth of its capital/labour ratio. Galicia, on the contrary, showed a notable stagnation, falling back from ninth to twelfth place.

(iv) To the last group belong the four regions with capital/labour values of less than 4 (Murcia, Castilla–La Mancha, the Balearics and the Canaries), which did not show substantial growth in intensity of capitalization.

Table 4.5.5. Ranking and impact on the capital/labour ratio

1978–85			1986–92			Change (%)
Ranking	Region	Capital/ labour	Ranking	Region	Capital/ labour	
1	Cantabria	8.5	1	Asturias	11.5	38.8
2	Asturias	8.3	2	Cantabria	9.5	11.3
3	País Vasco	6.7	3	País Vasco	8.2	23.6
4	Andalucia	5.5	4	Andalucia	5.9	7.7
5	Navarra	4.7	5	Castilla y Leon	5.4	16.8
6	Castilla y Leon	4.6	6	Navarra	5.3	12.8
7	Catalonia	4.4	7	Catalonia	4.9	12.8
8	Aragon	4.3	8	Madrid	4.7	21.8
9	Galicia	4.1	9, 10, 11	Extremadura,		23.5
10	Madrid	3.9		Rioja and		4.2
11 and 12	Valencia			Aragon	4.5	25.6
	and Extremadura	3.7	12	Galicia	4.4	7.5
13	Rioja	3.6	13	Valencia	4.3	16
14	Murcia	3.5	14	Murcia	3.6	2.9
15 and 16	Castilla–La Mancha		15	Baleares	3.4	12.7
	and Baleares	3	16	Castilla–La Mancha	3.1	16.8
17	Canarias	0.2	17	Canarias	0.3	59.2

The conclusions to be drawn from this evolution in relation to the impact of SMP are the following:

(a) To begin with, there was a growth in the capital/labour ratio that was shared by all the regions (though in some the increase was very small). An effort to capitalize and modernize the industrial fabric seemed to manifest itself in order to improve competitiveness and meet the challenges of integration into the EU. However, it was not possible, without a model to determine the factors that influenced the rise in the capital/labour ratio in the Spanish regions, to come to more precise conclusions as to the exact influence of the SMP on this process.

(b)   In fact, according to the studies conducted by IVIE (1995), the determining factor seemed to have been the recovery of economic activity after the crisis, causing strong growth of industrial capital, which showed pro cyclical behaviour:

(i)   following a period of strong growth of national private capital from 1965–75, the period of crisis had affected industrial capital very negatively;

(ii)   in the recovery period, from 1986 onwards, the fast pace of investment in the industrial sector led to general rises in the capital/labour ratio.

The best example of the relationship between economic recovery and capitalization is offered by Asturias, one of the regions where the capital/labour ratio rose most as the high growth rate of capitalization in Asturias is produced precisely by the heavy investments in the reconversion of industry and the restructuring of the steelmaking sector.

Inter-regional and intersectoral employment and investment flows

Four types of Herfindahl indices were calculated – two for employment and two for investment. In both cases they were of a sectoral and regional character.

The indices obtained and their evolution in time are shown in Tables 4.5.7–4.5.10. The tables referring to regional concentration (4.5.7 and 4.5.9) rank the regions/sectors in descending order of concentration, and sizes of changes that occurred for the whole period (1978–92) or for the subperiod 1984–92, in order to provide a comparison of the results obtained for Spain and for the other countries included in this report and for the subperiod 1985–92, as 1985, being the year immediately before Spain's accession to the EU, is a key year for analysing the structural adjustments undertaken by the Spanish regions.

Intersectoral employment flows

It can be deduced from looking at Table 4.5.6 that, in general, there was no increase in the sectoral concentration of employment in the Spanish regions after 1984–85. Most regions either presented relatively stable Herfindahl indices with small annual oscillations around a mean that did not alter significantly or showed a trend towards diversification of employment, reducing the value of the concentration index. Very few regions showed a trend towards increased concentration of employment.

In the most numerous group – that consisting of regions with a tendency towards diversification in employment – the region of Ceuta and Melilla stands out, in spite of which it continues to be the region with the highest concentration in employment. This extremely high concentration is due to the lack of industrial diversification resulting from the economic and territorial limitations of the region. The Castilla–La Mancha region experienced a similar fall in concentration (-24.5%), although it started with levels of concentration much lower than those of Ceuta and Melilla. Also outstanding for their clear trend towards diversification of industrial employment were the regions of La Rioja (-13.4%), Galicia (-13%), Aragon (-12%), and Asturias (-10.8%).

In four regions, going against the trend, there was an increase in concentration in employment for the period 1984–92 in Extremadura (12.4%), Navarra (12.3%), Cantabria (9.6%) and Murcia (5%). However, it cannot be inferred from these results that the increase in concentration of employment was due to the effects originated by economic integration and opening up to the European market. Except in Extremadura, which developed in a more irregular fashion, in the other three regions, the trend towards concentration was not a recent phenomenon, but merely the continuation of a trend that had been manifesting itself since 1978, the first year for which this data was recorded.

On the other hand, in many regions where concentration decreased, this trend towards diversification was exclusive to the second half of the 1980s – the regions had previously shown trends towards concentration. This occurred in Aragon, Asturias, the Balearics, Galicia, the Basque country and Rioja. Thus, the entry of Spain into the EU did seem to coincide with a change in the trend towards greater diversification. Nevertheless, we could not interpret this mere coincidence in time as purely an effect of entry, as, in order to reach conclusive results, it was necessary to go beyond this descriptive study and use analytical procedures.

Nevertheless, there were some regions with a trend towards diversification that did not show a change in behaviour in the second half of the 1980s, as their trend towards dispersion could be seen to have occurred from 1978, not only from 1984. These regions were the Canaries, Catalonia, Valencia and Ceuta and Melilla.

The changes that occurred in the concentration index from 1984 moderately altered the ranking of regions in terms of the degree of concentration of industrial employment. From Table 4.5.6 we drew the following conclusions.

(a)   There was a general trend towards a gradual decrease in sector concentration, common to regions starting with high levels of concentration and to regions with greater industrial dispersion.

(b)   It is the regions in Objective 1 that show higher levels of concentration of employment than the rest: the top 11 places are occupied by Objective 1 regions, excepting the Balearics (in sixth place) and Rioja (ninth). The highest degree of diversification occurred in regions excluded from Objective 1, with the exception of Valencia, which showed intense diversification, similar to that of Madrid and Catalonia, yet it was still in Objective 1.

(c)   There was no variation in the position of the four regions that had the highest sector concentrations of employment (Ceuta and Melilla, the Canaries, Extremadura and Asturias). In all of them, except Extremadura, there was a decrease in concentration. In Ceuta and Melilla and Asturias, it was notable, and it was much less intense in the Canaries.

(d)   The relative positions of the three regions that had the most diversified employment did not vary either: Catalonia continued to be the least concentrated region, followed closely by Madrid and Valencia. The absolute values of their respective Herfindahl indices hardly varied, showing, if anything, a slight trend towards yet greater diversification in employment. The greatest changes in the relative positions were produced in the regions with an intermediate degree of concentration (those in positions 5–15). In this group, three cases should be distinguished:

   (i)   regions that did not modify their relative positions: the Balearics (sixth), Castilla y Leon (tenth), and the Basque Country (twelfth), although they did experience a slight trend towards diversification;

   (ii)   four regions rose in the ranking, an increase in concentration occurring in nearly all of them: Murcia (from seventh place to fifth), Andalusia (from eighth place to seventh), Cantabria (from thirteenth to ninth) and Navarra (from fifteenth to fourteenth);

(iii) finally, four regions fell in the ranking, showing lower relative levels of concentration and significant falls in the absolute values of the Herfindahl indices, and these variations, tending towards greater dispersion, were much more intense than those shown in group (b) towards concentration: Castilla–La Mancha (from fifth place to eighth), Rioja (from ninth to eleventh), Galicia (from eleventh to thirteenth) and Aragon (from fourteenth to fifteenth).

Table 4.5.6.   The Herfindahl index of sectoral employment

CSF objective	1984			1992			Change 92/84 (%)
	Ranking	Region	HI	Ranking	Region	HI	
1	1	Ceuta and Melilla	0.390	1	Ceuta and Melilla	0.296	-24.2
1	2	Canarias	0.265	2	Canarias	0.251	-5.0
1	3	Extremadura	0.213	3	Extremadura	0.239	12.4
1	4	Asturias	0.213	4	Asturias	0.189	-10.8
1	5	Castilla–La Mancha	0.185	5	Murcia	0.178	5.0
5b, 2	6	Baleares	0.171	6	Baleares	0.164	-4.1
1	7	Murcia	0.167	7	Andalucia	0.150	-0.4
1	8	Andalucia	0.151	8	Castilla–La Mancha	0.140	-24.5
5b, 2	9	Rioja	0.136	9	Cantabria	0.135	9.6
1	10	Castilla y Leon	0.132	10	Castilla y Leon	0.132	0.2
1	11	Galicia	0.130	11	Rioja	0.117	-13.4
5b, 2	12	País Vasco	0.123	12	País Vasco	0.115	-6.3
1	13	Cantabria	0.123	13	Galicia	0.115	-13.0
5b, 2	14	Aragon	0.111	14	Navarra	0.113	12.3
5b, 2	15	Navarra	0.101	15	Aragon	0.097	-12.5
1	16	Valencia	0.070	16	Valencia	0.093	-4.0
5b, 2	17	Madrid	0.091	17	Madrid	0.089	-1.2
5b, 2	18	Catalonia	0.088	18	Catalonia	0.084	-3.2

Inter-regional employment flows

In this case, the Herfindahl index measured the concentration of regional employment in sectors of the NACE 2 classification for the period 1978-92. An increase in the values of such regional indices reflected a higher concentration of employment in the corresponding sectors.

The results are included in Table 4.5.7 and, in general, the previous conclusions regarding the sector Herfindahl index were ratified: employment did not tend towards regional concentration. On the contrary, regional dispersion of employment increased in most sectors. Of the 19 sectors shown, only in 6 did employment concentration increase, the behaviour of the chemicals sector (22/26) standing out with a growth of 22.5 points. In the 13 others, it was dispersed among the regions; in this sense the office materials sector (33) was the most outstanding, with a decrease of 38.8 points in its concentration.

With regard to the effects of the SMP, in the light of the evolution of the Herfindahl indices, it cannot be affirmed that the SMP directly affected the phenomenon of dispersion or concentration shown in the case of each sector as, except for the non-metallic minerals sector (23) and the chemicals sector (25/26), the behaviour was quite irregular, maintaining the same trend as for the previous period.

The ranking showed that it was in the metallic minerals sector (22), office materials and machinery (33) and the textile industry (43) that employment was more concentrated in certain regions, with very little variation during the period studied, the three first places staying the same. In turn, the sectors with regionally most disperse employment also maintained their position as the last five sectors in the ranking – food, beverages and tobacco (41/2), non-metallic minerals (23), wood, cane and cork (46), non-metallic minerals (24), and clothing and footwear (45), did not change their situation of concentration in the regions as a whole.

More particularly, it can be concluded that those sectors that showed concentration of employment did not, in general, alter their position in the ranking that figured in Table 4.5.7. Except for the leather sector (44), which improved by moving from tenth place to seventh, the others remained the same in the regional order of concentration.

There were no outstanding features among the sectors where employment showed a tendency to disperse, except in the cases of mechanical engineering (32) and rubber and plastics (48), indices of which evolved in opposite directions, and, although both had negative variation rates, the first went down in the ranking while the second went up.

Intersectoral investment flows

As occurred with industrial employment, the trend in most of the Spanish regions was a decrease in the concentration of industrial investment, as shown in Table 4.5.8 when, in each region, the average of the sectoral Herfindahl index for the period 1978–85 was compared with the same average for 1986–92, in 12 of the 18 Spanish regions its value decreased.[37] A trend towards diversification of industrial investment was therefore seen, which was more marked than that registered in employment (however, employment concentration indices were normally lower than those for investment).

Although the trend was general, the fall in the index did not occur in all regions to such an extent as to indicate an unequivocal structural change.

(a) The regions that most strongly reduced the concentration of sectoral investment were the Balearics (-30%), the Basque country (-25%), Aragon and Ceuta and Melilla (-20%), and Murcia (-15%). In seven other regions, the concentration index was also reduced, but to a lesser extent.

(b) Despite the general trend towards diversification, the concentration of investment increased significantly in three regions:

(i) The greatest variations occurred in Extremadura and Asturias, with an increase in the Herfindahl index of around 50%. These regions had started out with higher levels of concentration, so the situation of economic growth in the late 1980s and the process of opening up and liberalization abroad had a heavy impact on the sectoral distribution of investment, intensifying further in these regions levels of concentration that traditionally were already very high (in Asturias, due to the type of industrial specialization, it was concentrated in the mining and metal transformation sectors, and in Extremadura, because it was one of the least-

---

[37] Due to the great annual variability of sectoral Herfindahl indexes for investment, the comparison of the average values for the periods before and after entry offered more accurate information than simply taking the variation rate from the initial year to the final year.

developed regions, lacking, therefore, a diversified industrial structure).

(ii) Catalonia also appreciably increased its index of investment concentration, but, unlike the two previous regions, it started, as well as Madrid, with the lowest levels of concentration, as these were regions with a more diversified industrial structure.

(iii) Three other regions did not show significant changes in the concentration of industrial investment: Valencia and Madrid were the regions with the highest degree of diversification, and the Canaries, at the opposite extreme, had high levels of concentration that were only exceeded by Extremadura and Asturias.

Table 4.5.7. The Herfindahl index of regional employment

Sector	Ranking		
	1978	1984	1992
22	1	1	1
33	3	3	3
43	2	2	2
37	4	4	4
34	6	6	6
25/26	5	5	5
49	8	8	8
47	9	9	9
32	11	11	11
35	12	12	12
44	7	7	7
48	10	10	10
31	14	14	14
36	13	13	13
45	15	15	15
24	16	16	16
46	17	17	17
23	18	18	18
41/42	19	19	19

Sector	Change (%) 1978–92	Change (%) 1984–92	Change (%) 1985–92
22	-1.3	-1.0	-0.5
23	15.3	2.8	-0.4
24	7.6	6.2	6.3
25/26	22.5	22.3	27.4
31	-14.3	-16.9	-17.3
32	-11.2	-15.3	-14.1
33	-38.8	21.5	34.7
34	-11.1	-9.7	-9.1
35	-11.2	-5.3	-2.8
36	-7.0	-12.5	-11.3
37	0.1	-4.4	-3.2
41/42	7.6	7.8	4.3
43	-5.4	1.0	3.0
44	13.7	13.4	18.0
45	-11.8	-2.6	-9.4
46	-1.2	5.9	6.4
47	-1.6	3.1	9.1
48	-4.9	-6.2	3.4
49	-10.4	-11.2	-2.9

Table 4.5.8.   The Herfindahl index of sectoral investment

1978–85 average			1986–92 average			Change (%)
Ranking	Region	HI	Ranking	Region	HI	
1	Ceuta and Melilla	0.477	1	Asturias	0.513	45.7
2	Canarias	0.412	2	Extremadura	0.442	53.3
3	Asturias	0.352	3	Canarias	0.425	3.2
4	Baleares	0.293	4	Ceuta and Melilla	0.382	-20
5	Extremadura	0.289	5	Baleares	0.206	-29.9
6	Andalucia	0.195	6	Andalucia	0.181	-6.9
7	Murcia	0.191	7	Castilla y Leon	0.171	-10.3
8	Castilla y Leon	0.191	8	Rioja	0.168	-11.6
9	Rioja	0.190	9	Castilla–La Mancha	0.162	-13
10	País Vasco	0.188	10	Murcia	0.162	-15
11	Castilla–La Mancha	0.186	11	Cantabria	0.155	-16.6
12	Cantabria	0.186	12	Navarra	0.142	-6.5
13 and 14	Navarra/Aragon	0.152	13	País Vasco	0.140	-25.5
15	Galicia	0.137	14	Catalonia	0.139	22.4
16	Valencia	0.114	15	Galicia	0.128	-6.7
17	Catalonia	0.114	16	Aragon	0.122	-19.6
18	Madrid	0.112	17	Valencia	0.115	1.8
			18	Madrid	0.115	2.5

The changes observed did not significantly alter the ranking of regions by degree of concentration, given the relationship existing between the Herfindahl index of investment and the regional productive structure, which rarely adjusted in such a short time.

(a)   The five regions with the most concentrated investment continued to be the same ones, although there have been changes among them: Asturias and Extremadura took the first places from the Canaries and Ceuta and Melilla.

(b)   At the other extreme, Madrid was still the region with the most diversified industrial investment, now accompanied by Valencia. Catalonia, while still one of the most diversified regions, no longer showed index figures as close to those of Madrid, so that now Galicia and Aragon presented diversification of industrial investment greater even than that of Catalonia.

(c)   The intermediate regions remained very stable in their relative positions. The only movement of note was the change in the positions of Murcia and the Basque country. Both regions moved away from the top places in the ranking because they increased the diversification of investment notably.

To sum up, the influence of the SMP and the opening up of the Spanish economy on sectoral investment flows seemed to be positive, though it was not decisive. At all events, there was a majority trend towards decreased sectoral concentration of industrial investment. The differential regional impacts (strong growth of concentration in three regions and a notable increase in diversification in five of them) were not sufficiently heavy to substantially alter the regional ranking of sectoral concentration.

Inter-regional investment flows

Table 4.5.9 includes the results of the Herfindahl index that measures the concentration of regional investment. From them it can be observed that, in general, there was a parallelism between investment and employment in that, once again, the sectors of metals (22), office materials and machinery (33) and the textile industry (43) showed greater concentration for both variables.

Table 4.5.9. The Herfindahl index of regional investment

Sector	Ranking		
	1978	1984	1992
22	1	1	1
43	2	3	2
33	3	2	5
37	4	4	4
25/26	5	6	6
49	6	7	8
44	7	5	7
47	8	9	9
31	9	12	12
32	10	11	13
34	11	8	11
48	12	10	15
41/42	13	19	18
45	14	14	17
24	15	17	14
46	16	18	10
35	ND	15	3
36	ND	13	16
23	ND	16	19

Sector	Change (%) 1978–92	Change (%) 1984–92	Change (%) 1985–92
22	5.1	-4.1	-4.7
23	ND	-36.4	-49.7
24	28.3	5.0	29.5
25/26	7.7	30.1	17.8
31	-19.6	-4.8	-18.6
32	-18.0	-15.2	-24.4
33	-22.7	-55.9	-1.0
34	-3.9	-17.9	-29.7
35	ND	141.8	168.9
36	ND	-6.4	-27.0
37	11.1	28.7	-5.6
41/42	-21.4	20.3	14.9
43	20.1	66.6	45.7
44	1.6	17.9	7.8
45	11.2	-11.9	-21.5
46	92.9	66.0	100.2
47	-11.9	-3.5	51.5
48	-9.6	-22.0	-14.6
49	-25.1	-7.5	-14.0

In this case, the indices also revealed that the metals sector (22) showed the greatest regional concentration among the sectors, with values for its index very close to the maximum (0.989 in 1986). However, Spain's entry into the single market caused this concentration to decrease with the arrival of more investment to the regions in general. The trend of the office materials and machinery (33) sector was of the same type, even though, after a period of concentration until the years 1983–84, its subsequent dispersion caused it to fall to fifth place in the classification shown in Table 4.5.8.

In general terms, it can be emphasized that, just as for employment, a predominance of regional dispersion was observed in the case of investment, though both trends appeared to be quite level as dispersion covered ten sectors and concentration nine. In this sense, the sector that most increased its concentration was wood, cane and cork (46), and investment was most dispersed among the regions in the sector of other manufacturing industries (49).

The effect on investment of Spain's entry into the single market was different in different sectors, making it difficult to make general statements about its results. Heavy regional concentration took place in sectors such as vehicles and components (35), with 168.9 points, or in wood, cane and cork (46), with 100.2. The electronic material (37) and chemical products (25/26) sectors would also be included here. However, for others, the entry into the single market meant that investment was directed towards a wider spectrum of regions, thus allowing dispersion, as in the case of the office materials and machinery sector (33), with negative variation of its indices.

Trade flow indicators

The following trade flow indicators have been calculated (see also Chapter 3, Table 3.1):

M_{ei}/C_i, X_{ei}/Q_i: we generally refer to these as indicators of 'internal trade creation', even though an increase of these indicators may be due for M_{ei}/C_i to trade diversion from 'outside' to EU suppliers, and for X_{ei}/Q_i, to trade diversion from 'outside' to Spanish suppliers by other EU countries;
M_{oi}/C_i, X_{oi}/Q_i: we generally referred to these as indicators of 'trade diversion' or 'external creation of trade';
Grubel-Lloyd index (to measure IIT);
specialization index (SI);
RCA index.

Madrid

Specialization index (SI)

The region of Madrid presented high SI figures for exports in leather and leather goods (44), non-metalliferous minerals (23), other means of transport (36), office and machinery (33) and instrument engineering (37). All of them experienced a significant fall in the value of this index during the years covered by the sample (1988–92), which saw the simultaneous action of the liberalizing impact of the SMP and the intense process of the opening up of the Spanish economy after its entry into the EU. The fall in the value of the index was very sharp in the office materials and machinery (33) sector, followed by leather goods (44) and other means of transport (36), although Madrid's exports continued to be notably specialized in these types of products, more so than the EU average (the SI of these sectors was still over 100).

On the other hand, the SMP and the opening up of the Spanish economy had a positive influence on the SI value of five sectors that, though less outstanding than those just mentioned, also presented high SI values (between 100 and 150 approximately). These were the manufacture of metal articles (31), mechanical engineering (32), motor vehicles (35) sectors and, above all, the electrical machinery (34) and paper and graphic arts (47) sectors.

Lastly, the liberalizing impact was also very positive on the specialization of the metals (22), timber and wooden furniture (46), other manufacturing industries (49) and non-metallic mineral products (24) sectors. All of them have in common low indices of specialization. Although in these years the value of the SI increased notably in all of them, the increase was not enough to reach SI values close to 100. The only exception was the non-metallic mineral products (24) sector, the SI of which rose from 81.3 in 1988 to 197 in 1992.

In conclusion, the SMP and Spain's entry into the EU did seem to have caused a significant, though not spectacular, impact on the specialization pattern of Madrid's exports. This impact manifested itself in different ways in three groups of sectors. There was:

(a)   a notable reduction in the high SI values of the sectors in which Madrid was most specialized;

(b)   an improvement in the indices of sectors that were already beginning to stand out in their export specialization in previous years, sectors characterized by dynamic demand and a medium-high technology content;

(c)   an increase in the SI also of sectors in which Madrid was not, or not very, specialized.

Table 4.5.10. Madrid's trade indicators change 92/88

NACE 2	RCA	IIT	Specialization index	Trade creation (Xie/Qi)	Trade creation (Mei/Ci)	Trade diversion (Moi/Ci)	Trade diversion (Xoi/Qi)
22	48.1	182.0	32.6	98.0	-35.9	112.4	-28.6
23	4.7	-17.5	-20.8	-21.6	-40.5	-67.8	-15.8
24	43.1	85.7	31.5	30.0	-34.2	-27.1	9.1
25	0.9	1.9	18.9	42.7	28.5	8.2	21.0
31	8.7	25.5	4.9	30.5	1.9	21.4	61.4
32	28.6	92.7	19.8	32.1	-8.9	-1.3	62.4
33	-62.0	-73.6	-80.4	-84.6	-3.7	-21.1	426.0
34	15.4	26.5	33.6	-56.3	-32.5	-19.5	357.4
35	31.8	67.8	7.8	n.d.	n.d.	n.d.	n.d.
36	19.8	37.1	-43.1	65.5	37.6	-33.7	-17.4
37	-9.6	-28.6	-21.3	-90.5	-14.3	-10.6	-73.9
41-42	-9.9	-27.9	-21.5	2.0	40.1	-15.8	-13.4
43	0.8	5.2	22.2	15.6	-5.5	25.6	165.8
44	-154.6	20.7	-43.1	-43.4	3.4	287.3	1327.4
45	4.5	41.4	-14.9	34.2	-16.0	83.1	-49.7
46	14.1	39.9	35.1	83.4	22.8	-1.2	80.7
47	24.4	43.3	38.5	40.9	-7.1	-22.0	0.1
48	5.1	19.0	12.6	37.3	7.3	53.1	46.1
49	53.9	118.7	37.0	238.5	-29.2	260.6	27.4
Total	11.4	23.8	0.0	-15.9	-20.2	-14.3	16.8

RCA index

Of all the regions presented, Madrid was the one with the greatest growth in the competitiveness of its sectors. In the period analysed, it showed improvement in its disadvantaged situation, given that only four sectors showed weakness, their situation worsening, specifically the office materials and machinery (33), instrument engineering (37), food, beverages and tobacco (41-42) and leather goods (44) sectors. This last sector passed from a situation of positive comparative advantage in 1988, regional exports having exceeded imports, to the opposite situation, the trade indicator reflecting a result of -154.6%.

The remaining sectors, despite negative RCAs, improved their competitiveness, though they continued to be weak. Office materials and machinery (33), footwear and clothing (45), textiles and clothing (43) and instrument engineering (37) were confirmed as least competitive. It should also be mentioned that Madrid had a clear advantage in a single sector – non-metallic minerals (23) – which it preserved and even improved throughout the period. This good behaviour ratified for this region the fact that it was not one of the sectors included as sensitive in its commercial results to entry into the EU, and so it did not appear in Table 4.5.11. The vulnerability of the office materials and machinery (33) and instrument engineering (37) sectors was confirmed and, contrary to expectations, textiles and clothing (43) and footwear and clothing (45), considered initially as sectors of weak demand, were found to be competitively strong.

To sum up, the impact of liberalization improved the particular situation of each of the sectors included in our analysis, as index values rose in 78% of cases as a result of higher preference in the sales destination of such products for Member States.

Table 4.5.11. Competitive position of Spain's sensitive sectors

NACE code	Sector	Demand intensity
	Vulnerable competitive position	
24 (247)	Glass industry	Weak
25	Chemical industry	Strong
32	Mechanical engineering	Medium
33	Data processing machinery	Strong
34	Telecommunications	Strong
36	Other means of transport	Medium
37	Medical and surgical instruments	Medium
42 (427)	Beer	Medium
(428)	Non-alcoholic beverages	Strong
49 (493)	Photographic instruments	Strong
	Medium competitive position	
36 (361)	Shipment building	Medium
42 (421)	Chocolate and confectionery	Medium
43 (438)	Rugs and carpets	Weak
49 (491)	Jewelry	Medium
	Strong competitive position	
24 (248)	Ceramics and tile industry	Weak
34 (341)	Electric wires	Strong
(346)	Electrical appliances	Medium
35	Car industry	Strong
42 (425)	Wine	Medium
43	Cotton and wool textiles	Weak
45	Footwear and clothing	Weak
48 (481)	Rubber	Weak
49 (494)	Toys and sportswear	Weak

IIT

The construction of a Grubel-Lloyd index using a database with such a high level of aggregation (the figures were only to two digits) caused substantial limitations when we tried to obtain definitive conclusions as to the model of specialization followed in each region. For this reason, this first analysis has been restricted to merely underlining the behaviour of those sectors that stood out from the rest, such remarks being introductory in relation to a series of features that will be described via the other trade indicators dealt with here.

In the case of Madrid, in most sectors the value of the IIT index increased. Leather goods (44) stood out in this sense as it showed higher results in absolute terms, leading one to think intra-industry specialization had occurred in this particular sector. The sectors in which this type of model of specialization seemed to have lost importance during the period 1988–92 were metals (22), office materials and machinery (33), food, beverages and tobacco (41–42), which presented a lower index and the change experienced was of a negative character.

Static effects: trade creation and trade diversion

With the aim of analysing the probable presence of static effects deriving from the SMP and from Spain's entry into the EU, we constructed the four indicators proposed in the methodological part of this project.

(a)   *Mei/Ci* The aim of this ratio was to measure, approximately, the effect of the internal creation of trade, although it could only provide a very simplistic valuation of it. As we only studied the behaviour that in fact took place and there was no analytical model for this part of the study, at least two types of problems occurred to limit its explanatory and informative power:

   (i)   this indicator only showed whether or not the proportion of EU imports had risen, but did not enable us to differentiate what part of the increase was due to the trade creation effect (the substitution of home production by imports from a member country) and what part to the mere substitution of imports previously made from third countries (trade diversion effect), i.e. the total increase in the ratio included, as well as the internal trade creation effect, the possible diversion effect;

   (ii)   even supposing that the value of the ratio showed only the trade creation effect, it was not possible to distinguish what part of the increase in the share of imports in apparent consumption was due to the so-called 'production effect' (creation of trade caused by the substitution of goods previously produced internally by imports from member countries) and what part was due to the 'consumption effect' (creation of trade with member countries due to the net increase in apparent total consumption in the region; this increase in consumption was produced by the process of integration itself, by lowering internal prices).

(b)   *Moi/Ci* This enabled the presence of trade diversion to be detected if the variation of the ratio was negative, but, at the same time, a positive variation would indicate the existence of external trade creation, i.e. the increase in the share of non-EU imports following the process of liberalization within the EU. In the case of Spain, two important factors could have given rise to external creation of trade and, thus, would have substantially compensated for the possible diversion effect.

   (i)   Spain's entry into the EU meant adapting the country's protective tariff to the common external tariff (CET), which, in general, imposed lower duties than those previously applied by Spain, so that entry also led to liberalization with regard to third countries. *Ex post* studies on the effects of entry on Spain confirmed a high degree of external creation of employment as against a low volume of trade diversion for most of the big industrial sectors analysed (Martinez Mongay *et al.*, 1991; Roca, 1994).

(ii)   The SMP may also have stimulated the penetration of imports from third countries by means of the elimination of technical barriers. This stimulus only occurred if the elimination of barriers came about as a result of harmonization of technical norms and not through mutual recognition, as harmonization implies eliminating the segmentation of European markets, allowing firms from third countries to work with longer production runs and take advantage of economies of scale themselves, making them more competitive in European markets.

(c)   *Xei/Qi* and *Xoi/Qi* The increased share of Spanish products exported to the EU (EU export propensity) cannot be attributed simply to a trade creation effect, as echoing what occurred with the ratio *Mei/Ci*, such an increase may also have been due to the change of supplier country made by its EU customers, who stopped importing from a third country to the benefit of Spanish producers, in which case this would have been trade diversion (diversion from the point of view of the EU country, not from that of the Spanish region).

Internal trade creation effect

In the case of the Madrid region, there was a very significant rise in the ratio *Xei/Qi*, for nearly all the sectors analysed, outstanding among them being the increase in other manufacturing (49), metal products (22), wooden furniture (46) and other means of transport (36). Only instrument engineering (37), electrical machinery (34), leather goods (44) and office materials and machinery (33) showed a negative evolution of export share. Consequently, the opening up to the EU seemed to have affected the export propensity of firms in the Madrid region favourably.

The behaviour observed regarding imports contrasted with that concerned with exports: the share of industrial imports coming from the EU fell during the period analysed for all sectors. In 11 of the 18 sectors analysed, the value of the ratio decreased, so that, contrary to expectations, liberalization did not seem to have caused a generalized trade creation effect.

The shrinking in the share of EU imports was very intense in non-metallic minerals (23), metals (22) and non-metallic mineral products (24). However, four sectors greatly increased their share of imports, so that in them there was indeed creation of trade: chemicals (25), other means of transport (36), wooden furniture (46) and, above all other sectors, food, beverages and tobacco (41–42). The strong impact experienced by the food, drink and tobacco (41–42) sectors in the Madrid region was completely congruent with what happened in Spain as a whole, as these sectors had traditionally been heavily protected and therefore were very sensitive to the liberalization process. Trade creation, though not on the same scale, was also detected in the rubber and plastics (48), leather goods (44) and manufacture of metal articles (31) sectors.

To conclude, the impact of liberalization on the share of imports was very uneven. Although some sectors experienced a high increase in EU imports, others showed a clear trend towards a decrease in their share of EU imports. At any rate, it is possible that this decrease was not caused by the process of the opening up of trade.

Diversion effect and external creation of trade

On analysis of the effects generated by Spain's integration and the SMP on non-EU imports, three differentiated groups of sectors appeared.

(a)   Many sectors showed a shrinking in their share of non-EU imports (their *Moi/Ci* ratio), although it could not be inferred therefrom that such a shrinking was due in all cases to trade diversion. In several of these sectors, their share of EU imports also shrank, so it would be incorrect to affirm that the decrease in imports from the rest of the world was substituted by EU imports. This occurred in the non-metallic minerals (23), non-metallic mineral products (24) and electrical machinery (34) sectors, which reduced their share of imports from any origin. Office materials and machinery (33) and paper, printing and publishing (47) also reduced both ratios, but the reduction in their share of imports from third countries was much greater than that of EU imports.

(b)   Clear signs of trade diversion were presented only by those sectors in which, simultaneously, the *Moi/Ci* ratio shrank and the *Mei/Ci* ratio grew. The sectors that showed trade diversion according to this criterion were other means of transport (36) and food, beverages and tobacco (41–42). There were also signs of a small diversion of trade in the mechanical engineering (32) and other means of transport (36) sectors.

(c)   The share of imports from third countries increased in the other sectors so that, in the absence of a more rigorous analytical model to offer an alternative explanation for this phenomenon, we concluded that, in those sectors, an external trade creation effect had been produced. The increase was very great in the leather goods (44) and other manufacturing industries (48) sectors, and also fairly high in footwear and clothing (45) and rubber and plastics (48). This result agreed with the overall estimations of static effects for the whole of Spain and was, in large part, a response to the causal factors set out above, especially to the reduction in protectionist barriers against third countries in relatively labour-intensive sectors, where the competition of developing countries made itself felt.

Overall conclusions for the Madrid region

The results obtained for Madrid showed us a region with net importing sectors, as reflected by the negative values of the RCA indices. However, incorporation into the single market improved their competitiveness, which was also shown by the evolution of this indicator. Nevertheless, the office materials and machinery (33), instrument engineering (37), food, beverages and tobacco (41–42) and even leather goods (44) sectors were weakened by the process, thus ratifying the expectations of vulnerability anticipated in the study carried out previously by the Commission (Buigues *et al.* 1990).

The effects of internal trade creation were intense, but concentrated on a relatively small number of sectors (food, beverages and tobacco, the chemical industry, transport materials). In other sectors, on the contrary, the weight of EU imports in apparent consumption fell. Exports reacted strongly to liberalization, notably increasing the propensity to export to the EU. The combined analysis of import and export behaviours showed, in the absence of the study of other indicators and of regression analysis, that, in general, the industry of Madrid seemed to have responded favourably to the challenge of liberalization in that it maintained and increased its presence in EU markets at the same time as it safeguarded its home market, preventing massive penetration by EU imports (except in 'sensitive' sectors where the penetration of both EU and non-EU imports was intense).

Finally, it should be underlined that, for the sectors analysed, as a whole, there was a predominant fall in the share of third-country suppliers, even though in certain sectors this could not be fully attributed to a trade diversion effect.

Catalonia

Specialization index

Catalan exports mainly concentrated in the non-metallic mineral products (24), chemical (25), mechanical engineering (32) and motor vehicles and parts (35) sectors. In 1988, it was also highly specialized in traditional sectors, such as textiles and clothing (43), leather goods (44), footwear and clothing (45) and paper, printing and publishing (47) sectors. The years when the SMP was being set in motion and Spain's integration into the EU was complete were characterized by significant changes in traditional specialization.

(a)   The behaviour of these sectors, which accounted for 70% of total industrial exports, was divergent:

  (i)   in the traditional sectors of textiles and clothing (43), and leather goods, footwear and clothing (44–45), the specialization index decreased notably, though it was still above the EU average, i.e. these sectors still had specialization indices above 100;

  (ii)   the chemicals industry (25) continued to occupy first place, due to its high specialization index, but showed a slightly decreasing trend;

  (iii)   on the other hand, the motor vehicles and parts (35) and mechanical engineering (32) sectors, both catalogued as being in high demand, maintained and even improved their specialization indices, mainly motor vehicles and parts (35).

(b)   The impact of the opening up of Europe also originated structural adjustments in the exports of sectors that had started off with low levels of specialization.

  (i) The specialization index fell sharply for the office materials and machinery (33) sector, which had already started with very low values, and for the food, beverages and tobacco (41–42), other means of transport (36) and manufacture of metal articles (31) sectors.

The opening up of the Catalan economy originated, on the other hand, an increase in the specialization of exports in the electrical machinery (34), metals (22), and rubber and plastics (48) sectors. The electrical machinery (34) sector deserves special attention: it contained sensitive and vulnerable products, and at the same time other products situated a priori in a good competitive position. In the case of Catalonia, unlike what happened in other Spanish regions, the increase in the export specialization of the electrical machinery (34) sector was due to the favourable competitive evolution of the products that, a priori, were considered vulnerable at the national level (electronic materials, radios, televisions and telecommunications and while electrical machinery and materials, which apparently had greater potential according to Table 4.5.11, did not experience any improvement in their RCA. As a consequence of this favourable evolution, Catalonia stood at a level of specialization in the electrical machinery (34) sector that was very similar to the European average – a sector of high capitalization and technological intensiveness.

As a result of these changes, in Catalonia, an increase in specialization in sectors of high or medium demand – mechanical engineering (32), electrical machinery (34), motor vehicles and parts (35) and paper, printing and publishing (47) – was occurring to the detriment of traditional sectors that had, up until that point, had high specialization indices. Consequently, the evolution of this indicator showed signs that, in Catalonia, there was a strategy of intra-industry adjustment that was more marked than it was in other regions and one of de-specialization in sectors in which it seemed to enjoy high comparative advantages, which, above all, were in the textiles and clothing (43) and leather goods, footwear and clothing (44–45) sectors.

Table 4.5.12. Catalonia's trade indicators change 92/88

NACE 2	RCA	IIT	Specialization index	Trade creation (Xie/Qi)	Trade creation (Mei/Ci)	Trade diversion (Moi/Ci)	Trade diversion (Xoi/Qi)
22	5.9	12.0	33.4	143.0	89.5	-51.1	4.
23	6.5	24.0	13.3	32.5	9.1	-30.9	7.
24	-63.2	-7.1	-4.6	33.7	49.6	-37.6	-30.
25-26	-31.9	-13.9	-6.9	36.7	70.0	-50.3	-33.
31	-138.4	-20.4	-8.7	60.1	119.4	-9.0	-31.
32	-14.2	-9.1	4.2	59.6	79.7	-45.8	1.
33	-43.0	-29.7	-49.7	-9.2	6.0	-14.8	-81.
34	25.8	5.3	37.9	109.8	102.2	-30.3	-42.
35	-51.6	42.6	26.7	-99.6	-108.6	-100.9	-100.
36	-42.6	-11.4	-16.2	652.7	596.2	779.3	679.
37	-7.2	-11.3	4.1	270.0	156.7	13.5	125.
41-42	14.1	12.0	-21.3	74.9	49.7	-30.5	-19.
43	-135.7	14.2	-14.8	64.2	139.5	55.8	-33.
44-45	-159.2	26.6	-25.1	11.5	79.3	12.1	5.
47	-93.5	-17.2	3.5	16.1	56.1	-34.9	-11.
48	-153.9	-11.8	17.4	64.7	97.2	-26.7	-27.
46-49	-1304.5	-27.9	-6.6	65.1	93.1	1.3	8.
Total	-53.4			60.2	77.2	-37.6	-26.

RCA

The manufacturing sectors of Catalonia were in a weak competitive situation against Europe during the period studied as, except for the vehicles sector (35), all sectors produced negative results. However, in this single case of clear comparative advantage, the change experienced during the period indicated that it was losing its advantage because a greater number of European products were being bought. This led to a decline in IIT, as reflected in the previous section, so that this RCA indicator corroborated the predominance and growing trend of this specialization.

The manufacture of metal articles (31) sector was one of the sectors that showed greatest loss of competitiveness in this region. However, its initial comparative disadvantage led to a decrease in its intra-industrial specialization, inter-industrial trade predominating with comparative advantage for other members of the EU.

Mention should be made of the textiles and clothing (43) and leather goods, footwear and clothing (44–45) sectors, which both lost their advantage during the period 1991–92, but as they were sectors where demand was strong, they managed to recover. In the first case, this occurred immediately – a real example of a traditional industry that was sensitive to the effects of entry into the single market. Its thorough modernization led to improved competitiveness, which was reflected in the RCA indices. It managed to recover its initial comparative advantage without renouncing trade in similar products with other European countries, raising its IIT indices. However, the leather goods, footwear and clothing (44–45) sectors, despite their recovery, which was also immediate, did not manage to recover their initial comparative advantage altogether.

Finally, we concluded from the RCA indicator that Catalonia held a position of disadvantage in its manufacturing sectors compared with other EU countries, and, although its competitive situation improved, this was only in a limited number of sectors with strong demand.

IIT

For this indicator, in general, Catalonia showed high values. Specifically, 3 of its 17 sectors had values of over 70%. Nevertheless, along with the Basque country, this region had the greatest number of sectors that had experienced negative growth during the period 1988–92.

In the light of their results, the electrical machinery (34), non-metallic mineral products (24) and rubber and plastics (48) sectors showed the highest levels of intra-industrial specialization. However, the motor vehicles and parts (35) and leather goods, footwear and clothing (44–45) sectors developed this type of trade most in the years analysed, confirming expectations that they would be sectors sensitive to the changes due to entry into the single market, but they did so in a strongly competitive way.

Static effects

In the period analysed, there was a substantial increase in the proportion of Catalan exports to the EU, with an average rise in the *Xie/Qi* ratio of more than 60%. This increase in EU export propensity affected all types of NACE 2 sectors. The only one that showed a slight decreasing trend was the office materials and machinery (33) sector, which behaved as expected as it was classified among the sectors that were sensitive and vulnerable to entry into Europe and experienced a substantial fall in its RCA, IIT and specialization indices. Nevertheless, exports in this sector showed much more negative behaviour with respect to third countries than to the EU.

The other means of transport (36) sector was the one that intensified exports to the EU most in relation to production, followed at some distance by the instrument engineering (37), electrical machinery (34) and metals (22) sectors. These sectors were also those that most increased the EU's share of their imports in terms of apparent consumption. Therefore, it can be affirmed that these seemed to have been the sectors most affected by internal liberalization as the elimination of barriers caused an increase in EU trade in both directions.

Within the sectors that suffered the greatest impact in terms of exports to the EU, two groups could be distinguished, as growth in the *Xei/Qi* indicator was not always accompanied by a reduction in the share of exports going to third countries (*Xoi/Qi*).

(a)   In the first group, which contained most of the NACE 2 sectors, the discriminatory opening in favour of the member countries caused an increase in the share of exports going to the EU, at the expense of a reduction in the importance of customers from third countries. They were therefore sectors that combined positive variations in the Xei/Qi indicator with negative variations in the Xoi/Qi indicator. Within this group, three levels of intensity of this phenomenon were distinguished:

(i)   the electrical machinery (34) sector represented the most extreme case;

(ii)   the manufacture of metal articles (31), food, beverages and tobacco (41–42), textiles and clothing (43), paper, printing and publishing (47) and rubber and plastics (48) sectors were at an intermediate level;

(iii)   the non-metallic mineral products (24) and chemicals (25) sectors also increased their EU export propensity, though, at rates approaching 30%, these were lower than those of the previous levels.

Altogether, most NACE 2 sectors of Catalonia belonged to this group, causing a clear reorientation of Catalan exports to the EU market at the expense of third countries.

(b)   The two sectors with the greatest increase in the Xei/Qi indicator also increased their share of exports to the non-EU market, the other means of transport (36) and instrument engineering (37) sectors. Therefore, the increase in the Xei/Qi should not be interpreted as a pure effect of creation of trade with the EU, induced by the SMP or Spain's entry into the EU, but as forming part of a trend towards improvement of the overall export propensity of the sector.

The strong increase in the share of exports going to the EU was accompanied by a generalized internal trade creation effect with regard to imports as all the NACE 2 sectors, without exception, increased their relative weight of EU imports in the apparent consumption of Catalonia.

(a)   The electrical machinery (34), other means of transport (36) and instrument engineering (37) sectors were the ones that increased the weight of their exports to the EU most and stood out from among all the other sectors. An intense two-way trade creation effect therefore seemed to have been generated in these sectors.

(b)   However, in most NACE 2 sectors the increase in the penetration of imports from the EU was much less intense than the increase in the propensity to export to the EU (variation of $Mei/Qi > Xei/Qi$). This uneven behaviour explained the worsening that most of them experienced in their RCA against the EU.

Regarding the static effects with respect to third countries, in Catalonia trade diversion seemed to have predominated over external trade creation, which was unlike what happened in Spain as a whole. The Mo/C indicator fell nearly 40% on average of the industrial sectors of Catalonia. This was the result of a general fall in most NACE 2 sectors, reaching around 50% in three of them – metals (22), chemicals (25) and mechanical engineering (32). The value of the indicator only rose in the other means of transport (36) sector and in traditional sectors of weak demand that were very sensitive to the process of the liberalization of trade with third countries – textiles and clothing (43), leather goods (44), footwear and clothing (45) – so that an external trade creation effect could only be detected in these sectors.

Overall conclusions for Catalonia

Altogether, the results of the various trade indicators discussed enabled us to conclude that Catalonia was a region which, in comparison with other regions, presented greater intra-industrial specialization, but entry into the single market left it in a not very favourable competitive situation due to the high proportion of weak sectors in its industrial production.

This involved a strategy of intra-industrial adjustment in sectors of medium and high demand, which meant it lost specialization in traditional sectors. Thus, for sectors that traditionally exported goods, such as leather goods, footwear and clothing (44–45), although their specialization indices were still above the EU average, they lost competitiveness during the period 1988–92, which was underlined by their RCAs.

The favourable evolution of the electrical machinery (34) sector's specialization index result stood out, and placed it on a level similar to that of Europe. Last, we would underline that there was a group of sectors, among which electrical machinery (34) was the most extreme case, that was clearly reorientating its exports towards the EU market at the expense of trade with third countries. As to the static effects generated by the single market, in Catalonia there was a steep increase in the intra-EU flows, which increased its share of both imports and exports. This creation of trade was accompanied by an appreciable trade diversion effect and very little external creation, which was present only in traditional sectors. The impact on trade flows with the EU was much greater for imports than exports, which led to a generalized decrease in the RCAs of Catalonia against those of the EU.

The Basque country

Specialization index

The exports of the Basque country in 1988 were highly concentrated in the metals (22), mechanical engineering (32), rubber and plastics (48) and manufacture of metal articles (31) sectors. The value of the exports of these four sectors was 64% of total industrial exports. Consequently, they were more concentrated in this region than they were in other Spanish regions as this region had a powerful but not excessively diversified industrial structure: 50% of industrial GVA was generated in only three sectors – metals (22), manufacture of metal articles (31) and mechanical engineering (32).

As well as the sectors mentioned, the Basque country also had a high degree of specialization in the exports of the other means of transport (36) sector that was well above the EU average. The SMP and the process of integration into the EU has not reduced that high concentration of exports. In 1992, four sectors continued to dominate industrial exports: metals (22), mechanical engineering (32), manufacture of metal articles (31) and other means of transport (36). Between them, they accounted for nearly 72% of the total value of exports. The trend was thus towards intensification of concentration. All the exporting sectors increased their specialization indices even more, reaffirming their previous positions. The only exception was the rubber and plastics (48) sector, which suffered a drastic fall in its position from second place with a high specialization index to one of the last places.

The most outstanding changes did not, therefore, occur in the most highly specialized sectors, but in those that had little representation in Basque exports, ones that were well below the EU average.
(a)   The instrument engineering (37) sector – especially electrical machinery (34) – increased their specialization indices spectacularly, starting from very low levels to become two of the highest indices. The chemicals (25) and electrical machinery (34) sectors also increased their specialization indices, but by smaller amounts than the first two, so that they still had specialization indices below 100, far below the EU average.
(b)   On the other hand, the indices fell in most of the sectors where they were already low, so

that they stood at insignificant levels (in the non-metallic minerals (23), motor vehicles and parts (35) and food, beverages and tobacco (41–42) sectors) or even close to zero (in the office materials and machinery (33), timber and wooden furniture (46) and paper, printing and publishing (47) sectors).

Table 4.5.13. País Vasco's trade indicators change 92/88

NACE 2	RCA	IIT	Specialization index	Trade creation (Xei/Qi)	Trade creation (Mei/Ci)	Trade diversion (Moi/Ci)	Trade diversion (Xoi/Qi)
22	30.5	5.4	14.5	23.4	16.0	0.1	16.1
23	6.6	14.4	-29.1	-50.3	-49.5	-2.0	-69.5
24	-894.3	-7.0	14.4	-10.7	3.8	68.7	-7.0
25	36.6	23.2	35.2	24.6	-6.0	22.2	-9.0
31	-50.7	23.8	29.7	23.2	74.2	118.3	39.0
32	323.2	-3.4	39.8	12.4	-0.1	35.2	19.7
33	-65.0	-33.1	-38.7	n.a.	-21.3	52.7	n.a.
34	-53.5	-0.9	23.6	-8.6	-6.1	-12.6	13.5
35	-206.2	-4.8	-90.5	-99.9	107.7	192.1	-99.4
36	705.5	-66.7	149.6	1,110.6	129.8	89.5	-84.4
37	733.6	-43.7	829.3	-63.5	-108.9	-108.9	269.7
41-42	-1,678.9	-27.0	-86.4	-89.8	-82.3	-80.4	-93.6
43	12.9	7.9	34.9	41.6	29.5	-16.4	23.8
44	-66.2	-19.3	3,987.9	8,255.5	1,860.0	1,851.0	4,575.6
45	-10.8	-10.7	765.7	407.1	451.8	-72.5	1,432.3
46	-525.8	-41.1	-35.3	-50.8	65.2	-24.7	20.8
47	-605.9	-48.1	-97.4	-99.2	-96.7	-95.7	-92.6
48	-359.2	-58.1	-97.5	-96.5	-76.6	228.7	-98.8
49	-128.5	19.5	88.5	-27.2	12.1	-5.2	-47.4
Total	401.4	-0.7	-0.0	-10.5	-14.3	-3.3	-19.5

In conclusion, the opening up of the Spanish economy to the single market did not have significant effects on the traditional specialization of Basque exports, which were still highly specialized in three or four sectors. However, an increase in this concentration did indeed occur, as the specialization indices of these sectors rose even more and the indices of most of the sectors that started in 1988 with low levels of specialization fell further. Some specific changes were quite striking, such as the very steep increases in the indices of the instrument engineering (37) and leather goods (44) sectors, which were not always accompanied by improvements in the RCAs. In the instrument engineering (37) sector, the strength of exports helped to improve and change the sign of the RCA, which became positive, but in the leather goods (44) sector, the RCA worsened during the years analysed.

RCA

The weakness of the region's manufacturing sectors that were in competition with the countries of the EU was, in general, confirmed by the RCA indices for the Basque country. However, in the course of the period 1988–92, the following peculiarities were found to be worthy of mention.

(a)   As anticipated, in the analysis of the previous trade indicators, the other means of transport (36) and instrument engineering (37) sectors stood out among the Basque country's productive sectors in that they presented a change that was well above the overall average, as well as being sectors that could have been said to have been strengthened by the entry into the single market. Their competitiveness improved notably, changing their behaviour as net importing sectors, so that, in the case of this region, their former classification as vulnerable could be corrected, which was helped by the sector's having medium demand.

(b)   The mechanical engineering (32) sector also improved its competitive situation, changing its importing tendency from 1990 onwards. The remaining sectors, even though the variation of the indices during the period was positive, continued to be at a disadvantage compared to those of the other countries of the EU. In this sense, we could highlight the negative growth rate of the RCAs in the non-metallic mineral products (24), timber and wooden furniture (46) and paper, printing and publishing (47) sectors and, as a special case, the food, beverages and tobacco (41–42) sector.

IIT

The Basque country presented high results for its IIT index, but negative rates predominated in its growth. As in the case of Catalonia, the sectors that stood out for their higher level of intra-industrial specialization were electrical machinery (34) and non-metallic mineral products (24). During the years 1988–92, the chemicals (25) and metal products (31) sectors developed this type of trade most, which was supported by the fact that these products were in strong or medium demand. These sectors were closely followed by the textiles (43) sector. The rise in the IIT indices for other sectors was insignificant.

The other means of transport (36) and instrument engineering (37) sectors were affected by their entry into the single market in that their intra-industrial specialization decreased and their comparative advantage improved notably, as can be seen from the results presented for the next trade indicator.

Static effects

Unlike Catalonia, Spain's other great industrial region, in the Basque country there was no generalized increase in the propensity to export to the EU: the Xe/Q indicator fell, on average, by 10%.

(a)   Nevertheless, in all the sectors that were most important to the productive and export structure of the Basque country (metals (22), manufacture of metal articles (31), mechanical engineering (32) and other means of transport (36)) the EU export propensity increased notably. The same trend, though in lesser measure, was recorded for the metals (22), chemicals (25), textiles and clothing (43) and footwear and clothing (45) sectors.

(b)   In the remaining sectors, the proportion of exports going to the EU fell, but they were sectors that were of little importance to the industrial trade of the Basque country.

The increase in EU export propensity should not be interpreted purely as an effect of intra-EU liberalization as it was necessary to know the evolution of exports to third countries (Xoi/Qi) in the sectors where such an increase occurred.

(a)   In the other means of transport (36) and metals (22) sectors, an increase could indeed be detected in EU export specialization. In other means of transport, the increase in the *Xei/Qi* ratio was accompanied by a reduction of the third-country export propensity, while in metals, both indicators increased, but the EU export propensity did so at a greater rate.

(b)   In the manufacture of metal articles (31) and mechanical engineering (32) sectors, on the other hand, the export propensity to third countries increased more than it did to the EU. Therefore, the liberalization of the SMP did not seem to have had a crucial influence as no reorientation of exports towards the EU and away from third countries was perceived.

(c)   The instrument engineering (37) sector presented a yet more extreme case. The notable increase in its total exports was wholly devoted to third countries – indeed, it almost trebled its export propensity to these countries. On the other hand, the EU export propensity was reduced by more than 63%. Consequently this sector, with its medium-high demand and relatively technology-intensive way of working, was seen to be in a suitably competitive position to export to third countries, but to lack comparative advantages against the rest of the EU. This behaviour was congruent with its classification as a sector that, in Spain, was sensitive and vulnerable in its position *vis-à-vis* the EU by Martin in Buigues *et al.*, 1990). However, the pessimistic forecasts deriving from this classification have not been fully confirmed, as no trade creation effect via the penetration of imports has been detected, allowing even a slight improvement of the sector's RCA against those of the EU.

With respect to the evolution of exports, in the Basque country, in general, there was no intense internal trade creation effect, and a massive influx of imports was thus discarded, unlike what happened in other Spanish regions.

(a)   Nevertheless, in seven sectors there was a notable increase in the region's share of EU imports in terms of apparent consumption (*Mei/Ci*), but, at the same time, the penetration of non-EU imports also increased in all of them (*Moi/Ci*). Therefore, these sectors seem to have experienced a joint internal and external trade creation effect, external creation attaining greater importance than the internal one in the non-metallic mineral products (24) and manufacture of metal articles (31) sectors.

(b)   In trade with third countries, a slight average trade diversion was observed, although, as occurs with trade creation, there were many sectoral differences. In at least eight sectors, external trade creation predominated over diversion.

In conclusion, the direction and intensity of the static effects generated in the Basque country by the SMP and Spain's integration into the EU did not present a trend that was as clear as that manifested in other Spanish regions.

(a)   The most competitive sectors increased their EU export propensity, but also that to third countries.

(b)   There was an uneven internal trade creation effect that was not applicable to all sectors. However, this penetration of EU imports in apparent consumption was intense in the manufacture of metal articles (31), other means of transport (36), textiles and clothing (43), footwear and clothing (45) and wood and other manufacturing industries (46/49) sectors.

(c)   In relations with third countries, a moderate diversion effect seemed to prevail, although, in numerous sectors, there was a sharp increase in the penetration of imports (an external trade creation effect). On the whole, there was a shrinking of nearly 20% in export propensity to these countries, although, once more, this phenomenon was not applicable to all sectors.

General conclusions for the Basque country

Taking into account the behaviour of all the trade indicators, what was the impact of the SMP on the main production and export sectors of the Basque country?

(a) The metals (22) sector, which was not, *a priori*, classified as a sensitive sector, did not appear to have suffered a heavy impact as a consequence of the SMP, although it did follow a slightly positive trend in its trade flows:
  (i) the already high specialization index for exports rose yet more;
  (ii) the export propensity increased, both to the EU and to the rest of the world (more intensely to the EU than to third countries);
  (iii) although there was internal trade creation, with an increased penetration of non-EU imports in apparent consumption, this increase was less than the growth of the export propensity of the area;
  (iv) as a consequence of this evolution, the RCA indicator improved slightly against that for the EU, though without becoming positive, and the IIT indicator likewise increased.

(b) The manufacture of the metal articles (31) sector strengthened its leadership position in Basque exports – its specialization index rose nearly 30%. However, it seemed to have been affected by the SMP more intensely than did metals:
  (i) although it was not classified as sensitive either in Spain or in the EU as a whole, the internal creation of trade, in the form of the penetration of EU imports, was quite considerable;
  (ii) as a consequence of this effect, the RCA index fell against that for the EU because internal trade creation via imports was much greater than the increase in export propensity to the EU, but the RCA continued to be positive;
  (iii) the IIT index increased, due above all to the intensification of imports from the EU.

(c) The simple analysis of the indicators did not detect an intense effect of the SMP on the mechanical engineering (32) sector, which, unlike the preceding sector, was classified as sensitive:
  (i) there was no increase in IIT with the EU or a trade creation effect as the penetration of imports from the EU did not increase;
  (ii) the EU export propensity did increase, but less than the export propensity to the rest of the world;
  (iii) as a consequence of (i) and (ii), the RCA when compared with that for the EU improved greatly, changing its sign from a negative to a positive one, though it was still at a low level, and, consequently, this sector seemed to have withstood well the shock of liberalization, having increased its presence in EU markets and avoided massive penetration by EU imports, but an intense external trade creation effect was produced due to an increase in the penetration of EU imports.

Summing up, no general intense impact of the SMP on Basque external trade was detected, and it continued to be characterized by negative RCAs in nearly all sectors. However, the opening up to the EU:

(a)   seemed to have facilitated the exports of the sectors that started with a stronger competitive position, which propitiated a slight improvement in the average RCA;

(b)   caused a heavy penetration of imports into traditional sectors, reducing their traditionally positive RCAs (the wood and other manufacturing industries (46–49)).

Altogether, the SMP acted as a filter. The strong sectors behaved as such, maintaining or improving their positions, while the weak sectors lost weight in overall trade, their RCAs fell and they suffered, to a greater extent, the effects of internal trade creation.

All other regions

This aggregate included a very heterogeneous set of regions that had to be analysed together due to the difficulties of obtaining trade data, as explained in Section 4.5.2.

To this group belonged:

(a)   all the Objective 1 regions – Andalusia, Asturias, Canarias, Cantabria, Castilla–La Mancha, Castilla y Leon, Valencia, Extremadura, Galicia, Ceuta and Melilla and Murcia – altogether constituting 80% of the total surface area of the country and more than 60% of the population;

(b)   Aragon, Baleares, Rioja and Navarra, which did not meet the requirements for inclusion among the Objective 1 regions but contained territories that benefited from Objectives 2 and 5b.

The least-developed regions of Spain, with the lowest per capita sectoral value added (Andalusia, Extremadura) were thus mixed with some of the most developed ones (Baleares had the highest per capita sectoral value added in Spain, thanks to tourism; Valencia, although still included in the Objective 1 regions, had a strong productive and industrial fabric).

Consequently, the changes reflected by the trade indicators were merely averages that concealed behaviours and reactions with respect to the SMP that were even opposite in some cases. In fact, the analysis of this aggregate, instead of studying regional peculiarities, enabled us to find out what happened in Spain as a whole, but eliminated the bias introduced by the three most heavily industrialized regions (Catalonia, the Basque country and Madrid).

The specialization indices

In 1988, this group of regions concentrated 21.4% of the total value of exports in the motor vehicles and parts (35) sector, due to the location in several of them of multinationals that exported a large part of their production as part of their global strategy. The second place was occupied by the chemicals sector, with 17% of total exports. Also in high places were the food, beverages and tobacco (41–42, 9%), metals (22, 8.6%) and mechanical engineering (32, 6.3%) sectors, as well as a varied range of traditional industrial products (from the textiles and clothing (43) to other manufacturing industries (48) sectors), highly concentrated in particular regions and districts that traditionally had high RCAs in very specific products. The exports from these sectors together formed 20% of the total.

Table 4.5.14. All other regions' trade indicators change 92/88

NACE 2	RCA	IIT	Specialization index	Trade creation (Xie/Qi)	Trade creation (Mei/Ci)	Trade diversion (Moi/Ci)	Trade diversion (Xoi/Qi)
22	-87.3	7.4	-2.8	57.8	59.9	54.3	14.6
23	-16.9	3.5	-16.6	-11.0	2.9	-28.7	-20.9
24	-7.6	2.8	2.8	20.4	21.4	83.3	2.0
25-26	-16.4	-9.3	-8.2	32.9	-2.1	54.0	37.1
31	-3,316.6	-25.2	-9.5	16.9	66.5	90.9	3.4
32	13.0	15.5	1.3	1.5	-10.1	51.3	-4.3
33	-48.1	58.1	58.8	102.4	407.7	353.6	279.7
34	12.7	6.1	28.4	103.6	46.2	11.0	42.9
35	77.0	-8.0	19.8	-60.6	-94.5	-85.1	-76.7
36	-493.2	-23.2	-6.1	47.7	167.9	249.0	278.4
37	17.6	12.1	-0.0	554.5	10.0	81.6	373.7
41-42	-501.1	-9.7	-27.0	-4.3	22.7	-14.8	-24.6
43	-356.9	-24.4	-8.0	27.0	65.7	344.2	13.9
44-45	-40.0	118.3	-19.7	-7.6	46.6	44.7	-15.5
47	-167.0	4.0	-12.8	-6.0	9.2	69.2	20.0
48	-9,855.3	-10.7	7.4	60.1	54.3	127.5	-5.2
46-49	-69.0	37.8	5.2	6.5	50.0	30.5	10.3
Total	-20.3			54.1	3.7	26.8	-8.5

When the specialization index was taken into consideration, thus placing these shares of exports in relation to the average specialization of EU exports, the classification changed slightly.

(a)   The highest index figure by a long way was that for the leather goods, footwear and clothing (44–45) sector (1,255 in 1988) – one in which Spain has traditionally enjoyed high comparative advantages.

(b)   These regions were also more specialized than the EU average in the metals (22) to chemicals (25), motor vehicles and parts (35) and timber and wooden furniture (46), rubber and plastics (48) and other manufacturing industries (48) sectors. In the other means of transport (36) sector, the specialization index equalled the EU average (close to 100).

(c)   In the remaining NACE 2 sectors, these regions had very low specialization indices.

From this classification it could be deduced that specialization was localized in products that had medium or weak demand and low or medium technological content, with the sole exceptions of the chemicals (25) and motor vehicles and parts (35) sectors, which were considered to have strong demand.

This type of export specialization led to forecasts that there would be a notable impact from the opening up of the EU: most were products sensitive to the SMP, some of them classified as vulnerable (the chemicals (25) and other means of transport (36) sectors) and others in a strong position (the ceramic products (248), motor vehicles and parts (35), 425, textiles and clothing (43), footwear and clothing (45), rubber and plastics (48) 494 sectors; see Table 4.5.11).

From 1988 to 1992, there were changes in the indices, but they were not of excessive magnitude. The sectors where the figures decreased were more numerous than those where they rose.

(a)   Three of the NACE 2 sectors (office materials and machinery (33), electrical machinery (34) and motor vehicles and parts (35)) notably increased their indices, by percentages from 20% in the motor vehicles and parts (35) sector to 60% in the mechanical engineering (32) sector. The growth of total exports was intense in all of them.

(b)   The most negative impact on the indices was experienced by the food, beverages and tobacco (41–42) sector, followed, at some distance, by the leather goods, footwear and clothing (44–45), non-metallic minerals (23) and paper, printing and publishing (47) sectors.

(c)   The variations in the figures for the remaining sectors, both positive and negative, did not reach sufficient magnitude to identify structural change. In general, falls in the specialization indices predominated, although the timber and wooden furniture (46), rubber and plastics (48) and other manufacturing industries (48) sectors seemed to have maintained it, showing a slight trend towards growth.

In summary, the sectors that started with high indices maintained their positions, indeed, slightly strengthened them (see (c)) or else experienced falls so small that they were totally insufficient to make them lose their leading positions (as was the case for the chemicals (25), metals (22), non-metallic minerals (23), leather goods, footwear and clothing (44–45) sectors). The only important change was that in the motor vehicles and parts (35) sector, discussed in (a.)

RCA

Even though the diverse regions included in this group combined strong competitive situations and sector vulnerability, the results of such an aggregation of regions led us to conclude that the comparative advantages of this grouping and that of Catalonia were the ones most affected by the entry into the single market. In the case of the latter, too, the sectors most affected by loss of competitiveness were the rubber and plastics (48) and manufacture of metal articles (31) sectors.

The other means of transport (36) sector lost its comparative advantage after 1991 – the RCA indicator showing negative values – with an overall loss of competitiveness for the years 1988–92 of 493 points, fulfilling all expectations of its vulnerability, which was also confirmed by other trade indicators.

At the other extreme, there was the motor vehicles and parts (35) sector, which achieved the greatest progress in competitiveness, as well as the electrical machinery (34), mechanical engineering (32) and instrument engineering (37) sectors – the only ones to have achieved it during the period analysed despite having been considered among the most vulnerable in the face of the single market – the demand from EU countries exercised a notable influence in this respect.

IIT

The inclusion of a set of regions with such heterogeneous characteristics, together with the peculiarities mentioned for the calculation of these IIT indices, restricted our knowledge of the trade model and the evolution followed by the manufacturing sectors with respect to their entry into the single market. Nevertheless, it was the metals (22) and paper, printing and publishing (47) sectors that presented the highest values in this indicator, with figures close to the maximum. The leather goods, footwear and clothing (44–45) and office materials and machinery (33) sectors were those that most developed this model of specialization during 1988–92, starting with lower levels of IIT.

The manufacture of metal articles (31) and textiles and clothing (43) sectors stood out among the sectors where this type of trade lost importance due to the specialization of other EU countries, though these aspects needed to be studied in greater depth with other indicators, such as those dealt with here.

Static effects

In this set of regions as a whole, there was a very sharp increase in the propensity to export to the EU, the average of the indicator rising by 54%, which was far above the national average and exceeded only by Catalonia.

At the same time, the share of exports going to third countries fell by 8.5%. Therefore, without entering into sectoral nuances, there was a change in export orientation towards the EU area that could be attributed in large part to the effect of the opening up of the EU markets.

(a)   Most sectors improved their EU export propensity, especially the metals (22), rubber and plastics (48) and other means of transport (36) sectors.

(b)   The value of the Xei/Qi indicator fell in only four sectors, all with insignificant variations, non-metallic minerals (23) experiencing the greatest fall (-11%).

The increase in EU export propensity was accompanied by an average decrease of more than 8% in the Xo/Q indicator. However, there were important sectoral differences in this respect.

(a)   In numerous sectors (the chemicals (25), office materials and machinery (33), electrical machinery (34), other means of transport (36) and instrument engineering (37) sectors), there was a rise in the export propensity not only to the EU but also to third countries, so that there was not such an intense change in the geographical specialization of exports. Consequently, not all of the increase in the Xei/Qi indicator could be attributed to the effect of the SMP.

(b)   There was outstandingly negative behaviour in the export propensity of the food and drink sector (food, beverages and tobacco (41–42)), one of those that traditionally enjoyed a greater comparative advantage in these regions. The Xei/Qi ratio fell and so did the Xoi/Qi ratio, though proportionately more than the former. Similar behaviour occurred in the leather goods (44) and footwear and clothing (45) sectors, which were sensitive traditional sectors but classified among those with a strong competitive position. These sectors did not therefore fulfil expectations, and there was a process of despecialization and growing difficulties in exports, to both EU and non-EU markets. Therefore, the high RCAs were partly the result of a high degree of protection rather than of a genuine comparative advantage, which was much eroded by the new producers of PVD – an advantage that may, perhaps, be recovered only by 'upgrading'.

The vulnerability in the competitive position of most of the regions' industrial fabric was confirmed by the great increase in the penetration of imports from both the EU and third countries. The SMP and the liberalizing measures of the transition process of Spain's incorporation into the EU generated a strong internal and external trade creation effect in nearly all sectors (on average, the impact of external trade creation seemed to have been greater than that of internal creation). By sectors, the internal trade creation effect was almost unanimous, and only in the chemicals (25) and mechanical engineering (32) sectors was a small fall in the *Mei/Ci* indicator detected.

With respect to third countries, the effect in the majority of the regions was one of external creation of trade and not diversion. Non-EU imports shrank only in the non-metallic minerals (23) sector and, to a lesser extent, in the food, beverages and tobacco (41–42) sector.

Conclusions for all other regions

In conclusion, all the trade indicators showed the vulnerability of the industrial structure of this type of regions:

(a)   the incorporation into the single market had a marked impact, with generalized falls in the RCA index;

(b)   specialization in the export of traditional goods (in the leather goods, footwear and clothing (44–45), non-metallic minerals (23) 27 and, above all, food, beverages and tobacco (41–42) sectors) was also reduced, but in sectors with strong demand (the chemicals (25) and motor vehicles and parts (35) sectors) export specialization was maintained and even increased;

(c)   trade creation was intense, both internal and external, and this behaviour contrasted with the effects of integration in the more industrialized regions: in Catalonia, although the penetration of EU imports (*Mei/Ci*) increased, trade was diverted to the detriment of third-country suppliers, and in the Basque country the penetration of EU imports was acceptably reduced.

The automobiles (35) sector was the one that most strengthened its position of hegemony, increasing its RCA most of all, and also increasing its specialization index notably (by 30%). This sector therefore fulfilled forecasts that attributed to it a strong competitive position. The chemicals (25) sector, which had the second highest value for exports, did not show such a positive evolution as that of the automobile sector. Its RCA fell against the EU's as, although its export propensity increased, this was not sufficient to compensate for the notable penetration of imports. Furthermore, no increase was observed in the role of the European markets as the increase in the export propensity to third countries was greater than that experienced in the export propensity to the EU.

The traditional sectors suffered a much more negative impact, the food and beverages (41–42) sector standing out. The RCA indicator fell, as did the specialization index and the export propensity (both to the EU and to third countries), and it suffered intense trade creation, a large volume of EU imports penetrating.

Although the evolution of most traditional sectors was negative, a detailed analysis of specific regions and products seemed necessary, as there were products that, in certain regions, were evolving very favourably, indicating that specialization based on comparative advantages as opposed to intra-industrial specialization might not be completely impossible, as long as the quality and design of traditional products were improved.

Horizontal analysis of trade indicators

In this part of the review, a more detailed study is made of regional sectoral behaviour in order to assess whether or not expectations arising from the SMP were fulfilled, especially in those sectors that had been identified as sensitive by the *ex ante* studies (Commission, 1990; Collado, 1992; Martin in Buigues *et al.*, 1990). For this purpose, we have produced a table for each trade indicator, comparing the behaviour of each sector across the regions, and then given a national total (last column). The analysis of these tables also enabled it to be distinguished whether or not a single sector reacted in different ways in different regions or if, on the contrary, the behaviour was similar, the intrinsic competitive characteristics of a sector prevailing over regional peculiarities.

It was thus intended to discover whether or not the initial expectations regarding the impact of the SMP were fulfilled and whether or not in Spain, as a country included in the group of other southern countries, it had an impact that was different from that in Greece and Portugal.

(a) According to the *ex ante* studies mentioned, a lesser impact than the EU average was expected in the Spanish regions as the 40 sectors identified as sensitive by the Commission only represented 41% of GVA in Spain, whereas in the EU as a whole they represented 50% of GVA. This lower percentage could be explained by the lesser presence in Spain of sectors linked to public markets and high technology. However, this percentage rose to 48% if we added sectors that were sensitive specifically in Spain, though, in the event, it continued to be lower than the relative weight of sensitive sectors in Greece (61.5%) and Portugal (68%).

(b) Spain was also distinguished from Greece and Portugal in that its comparative advantages occurred not only in traditional industries with weak demand, but also in some industries with medium demand, which are more capital-intensive and skilled labour-intensive (household appliances, electrical materials, automobiles). This duality meant that, for Spain, the sectors with the best outlook were different when the EU market (where the comparative advantages lay in labour-intensive products) or the non-EU market (where there were good prospects in some capital-intensive products, such as automobiles and household appliances) was considered. Furthermore, Spain already started with IIT indices that were higher than those of Greece and Portugal. Indeed, a sharp rise in these indices was even expected, given that the strong increase in FDI following Spain's integration into the EU was concentrated in sectors that had strongly growing demand and a high technology content (computers, electronics, chemicals and pharmaceuticals).

(c) Given these specific characteristics it was expected that, in Spain, the strategy of adjustment to the impact of liberalization, caused not only by the SMP but also by integration into the EU, would follow the intra-industrial path rather than the inter-industrial one, which would be reflected in the trade indicators by:

  (i) a reduction in the specialization indices for traditional sectors (a negative variation in the index of export specialization);

  (ii) worsening of the RCA with respect not only to the EU but also to third countries, due to a sharp increase in imports from non-EU suppliers;

  (iii) improvement in the competitive position of the sectors with a higher technology content or more highly skilled labour when compared with both third countries and the EU.

With the aim of testing the fulfilment of these forecasts in the regions covered by this review, below are presented tables that translate into two-digit NACE, approximately, the three-digit classification of sensitive sectors compiled by Martin (in Buigues *et al.*, 1990). The sensitive sectors were classified in terms of their competitive position, based on the coverage rate they presented in 1986, the first year in which the influence of Spain's integration into the EU made itself felt.

By comparing these tables with the tables of regional trade indicators it was possible to detect whether or not the sensitive sectors in each region behaved according to the classification assigned to them or if, on the contrary, there were changes in the classification itself (for example, if a sector classified as sensitive in 1986 improved its competitive position in subsequent years to the extent of passing into the group of intermediate or strong competitiveness).

These tables also enabled the behaviour of the external flows of sensitive sectors to be related to the sectors with low, medium or strong demand, thus enabling verification of the structural adjustment path followed by each region in the process of integration, and testing of the hypotheses of inter-industrial or intra-industrial adjustment.

On the basis of these tables and of the forecasts made for Spain (Martin in Buigues *et al.*, 1990), it could be deduced that, *a priori*, the expectations of the impact of the integration of the SMP were not totally favourable as:

(a)   of the 40 sensitive sectors, non-metallic mineral products (24) was classified as vulnerable because of its negative competitive position, a worsening of the indicator of its coverage rate; a clearly favourable impact of the SMP was foreseen in only 12 sectors;

(b)   most sectors that were vulnerable because of their low competitiveness were sectors of strong demand and, in general, were high-tech, whereas nearly all of the sensitive sectors in which Spain started with a favourable competitive position were those that had medium or weak demand.

Nevertheless, there were notable exceptions to brighten this gloomy scenario and differentiate Spain from the other southern EU countries. There was a strong competitive position in some sectors of strong demand in the context of the EU, such as the automobiles (35) sector and part of the electrical materials and household appliances (34) sector.

Did the facts confirm these expectations? The main problem with the comparison between expectations and achievements lay in the fact that the sensitive sectors were defined by a three-digit NACE disaggregation, whereas our regional study could only apply to them a two-digit disaggregation. For this reason, there were NACE 2 sectors (such as electrical engineering (34)) that simultaneously contained weakly competitive NACE 3 subsectors (such as telecommunications (344)) and others with a strong competitive position (such as electrical cables (341) and household electrical appliances (346)). The analysis of trade indicators in these specific cases prevented a precise identification of the behaviour of some subsectors.

The analysis for each indicator is shown in Tables 4.5.16 to 4.5.22. In all of them, the period analysed is that of 1988–92. The information figuring in each box corresponded to the total variation of that period, with the aim of reflecting the change experienced by each of these indicators during the five years we studied.

The specialization indices

On the basis of the analysis of variations in the specialization of total exports it was intended to demonstrate:

(a)   whether or not the sensitive sectors were the ones that showed most variation (positive or negative) in the specialization index;
(b)   which type of sectors presented a more dynamic index, those of strong, medium or weak demand.

In other words, we attempted to find out whether or not specialization in traditional sectors decreased in favour of those for which there was strong demand as an affirmative response would have provided a first indication that the path of adjustment was intra- rather than inter-industrial.

Table 4.5.15 shows that, in Spain as a whole, 10 of the 16 sectors into which we finally grouped industrial products[38] experienced a decrease in the specialization index. Among them, the most important reductions corresponded to sensitive sectors: the food, beverages and tobacco (41–42) and leather goods, footwear and clothing (44–45) sectors. Also notable, though not so intense, was the fall of the index in two sectors not included in the classification of sensitive products (non-metallic minerals (23) and paper, printing and publishing (47)).

The remaining sectors increased their specialization indices, the heaviest impact falling on three sensitive sectors: electrical machinery (34), instrument engineering (37) and motor vehicles and parts (35). Especially outstanding was the increase in the electrical machinery (34) sector, in which Spain presented products with a weak competitive position together with others that started from a strong position (electrical materials, household appliances).

This preliminary analysis of nationwide changes confirmed expectations of the impact of the SMP as it was the sectors classified as sensitive in the *ex ante* studies that experienced the most intense variations in the value of their specialization indices with both positive and negative signs.

The behaviour of the specialization index presented peculiarities at regional level, but these differences were not sufficiently important to alter the national conclusions. Although it was unusual for the variations in the indices for one sector to be of the same sign in all the regions analysed, there was, however, unanimity in the case of extreme variations. Thus, the sectors that stood out most at national level for the rise or fall of their specialization indices did the same in each of the regions:

(a)   in all the regions analysed, there was a fall in specialization in the exports of the food, beverages and tobacco (41–42) and leather goods, footwear and clothing (44–45) sectors

---

[38]   As the tables in this section present information for all the regions simultaneously, it was necessary to form an aggregate of the following NACE sectors: leather goods (44) and footwear and clothing (45), and of timber and wooden furniture (46) and other manufacturing industries (48), in order to homogenize the classification with that for Catalonia, which did not allow for a finer distinction.

that have in common that they are sensitive sectors with weak demand (except for a few food and consumption products of high income elasticity;

(b)   there was a steep increase in the specialization index for the electrical machinery (34), instrument engineering (37) (except, in this case, Madrid, the index for which fell) and motor vehicles and parts (35) sectors (except the Basque country) – all these sectors were classified as having high demand and greater intensity of technology and physical and human capital.

Table 4.5.15. The impact of the SMP on the specialization index change 92/88

NACE 2	Madrid	Catalonia	País Vasco	Other regions	Totals for Spain
22	32.6	33.4	14.5	-2.8	-2.6
23	-20.8	13.3	-29.1	-16.6	-15.1
24	31.5	-4.6	14.4	2.8	3.6
25-26	18.9	-6.9	35.2	-8.2	-6.0
31	4.9	-8.7	29.7	-9.5	-7.6
32	19.8	4.2	39.8	1.3	4.3
33	-80.4	-49.7	-38.7	58.8	7.1
34	33.6	37.9	23.6	28.4	30.7
35	7.8	26.7	-90.5	19.8	19.3
36	-43.1	-16.2	149.6	-6.1	-3.5
37	-21.3	4.1	829.3	-0.0	21.9
41-42	-21.5	-21.3	-86.4	-27.0	-27.5
43	22.2	-14.8	34.9	-8.0	-9.1
44-45	-29.4	-25.1	2,077.1	-19.7	-15.7
47	28.1	3.5	-97.6	-12.8	-12.2
48	13.2	17.4	-97.5	7.4	-8.7
46-49	42.9	-6.6	16.1	5.2	6.6

However, this general tendency must be seen in perspective by paying attention to two types of considerations.

The aggregate 'all other regions' included a very heterogeneous set of regions, many of which did not seem to have comparative advantages in sectors of medium or high demand but did seem to have possibilities of specialization in traditional sectors (agriculture and foods in Andalusia, for example). In others, such as the Valencia region, there was a combination of competitive possibilities in traditional sectors, which were trying to 'upgrade', and in others of medium and high demand. For these reasons, it would have been very risky to affirm, without entering into a more detailed analysis of the peculiarities of each region and of the behaviour of more finely disaggregated products, that the adjustment undertaken by the Spanish regions as a whole was fully of the intra-industrial kind.

Regions like Catalonia, and especially Madrid, increased their specialization not only in the above-mentioned sectors but also in others that could not be classified as being ones for which there was a high demand: metals (22) in Catalonia and Madrid, non-metallic mineral products (24) and textiles and clothing (43) in Madrid.

RCA

With this indicator, we could discover the influence exercised by membership of the single market on the RCAs of the sectors and regions that figure in Table 4.5.16.

On the basis of the results that appear in the last column, it can be affirmed that, in general, there was a worsening at national level as 10 of the 17 sectors lost competitiveness, i.e. their RCAs decreased and the inter-industrial trade model thus loses relevance with respect to such sectors. The greatest decreases corresponded first to the textiles and clothing (43) and paper, printing and publishing (47) sectors and then, though with a smaller loss, the manufacture of metal articles (31) and leather goods (44) sectors. The motor vehicles and parts (35) sector stood out nationwide for the improvement in its RCA, while the electrical machinery (34) sector increased its competitiveness with the EU in practically all the regions.[39]

Table 4.5.16. The impact of the SMP on the RCAs change 92/88

NACE 2	Madrid	Catalonia	País Vasco	Other regions	Totals for Spain
22	48.1	5.9	30.5	-87.3	-25.6
23	4.7	6.5	6.6	-16.9	-6.9
24	43.1	-63.2	-894.3	-7.6	5.0
25-26	0.9	-31.9	36.6	-16.4	-15.9
31	8.7	-138.4	-50.7	-3,316.6	-205.1
32	28.6	-14.2	323.2	13.0	15.9
33	-62.0	-43.0	-65.0	-48.1	0.6
34	15.4	25.8	-53.5	12.7	22.6
35	31.8	-51.6	-206.2	77.0	234.1
36	19.8	-42.6	705.5	-493.2	1.3
37	-9.6	-7.2	733.6	17.6	6.9
41-42	-9.9	14.1	-1,678.9	-501.1	-138.5
43	0.8	-135.7	12.9	-356.9	-1,602.3
44-45	-42.5	-159.2	2.5	-40.0	-80.5
47	24.4	-93.5	-605.9	-167.0	-1,027.0
48	5.1	-153.9	-359.2	-9,855.3	-192.0
46-49	38.8	-1,304.5	-294.4	-69.0	-109.0
Total	11.4	-53.4	401.4	-20.3	0.9

With respect to regional differences, it can be underlined that Catalonia and other regions are the groups that, as a whole, show a greater loss of competitiveness for industrial sectors due to the increase in imports from EU countries, as shown by the indicators that quantify the trade creation effects for such regional groupings. The loss of comparative advantage for Madrid and the Basque country was less, as it was centred, in the main, on the leather goods, footwear and clothing (44–45) and office materials and machinery (33) sectors in the first region whereas for the second the loss was more evenly spread over the sectors.

---

[39] The result for the Basque country (-53.5) was not very relevant as the index started with a very low value, so it can be considered that it practically maintained its situation.

This decrease in the competitiveness of products manufactured in Spain, quantified by means of the RCA indices, confirmed the results obtained by measuring trade creation, reflecting the penetration of imports from EU countries anticipated by recent studies of the effects of the single market on Spanish productive sectors. Within these sectors, there was a notable relative weight of imports of products with a medium technology level. The vehicles (35) sector was consolidated as the leading export sector of Spanish industry, with a share of around 25% in the total for industrial exports, as well as the sale of manufactured products with high technology content (Collado, 1992; Sancho, 1994).

Finally, we should ask ourselves if the figures for this indicator confirmed expectations as to whether or not the sectors initially classified as the weakest with respect to entry into the single market did indeed turn out to be of this type and therefore register a loss of their competitiveness against those of the EU. The reply cannot be generalized as it is necessary to make particular observations about sectors and regions. However, of the sectors considered as strongly competitive in Table 3.12, the motor vehicles and parts (35) sector was the one that behaved best during the period – the regions of Madrid and all others, containing the multinationals General Motors and Ford, were the ones that showed the highest competitiveness. Among sectors for which there were forecasts of loss of competitiveness, we can highlight the behaviour of the mechanical engineering (32) sector that, contrary to expectations, was, in fact, strengthened by the situation of competition with other EU countries.

IIT

Table 4.5.17 presents information relating to IIT, with the aim of verifying whether or not entry into a wider market originated an intensification of this type of trade with EU countries. However, the limitations of the level of disaggregation used in the information (two-digit NACE) meant that the construction of a Grubel-Lloyd index of these characteristics produced very high results, showing a high proportion of IIT compared to inter-industrial trade. Despite such limitations, it was useful in the analysis of the sectors and regions that experienced growth or reduction of intra-industrial specialization as a consequence of entry into the single market. It therefore allowed the corroboration of affirmations to this effect resulting from the study of other trade indicators.

At the national level, there was a growth in intra-industrial specialization in sectors with strong or medium intra-EU demand and vulnerable competitive position, as there was for the mechanical engineering (32), office materials and machinery (33), electronic materials (34), electronic engineering (37 (instrument engineering)) sectors, or strong, as for the leather clothing and footwear (44, 45) and others (46–49 (wood and other manufacturing industries)) (according to the grouping criteria in Table 4.5.11; Martin in Buigues *et al.*, 1990).

The sector in which intra-industrial specialization was most clearly detected in all regions was electronic materials (34), a sector with strong competitiveness and for which there was strong demand, while in the remaining sectors there were greater regional differences. Thus, the regions of Madrid and the others were the ones where a greater number of sectors increased their specialization, confirming, in general, that an intensification of this trade model occurred with Spain's entry into the single European market.

Static effects

An analysis of the indicator *Xei/Qi* and of other indicators of the creation and diversion of trade enabled us to become more precise about our provisional conclusions drawn from the changes in the RCAs, IIT and specialization indices regarding the types of structural adjustment undertaken by the Spanish regions.

For Spain as a whole (see Table 4.5.18), the increase in the total *Xe/Q* ratio (average of industrial exports) was very notable (a variation of +30% was achieved in only four years), indicating a high degree of intensification of exports to EU countries. Catalonia, the Basque country and all other regions experienced total growth above this average. Only Madrid showed greater dynamism in the growth of exports to the EU, experiencing a change that was positive but below the average. At the same time, Madrid was the only region of those analysed where the *Xoi/Qi* ratio decreased (see Table 4.5.20), thus showing a reorientation of exports towards third countries, the opposite of the predicted effect of a process of integration.

Table 4.5.17. The impact of the SMP on IIT (the Grubel-Lloyd index) change 92/88

NACE 2	Madrid	Catalonia	País Vasco	Other regions	Totals for Spain
22	182.0	12.0	5.4	7.4	-2.0
23	-17.5	24.0	14.4	3.5	0.9
24	85.7	-7.1	-7.0	2.8	-0.8
25–26	1.9	-13.9	23.2	-9.3	-9.4
31	25.5	-20.4	23.8	-25.2	-20.0
32	92.6	-9.1	-3.4	15.5	17.8
33	-73.6	-29.7	-33.1	58.1	0.2
34	26.5	5.3	-0.9	6.1	13.8
35	67.8	42.6	-4.8	-8.0	-9.7
36	37.1	-11.4	-66.7	-23.2	0.3
37	-28.6	-11.3	-43.7	12.1	8.2
41–42	-27.9	12.0	-27.0	-9.7	-14.6
43	5.2	14.2	7.9	-24.4	-29.7
44–45	-47.8	26.6	2.0	118.3	78.7
47	43.3	-17.2	-48.1	4.0	-15.8
48	19.0	-11.8	-58.1	-10.7	-12.4
46–49	93.3	-27.9	-15.7	37.8	21.9

Such a notable increase in the national indicator was due to the fact that the share of total exports going to the EU decreased in only four sectors. In the other sectors, the ratio increased notably – the electrical machinery (34) and motor vehicles and parts (35) sectors standing out among all the other sectors.

(a)　The automobiles (35) sector thus confirmed its positive expectations as it was classified as sensitive, an area for which there was high demand and in a strong competitive position. Given the lack of reliable production data for this sector at the regional level, it was not possible to calculate the exact variation rate in all of them. Nevertheless, from the export data of the multinationals, it was possible to conclude that the sign was positive in each one of them. This was so even in the aggregate 'all other regions' because this group included at least two regions with powerful multinationals that were big exporters to the EU area: Aragon, where General Motors is based, and Valencia with Ford.

(b)   The increase in the ratio of the electrical machinery (34) sector posed more problems of interpretation as this sector consisted of NACE 3 subgroups that were sensitive but classified *a priori* in opposite ways according to their competitive position. Therefore, the expectations of each subgroup with respect to the SMP were opposed: favourable for the electric cables (341) and household appliances (346) subgroups and pessimistic for the telecommunications (342 and 344) subgroups. As the available information on the evolution of the indicator was not individualized by subgroups, it was not possible to test these forecasts with precision. The only thing that we could infer was that such a positive variation of the ratio was due to the performance of the sectors placed in a strong competitive position and not to the telecommunications sector.

Table 4.5.18. The effect of the SMP on trade creation (*Xie/Qi*) change 92/88

NACE 2	Madrid	Catalonia	País Vasco	Other regions	Totals for Spain
22	98.0	143.0	23.4	57.8	37.6
23	-21.6	32.5	-50.3	-11.0	-8.7
24	30.0	33.7	-10.7	20.4	26.5
25-26	42.7	36.7	24.6	32.9	2.5
31	30.5	60.1	23.2	16.9	19.8
32	32.1	59.6	12.4	1.5	18.0
33	-84.6	-9.2	n.a.	102.4	27.5
34	-56.3	109.8	-8.6	103.6	77.7
35	n.a.	n.a.	n.a.	n.a.	64.2
36	65.5	652.7	1,110.6	47.7	-10.6
37	-90.5	270.0	-63.5	554.5	16.6
41-42	2.0	74.9	-89.8	-4.3	29.6
43	15.6	64.2	41.6	27.0	35.8
44-45	-53.5	11.5	1,564.2	-7.6	-7.3
47	40.9	16.1	-99.2	-6.0	-23.3
48	37.3	64.7	-96.5	60.1	30.3
46-49	167.7	65.1	-24.9	6.5	14.6
Total	9.0	60.2	-10.0	54.1	29.8

There was also intense growth in the share of exports going to the EU in the metals (22) and textiles and clothing (43) – a growth shared by all the regions analysed – rubber and plastics (48) – growth in all regions except the Basque country – and food, beverages and tobacco (41–42) sectors. In this latter sector, the growth was limited to Catalonia and Madrid, where the most competitive multinationals in the food sector are located; in the remaining regions, the pessimistic expectations for a large number of food products were confirmed.

The most marked differences between regions related to the number of sectors in which the EU lost importance as a customer:

(a)   in Catalonia, all the NACE 2 sectors increased the value of the indicator, and showed a more intense impact than did other Spanish regions;

(b)   at the other extreme stood the Basque country, where, in a great majority of sectors, the *Xei/Qi* ratio shrank and trade with the EU was only created in the metals (22), chemicals (25) and, especially, non-metallic minerals (23) and non-metallic mineral products (24) sectors;

(c)   Madrid was in an intermediate situation, though closer to Catalonia as the value of the ratio fell in only four sectors: non-metallic minerals (23), electrical machinery (34), instrument engineering (37) and leather goods, footwear and clothing (44–45);

(d)   in the other regions, there were generalized intense increases in exports to the EU in nearly all sectors, but in the sectors where the percentage of exports going to the EU fell, the fall was not very steep (these sectors were mechanical engineering (32), non-metallic minerals (23), manufacture of metal articles (31), food, beverages and tobacco (41–42) and leather goods, footwear and clothing (44–45).

The trade creation effect, strictly speaking (see Table 4.5.19), which the *Mei/Ci* indicator attempted to reflect, was very intense and widespread. There was a high penetration of EU imports, thus continuing the trend that all the studies subsequent to Spain's entry into the EU had pointed out. This intense effect, detected for the period 1988–92, was due to the synergy caused by the SMP and the effects of the tariff removal after Spain's entry in 1986, and about 1992 the transition period for the expansion was completed.

Table 4.5.19. The effect of the SMP on trade creation (*Mei/Ci*) change 92/88

NACE 2	Madrid	Catalonia	PaísVaso	Other regions	Totals for Spain
22	-35.9	89.5	16.0	59.9	39.2
23	-40.5	9.1	-49.5	2.9	-2.3
24	-34.2	49.6	3.8	21.4	25.6
25-26	28.5	70.0	-6.0	-2.1	12.8
31	1.9	119.4	74.2	66.5	69.2
32	-8.9	79.7	-0.1	-10.1	1.7
33	-3.7	6.0	-21.3	407.7	20.6
34	-32.5	102.2	-6.1	46.2	46.2
35	n.a.	n.a.	n.a.	n.a.	48.0
36	37.6	596.2	129.8	167.9	-4.1
37	-14.3	156.7	n.a.	10.0	7.8
41-42	40.1	49.7	-82.3	22.7	68.3
43	-5.5	139.5	29.5	65.7	96.3
44-45	-14.8	79.3	812.1	46.6	165.5
47	-7.1	56.1	-96.7	9.2	0.7
48	7.3	97.2	-76.6	54.3	66.1
46-49	-7.6	93.1	65.1	50.0	48.1
Total	-19.7	77.2	-14.2	3.7	29.0

Nevertheless, there were great regional differences in the effects of internal trade creation via imports, differences that were more acute than in the case of the export flows already discussed.

(a)   Catalonia increased this penetration much more than the national average, trade creation being very intense in the manufacture of metal articles (31), electrical machinery (34), other means of transport (36), instrument engineering (37) and textiles and clothing (43) sectors. Furthermore, no NACE 2 sector decreased its relative weight of EU imports in apparent consumption.

(b)   The 'all other regions' group also experienced intense internal trade creation in most sectors, with the exception of chemicals (25) and mechanical engineering (32).

(c)   Madrid, on the contrary, went against the general trend, with a predominance of sectors that had decreased values for the *Mei/Ci* indicator. A notable creation of trade effect was observed only in the chemicals (25), other means of transport (36) and food, beverages and tobacco (41–42) sectors.

(d)   The Basque country, like Madrid, did not register widespread trade creation effects, as the indicator shrank in many sectors. However, in some sectors – manufacture of metal articles (31), other means of transport (36), wood and other manufacturing industries (46–49) – it presented very steep increases in the *Mei/Ci* ratio, ones of much greater magnitude than in the case of Madrid.

The trade diversion effect (see Table 4.5.20) in industrial products was insignificant at national level, to judge by the evolution of the *Moi/Ci* ratio, which increased in all sectors except non-metallic minerals (23) and other means of transport (36). Thus, there was a preferable external trade creation effect, which amply compensated the small trade diversion effect that could perhaps have been generated.

In one of the only two sectors where the value of the indicator decreased, it was not possible to state with total certainty that the fall was due wholly to a diversion effect. In that sector, instrument engineering (37), the ratio decreased by 3.7%, but at the same time, the percentage of imports from the EU also shrank (-4.1%). Therefore, it was not possible to affirm that the fall in the percentage share of third-country suppliers was substituted by an increase in that of EU producers.

The only sector where there was an intense trade diversion effect, which was shared by all the regions analysed, was non-metallic minerals (23), as in this case the shrinkage in the *Moi/Ci* ratio, -28.1%, was much more intense than that experienced for the imports from the EU as the *Mei/Ci* was -2.3%.

At regional level, however, it was possible to detect sectors that seemed to have generated trade diversion as there was an abundance of negative signs in the evolution of the index, especially in Catalonia and Madrid. In the remaining regions, however, the evidence pointed to a definite predominance of external trade creation, though this increase in the participation of EU suppliers was not due mainly to effects of the SMP but to the liberalization of the post-accession transition process and to factors alien to economic integration.

Table 4.5.20. The effect of the SMP on trade diversion (*Moi/Ci*) change 92/88

NACE 2	Madrid	Catalonia	País Vasco	Other regions	Totals for Spain
22	112.4	-51.1	0.1	54.3	20.6
23	-67.8	-30.9	-2.0	-28.7	-28.1
24	0.0	-37.6	49.1	83.3	86.8
25-26	8.2	-50.3	22.2	54.0	10.5
31	21.4	-9.0	118.3	90.9	52.2
32	-1.3	-45.8	35.2	51.3	5.6
33	-21.1	-14.8	52.7	353.6	3.6
34	-19.5	-30.3	-12.6	11.0	10.2
35	n.a.	n.a.	n.a.	n.a.	38.3
36	-33.7	779.3	89.5	249.0	-3.7
37	-10.6	13.5	n.a.	81.6	8.2
41-42	-15.8	-30.5	-80.4	-14.8	7.1
43	25.6	55.8	-16.4	344.2	113.9
44-45	96.7	12.1	180.7	44.7	195.7
47	-22.0	-34.9	-95.7	69.2	1.6
48	53.1	-26.7	228.7	127.5	77.4
46-49	169.7	1.3	4.2	30.5	39.5
Total	-13.7	-37.6	-3.2	26.8	19.1

Table 4.5.21. The effect of the SMP on trade diversion (*Xoi/Qi*) change 92/88

NACE 2	Madrid	Catalonia	País Vasco	Other regions	Totals for Spain
22	-28.6	4.4	16.1	14.6	0.6
23	-15.8	6.8	-69.5	-20.9	-17.8
24	9.1	-29.7	-7.0	2.0	4.7
25-26	21.0	-33.4	-9.0	37.1	-7.7
31	61.4	-30.7	39.0	3.4	4.1
32	62.4	1.4	19.7	-4.3	7.2
33	426.0	-80.7	n.a.	279.7	52.7
34	357.4	-42.3	13.5	42.9	37.8
35	n.a.	n.a.	n.a.	n.a.	-9.1
36	-17.4	678.8	-84.4	278.4	11.7
37	-73.9	124.7	269.7	373.7	44.7
41-42	-13.4	-18.6	-93.6	-24.6	-2.3
43	165.8	-32.5	23.8	13.9	-0.9
44-45	31.3	4.8	2151.0	-15.5	-12.4
47	0.1	-11.2	-92.6	20.0	-11.0
48	46.1	-27.4	-98.8	-5.2	-27.5
46-49	24.9	7.7	4.1	10.3	10.7
Total	19.8	-26.4	-19.5	-8.5	-0.2

4.5.4. The main conclusions drawn from the indicator analysis

The analysis of the indicators of flows of goods and factors showed, in general, important changes in the behaviour of most Spanish regions and sectors, changes that were very important in the case of trade flows and of less intensity in the case of factor flows. Even though this was confirmed by the regression analysis (see next section) it would still have been premature to state that the impact of the SMP was very strong in the case of Spain as it was necessary to take into account at least two types of factors that limited the explanatory capacity of the analysis.

(a)   In the case of Spain, the changes observed in the patterns of trade and specialization, as well as the static effects, were probably of a much greater magnitude than in most other countries as, in the period analysed, two powerful processes acting in the same liberalizing direction were superimposed: the SMP and, even more influential, the transitional process of integration of the Spanish economy into the EU, beginning in 1986 and culminating precisely in the years covered by this review. This thoroughgoing opening-up of the Spanish economy, brought about by entry into the EU was, in fact, the cause of the majority of changes observed, as corroborated by the *ex post* studies carried out in Spain on the effects of integration. Therefore, the influence of the SMP on these changes was probably much less than the present analysis would seem to suggest.

(b)   The level of aggregation used in this analysis, though imposed by the problems of the availability of the statistical sources, was not the most suitable for determining the sectoral and regional effects of the SMP as:

   (i)   to verify the fulfilment of the forecasts made for the 40 sensitive sectors a three-digit NACE disaggregation would have been necessary, not only the two-digit NACE we were able to use;

   (ii)   in the case of Spain, when working with the aggregate 'all other regions' we lost much information on the behaviour of certain products and subsectors that started with very high comparative advantages.

Taking these factors into account, the main conclusions that we could draw on the impact of the SMP in the case of Spain were that:

(a)   the specific impact of the SMP on factor flows did not seem to have been very intense, although a process of moderate structural change was clearly perceptible;

(b)   all the regions increased their capital/labour ratio between 1978–85 and 1986–92, evidence of the efforts made in the capitalization and modernization of the industrial fabric to improve competitiveness in view of the single market.

The analysis carried out on the regional and sectoral concentration of employment and investment by means of Herfindahl indices enabled us to conclude that:

(a)   there was a trend towards diversification in both employment and investment, although the decrease in concentration was more pronounced in investment than in employment, but in most sectors and regions this change could not be attributed to the impact of the SMP as this trend had been observed since 1978, so, in this sense, the food, beverages and tobacco (41–42) and non-metallic minerals (23) sectors had the lowest regional concentrations of such variables;

(b)   nevertheless, there was a localized increase of concentration in certain regions –

Extremadura, Asturias – and sectors – metals (22), textiles and clothing (43) and office materials and machinery (33) – had the highest concentration of employment and investment;

(c) Spain's entry into the single market seems to have influenced investment, but not decisively:

(i) there were different impacts from one region to another (strong growth in three of them and a notable increase of diversification in five of them) and they were not on a large enough scale to substantially alter the regional ranking of sectoral concentration;

(ii) the differences among sectors with regard to regional concentration made it difficult to come to conclusions of a general character, so the observations must remain at the level of the particular.

With regard to the behaviour of trade flows, as confirmed by the regression analysis, in general there was a strong impact, one that was much more intense than in the case of the factor flows. There were generalized falls in the RCA indices, significant changes in the indices of sectoral specialization in exports, increases in the already high indices of IIT and a high degree of trade creation, both internal and external. The trade diversion effect, though present, reached lesser dimensions. There were also changes in export propensity, but not always towards an increase in the share of European customers to the detriment of third countries, reflecting the difficulties that Spanish products in general have had in penetrating the EU market. This fact, together with the high level of EU imports, explained the heavy falls in the RCA indices against those of the EU. However, this general view needed to be moderated by the notable sector and regional differences observed, which are outlined below.

By region

(a) Madrid, despite weak competitiveness (most of its RCAs were negative), experienced a positive impact from liberalization, which improved its indices. This improvement was due to the positive reaction of exports to the opening up of Europe, with a notable increase in the propensity to export to the EU, combined with a very weak internal trade creation effect that avoided the massive penetration of EU imports (except in 'sensitive' sectors where the penetration was intense on all fronts).

(b) In Catalonia, which had high specialization in weak- and medium-demand sectors, the entry into the single market led to an unfavourable competitiveness situation regarding outside competition, as shown by its RCAs and sector specialization indicators. Nevertheless, it followed a strategy of intra-industrial adjustment in sectors of medium-high demand, losing specialization in traditional sectors. Catalonia was, furthermore, the region that showed most trade creation effects, internal trade creation being combined with trade diversion, unlike other regions where external creation predominated.

(c) In the Basque country, unlike Catalonia, no such intense and generalized impact of the SMP was detected as there were notable differences between the reactions of the strong sectors and of the weak ones. The opening up of the EU facilitated exports of the sectors that started from a stronger competitive position (the metals (22), manufacture of metal articles (31) and mechanical engineering (32) sectors) and a slight improvement in the average RCA, but led to a heavy penetration of imports in traditional sectors, which also reduced its share of overall exports.

(d) The 'all other regions' group, owing to the heterogeneity of the regions concerned, combined highly competitive sectors with other very vulnerable ones. However, most of its export structure was oriented towards sectors of weak demand, with the exception of the chemicals (25) and automobiles (35) sectors. Therefore, almost all the trade indicators showed the vulnerability of this productive specialization: there were generalized falls in the RCAs and a strong internal and external trade creation effect. Specialization in the export of traditional goods fell, especially in the food, beverages and tobacco (41–42) sectors but export specialization in sectors of strong demand was maintained and even increased.

By sector

(a)   The export specialization index fell most in the sectors described as sensitive and having weak demand, such as food, beverages and tobacco (41–42) and leather goods, footwear and clothing (44–45), which decreased in all regions. On the other hand, the steep rise of specialization in the automobiles (35) sector confirmed that the sectors with greater intensity of technology and for which there was high demand offered better results for this indicator.

(b)   The RCA indicator showed the worsening of competitiveness in the Spanish manufacturing sectors, confirming the loss of importance of the inter-industrial trade model in these sectors as a whole. Catalonia and the other regions group reflected a greater loss of competitiveness against the increase in imports from EU countries, and in terms of sectors, automobiles (35) stood out as having the greatest rise in RCA, while the textiles and clothing (43) and paper, printing and publishing (47) sectors were at the opposite extreme, experiencing substantial falls in their competitiveness.

(c)   The IIT indices showed that there was an intensification of the IIT model on entry into the EU, and the trend was towards specialization in sectors for which there was strong or medium demand. In this sense, specialization implied differences in regional preferences, but for all regions the electrical machinery (34) sector experienced the greatest specialization.

(d)   The trade creation effect resulting from the process of integration of the Spanish economy into the EU was intense and widespread. There was high penetration of EU imports, as revealed by other studies made after entry, Catalonia and the 'all other regions' group experiencing the greatest creation of trade. The growth of penetration of imports in the food, beverages and tobacco (41–42) sector stood out among the traditional sectors, and the high level of trade creation in the electrical machinery (34), other means of transport (36) and instrument engineering (37) sectors among those for which there was medium and high demand. There were, however, notable regional differences within single sectors. For example, in the chemicals (25) sector, intense trade creation was generated in Madrid, but not in the 'all other regions' group, where this sector was one of the most competitive and important to the region's exports.

(e)   Finally, in trade with third countries, the diversion of trade in industrial products was insignificant and it seemed likely that the external trade creation effect compensated for the small trade diversion effect generated by the process of integration. Catalonia and Madrid were the regions where it was possible to detect most cases of diversion and, at the sectoral level, the non-metallic minerals (23) sector was the only one for which a clear diversion effect could be distinguished.

4.5.5. Regression analysis

Introduction

In the case of Spain, the regression analysis could not be performed for all regions and sectors as, in many regions, lots of variables were missing or were characterized by a very incomplete data set. We analysed the following regions:

(a)   Catalonia (C);
(b)   Madrid (M);
(c)   País Vasco (V);
(d)   the aggregate of the rest of Spain (A), which contained all the other regions, namely Andalucia, Aragon, Asturias, Baleares, Canarias, Cantabria, Castilla y Leon, Castilla–La Mancha, Valencia, Extremadura, Galicia, Murcia, Navarra, Rioja and Ceuta and Melilla.

For these regions, statistical observations were available for the sample size (for the period 1988–92) and for all tradable sectors, with the exception of the agricultural and energy sectors (NACE 01–11). Also, the available observations on FDI were aggregated, that is, we had the total amount of FDI for all the regions and sectors, but not how they were distributed within the sectors.

Objectives and model specification

The regression analysis was designed to achieve the following four main goals.

(a)   **To quantify the impact of the SMP on some trade indicators and factor flows**, which was done by analysing the value of ρ in the following regressions:

Equation 1 $XE_t/Y_t = b_0 + X_t\psi + \rho I_t + \varepsilon_{1t}$

Equation 2 $B_t = b_0 + X_t\psi + \rho I_t + \varepsilon_{2t}$

Equation 3 $RCA_t = b_0 + X_t\psi + \rho I_t + \varepsilon_{3t}$

Equation 4 $FDI_t = b_0 + X_t\psi + \rho I_t + \varepsilon_{4t}$

where trade creation (XE_t/Y_t), IIT (B_t), RCA (RCA_t) and FDI (FDI_t) were the main indicators of trade and factor flows that we selected. The vector of explanatory variables, X_t, contained proxies for cyclical and globalization effects (the growth rate of industrial production and world trade growth respectively). In the set of explanatory variables, X_t, we also included the other variables that were used in the indicator analysis – labour productivity, sectoral specialization and capital intensity (the capital/labour ratio). Finally, we also accounted for CSF support in all regions. These variables enabled us to disentangle the effect of the SMP (quantified by the parameter ρ) on trade and factor flows from the effects of cyclical and globalization variables and of variables capturing the specificity of each sector (capital intensity, labour productivity and specialization).

(b)   **To assess whether or not the SMP, by changing the pattern of trade flows, also modified the accumulation of (physical and human) capital in the Spanish regions considered in this study**. To achieve this goal we ran the following regressions:

Equation 5 $k_t = s_0 + s_1 Y_t + s_2 K_t + s_3 \Delta XE_t/Y_t + s_4 \Delta B_t + s_5 \Delta RCA_t + s_6 \Delta FDI_t + \varepsilon_{5t}$

Equation 6 $h_t = r_0 + r_1 Y_t + r_2 H_t + r_3 \Delta XE_t/Y_t + r_4 \Delta B_t + r_5 \Delta RCA_t + s_6 \Delta FDI_t + \varepsilon_{6t}$

where the dynamics of the growth rate of physical (k_t) and human (h_t) capital is explained stock (K_t) and flow (Y_t) characteristics of each region and sector (Baldwin and Venables, 1995) and for possible effects of trade creation (XE_t/Y_t), IIT (B_t), international competitiveness (RCA_t) and EU FDI (FDI_t). Notice that all these variables enter into Equations 5 and 6 as first differences (Δ) of the original variables endogenized by Equations 1 to 4. As explained in Baldwin and Venables (1995), the rationale of Equations 5 and 6 was that capital accumulation is likely to be pro cyclical (in the empirical specification we also used the rate of change of Y_t) and faster when capital is small, i.e. regions with a low level of capital stocks are likely to grow more rapidly. This argument implicitly embodies the assumption of a technology characterized by decreasing returns. As this may not be the case in some sectors, we did not expect the coefficients r_2 and s_2 to be necessarily negative.

Note that, given the available data, Equation 5 was run for all regions *and* sectors, whereas Equation 6 was run for all regions only. Moreover, remember that only the *total* amount of FDI was available for each region and sector. Therefore, in Equations 5 and 6, we introduced the level of this variable (rather than the change). The cross-section dimension of FDI helped us identify region-specific effects.

(c)   **To assess the impact of the SMP on the growth rates of per capita sectoral value added in the different sectors in all regions.** Therefore, the following regression was also run:

Equation 7 $y_t = a_t + \alpha k_t + \beta h_t - (1-\gamma)l_t + \varepsilon_{7t}$

where y_t is per capita GDP growth, a_t is the rate of growth of technical progress, k_t and h_t of physical and human capital, respectively, and l_t is the growth rate of unskilled labour. This regression was done for all regions and sectors. However, data on technical progress was available only at country level, whereas for physical capital we used data at regional level.

(d)   **Finally, the ultimate goal of our analysis was to verify in which sectors the implementation of the SMP increased or reduced the speed of convergence between the regions considered in this study.** To do that we had to calculate the *antimonde* growth path of sectoral per capita value added (see Chapter 3) and then run the following regression:

Equation 8 $IM_{j,avg} = cost°_j + (\alpha-\alpha^*)INV_{j,avg} - (\beta-\beta^*)RGDP_{j,85} + (\gamma-\gamma^*)GPO_{j,avg} (\delta-\delta^*)SEC_{j,85} + (\varphi-\varphi^*)TECH_{j,avg} + (\theta-\theta^*)DUMMIES_j + \alpha^*(INV_{j,avg} - INV^*_{j,avg}) + \eta_j$

where the dependent variable is defined as the difference between the actual average relative rate of growth of sectoral per capita value added and the average *antimonde* rate of growth, determined as explained in Section 3.7.[40]

The lack of data, both in terms of the time range (which did not permit us to identify the economic state *before* the implementation of the SMP and the *antimonde* situation needed to evaluate the convergence) and the number of regions (that we could not disentangle the aggregate effects), led us not to include the data for the Spanish regions in Equation 8 (see also Chapter 5).

Methodology

From a methodological viewpoint, Equations 1 to 7 were estimated using the techniques described in Chapter 3. In particular, in the estimation process we accounted for:

(a) **co-integration**, by using the two-step Engle and Granger estimator (the one-step estimator proposed by Davidson and McKinnon proved to be less efficient);

(b) **simultaneity**, by using instrumental variables for the endogenous variables appearing among the explanatory ones;

(c) **regional heterogeneity** in the panel of data used to estimate Equations 1 to 7 (regional heterogeneity was tested by introducing regional dummies among the regressors);

(d) **structural breaks** related to the implementation of the SMP, by using the liberalization index as the explanatory variable for the dynamics of the equation coefficients;

(e) **heteroscedasticity**, by using a White-consistent estimator;

(f) **technical progress**, by constructing an index that reflected the dynamics of economic indicators such as R&D, relative prices, GDP growth, patents etc.;

(g) **structural funds**, by explaining regional differences, also by means of a measure of CSFs in each region.

The actual specification of the model was achieved following the 'encompassing principle' approach. That is, we started from the most general model in which all available variables were included and then we reduced the number of variables of the regressions by performing a cascade of t and F tests. If the 'true' model is 'encompassed' by the initial general model, this method leads the specification process just described to identify the 'true' model. Of course, the small number of degrees of freedom does not guarantee this outcome, which holds asymptotically. Therefore, once we had identified the 'true' model, we tested its robustness by using Pagan and Hall's residual analysis, that is, we regressed the residuals on the excluded coefficients).

This procedure (encompassing approach plus residual analysis), designed to guarantee the robustness of the estimated model, was followed for both the explanatory variables included in each of the regressions and the regional dummies, which captured the difference between the region-specific effects and the average effects in the panel of regions. Note that when we applied this procedure we did not use a rigid criterion to define the significance level of the various tests. In particular, the constants CO, $C1$ and $C2$ (see Appendix A1 to Section 4.5) and the lagged variable of the second stage of the Engle and Granger procedure were maintained in

---

[40] The starred parameters and variables are those generated within the *antimonde* analysis, that is, assuming that the liberalization index is equal to 1 over the whole sample.

the regression even when they were statistically non-significant. A few explanatory variables also appeared with low t statistics.

This was done because our main goals were the robustness and the theoretical consistency of the model. Therefore, given the small number of degrees of freedom, in the selection of the variables, priority was given to these two objectives rather than to the choice of a given (say, 10%) significance level.

Robustness was also an issue as far as co-integration and structural breaks were concerned. In the case of co-integration, the small quantity of data did not enable us to perform the usual Dickey and Fuller's tests. However, we used a graphical representation of the time series as evidence of the presence of a common trend. Moreover, we exploited the super-consistency properties of the estimates of the co-integration vector in the Engle and Granger two-stage procedure in order to exclude from the co-integration regression those variables for which the coefficients were not statistically significant in the first stage. These variables were then tested to check that they belonged to the 'true' model as stationary non-co-integrated variables. When this hypothesis could be accepted, the variables were maintained in the regression (their first difference was not introduced in the second stage of the Engle and Granger procedure).

In the case of structural breaks, we tested the robustness of the model in two ways: by running t tests on the significance of the coefficients, explaining the variability of the coefficients, and by comparing the model in which structural variability was assumed with the model in which coefficients were assumed to be constant. The computed likelihood ratio always led us to accept the hypothesis that the correct specification was the one that assumed structural variability. The power of these tests was certainly limited by the small size of the sample. However, the panel approach and the non-significance of many of the regional dummies provided us with a sufficient number of degrees of freedom for the estimation and the robustness check of the final model.

Trade and factor flows

The four equations describing the dynamics of trade flows were estimated using the methodology described above. The notable exception in the case of Equations 1–4 was that only the constant term was assumed to be time-varying, that is, the liberalization index was introduced into these equations in an additive way. A panel data approach was used in order to increase the efficiency of our estimates. Therefore, all equations were estimated sector by sector, by stacking regional data. Regional dummies (both on constant and slope parameters) were introduced when they were statistically significant.

Let us consider the first equation, which captures the dynamics of trade creation. The eight parameters presented in Appendix A1 to Section 4.5 are the impact on trade creation of the following:

(a)   world trade index ($x1$);
(b)   specialization index ($x2$);
(c)   capital/labour ratio ($x3$);
(d)   labour productivity ($x4$);
(e)   GDP growth rate ($x5$);
(f)   liberalization index ($x6$);

(g) FDI (*x7*);
(h) CSFs (*x8*).

In order to understand the results reported in Appendix A1 to Section 4.5 (Tables A1.4.5.1, A1.4.5.2), note that the set of regressors is divided into two parts: the first block contains the regressors that were shown to be co-integrated (their coefficients were estimated in the first step); the second block contains the regressors that are not co-integrated (the constants and some explanatory variables) and the lagged dependent variable, which must be introduced into the second step (we do not show the coefficients related to the first differences of the co-integrated variables, because they are relevant only to performing a correct inference on the other parameters). Note that the second block of coefficients is shown after the constant *CO* and the coefficient of the lagged variable (*RIT*).

Let us focus on the impact of the liberalization index – which captured the progressive implementation of the SMP – on trade creation. It can be seen that a generalized positive and significant effect was found in most of the sectors and regions considered. The only exceptions were the paper products sector, which showed a negative influence, and the textiles and clothing sector, the only one for which the effect was not statistically significant. The food, beverages and tobacco sector presented a diminishing correction dummy for the País Vasco region to the aggregate and positive effect.

Let us now move to the indicator of IIT. The liberalization index seemed to have had a more generalized and positive impact on this index, too. Actually, its effect was always statistically significant and the metal products sector was the only one to show a negative parameter.

It is worth noting also that the specialization index and the GDP growth rate were always positively correlated to IIT, although they were not statistically significant in all sectors. In particular, this positive effect was evident for the non-metal minerals, transport equipment and food, beverages and tobacco products sectors, which were influenced by the GDP growth rate; the metal products, textiles and clothing and wood and rubber sectors were influenced by the specialization index; finally, the chemicals sector showed a positive correlation with respect to both indices.

Less favourable results were found when we focused on the RCA indicator. In this case, the only sectors for which there was a significant and positive effect linked to the liberalization index were the transport equipment, food, beverages and tobacco products, textiles and clothing and wood and rubber sectors. The metal minerals and paper products sectors showed a negative correlation, while for the remaining sectors (non-metal minerals, metal products and chemical products) there was no significant impact.

The RCA was also influenced by changes in the level of labour productivity. With the exception of the non-metal minerals and chemical products sectors, all other sectors showed a positive correlation with the labour productivity.

Finally, a unique equation for total FDI was estimated for all sectors, without distinguishing either their origin/destination – EU or the rest of the world – (because data were available only in aggregate form with respect to their origin) or the specific sectoral level. Therefore, one equation with regional dummies was used to capture the dynamics of FDI.

The results showed that the investment from/to abroad for all regions was positively correlated to the accumulation factor, the productivity level and to the growth rate of GDP. Also, in this case, the SMP had a significant and positive impact, although Madrid and País Vasco had dummies that dampened the aggregate effect.

We could therefore conclude that the implementation of the SMP in Spain seemed to have had a generalized positive effect on trade and factor flow indicators. The majority of sectors were positively influenced by the SMP in each indicator. Only the RCA indicator had more than one sector that was negatively correlated with the SMP. At the same time, only in a few sectors did we identify a significant negative impact for each indicator. Actually, only the paper products sector showed negative impacts in more than one of the indicators adopted. By contrast, there were three sectors (transport equipment, food, beverages and tobacco, and wood and rubber) that, in each indicator, had been stimulated by the SMP.

Factor accumulation

Equations 5 and 6 were designed to assess the impact of trade and factor flow changes on the accumulation of physical and human capital in the different regions and sectors. Capital accumulation (the growth rate of physical and human capital) was therefore explained by the standard stock flow law of motion and by the possible effects of changes of trade and factor flow indicators. In the estimation of these two equations, we accounted for heteroscedasticity due to regional variability, for structural breaks induced by the implementation of the SMP (both on constants and slope parameters), for regional dummies, for co-integration (using the Engle and Granger two-step estimator) and for simultaneity (by means of the available instrumental variables).

The estimation results for Equation 2 are shown in Appendix A1 to Section 4.5. The regressors are as follows:

(a)   regional value added ($x1$);
(b)   level of the physical capital stock ($x2$);
(c)   trade creation ($x3$);
(d)   FDI ($x4$);
(e)   IIT ($x5$);
(f)   RCA ($x6$).

Moreover, the coefficient C_0 accounts for regional differences due to the initial 1988 level of the capital stock, whereas C_2 accounts for regional differences due to CSF. The coefficient C_1 measures the break induced on the panel fixed effect by the increase in the liberalization index.

Looking at the results (see Appendix A1 to Section 4.5), note that an increase in regional value added had a positive impact on capital accumulation in all regions and sectors. Moreover, the parameters related to the level of the capital stock have the expected negative sign, thus showing that capital accumulation was faster when the level of the capital stock was lower.

As far as our objectives are concerned, the most interesting results are those that showed the impact of trade and factor flow indicators on capital accumulation.

Considering the role of trade creation, we can see that this indicator, although it had a significant impact only for few sectors, always had a positive effect on the accumulation of capital. This was the case for the metal minerals, paper products and wood and rubber sectors.

By contrast, the other two trade indicators showed different impacts on different sectors. The intra-industry indicator had a positive effect on the metal minerals, metal products, chemical products and the textiles and clothing sectors, while it was negatively correlated to the capital accumulation of transport equipment, paper products and wood and rubber sectors.

The RCA indicator had a positive effect on the food, beverages and tobacco and textiles and clothing sectors, while it had a negative influence on the chemical products, paper products and the wood and rubber sectors.

Moving forward in the analysis of the impact of SMP on factor accumulation, as we found a generalized positive impact of the SMP on the trade indicators (particularly on trade creation and IIT), we concluded that, indirectly, this effect was frequently transmitted to capital accumulation via the trade indicators themselves. This was the case, for example, for the metal minerals sector, where capital accumulation was stimulated positively by the IIT and by the IIT indicators that, in turn, were both positively influenced by the implementation of the SMP.

This result was even more evident considering the role of FDI on capital accumulation. The indicator of factor flows showed a positive impact in most of the sectors considered. Actually, the only exception was the transport equipment sector in which the effect was not statistically significant. As we registered the SMP as having a positive impact on the total FDI indicator, this effect was constantly transmitted to the capital accumulation in all the sectors considered but transport equipment. Therefore, among trade and factor flow indicators, the RCA was the most ambiguous in its relation to the SMP and to capital accumulation. Our analysis suggested that liberalization had a positive impact on factor accumulation concentrated mainly in those sectors capturing the changes in the other trade indicators.

Direct effects due to the implementation of the SMP could be detected by means of the generalized structural breaks on the model coefficients by the increase in the liberalization index and via the coefficient linked to the CSFs.

In particular, the coefficient C_1, which measured the break induced on the panel fixed effect, shows a positive value for non-metal minerals, food, beverages and tobacco and the textiles and clothing sectors, while it was negative for metal minerals, transport equipment and the wood and rubber sectors; in the other sectors, it was not statistically significant.

More favourable results were found when we focused on the effect of the CSFs. Results suggested that capital accumulation grew faster because it was stimulated by the CSFs. The coefficient C_2 was positive and significant in most of the sectors (metal minerals, chemical products, transport equipment, food, beverages and tobacco and paper products). The only exception was wood and rubber, while in the other sectors there was no statistical significance.

Let us now move to human capital. This variable was proxied by the number of students in the secondary school, a variable that was obviously defined at the regional level (it was meaningless to disaggregate this variable for each sector). This proxy has been the one most used in the literature on convergence (see Levine and Renelt, 1992, and Baldwin and

Venables, 1995). The fact of using only regional observations implied that only one regression was run, where regional data were considered as a panel. The results are shown in Appendix A1 to Section 4.5. Again, the growth rate of the stock of human capital was negatively related to its level, thus indicating that human capital increased faster when the level was low. The effect of value added growth on human capital growth was positive, as expected.

As far as trade and factor flow indicators were concerned, we found a positive impact on human capital accumulation of changes in the trade creation and IIT indicators. A positive, albeit slightly significant, effect was found for FDI. The effect of changes in RCA was not statistically significant.

These results were therefore similar to those found for physical capital: trade creation and FDI together with IIT have had a generalized positive effect; via these indicators the positive effect of the SMP was transmitted to human capital accumulation; the role of the RCA was, again, the most ambiguous.

The indirect positive effect transmitted through the trade and factor flow indices balanced the negative SMP-induced structural break on the panel fixed effect measured by the parameter C_1. The positive and significant value of the C_0 parameter showed that the human capital accumulation grew faster in the regions with higher initial capital stock. The CSFs did not have significant effects.

Regional growth

The previous analysis did not provide any behavioural link between the implementation of the SMP and economic growth. However, it may be worth looking at the existence of a structural link, that is, an increase in the economic growth induced by the SMP via a structural change of the coefficients in the growth equation. Consider, therefore, the last equation in our regression model, which linked the growth rate of per capita income to technical progress ($x1$), the accumulation of physical ($x2$) and human ($x3$) capital, and to the growth rate of labour force ($x4$), which was assumed to be exogenous.

The crucial question is whether or not, and in which sector, there have been positive effects induced by the implementation of the SMP. As for the accumulation factors, these effects are direct (because of the structural break induced by the implementation of the SMP and/or via CSFs) and indirect, as we have seen that factor accumulation has itself been stimulated by the SMP.

Looking at the results shown in Appendix A1 to Section 4.5, a positive and statistically significant break occurred only in the non-metal minerals and in the wood and rubber sectors. In all other sectors, the coefficient C_1 was either negative (as it was for metal products and chemical products) or statistically non-significant. No positive effect was found for CSFs.

The growth equation provided more interesting information. There was evidence of convergence in economic growth in the transport equipment, food, beverages and tobacco and the paper products sectors. In all other sectors, the coefficient C_0 was statistically non-significant.

Economic growth in Spanish regions was mainly explained by the dynamics of the human capital (in all sectors except metal minerals, food, beverages and tobacco and textiles and clothing) and of the technical progress (all sectors except metal minerals, metal products and chemical products). Positive effects on growth were also related to the labour force (positive in metal products, food, beverages and tobacco and wood and rubber; negative in metal minerals, chemical products and textiles and clothing). Finally, the physical capital influence is limited to transport equipment and paper products sectors.

The positive role played by the human capital and, to a lesser extent, by the physical capital, partly balanced the lack of direct effects induced by the SMP on the per capita GDP growth rate. In particular, it was possible to identify sectors (metal minerals, food, beverages and tobacco and textiles and clothing) in which there were no effects, direct or indirect, of the implementation of the SMP on economic growth.

Conclusions

There are a few conclusions that the regression analysis seemed to support:

(a) The implementation of the SMP had many positive effects on trade and factor flows. Most of these effects have been identified as relating to trade creation and IIT. The impact on RCA was less clear, while the aggregate by sector FDI was positively influenced.

(b) As far as human capital was concerned, the relation of its accumulation rate to trade and factor flows showed that it was positively related to the changes in trade creation, IIT and FDI indicators. The RCA was not statistically significant. The conclusions were similar when we considered physical capital, for which, again, trade creation and IIT had a generally positive effect on its accumulation rate, whereas the RCA had an uncertain effect.

(c) A significant and positive influence on the accumulation of physical capital was produced by the different CSF values for different regions. There was no statistical evidence for the relation between human capital accumulation and CSFs. There was evidence of a positive SMP-induced structural break only for physical capital but for a few sectors.

(d) By coupling the above results, we concluded that the regression analysis for the Spanish regions suggested that most of the positive impacts of the implementation of the SMP on human capital accumulation were likely to have occurred via trade and factor flows. In the case of physical capital, a less clear influence of the trade indicators was balanced by the stimulating effect of the CSFs.

(e) There was evidence of convergence in economic growth in some sectors (transport equipment, food, beverages and tobacco and paper products). The impact of the implementation of the SMP on economic growth was mostly not significant. No positive effect on growth was found for CSFs.

(f) Economic growth was influenced mainly by the human capital changes and technical progress; few effects came via the physical capital.

4.5.6. Appendix A1 to Section 4.5.

Explanatory note regarding the regression analysis

The regression parameters, *Xijk*, have to be read as follows:

(a)   *i* is the index of the regressor (according to the three types of equation) for:
-    (i)   trade and factor flows:
     - world trade index;
     - specialization index;
     - capital/labour ratio;
     - labour productivity;
     - GDP growth rate;
     - liberalization index;
     - FDI;
     - CSFs;
-    (ii)   human and physical capital:
     - 1 regional value added;
     - 2 level of the physical capital stock;
     - 3 trade creation;
     - 4 FDI;
     - 5 IIT;
     - 6 RCAs;
-    (iii)   economic growth:
     - 1 technical progress;
     - 2 accumulation of physical capital;
     - 3 accumulation of human capital;
     - 4 growth rate of labour force;

(b)   *j* is the index of the region:
- *C*atalonia;
- *M*adrid;
- Pais *V*asco;
- *A*ggregate of the rest of Spain;

(c)   *k* is the index of the sector:
- AGR;
- CHP;
- ENP;
- FBT;
- MEM;
- MEP;
- NMM;
- PAP;
- TEC;
- TOT;
- TRE;
- WOR.

Table A1.4.5.1. Sectoral regression parameters for Spain

Sector MEM

Growth equation

	Param	t student
X4MEM	-3.427	-3.981
X4CMEM	3.315	3.782
X4MMEM	2.831	1.745
X4PMEM	-3.262	-2.323
C0MEM	-1.668	-0.361
C1MEM	0.033	0.286
C2MEM	-0.005	-4.314
R1TMEM	-0.047	-9.319
R-squared =	0.903	

Physical capital equation

	Param	t student
X2MEM	-0.059	-2.451
C0MEM	3.283	1.534
C1MEM	-0.186	-2.060
C2MEM	0.106	2.075
R1TMEM	-0.014	-4.061
X1MEM	0.111	0.993
X3MEM	0.797	2.564
X4MEM	0.152	3.288
X5MEM	0.286	3.114
R-squared =	0.519	

IIT-E equation

	Param	t student
X1MEM	0.024	41.583
X6MEM	0.003	7.028
X7MEM	0.003	6.183
C0MEM	-0.503	-1.424
R1TMEM	-0.895	-1.980
X3MEM	0.325	1.598
X4MEM	0.067	1.501
X8MEM	0.012	2.600
R-squared =	0.655	

RCA-E equation

	Param	t student
X1MEM	0.029	15.827
X6MEM	-0.005	-1.899
X6CMEM	0.002	5.279
X6MMEM	-0.002	-4.769
X8MEM	0.053	2.462
C0MEM	-0.903	-3.755
R1TMEM	-0.629	-4.595
X4MEM	0.081	3.733
R-squared	0.862	

TC equation

	Param	t student
X4MEM	0.088	10.403
X6MEM	0.018	12.035
C0MEM	0.200	3.074
R1TMEM	-0.273	-1.471
X2MEM	-0.001	-1.527
X3MEM	0.750	2.248
R-squared	0.523	

Sector NMM

Growth equation

	Param	t student
X1NMM	0.225	2.378
X3NMM	0.747	2.471
C0NMM	-0.118	-0.278
C1NMM	0.093	5.058
C2NMM	-0.002	-8.081
R1TNMM	0.007	3.516
R-squared =	0.746	

Physical capital equation

	Param	t student
X1NMM	0.262	3.013
X2NMM	-0.125	-2.364
C0NMM	-4.644	-5.091
C1NMM	0.191	6.434
C2NMM	-0.111	-0.963
R1TNMM	-0.042	-8.295
X4NMM	0.031	1.763
R-squared =	0.839	

IIT-E equation

	Param	t student
X1NMM	0.074	6.282
X1CNMM	0.015	2.538
X1MNMM	-0.017	-2.266
X3NMM	0.893	3.918
X4NMM	-0.068	-2.073
X5NMM	0.020	4.641
X6NMM	0.017	11.419
C0NMM	0.210	4.260
R1TNMM	-0.553	-2.731
R-squared =	0.984	

RCA-E equation

	Param	t student
X1NMM	0.062	13.700
X1CNMM	0.019	3.818
X8NMM	0.043	2.700
C0NMM	0.510	0.809
R1TNMM	-0.966	-2.251
X2NMM	-0.010	-1.005
X7NMM	0.018	1.409
R-squared	0.450	

TC equation

	Param	t student
X1NMM	0.138	3.039
X2NMM	-0.005	-2.051
X4NMM	-0.175	-2.138
X6NMM	0.023	15.523
C0NMM	-0.007	-0.162
R1TNMM	-0.881	-1.718
X3NMM	1.031	4.019
X7NMM	0.002	1.830
R-squared	0.941	

Sector CHP

Growth equation

	Param	t student
X4MEP	3.638	2.405
X4CMEP	-9.917	-3.599
X4MMEP	-2.670	-1.764
X4AMEP	-3.269	-1.551
C0MEP	1.181	0.540
C1MEP	-0.109	-1.693
C2MEP	-0.001	-1.295
R1TMEP	-0.013	-1.183
X3MEP	1.012	1.735
R-squared =	0.672	

Physical capital equation

	Param	t student
X1MEP	0.133	4.105
X2MEP	-0.109	-3.970
C0MEP	-0.222	-0.306
C1MEP	0.015	0.705
C2MEP	0.025	0.600
R1TMEP	-0.025	-2.668
X4MEP	0.024	2.892
X5MEP	0.006	2.742
R-squared =	0.609	

IIT-E equation

	Param	t student
X1MEP	0.004	5.481
X2MEP	0.002	3.566
X3MEP	-1.757	-3.210
X4MEP	-0.143	-2.793
X6MEP	-0.008	-3.148
X7MEP	0.004	2.395
X8MEP	0.010	1.604
C0MEP	0.196	1.148
R1TMEP	-0.945	-1.359
R-squared =	0.864	

RCA-E equation

	Param	t student
X1MEP	0.001	6.103
X2MEP	-0.001	-1.574
X4MEP	0.125	4.841
C0MEP	0.473	2.243
R1TMEP	-0.125	-1.219
X3MEP	-2.356	-3.071
X5MEP	0.038	4.537
R-squared	0.365	

TC equation

	Param	t student
X1MEP	0.002	6.527
X3MEP	-1.233	-1.242
X6MEP	0.023	8.193
X6MMEP	-0.007	-2.689
X6PMEP	-0.005	-2.027
C0MEP	0.677	3.146
R1TMEP	-0.994	-2.682
X4MEP	-0.094	-2.135
R-squared	0.948	

Sector MEP

Growth equation			Physical capital equation			IIT-E equation			RCA-E equation			TC equation		
	Param	t student		Param	t student		Param	t student		Param	t student		Param	t student
X3CHP	0.839	4.269	X1CHP	0.468	2.600	X1CHP	0.001	4.586	X1CHP	0.003	5.444	X1CHP	0.003	5.751
X3PCHP	-1.601	-1.689	X2CHP	-0.258	-2.009	X2CHP	0.001	6.002	X2CHP	0.001	1.583	X2CHP	0.001	3.189
X3ACHP	0.194	1.651	COCHP	-1.472	-0.658	X3CHP	-0.656	-3.805	X8CHP	0.021	1.574	X4CHP	-0.018	-1.860
X4CHP	-0.101	-1.019	C1CHP	0.062	0.938	X4CHP	0.047	6.203	COCHP	0.076	1.386	X6CHP	0.013	8.803
X4MCHP	0.902	13.674	C2CHP	0.138	3.456	X6CHP	0.010	10.496	R1TCHP	-0.753	-2.319	X7CHP	0.007	10.127
COCHP	0.370	0.447	R1TCHP	-0.004	-0.259	X6CCHP	0.004	1.064	X3CHP	-1.377	-4.154	COCHP	-0.072	-0.898
C1CHP	-0.023	-1.288	X4CHP	0.056	1.042	X6MCHP	0.003	3.112	X5CHP	0.009	2.441	R1TCHP	-0.418	-1.935
C2CHP	-0.004	-2.129	X5CHP	0.018	1.107	COCHP	-0.095	-1.432				X8CHP	-0.009	-1.850
R1TCHP	-0.026	-2.574	X6CHP	-0.731	-1.632	R1TCHP	-0.374	-0.943						
						X5CHP	0.008	2.636						
						X1CHP	0.003	7.557						
						X8CHP	0.030	3.791						
R-squared =	0.726		R-squared =	0.387		R-squared =	0.998		R-squared	0.692		R-squared	0.981	

Sector TRE

Growth equation			Physical capital equation			IIT-E equation			RCA-E equation			TC equation		
	Param	t student		Param	t student		Param	t student		Param	t student		Param	t student
X1TRE	0.333	2.041	X1TRE	1.152	1.759	X4TRE	0.152	75.791	X1TRE	0.000	0.514	X1TRE	0.001	1.695
X2TRE	0.065	1.338	X2TRE	-0.739	-1.654	X6TRE	0.019	101.269	X2TRE	-0.011	-2.469	X2TRE	0.009	2.356
X3TRE	0.445	1.454	COTRE	3.975	2.151	X6CTRE	0.023	2.482	X3TRE	-0.412	-5.198	X4TRE	-0.253	-2.272
COTRE	-1.813	-2.385	C1TRE	-0.273	-4.542	X6MTRE	-0.009	-45.162	X4TRE	0.404	2.261	X6TRE	0.019	3.398
C1TRE	-0.011	-0.240	C2TRE	0.289	1.869	X6PTRE	-0.009	-3.683	X5TRE	0.008	1.531	X7TRE	0.005	2.007
C2TRE	0.000	-0.024	R1TTRE	-0.009	-1.703	COTRE	-0.820	-2.430	X6TRE	0.016	1.657	X8TRE	0.019	1.257
R1TTRE	-0.007	-2.719	X5TRE	-0.021	-3.853	R1TTRE	-0.500	-1.145	X8TRE	0.109	3.074	COTRE	-0.922	-3.770
						X1TRE	0.001	2.315	COTRE	-0.129	-1.089	R1TTRE	-0.951	-2.089
						X5TRE	0.007	1.278	R1TTRE	-0.926	-3.398	X3TRE	0.207	2.112
												X5TRE	0.042	3.232
R-squared =	0.529		R-squared =	0.737		R-squared =	0.987		R-squared	0.860		R-squared	0.955	

Sector FBT

Growth equation			Physical capital equation			IIT-E equation			RCA-E equation			TC equation		
	Param	t student		Param	t student		Param	t student		Param	t student		Param	t student
X1FBT	0.504	11.006	X1FBT	0.265	5.733	X4FBT	0.099	30.305	X2FBT	-0.007	-2.152	X2FBT	-0.006	-2.827
COFBT	-0.854	-2.570	X2FBT	-0.254	-5.811	X6FBT	0.025	67.988	X3FBT	5.384	2.856	X3FBT	-3.582	-2.968
C1FBT	0.015	0.770	COFBT	-1.800	-1.786	X6CFBT	-0.003	-3.782	X4FBT	0.191	3.967	X4FBT	0.276	5.859
C2FBT	0.000	-0.192	C1FBT	0.071	2.358	X6PFBT	-0.020	-4.183	X6FBT	0.011	4.004	X6FBT	0.022	7.362
R1TFBT	-0.010	-2.365	C2FBT	0.177	3.012	X7FBT	0.003	6.391	X8FBT	0.074	2.232	X6PFBT	-0.032	-8.648
X4FBT	0.160	1.750	R1TFBT	-0.013	-2.165	COFBT	0.110	3.162	COFBT	-15.630	-1.891	COFBT	-11.184	-2.294
X4PFBT	-0.357	-3.236	X4FBT	0.072	2.529	R1TFBT	-0.782	-1.992	R1TFBT	-0.465	-1.285	R1TFBT	-0.997	-5.116
			X6FBT	0.440	1.567	X5FBT	0.015	1.954	X1FBT	0.059	1.876	X1FBT	0.043	2.336
									X5FBT	0.061	1.648			
									X7FBT	0.014	1.746			
R-squared =	0.590		R-squared =	0.738		R-squared =	0.990		R-squared	0.795		R-squared	0.919	

Sector: TEC

Growth equation			Physical capital equation			IIT-E equation			RCA-E equation			TC equation		
	Param	t student		Param	t student		Param	t student		Param	t student		Param	t student
X1TEC	0.448	4.623	X1TEC	4.312	4.218	X1TEC	0.001	1.756	X1TEC	0.001	1.281	X1TEC	0.013	4.754
X4TEC	-0.076	-1.564	X1MTEC	-3.340	-3.679	X2TEC	0.002	2.761	X1CTEC	-0.004	-1.881	X1PTEC	0.011	4.265
C0TEC	-0.471	-0.490	X2TEC	-4.539	-4.330	X6TEC	0.022	12.693	X1MTEC	0.000	1.861	X4TEC	-0.537	-2.746
C1TEC	-0.025	-0.639	X2PTEC	2.490	2.142	X7TEC	0.008	5.633	X2TEC	-0.003	-1.802	X5TEC	0.061	1.867
C2TEC	0.000	0.261	C0TEC	-7.310	-2.405	X8TEC	0.015	1.888	X4TEC	0.236	3.138	C0TEC	0.038	0.097
RITTEC	-0.019	-2.526	C1TEC	0.287	2.313	C0TEC	-0.032	-0.409	C0TEC	-1.015	-4.603	RITTEC	-0.373	-2.529
			C2TEC	0.026	0.806	RITTEC	-0.230	-1.205	RITTEC	-0.045	-1.184	X2TEC	0.009	2.927
			RITTEC	-0.023	-8.685				X6TEC	0.008	3.299	X3TEC	4.591	3.484
			X4TEC	0.265	3.027							X7TEC	0.014	2.406
			X5TEC	0.671	2.711							X8TEC	0.098	4.012
			X6TEC	0.718	2.149									
R-squared =	0.615		R-squared =	0.969		R-squared =	0.983		R-squared	0.600		R-squared	0.917	

Sector: PAP

Growth equation			Physical capital equation			IIT-E equation			RCA-E equation			TC equation		
	Param	t student		Param	t student		Param	t student		Param	t student		Param	t student
X1PAP	1.153	6.375	X1PAP	0.434	6.101	X1PAP	0.004	22.571	X1PAP	0.006	7.704	X1PAP	0.008	2.605
X3PAP	1.176	1.876	X2PAP	-0.231	-5.960	X1CPAP	0.000	1.124	X6PAP	-0.017	-3.182	X3PAP	-1.223	-1.974
C0PAP	-29.112	-2.536	C0PAP	1.150	1.571	X1PPAP	-0.003	-2.695	X6PPAP	-0.079	-3.981	X4PAP	-0.150	-1.389
C1PAP	-0.032	-0.476	C1PAP	-0.029	-1.280	X1APAP	0.000	1.436	X6APAP	-0.131	-5.897	X6PAP	-0.025	-1.612
C2PAP	-0.001	-1.541	C2PAP	0.503	7.433	X3PAP	0.463	4.218	C0PAP	-5.150	-1.971	X6CPAP	0.026	3.342
RITPAP	-0.031	-2.539	RITPAP	-0.053	-4.615	X6PAP	0.008	6.793	RITPAP	-0.354	-1.198	X8PAP	0.127	3.167
X2PAP	3.370	2.823	X3PAP	0.211	1.902	C0PAP	-2.137	-4.253	X2PAP	-0.006	-3.314	C0PAP	-2.247	-10.221
			X4PAP	0.018	2.833	RITPAP	-0.615	-2.169	X4PAP	1.310	2.235	RITPAP	-0.205	-1.595
			X6PAP	-0.069	-3.907	X4PAP	0.401	3.859				X2PAP	0.005	3.974
						X7PAP	0.014	5.475				X7PAP	0.015	5.431
R-squared =	0.590		R-squared. =	0.938		R-squared. =	0.942		R-squared	0.814		R-squared	0.956	

Sector: WOR

Growth equation			Physical capital equation			IIT-E equation			RCA-E equation			TC equation		
	Param	t student		Param	t student		Param	t student		Param	t student		Param	t student
X1WOR	0.214	2.831	X1WOR	0.567	7.257	X1WOR	0.001	12.734	X2WOR	-0.053	-3.627	X1WOR	-0.002	-1.541
X3WOR	0.366	1.690	X2WOR	-0.383	-7.095	X1CWOR	0.000	1.955	X3WOR	18.679	6.696	X2WOR	0.017	2.099
C0WOR	0.358	0.852	C0WOR	0.826	3.693	X6WOR	0.019	18.693	X4WOR	1.656	4.243	X4WOR	-0.169	-1.008
C1WOR	0.105	4.685	C1WOR	-0.046	-4.765	X6PWOR	-0.015	-3.941	X6WOR	0.018	3.855	X6WOR	0.024	9.771
C2WOR	-0.002	-3.168	C2WOR	-0.730	-2.642	X7WOR	0.005	6.502	X6CWOR	0.022	1.640	X6PWOR	-0.042	-8.042
RITWOR	-0.005	-1.655	RITWOR	-0.041	-2.885	C0WOR	-0.355	-4.237	C0WOR	-0.446	-1.380	C0WOR	-0.106	-1.510
X4WOR	0.068	1.055	X3WOR	0.418	2.254	RITWOR	-0.964	-3.374	RITWOR	-0.789	-2.345	RITWOR	-0.704	-3.544
			X4WOR	0.081	3.584	X2WOR	0.016	4.306	X7WOR	0.046	1.570			
			X5WOR	-0.011	-4.995	X3WOR	-3.126	-2.325						
			X6WOR	-0.314	-2.399	X4WOR	-0.318	-5.848						
R-squared =	0.818		R-squared. =	0.978		R-squared. =	0.981		R-squared	0.664		R-squared	0.858	

Note: A=other regions; M=Madrid; C=Catalonia; P=PaisVasco.

Table A1.4.5.2. Non-sectoral regression parameters for Spain

Sector	FDI equation			Human capital equation		
		Param.	*t* student		Param.	*t* student
TOT						
	X3TOT	7.756	6.479	X1TOT	0.004	2.940
	X4TOT	0.140	3.949	X1ATOT	0.003	2.341
	X5TOT	0.116	2.750	X2TOT	-0.129	-2.131
	X6TOT	0.046	8.579	X2MTOT	0.114	1.795
	X6MTOT	-0.010	-2.543			
	X6PTOT	-0.019	-2.015	C0TOT	1.892	5.712
				C1TOT	-0.064	-9.001
	C0TOT	0.628	1.187	C2TOT	0.000	0.252
	RITTOT	-0.613	-1.068	RITTOT	-0.024	-2.461
				X3TOT	0.099	2.544
				X4TOT	0.008	1.323
				X5TOT	0.001	1.743
	R-squared	0.929		R-squared	0.869	

Note: A=other regions; M=Madrid; C=Catalonia; P=País Vasco.

4.6. East Germany[41]

4.6.1. Background

Economic integration within the bounds of the Council for Mutual Economic Aid (Comecon) was, for the former German Democratic Republic (GDR), an important element in its effort to increase wealth with the help of the international division of labour. Nevertheless, foreign trade within Comecon did not come into being by virtue of marketable relations between the enterprises, as is usual in Western countries. Rather, it was the expression of the dirigistic planning bureaucracies of the Comecon countries. Foreign trade relations of the former GDR had been distorted in terms of its regional as well as of its sectoral structure. The GDR had been a member of Comecon since 29 September 1950. Comecon was an organization that was founded as a counterpart of the EU and tried to organize a 'socialist' division of labour. Trade within Comecon was not based on the idea of market relations, but it was determined by the planning authorities, codified in five-year plans and a yearly protocol on trade. The division of labour was organized in the form of specialization agreements that assigned specific goods to each of the Comecon members. The selection of these goods was not only motivated by comparative advantages, but also by development policy considerations. Thus, the GDR was, within Comecon, an exporter of – relative to Eastern standards – high-tech goods. Nevertheless, none of these had been competitive in Western markets (Neven and Roller, 1990).

Altogether, it was therefore not very surprising that East Germany's foreign trade was very much affected by the end of the central planning era. On the other hand, in terms of analysing changes in its trade structure post-1989, we faced the problems that, prior to 1989, there was very little information about future trade trends and there were statistical problems involved when we tried to compare the data generated for the purpose of central planning with those for a market economy.

Since the fall of the Iron Curtain, the basic conditions have changed drastically as there has been a transition from a centrally planned economy to a market economy. Up to 1989, foreign trade with the European member countries of Comecon was, for the GDR, an important element to its economic development. The share these countries had of total exports from the GDR amounted to 70.3% (of which the former USSR alone had a share of 40.3%); the share in total imports amounted to 65.1% (USSR: 37.4%). However, these shares may appear larger than they actually were owing to the overvaluation of the transfer rouble, which was used as a unit of account in Comecon trade. After 1991, when Comecon had disbanded and the trade took place according to free market rules and with convertible currencies, the structure and scale of trade changed rapidly. In 1991, for example, trade with the former partners of Comecon only reached just under one third of the previous year's level. Especially clear was the slump in imports, which decreased to one quarter. The most important reason for that development might have been the new access to better Western products (IAW, 1991).

Trade with the Western industrialized countries played a secondary role for the GDR. Nevertheless, exports to Western economies first of all aimed to earn 'hard currencies', which were scarce and necessary to import primary goods that were not available in the required

---

[41]   The primary data and calculations for this section were produced by RWI, Essen, Germany. The report was written by RWI in collaboration with the coordinator, CERES, Greece.

quantity or quality within Comecon. Its regional pattern was clearly dominated by the so-called 'inner zone trade' with West Germany. Its sectoral pattern was shaped by standardized products that could be sold at a standardized price. Thus, exports consisted mainly of raw materials and primary products that the GDR itself imported from the USSR or at least were produced on the basis of such imports (Lorenz, 1991). Taking the sectoral structure into consideration, it became obvious that this structure showed untypical specializations for an industrialized country. For example, basic products and producer goods dominated, which meant that the specialization of the former GDR lay in products with a relatively low vertical range of manufacture and technologically sophisticated production structures (Beyfuß, 1990). With regard to the factor content of the exports, a similar statement can be made. The share of human capital-, research- and technology-intensive goods in the exports was relatively small and did not reflect the high level of training of the GDR's workforce. In contrast, the share of energy-intensive goods was particularly large – a fact that has to be seen in connection with the corresponding ecological damage. Iron and steel, for example, as well as mineral fuels – with a share in exports to the West of almost one third – were especially important to the GDR (Mobius and Schumacher, 1990). That is why it is not surprising that the IIT – at just above 50% – was relatively small. For comparison we may note that in the Federal Republic of Germany (FRG) it was 80%.

The changes in the regional and sectoral foreign trade structures since 1989, analysed in this review, were not only a consequence of the economic integration in the EU, but also, and mainly, the result of the transformation from a planned economy into a market economy (Wohlers, 1992). In the first phase of the reallocation process, the slump in production may not have been without any consequences to foreign trade. The growth process, which was initiated by the transformation, was accompanied by strong increases in production that improved the international competitiveness of the affected sectors significantly and raised their shares of the markets concerned. Additionally, with the further modernization of the capital stock, relative competitiveness will increase again, which will have an influence on imports.

It is clear from the above that it is impossible to disentangle the EU's influence on East Germany's trade at present, and given the data problems detailed in the next section. Exactly in the period under consideration, the transformation effects outlined above may well have dominated changes in East Germany's economy.

4.6.2. Data

Since the German reunification, the Federal Bureau of Statistics has been recording economic processes in East Germany separately. In some areas, especially with respect to foreign trade, it also tried to calculate comparable data for the last years of the former GDR. Thus, sectoral data for East Germany can be found for the period since 1989. Nevertheless, there were many statistical problems connected with these figures. For example, goods imported via the West German border were not attributed to East Germany's foreign trade statistics, but to West Germany's. This meant that there were considerable distortions and the significance of the foreign trade statistics and the indicator calculations based on them was reduced. Therefore, calculations that attempted to capture changes in international competitiveness might well overestimate the trends in RCA. On the other hand, the IIT indicator was biased in both directions, i.e. inter- and intra-trade.

Additional problems occurred because the sample period (1989–94) was rather short. Furthermore, the regional structure of East Germany's trade on a sectoral basis was unknown.

Therefore, indicators could be calculated only in relation to total trade and not in relation to trade with the EU. In contrast, regional connections in the case of the specialization index and shares of the export market could not be taken into account. In order to get more concise information, the data used for the calculations were SITC revised 2-digit-level data in conformity with Leamer (1995) that was pooled in ten commodity groups according to their factor intensity (see also Appendix A1 to Section 4.6, Table A1.4.6.8).

The situation concerning FDI data for East Germany was unsatisfactory as well. The only data available referred to stocks classified by East German *Länder* for the period 1991–93. Due to secrecy, these data could not be aggregated with respect to country of origin or sector. (However, the Deutsche Bundesbank announced that that data would be available after June 1996.) Furthermore, it should also be pointed out that the informative value of this data was limited. For example, an enterprise that had already been active in Germany and became committed in East Germany would not be recorded in the direct investment statistics at all, or the investment would be attributed to the enterprise's headquarters, which was situated, as a rule, in West Germany. Additionally, the data was strictly recorded according to the legal domicile of the investment project. Therefore, if a foreign enterprise established a holding company in West Germany for coordinating its East German activities, the whole operation was counted as investment in West Germany. All in all, this led to a substantial underestimation of FDI in East Germany.

Concerning labour migration flows, these were available for the period 1989–94, subdivided into figures for Germans and foreigners. This data was not further differentiated by nationalities.

Finally, and most importantly, it should be noted that data of production and consumption for East Germany only existed in real terms for the period 1991–95, in the form of the German 1-digit industrial sector's nomenclature. This had the consequence that there was no correspondence between the production and the trade data of commodity groups, so the indicators of trade creation and trade diversion could not be calculated.

4.6.3. Indicator analysis

In the following section, as a first step, the indicators of IIT, RCA as well as specialization will be analysed. The indicators for trade creation/diversion cannot be calculated because, as mentioned above, there was a lack of data. In a second step, some factor flows – labour and FDI flows – are analysed.

IIT

With respect to the analysis of IIT (see Table 4.6.1) – with the exception of petroleum, raw materials and chemicals – a more intra-industrially shaped trade pattern is clearly developing. However, significant shifts in the importance of IIT could be observed over time. Up until 1991/92, there was a reduction of IIT, this being a trend that was particularly pronounced in the product groups of animal, labour- and capital-intensive as well as machinery products. After 1992, in almost all product groups an increase in IIT could be discerned. All in all, the relatively high initial level of IIT was a bit surprising as a major part of East Germany's foreign trade took place with centrally planned economies, and this trade was strongly complementary. One explanation of these results might be the high aggregation level of the data. An analysis at a lower level of aggregation may lead to more differentiated results.

However, such analysis could not be undertaken as appropriate data at the 3- and 4-digit SITC level were missing.

Table 4.6.1.   IIT in East Germany, 1989–94 (Grubel-Lloyd index)

Product group	1989	1990	1991	1992	1993	1994
Petroleum	46.3	27.8	8.5	4.3	4.8	8.8
Raw materials	45.4	43.5	39.8	40.9	29.9	36.1
Forest products	70.5	80.2	90.0	94.2	92.5	98.7
Tropical agriculture	42.1	54.7	99.1	94.9	96.5	79.8
Animal products	73.2	32.7	29.9	74.4	79.4	90.4
Cereals	56.0	53.5	64.4	45.5	57.7	72.7
Labour-intensive	83.6	59.7	67.0	87.4	99.3	93.6
Capital-intensive	93.0	79.3	68.9	79.4	91.2	95.4
Machinery	81.1	48.6	47.7	57.1	58.6	70.6
Chemicals	69.9	50.8	38.7	39.8	44.5	47.9

Note: Author's calculations from Statistisches Bundesamt sources.

RCA

The figures in Table 4.6.2 indicate that East Germany had considerable competitive disadvantages in petroleum and raw materials. These disadvantages worsened in the course of time. This result was to be expected, in so far as the existing factor endowment in East Germany did not favour these products. Concerning tropical agriculture, cereals and forest products, the former disadvantages had been partially changed into considerable competitive advantages. It is to be assumed here that the EU's agricultural policy influenced the development considerably. It should be pointed out also that the product group 'tropical agriculture' is a misleading name because this group also contains vegetables, which are even dominant in this case. However, the competitiveness of labour- and capital-intensive products worsened, and in 1994 the former advantage turned into a competitive disadvantage.

On closer consideration, however, only a few products – such as furniture, footwear, leather, as well as iron and steel – were the cause for this development. These were products in which the developing countries, but also the former Eastern European Comecon countries, had relatively high competitiveness, so, with the introduction of free market rules, a loss in their shares of the export market was to be expected.

On the other hand, there was an almost constant high level of competitiveness for items like chemicals and, with some restrictions, machinery. This reflected the government's priority of the GDR's planned economy, on the one hand, and the comprehensive West German and foreign direct investment of the last years, on the other. At this point it should be mentioned again that, due to the statistical problems described above, the competitiveness was likely to have been overestimated.

Table 4.6.2.   RCA for East Germany, 1989–94

Product group	1989	1990	1991	1992	1993	1994
Petroleum	-53.7	-72.2	-91.5	-95.7	-95.2	-91.2
Raw materials	-54.6	-56.5	-60.2	-59.1	-70.1	-63.9
Forest products	-29.5	-19.8	10.0	5.8	7.5	-1.3
Tropical agriculture	-57.9	-45.3	0.9	-5.1	3.5	20.2
Animal products	-26.8	67.3	70.1	25.6	20.6	-9.6
Cereals	-44.0	-46.5	35.6	54.5	42.3	27.3
Labour-intensive	16.4	40.3	33.0	12.6	0.7	-6.4
Capital-intensive	7.0	20.7	31.1	20.6	8.8	-4.6
Machinery	18.9	51.4	52.3	42.9	41.4	29.4
Chemicals	30.1	49.2	61.3	60.2	55.5	52.1

Note: Author's calculations from Statistisches Bundesamt sources.

The specialization index

In 1989, the main areas of export specialization that were above average in relation to the EU could be detected in the cases of the petroleum and machinery product groups (see Table 4.6.3). While machinery kept up this outstanding position and even slightly strengthened its position over the whole period, in the case of petroleum a decreasing trend could be seen. Petroleum exports of the former GDR existed almost exclusively in the form of re-exports of products imported from the Soviet Union. A continuing improvement in the specialization position was established in the forest products and chemicals groups, the latter – with the exception of 1993 – lying significantly above average. In the cases of the remaining product groups, a mostly unstable development of the main areas of export specialization was to be observed. However, these product groups remained constantly under the EU average.

Table 4.6.3.   The specialization index for East Germany, 1989–93

Product group	1989	1990	1991	1992	1993
Petroleum	153.0	49.2	27.8	11.3	9.0
Raw materials	100.0	75.4	74.4	101.3	72.7
Forest products	48.1	46.5	80.9	92.5	109.1
Tropical agriculture	39.4	24.4	41.6	59.9	63.2
Animal products	33.7	59.6	153.6	95.1	62.7
Cereals	60.0	31.6	60.7	89.0	52.4
Labour-intensive	71.2	90.6	67.7	52.7	45.7
Capital-intensive	91.3	77.2	81.4	100.6	85.6
Machinery	132.3	140.7	121.8	115.5	144.3
Chemicals	90.2	85.2	118.7	136.6	96.9

Note: Author's calculations from Statistisches Bundesamt sources.

This specialization structure, deviating from the EU average, could be interpreted as follows. For example, the significant specialization – even an overproportionate one in relation to the

EU – that took place in favour of the machinery and chemicals groups, should be considered as anticipated because, especially in these sectors, comparative advantages were expected owing to the East German factor endowments. This was confirmed by the RCA analysis. On the other hand, the observed increasing specialization in the case of tropical agriculture should be treated very cautiously.

Shares of the export market

East Germany's shares of the export market to the EU (see Table 4.6.4) decreased in all product groups during the period of the analysis. Consequently, East Germany's overall shares decreased from almost 2% to only 0.5% in 1993. In 1993, there was a turnaround in the forest products and machinery products groups. In these groups, there was a slightly increasing trend.

Table 4.6.4.   East Germany's shares of the export market to the EU (in %), 1989–93

Product groups	1989	1990	1991	1992	1993
Petroleum	2.98	0.86	0.21	0.07	0.05
Raw materials	1.95	1.32	0.57	0.62	0.38
Forest products	0.94	0.82	0.62	0.57	0.58
Tropical agriculture	0.77	0.43	0.32	0.37	0.33
Animal products	0.66	1.05	1.19	0.58	0.33
Cereals	1.17	0.56	0.47	0.55	0.28
Labour-intensive	1.39	1.59	0.52	0.32	0.24
Capital-intensive	1.78	1.36	0.63	0.62	0.45
Machinery	2.57	2.47	0.94	0.71	0.76
Chemicals	1.76	1.50	0.92	0.84	0.51
Total	1.95	1.76	0.77	0.61	0.53

Note: Author's calculations from Statistisches Bundesamt sources.

The structures of exports and imports

As indicated in Table 4.6.5, during the total period, the machinery sector was the most important to exports with a share of more than 50%. Adding to this the chemicals (about 13%) and capital-intensive manufactured products (about 10%), these items represented more than three quarter's of East Germany's exports, which means that there was a high level of concentration in these product groups.

The import structure turned out to be more diversified than the exports, though the machinery sector dominated once again with a share that was slightly above one third. Furthermore, petroleum, raw materials and labour- and capital-intensive manufactured products had – with a share of 10 to 15% each – a higher share than they did of exports. In contrast to exports, though, the chemicals sector, with a share of less than 5%, only played a secondary role in imports.

Table 4.6.5. **East Germany's sectoral distribution of exports and imports (in %), 1989–94**

Product group	Exports					
	1989	1990	1991	1992	1993	1994
Petroleum	4.1	1.5	0.8	0.3	0.3	0.4
Raw materials	3.8	2.6	2.4	3.1	2.2	2.9
Forest products	1.3	1.2	2.1	2.4	2.7	3.5
Tropical agriculture	1.5	1.0	1.7	2.4	2.7	4.3
Animal products	1.6	2.6	7.0	4.5	3.0	2.3
Cereals	2.1	1.1	2.1	3.2	1.9	1.9
Labour-intensive	9.6	12.4	9.3	7.3	6.6	7.4
Capital-intensive	11.5	9.4	9.7	11.7	9.6	8.6
Machinery	53.3	57.8	50.4	48.2	58.8	56.0
Chemicals	11.3	10.4	14.5	17.0	12.3	12.7
Total	100	100	100	100	100	100
Product group	Imports					
	1989	1990	1991	1992	1993	1994
Petroleum	13.6	15.5	28.8	17.8	14.4	9.9
Raw materials	12.9	15.3	15.6	17.3	17.4	15.7
Forest products	2.3	3.1	2.8	3.1	3.1	4.2
Tropical agriculture	5.8	4.3	2.7	3.8	3.4	3.4
Animal products	0.9	0.9	2.0	3.8	2.7	3.3
Cereals	5.3	4.8	1.6	1.3	1.0	1.3
Labour-intensive	6.9	8.8	7.5	8.1	8.8	10.0
Capital-intensive	10.0	10.3	8.1	11.0	11.0	11.2
Machinery	36.3	31.0	25.4	27.6	33.3	36.2
Chemicals	6.1	5.9	5.6	6.1	4.8	4.7
Total	100	100	100	100	100	100

Note: Author's calculations from Statistisches Bundesamt sources.

FDI

In view of the problems regarding the statistical data mentioned above, the FDI balance sheet (see Table 4.6.6) has underestimated the foreign entrepreneurial commitment that has been made in East Germany. FDI in the whole of Germany grew between 1991 and 1993. However, East Germany's share of it accounted for only just 2% of this total. The main regions for FDI were Saxony and Brandenburg. Data regarding the sectoral structure and the origin of investors was impossible to obtain, so we could not analyse FDI further.

Table 4.6.6.   FDI in East Germany, 1991–93 (stocks in billion DM)

Areas allocated to	1991	1992	1993	1994
Brandenburg	0.3	0.6	1.1	1.3
Mecklenburg-Vorpommern	0.6	0.9	1.6	1.4
Sachsen	0.2	0.7	1.6	1.9
Sachsen-Anhalt	0.1	0.1	0.6	1.7
Thüringen	0.1	0.3	0.5	0.5
Total	1.3	2.6	5.4	6.8

Note: Author's calculations from Deutsche Bundesbank sources.

Labour flows

As indicated in Table 4.6.7, after a large migration wave shortly after the fall of the Iron Curtain between 1989 and 1991 – with a peak in 1990 – the migration balance became slightly positive during the period following 1992, which meant, that, for this period, immigration turned out be higher than emigration. The migration of German nationals has therefore almost levelled out and the migration flows are increasingly influenced by foreigners. As to the qualifications of the migrants, the German statistics contain no information on this subject.

Table 4.6.7.   Migration flows for East Germany, 1989–94

Year	Immigration		Emigration		Balance
	German	Foreigner	German	Foreigner	
1989	5,300	47,700	390,700	34,700	-372,400
1990	36,800	39,900	389,900	102,300	-415,500
1991	90,800	37,800	247,000	29,400	-147,800
1992	134,200	94,900	191,500	35,300	2,300
1993	151,000	111,500	169,900	88,500	4,100
1994	155,800	99,900	155,000	65,700	35,000

Note: Author's calculations from Statistisches Bundesamt sources.

4.6.4. The main conclusions drawn from the indicator analysis

Clearly the severe data problems we faced for the region of East Germany meant that the indicator analysis was necessarily of limited scope, covering only a very limited number of trade and factor flow indicators. The main tentative conclusions that emerged from this analysis, however, were the following.

So far, East Germany has been driving on its integration into the EU and the world economy successfully with its exports of mechanical engineering and chemical products. The changes in the structure of its exports as well as imports since reunification indicated that we may anticipate, in the course of a further reconstruction of the capital stock as well as due to the relatively extensive use of high-quality human capital, that the comparative advantage of East Germany in the sectors of mechanical engineering and chemical goods could be strengthened even further in the medium term. Also, the still relatively more well-developed inter-industrial division of labour may turn more and more into an intra-industrial division of labour between East Germany and the Western industrialized countries. This trend could already be observed in the Grubel-Lloyd indices calculated. In almost all groups of goods, a stronger increase in IIT was to be seen. If the changes in the specialization and trade patterns took place in the expected direction, this might encourage a speedier integration into the world economy than would otherwise occur, as a well-developed intra-industrial division of labour in the course of integration processes tends to cause lower adjustment costs than a well-developed inter-industrial division of labour.

Concerning factor flows, FDI in Germany as a whole grew between 1991 and 1993, but East Germany's share still accounted for only 2% of total FDI. Labour migration, after the large outflow following 1989, levelled out and migration flows latterly have been increasingly influenced by foreigners.

4.6.5. Appendix A1 to Section 4.6.

Table A1.4.6.1. The components of ten commodity aggregates

Aggregate	SITC	Aggregate	SITC
Petroleum (PETRO)		**Cereals, etc. (GER)**	
Petroleum and derivatives	33	Cereals	4
		Feeds	8
		Miscellaneous	9
		Tobacco	12
		Oil seeds	22
		Textile fibres	26
		Animal oils and fats	41
		Fixed vegetable oils	42
Raw materials (MAT)		**Labour-intesive (LAB)**	
Crude fertilizers and minerals	27	Non-metal minerals	66
Metalliferous ores	28	Furniture	82
Coal, coke	32	Travel goods, handbags	83
Gas, natural and manufactured	34	Art apparel	84
Electrical current	35	Footwear	85
Non-ferrous metals	68	Miscellaneous manufactured articles	89
		Postal packaging, not classified	91
		Special transactions, not classified	93
		Coins (non-gold)	96
Forest products (FOR)		**Capital-intensive (CAP)**	
Lumber, wood and cork	24	Leather	61
Pulp and waste paper	25	Rubber	62
Cork and wood manufactured products	63	Textiles, yarn, fabric	65
Paper	64	Iron and steel	67
		Manufactured metal n.e.s.	69
		Sanitary fixtures and fitting	81
Tropical agriculture (TROP)		**Machinery (MACH)**	
Vegetables	5	Power generating	7
Sugar	6	Specialized	72
Coffee	7	Metalworking	73
Beverages	11	General industrial	74
Crude rubber	23	Office and data processing	75
		Telecommunications and sound	76
		Electrical	77
		Road vehicles	78
		Other transportation vehicles	79
		Professional and scientific instruments	87
		Photographic apparatus	88
		Firearms and ammunition	95
Animal products (ANL)		**Chemicals (CHEM)**	
Live animals	0	Organic	51
Meat	1	Inorganic	52
Dairy products	2	Dyeing and tanning	53
Fish	3	Medical and pharmaceutical products	54
Hides, skins	21	Essences and perfumes	55
Crude, animals and vegetables	29	Fertilizers	56
Processed animal and vegetable oils	43	Explosives and pyrotechnics	57
Animal products n.e.s.	94	Artificial resins and plastics	58
		Chemical materials n.e.s.	59

5. Comparative analysis and the issue of convergence

5.1. Comparative analysis

Having completed the empirical analysis of each of the less developed regions of the EU in Chapter 4, it is now time to consider whether any general, overall messages can be drawn from the totality of our empirical findings by comparing the results concerning the impact of the SMP that we obtained for each of the countries.[42]

Right at the outset, it should be noted that such comparative analysis is particularly difficult here. Further, and perhaps more importantly, it is not even always very meaningful to try to make detailed comparisons on the basis of the results of the indicator analysis, given the heterogeneity between countries/regions in a number of very important dimensions that are likely to influence the impact of the SMP on trade and factor flows. These dimensions are:

(a)   initial conditions, particularly the initial economic development stage;
(b)   macro-economic environment and cyclical effects;
(c)   accession effects (these were particularly important for Portugal and Spain);
(d)   proximity to the core of the developed regions of the EU (this was particularly important for Greece);
(e)   special factors (such as the extent of the presence of multinational corporations in Ireland);
(f)   other factors that may act simultaneously with the SMP but not with the same intensity for different regions (such as globalization).

A last, though certainly not unimportant, factor that makes it particularly difficult to undertake comparative analysis is the heterogeneity in data quantity and quality for each country/region. This has two major aspects. First, the set of relevant sectors under investigation differs as we move from country to country. Second, due to differing data availability and/or quality it was not possible to calculate the same number or type (in a given category) of indicators for all countries.

There is an additional important implication arising from the differing quantity and quality of data used for each country. It makes it very hard to know whether or not the different conclusions drawn for different countries, whenever they arise, are genuine or depend on data quality. One thing that should be mentioned here is that we carefully analysed the robustness of the regression analysis. For all countries, a robustness test of all regressions was performed. Additional variables were added to check whether robust inference was achieved and alternative selections of co-integrated variables were tried. We also tried simple regression methods. An accurate specifications search for each sectoral regression was also performed. However, we had statistical problems with Greece's data, probably because the regional data were generated by means of a regression approach. By contrast, the pooling of Ireland and Portugal's data did not increase the magnitude of the problem because we always tested whether or not we could accept the assumption of the problem by testing whether or not we

---

[42]   The region of East Germany was considered as a special case and so is not taken into account in the following discussion.

could accept the assumption of homogeneity between the coefficients for the Portuguese regions and those of Ireland. Note that, in any case, the regression analysis could not be done for Ireland alone because Ireland was treated as one region.

Notwithstanding all the above difficulties, it is still worth asking whether or not – if we now take into account the findings for all the countries under investigation – we can obtain support for the main hypotheses expressed in Chapters 2 and 3 of this review about the anticipated effects of the SMP on trade and factor flows.

Overall, on the basis of the theoretical background discussed in Chapters 2 and 3, we would expect that the SMP will generate allocation, location and accumulation effects that will have a positive impact on economic growth and possibly on convergence between the different countries and regions of the EU. The issue of convergence is examined in quite a lot of detail in the other sections of this chapter, so here we shall examine the issue of the association between the above effects and trade and factor flows[43] on the basis of the qualitative indicator analysis undertaken for each country. As mentioned in Chapter 2, economic theory suggests, though not unambiguously, that the SMP is expected to have positive effects on 'internal' trade creation and negative effects on trade diversion, that it will increase IIT and that will affect sectoral and regional relative competitiveness and specialization. Also, the SMP is expected to increase FDI, the capital/labour ratio (especially for less developed regions), labour migration (but little effect on this was anticipated to have occurred within the timespan considered in this review) and employment and capital flows into sectors of new intra-industry or inter-industry specialization. In the longer run, the SMP is expected to affect positively factor accumulation and, thus, growth (the reasons for these anticipated effects were detailed in Chapter 2).

Our main objective in this subsection is to see whether a 'horizontal' reading of our empirical findings across the less developed regions of the EU provides support for the above theoretical expectations. Additionally, by exploiting the regional dimension of the present review, what can we say about the strength (if any) of the impact of the SMP in terms of its *consistency* across the regions?

To answer these questions, we will, mainly for expositional reasons, divide the effects of the SMP into three broad categories.

(a)   **Static effects** Under this heading we will consider the movements of all trade and factor flow indicators other than those we used to measure location effects, the capital/labour ratio and the factor accumulation movements examined in the regression analysis. Thus, we consider that the importance of the static (mainly allocation) effects of the SMP can be captured by looking at the movements in:

   (i)   trade creation/diversion indicators;
   (ii)   IIT indicators;
   (iii)   RCA;

---

[43]   Of course, the convergence analysis also accounted for these effects, directly by looking at their impact on the regional per capita value added accounted for by the sectors under consideration and indirectly by analysing the impact on trade and factor flow indicators (including factor accumulation).

(iv)   FDI;
(v)   other factor flows.

(b)   **Location effects** We used movements in the Herfindahl indices of regional and sectoral concentration of employment and investment to try to capture these effects.

(c)   **Factor accumulation and growth effects** For the effects of the SMP on factor accumulation and growth, we used qualitative analysis of movements in the capital/labour ratio and the regression analysis.

Below we deal with each of these three categories of effects in turn. We will then consider briefly a number of other related 'horizontal' issues, such as the relative strength of trade versus factor flows and the effects of the CSF.

5.1.2. Static effects

Trade creation/trade diversion

The overall picture that emerges here is, to a large extent, consistent with the theoretical anticipations, though the effects have rarely been very strong and there were also some surprises, especially with regard to some aspects of trade diversion. The latter, as measured by exports to 'other countries', has increased in some instances (sectors), this being true, though, with differing significance, for *all* countries. There has been, however, a positive 'internal' trade creation effect, as anticipated, that has been more significant for Spain, Ireland and Portugal than for Greece and Southern Italy.

IIT

Results were, again, broadly in accordance with the theoretical expectations and, in this case, they were consistently strong, at least for Spain, Greece, Southern Italy and, more doubtfully, for Portugal. The exception was Ireland, but this is likely to reflect fundamental inter-industry specialization forces that have been dominant in the Irish economy for much longer and generally continued to be strong up to 1992.

RCA

Here, results were mostly negative, giving, with the exception of Ireland, a consistently rather bleak picture for the countries under consideration. Thus, in Southern Italy there was an effect in very few sectors, which may be the result of a cyclical upswing. In Ireland, the RCA increased for all manufacturing, but notably among its high-tech sectors dominated by foreign-owned firms. In Greece, the effect on its RCA across most sectors was not particularly encouraging, though there were some important exceptions (such as with respect to the non-metallic minerals sector, which is very important to Greece's external trade). The effect was also discouraging – if anything even more so – for Spain and Portugal.

FDI

While there are indications that the SMP has positively affected FDI, as we would anticipate, so that in Portugal and Spain this boosted economic growth and convergence, no such conclusion could be reached for Southern Italy, Greece and Ireland. Thus, there has been no consistently strong effect of the SMP on FDI in the Objective 1 regions of the EU.

Other factor flows

There was quite a large divergence in the availability of data concerning other factor flows across countries. Labour migration flows could be measured only in Ireland, Italy and Spain,[44] and very tentatively we can say that, in all these cases, for the period 1985–92, these flows increased, though we could not show that these increases *are* linked to the SMP.

5.1.2. Location effects

The picture concerning movements in regional and sectoral concentration of employment and investment is also mixed, suggesting that the location effects of the SMP have not, up until 1992, been consistently strong for the less developed regions of the EU. There are quite strong effects in just Portugal and Spain, but in opposite directions – towards increased concentration in Portugal but towards decreased concentration in Spain – and more pronounced in investment than in employment.

5.1.3. Factor accumulation and growth effects

The capital/labour ratio does not show significant changes in Ireland, but it does for many sectors in Greece and Spain, suggesting at least tentatively that the SMP has been a modernizing stimulus for these countries.

Concerning factor accumulation effects, the regression analysis suggests that, for both human and physical capital, there was an overall positive effect for Portugal and Southern Italy, but for Spain there was an effect only on physical capital (not human capital) and this only in some sectors.[45] Further, such a conclusion could not be reached for Greece (the above being the four countries for which we could provide credible tests for such effects).

Finally, let us consider the growth effects on the industrial sectors (excluding agriculture) stemming from the implementation of the SMP. For the regions of Southern Italy, the positive effect on capital accumulation induced by the effect of the SMP on trade flows (mainly on IIT) in turn had a positive effect on growth in four sectors (metal minerals, chemical products, metal products, food, beverages and tobacco). Growth, via human capital accumulation, was also found for the wood and rubber sectors. For Greece, as should be evident from the above remarks, no link was found between the SMP and sectoral growth induced by factor accumulation. However, the SMP may have induced growth via a structural break in the paper sector. For Portugal, the positive effects of the SMP on capital accumulation had a statistically significant impact on the growth of paper, non-metal minerals, wood and rubber, metal products and food, beverages and tobacco. Further, the growth of all the above sectors except paper benefited from the SMP via a structural break in the growth equations. For Spain, as for

---

[44]   As already noted, the distinct case of East Germany has not been included in the analysis in this chapter.

[45]   There was, however, for Spain an indication of indirect effects of the SMP on factor accumulation via its effect on trade flows.

Greece, there does not seem to have been a link between the SMP and sectoral growth induced by factor accumulation, but a positive effect by means of a structural break was found for the non-metal minerals and in the wood and rubber sectors.

5.1.4. Other related issues

Trade flows versus factor flows

Do the results suggest that the SMP had a stronger and/or more consistent effect on trade or on factor flows? The answer is that it depends on which region you are considering. For the regions of Southern Italy, the SMP consistently affected more trade flows than factor flows (indeed, the latter effects were negative or statistically insignificant), while exactly the reverse was true for Portugal. For Spain and Greece the results were mixed and, for the latter, not significant.

The effects of CSFs

Finally, we should comment on the lack of uniform results for the effects CSFs produced for each country. For Southern Italy, the overall effect has been positive, while a positive effect was found in Greece only for textiles and clothing, and in Portugal and Ireland only for wood and rubber, food, beverages and tobacco. This clearly does not reflect any differences in the methodological approach as the same methodology was used for all regions and countries. Data availability problems, however, may be at least partly responsible for the differences as they diminished the quality of the regressions. Thus, the degrees of freedom available to identify the CSF constant were very limited, particularly for Portugal and Ireland, which explains why, in many cases, it was not statistically significant. A new study, which focuses specifically on the role of CSFs, would be necessary to improve the quality of the regressions with respect to CSFs.

5.2. An introduction to the convergence issue

The last issue that may be addressed in this review is that of convergence. Is there a convergence process that is taking place at the sectoral levels in the less developed regions of the EU? Did the SMP provide a positive boost to the convergence path, i.e. did the SMP accelerate sectoral convergence? These questions are certainly relevant, even if doubts can be raised regarding the use of sectoral data to analyse the convergence of per capita incomes. In most studies, indeed, the issue of convergence has been analysed using aggregated data because the final crucial information to be obtained is the assessment of convergence of aggregate per capita incomes in the different EU regions. However, what we can do, using the relevant amount of data and information that we collected, is to analyse in which sectors a convergence process is taking place. These sectors are also likely to drive the overall convergence of per capita incomes. Therefore, the analysis carried out in this section can provide some complementary information by identifying those sectors in which the level of GDP follows a convergent dynamic process. Were this true for all sectors, we could argue that the structure of the regional economies considered in this review tends to become approximately similar (in the medium-long run). In other words, our results can be interpreted either as the contribution of each sector to the convergence of a given region (if this is actually taking place) or as a measure of convergence/divergence in the structure of production across regions.

To answer the above questions – namely does sectoral convergence take place, and is this linked to the SMP? – we needed to apply the methodology proposed in Chapter 3 to the data set provided by each of the country reports. In particular, we needed to compute the average value in the sample period of all the variables necessary to perform the convergence analysis for all regions and sectors considered in these different country reports. Moreover, it was necessary to compute the *antimonde* values of per capita sectoral value added growth in all regions and sectors. To clarify our approach, let us summarize the methodology we used for the analysis of convergence in the next section. Then, in Section 5.4, we will show the results derived from applying this methodology to a cross-section of Greek, Portuguese, Irish and Italian data.[46] This explains why this analysis had to be performed after the country reports presented in Chapter 4. A final section will summarize the main conclusions of the convergence analysis.

5.3. Methodology

We first of all had to select a convergence criterion. There has been a wide debate in the economic literature (see Barro and Sala-i-Martin, 1992; de la Fuente, 1995) on the merits of alternative definitions of convergence (β convergence, σ convergence, conditional versus unconditional convergence).[47] As far as this work is concerned, it seemed appropriate to select β rather than σ convergence as the criterion to be used to study convergence here. The reasons for this can be summarized as follows.

(a) σ convergence, in which a regression is designed in order to identify whether or not and why the (root of the) variance (σ) of per capita income of a group of regions becomes smaller and smaller is probably the concept closest to the intuitive notion of convergence. Moreover, β convergence – the alternative concept proposed in the literature – is only a necessary, but not a sufficient, condition for σ convergence (Friedman, 1992; Quah, 1993; Sala-i-Martin, 1994). However, for an appropriate analysis of σ convergence, much longer time series should be available than we have here.

(b) β convergence has been designed to understand whether or not poorer countries tend to catch up with richer ones (Sala-i-Martin, 1994). This is indeed one of the two pieces of crucial information we wanted to provide, i.e. whether or not peripheral EU regions are catching up with the most developed EU regions. The second crucial piece of information we wanted to discover was whether or not the implementation of the SMP has helped the convergence process. Again, β convergence seems to be more appropriate here than σ convergence as it can be analysed simply using a cross section of regions.[48]

Our methodological approach to the study of convergence therefore paralleled the one proposed by Barro (1991), Barro and Sala-i-Martin (1992) and used in Levine and Renelt

---

[46]   Data for Spain were not avaible before 1988 and, because of this, Spain has been excluded from the convergence analysis undertaken in this chapter. Of course, East Germany is not included either as the SMP only affected it after its accession in 1991.

[47]   A formal comparison of different definitions of convergence is provided in Sala-i-Martin (1994).

[48]   A good explanation of why β convergence may be informative than σ convergence is contained in Sala-i-Martin (1994).

(1992). First, as stated above, we considered the cross-section defined by the 22 regions[49] analysed in this review. Second, we ran the following regression (Levine and Renelt, 1992; Baldwin and Venables, 1995):

Equation 1 $\quad (y_j - l_j)_{avg} = cost_j + \alpha INV_{j,avg} - \beta RGDP_{j,85} + \gamma GPO_{j,avg} - \delta SEC_{j,85}$

$$+ \varphi TECH_{j,avg} + \theta DUMMIES_j + u_j$$

where *INV, GPO, SEC, RGDP, TECH* are the average (1987–92) investment to GDP ratio, the average population growth, the 1985 secondary enrolment rate, the 1985 GDP per capita, and the average indicator of technical progress described in Section 3.3, respectively. The dependent variable is the average growth rate of per capita sectoral value added in region j. Note that the introduction of the initial values for GDP and the enrolment rate implies that we are going to analyse conditional β convergence (as opposed to absolute convergence; see Sala-i-Martin, 1994).

As explained in Baldwin and Venables (1995), Equation 1, which is similar to the standard Barro-type equation, can be rationalized in terms of Lucas' (1988) endogenous growth model, where SEC is a proxy for human capital. With respect to the specification used in Levine and Renelt (1992), we introduced into Equation 14 of Section 3.3.8 an indicator of technical progress to account for the remarks on omitted variables contained in Baldwin and Venables (1995), and a few dummies to capture accession effects.

As is well known, a positive value for β provides evidence that convergence is taking place among the studied regions and the EU average. Moreover, the speed of convergence increases with β. Alternatively, the engine of convergence may be human capital (as in Lucas' (1988) model and as suggested by Barro's (1991) results). In this case, the value of δ would be positive.

In order to verify whether or not the SMP had a positive impact on convergence, let us consider the following regression:

Equation 2 $\quad (y^*_j - l^*_j)_{avg} = cost^*_j + \alpha^* INV^*_{j,avg} - \beta^* RGDP_{j,85} + \gamma^* GPO_{j,avg}$

$$- \delta^* SEC_{j,85} + \varphi^* TECH_{j,avg} + \theta^* DUMMIES_j + v_j$$

where the dependent variable is the *antimonde* relative per capita sectoral value added derived from the simulation described in Section 3.7, i.e. by running a simulation of the whole model in which the liberalization index is assumed to be constant and equal to 1 throughout the whole period of the implementation of the SMP. Note that we also considered the impact of the SMP on the explanatory variables. This is why the value of the investment/GDP ratio was also derived from the *antimonde* regression equations. However, we assumed the effect of the SMP on technical progress not to be significant.

Taking the difference between Equations 1 and 2 yielded:

---

[49]   Made up of 8 regions each for Italy and Greece, 5 regions for Portugal and 1 region for Ireland.

Equation 3 $IM_{j,avg} = cost°_j + (\alpha-\alpha^*)INV_{j,avg} - (\beta-\beta^*)RGDP_{j,85} + (\gamma-\gamma^*)GPO_{j,avg}$

$- (\delta-\delta^*)SEC_{j,85} + (\varphi-\varphi^*)TECH_{j,avg} + (\theta-\theta^*)DUMMIES_j$

$+ \alpha^*(INV_{j,avg} - INV^*_{j,avg}) + \eta_j$

where the dependent variable is defined as the difference between the actual average relative rate of growth of per capita sectoral value added and the average *antimonde* rate of growth.

The null hypothesis was that the coefficient $\pi_1 \equiv \beta-\beta^*$ (and/or $\pi_2 \equiv \delta-\delta^*$) was statistically significant and positive. This hypothesis could easily be tested using standard inference technique.

Summing up, the convergence analysis aimed to test two hypotheses that reflected the basic questions raised at the beginning of this section:

- H^1_0: $\beta > 0$ and/or $\delta > 0$

- H^2_0: $\pi_1 > 0$ and/or $\pi_2 > 0$

Note that the above tests were performed for 11 two-digit sectors. As we already noted (Section 3.3.8), we are certainly aware of the limits of the regression approach to the analysis of convergence. However, we do believe that the regressions described in this section are a very useful complement to the analysis undertaken in the previous sections.

5.4. A test of the impact of the SMP on convergence

Before measuring the impact of the implementation of the SMP on sectoral convergence for the regions of Greece, Portugal, Ireland and Southern Italy, let us verify whether or not a convergence process is actually taking place. To this end, let us run Equation 1 – which is the standard equation used in the literature on convergence – in order to estimate the parameters β and δ for all sectors.

The estimates of Equation 1 are shown in Appendix A1 to Section 5.4. The relevant coefficients we analysed are *B1* and *D1*, which measure the level of the estimated β and δ coefficients. Note that the whole set of necessary data was not available for all 22 regions in all sectors. Therefore, for some sectors, a smaller number of regions had to be considered in the regression. For example, data for agriculture and energy products were not available for Greece and Ireland. For these sectors, only 13 regions (Southern Italy and Portugal) were able to be considered. For metal products, the data for four regions in Greece and one in Portugal were missing. For non-metal minerals, transport equipment, and metal products the data for only one region in Greece was missing. The data for two Greek regions were missing for the wood and rubber sectors, whereas the data for one Portuguese region was missing for the textiles and clothing sector, and for Ireland for food, beverages and tobacco. Finally, the data for three Greek and one Portuguese regions were missing for the paper sector, whereas this was so for one region in Greece, one in Portugal and Ireland regarding the chemical products sector.

The estimated values for the coefficients β and δ, which are shown in Appendix A1 to Section 5.4 provide evidence that a convergence process is taking place. Indeed, the coefficients β (*B* in Appendix A1 to Chapter 5) are positive and significantly different from zero in the following sectors:

(a)   textiles and clothing;
(b)   chemical products;
(c)   paper;
(d)   wood and rubber.

A statistically significant negative coefficient is shown only for the metal products sector. Moreover, if we also consider δ convergence, the following sectors also appear to show a dynamic convergence process (see the positive coefficient D in Appendix A2 to Chapter 5):

(a)   metal minerals;
(b)   transport equipment.

A contradiction between β and δ convergence appears only for the paper sector.

Therefore, we can say that in 6 out of 11 sectors there is evidence that a convergence process is taking place. This result must be coupled with those given in the country reports, which also provide support for the conclusion that convergence is taking place among the different regions that were analysed.

However, the crucial question is whether or not the implementation of the SMP contributed to this convergence process. Therefore, the final step of our analysis was the assessment of the impact of the implementation of the SMP on the speed of convergence among the regions considered in this study. The estimates of Equation 3 for all sectors are shown in Appendix A2 to Chapter 5 The relevant coefficients are $B1$ and $D1$, which measure the changes in the coefficients β and δ produced by the implementation of the SMP. Again, the number of regions for which this could be done is not the same in all sectors. The available data set is the one already described for the convergence equation.

As was previously mentioned, the null hypothesis is that the coefficient $\pi_1 \equiv \beta - \beta^*$ (and/or $\pi_2 \equiv \delta - \delta^*$) is statistically significant and positive. The results of the tests for the 11 sectors were as follows:

agriculture:	$\pi_1 = -0.039$	t statistics $= -1.509$
	$\pi_2 = 0.030$	t statistics $= 0.423$
energy products:	$\pi_1 = 0.037$	t statistics $= 0.643$
	$\pi_2 = 0.414$	t statistics $= 1.967$
metal minerals:	$\pi_1 = -5.006$	t statistics $= -1.456$
	$\pi_2 = -0.271$	t statistics $= -0.162$
non-metal minerals:	$\pi_1 = -0.160$	t statistics $= -3.255$
	$\pi_2 = 0.0002$	t statistics $= 0.024$
chemical products:	$\pi_1 = 0.380$	t statistics $= 1.677$
	$\pi_2 = -0.057$	t statistics $= -0.184$
metal products:	$\pi_1 = -0.064$	t statistics $= -1.393$
	$\pi_2 = 0.289$	t statistics $= 1.814$
transport equipment:	$\pi_1 = 0.308$	t statistics $= 0.988$
	$\pi_2 = 1.577$	t statistics $= 3.111$

food and beverages: $\pi_1 = 0.025$ t statistics $= -1.413$
                       $\pi_2 = -0.152$ t statistics $= -2.631$
textiles and clothing: $\pi_1 = 0.293$ t statistics $= 1.316$
                       $\pi_2 = -2.090$ t statistics $= -1.777$
paper: $\pi_1 = 0.056$ t statistics $= 0.515$
                       $\pi_2 = -0.112$ t statistics $= -1.767$
wood and rubber: $\pi_1 = 0.454$ t statistics $= 1.905$
                       $\pi_2 = 0.147$ t statistics $= 0.850$

Note that convergence was speeded up by the implementation of the SMP only in a few sectors. If we consider the test on the parameter β (i.e. the value of π_1), the test provided statistically significant evidence of a positive impact of the SMP on convergence only for the wood and rubber sector. There was no statistical evidence of a change in β for all other sectors, with the exception of the non-metal minerals sector where the $D1$ coefficient showed a negative impact of the SMP.

If we consider the test on the parameter δ (i.e. the value of π_2, which implies, when negative, convergence related to the level of human capital), we found that the implementation of the SMP increased 'δ convergence' only in the transport equipment, metal products and energy products sectors. In all other sectors there was no statistically significant evidence of any impact of the SMP on δ convergence, with the exception of the food, beverages and tobacco sector where the $D1$ coefficient showed a negative impact of the SMP.

Summing up, this final regression suggests that convergence (either β or δ convergence) among the less developed regions of Greece, Ireland, Italy and Portugal is likely to have increased in the following sectors:

(a)   wood and rubber;
(b)   transport equipment;
(c)   metal products;
(d)   energy products.

A negative impact on convergence is instead likely in the non-metal minerals and food, beverages and tobacco sectors.

5.5. Conclusions

The empirical evidence provided in the previous subsections, despite the caveats regarding the meaning of sectoral convergence, suggests that the speed of convergence (either β or δ convergence) among the less developed regions of the EU examined in this chapter is unlikely to have increased, because of the implementation of the SMP, as we found an increase in the speed of convergence in only a few sectors (wood and rubber, transport equipment, metal products, energy products). In particular, β convergence increased only in the wood and rubber sector.

We have shown that, even though a convergence process *is* taking place among some sectors of the less developed regions of Greece, Portugal, Ireland and Southern Italy, this convergence process was largely unaffected by the implementation of the SMP. Also when a positive impact occurred, it was induced more by a positive change in the effect of human capital on convergence than by a change in the effect related to sectoral growth.

With respect to this issue, note that convergence seems to have been driven mainly by the direct effect of sectoral growth, whereas the *additional* convergence induced by the implementation of the SMP mainly occurred via human capital, as stated above.

5.6.   Appendix A1 to Chapter 5

Table A1.5.   The estimates of Equation 1 used to measure convergence

Sector	Param.	t student	Sector	Param.	t student	Sector	Param.	t student
AGR			MEM			MEP		
CAGR	0.05	1.70	CMEM	0.30	1.87	CMEP	0.19	3.48
AAGR	1.05	2.32	AMEM	0.17	1.68	AMEP	-0.06	-1.24
BAGR	-0.01	-0.57	BMEM	-0.39	-1.32	BMEP	-0.05	-2.67
GAGR	-3.63	-2.14	GMEM	-30.15	-2.62	GMEP	-15.80	-2.36
DAGR	-0.12	-1.51	DMEM	0.36	2.45	DMEP	0.18	1.23
FAGR	-0.07	-5.56	FMEM	-98.00	-1.43	FMEP	-0.06	-5.08
R sq.	0.81		R sq.	0.36		R sq.	0.53	
ENP			NMM			TEC		
CENP	0.16	1.11	CNMM	0.02	0.26	CTEC	-0.70	-1.42
AENP	-0.11	-0.75	ANMM	0.36	1.55	ATEC	-0.03	-0.49
BENP	0.11	0.04	BNMM	0.15	0.88	BTEC	0.41	1.92
GENP	13.31	1.58	GNMM	10.36	1.82	GTec	32.39	1.13
DENP	-0.01	-0.04	DNMM	-0.02	-0.15	DTEC	-1.91	-1.57
FENP	-0.08	-1.74	FNMM	-0.00	-0.23	FTEC	0.18	1.28
R sq.	0.74		R sq.	0.28		R sq.	0.44	

Table A1.5. (continued)   The estimates of Equation 1 used to measure convergence

Sector		Param.	t student	Sector		Param.	t student	Sector		Param.	t student
CHP	CCHP	0.13	1.14	TRE	CTRE	0.73	3.21	PAP	CPAP	-0.05	-1.50
	ACHP	-0.21	-3.67		ATRE	-0.32	-1.45		APAP	0.15	1.13
	BCHP	0.31	1.68		BTRE	0.05	0.13		BPAP	0.42	1.98
	GCHP	-12.74	-1.37		GTRE	-82.37	-3.07		GPAP	11.11	2.78
	DCHP	0.08	0.28		DTRE	1.37	2.73		DPAP	-0.32	-3.23
	FCHP	0.00	0.03		FTRE	-0.06	-0.95		FPAP	-0.00	-0.27
	R sq.	0.32			R sq.	-0.63			R sq.	0.39	
FBT	CFBT	0.09	2.21	WOR	CWOR	0.33	2.77				
	AFBT	0.20	3.12		AWOR	0.18	1.08				
	BFBT	0.03	0.57		BWOR	0.83	2.90				
	GFBT	5.68	1.27		GWOR	-31.62	-2.24				
	DFBT	0.02	0.15		DWOR	0.12	0.52				
	FFBT	-5.69	-4.34		FWOR	-0.06	-2.70				
	R sq.	0.68			R sq.	0.65					

5.7.　Appendix A2 to Chapter 5

Table A2.5.　The estimates of Equation 3 used to measure convergence

Sector		Param.	t student	Sector		Param.	t student	Sector		Param.	t student
AGR	C1AGR	-0.03	-1.75	MEM	C1MEM	1.21	1.02	MEP	C1MEP	0.19	2.49
	A1AGR	0.96	3.40		A1MEM	1.26	0.78		A1MEP	-0.72	-2.69
	B1AGR	-0.04	-1.51		B1MEM	-5.01	-1.46		B1MEP	-0.06	-1.39
	G1AGR	-2.41	-1.09		G1MEM	-221.82	-1.13		G1MEP	-25.66	-3.43
	D1AGR	0.03	0.42		D1MEM	-0.27	-0.16		D1MEP	0.29	1.81
	F1AGR	-0.00	-0.07		F1MEM	-0.96	-1.11		F1MEP	-0.03	-1.50
	A%1AGR	0.03	0.10		A%1MEM	-1.09	-0.74		A%1MEP	-0.00	-2.50
	R sq.	0.65			R sq.	0.21			R sq.	0.69	
ENP	C1ENP	0.15	1.24	NMM	C1NMM	-0.03	-0.47	TEC	C1TEC	-1.00	-2.05
	A1ENP	-0.16	-0.58		A1NMM	-0.16	-0.92		A1TEC	0.96	0.96
	B1ENP	0.04	0.64		B1NMM	-0.16	-3.26		B1TEC	0.29	1.32
	G1ENP	0.08	0.02		G1NMM	3.29	0.87		G1Tec	53.52	1.84
	D1ENP	0.41	1.97		D1NMM	0.28	0.02		D1TEC	-2.09	-1.78
	F1ENP	0.00	0.16		F1NMM	-0.00	-0.12		F1TEC	0.27	1.96
	A%1ENP	0.07	0.24		A%1NMM	0.00	0.77		A%1TEC	0.00	1.51
	R sq.	0.36			R sq.	0.32			R sq.	0.48	

Table A2.5. (continued)   The estimates of Equation 3 used to measure convergence

Sector	Param.	t student	Sector	Param.	t student	Sector	Param.	t student
CHP			TRE			PAP		
C1CHP	-0.00	-0.05	C1TRE	0.92	3.63	C1PAP	-0.02	-0.59
A1CHP	-0.17	-2.67	A1TRE	-0.39	-2.30	A1PAP	-0.11	-1.17
B1CHP	0.38	1.68	B1TRE	0.31	0.99	B1PAP	0.06	0.52
G1CHP	-27.21	-2.26	G1TRE	-106.63	-3.70	G1PAP	0.87	0.25
D1CHP	-0.06	-0.18	D1TRE	1.56	3.11	D1PAP	-0.11	-1.77
F1CHP	0.09	2.51	F1TRE	-0.10	-1.87	F1PAP	0.00	0.00
A%1CHP	-0.00	-0.61	A%1TRE	-0.08	-3.84	A%1PAP	-0.02	-0.58
R sq.	0.65		R sq.	0.74		R sq.	0.24	
FBT			WOR					
C1FBT	-0.05	-1.63	C1WOR	0.18	1.92			
A1FBT	0.16	2.85	A1WOR	-0.07	-0.52			
B1FBT	-0.03	-1.41	B1WOR	0.45	1.91			
G1FBT	2.66	0.99	G1WOR	-24.94	-2.32			
D1FBT	-0.15	-2.63	D1WOR	0.15	0.85			
F1FBT	-0.00	-0.38	F1WOR	-0.00	-0.30			
A%1FBT	0.00	4.83		-0.09	-1.29			
R sq.	0.41		R sq.	0.65				

Bibliography

AA.VV. *L' integrazione economica nella Comunità Europea: orientamento degli scambi e degli squilibri commerciali*, Rapporto sul Commercio Estero, ICE, 1989.

Attanasio, O. P. and Padoa Schioppa, F. 'Regional inequalities, migration and mismatch in Italy, 1960–86', in *Mismatch and Labour Mobility*. F. Padoa Schioppa (ed.), Cambridge, Cambridge University Press, 1991.

Balassa, B. 'Economic Integration in Eastern Europe', *Structural Change and Economic Dynamics*, Vol. 3, No. 1, 1992, pp. 3–15.

Baldwin, R. 'The Growth Effects of 1992', *Economic Policy*, 9, 1989, pp. 247–82.

Baldwin, R. 'Measurable Dynamic Gains from Trade', *Journal of Political Economy*, Vol. 100, No. 1, 1992a, pp. 162–74.

Baldwin, R. 'On the Growth Effects of Import Competition', NBER Working Paper No. 4045, 1992b.

Baldwin, R. and Venables, A. 'International Migration, Capital Mobility and Transitional Dynamics', GIIS and LSE mimeo, 1994.

Baldwin, R. and Venables, A. 'Methodologies for an Aggregate ex post Evaluation of the Completion of the Internal Market', study for the European Commission (DG II), 1995.

Banerjee, A. and Urga, G. 'Looking for Structural Breaks in Co-integrated Systems', CEF Discussion Paper No. 18–95, 1995.

Barro, R. 'Economic Growth in a Cross-section of Countries', *Quarterly Journal of Economics*, 1991, pp. 407–43.

Barro, R. and Sala-i-Martin, X. 'Economic Growth and Convergence Across the United States', NBER Working Paper No. 3419, 1990.

Barro, R. and Sala-i-Martin, X. 'Convergence', *Journal of Political Economy*, Vol. 100, No. 2, 1992, pp. 223–51.

Barros, P. and Garoupa, N. 'Convergencia Portugal CEE: Alguma evidencia', WP number 204, UNL, 1993.

Ben-David, D. 'Equalizing Exchange: Trade Liberalization and Income Convergence', *Quarterly Journal of Economics*, 1993, pp. 652–79.

Bentolila, S. and Jimeno, J. F. *Regional Unemployment Persistance (Spain, 1976-1994)*, Working Paper 95–09, FEDEA, 1995.

Beyfuß, J. 'Entwicklung und Struktur des DDR-Außenhandels', in IW-Trends, Vol.1, 1990, pp. 13–26.

Beyfuß, J. 'Position der Reformländer in der internationalen Arbeitsteilung – Stand und Perspektiven', in IW-Trends, 1/93, 1993, pp. 31–48.

Boone *et al.* 'Endogenous Technical Progress in Fossil Fuel Demand: the case of France', CEF Discussion Paper No. 21–93, 1992.

Bowen, H. P. 'Changes in the International Distribution of Resources and their Impact on US Comparative Advantage', *Review of Economics and Statistics*, 1983.

Brülhart, M. and McAleese, D. 'External trade and industrial performance: how Ireland adjusted to European integration', presented at the 6th SPES Workshop on 'Trade, Specialisation and Market Structure', Nottingham, September 1994.

Buigues, P. *et al.* 'The impact of the internal market by industrial sector: the challenge for the Member States', *European Economy (Social Europe)*, Luxembourg, Office for Official Publications of the EC, 1990.

Canova, F. and Marcet, A. 'The poor stay poor: convergence across countries and regions with a Bayesian panel data approach', mimeo, Universitat Pomepu Fabra, 1995.

Carraro, C. 'Regression and Kalman Filter Methods for Time Varying Econometric Models', Econometric Research Program Memorandum No. 319, Princeton University, September 1985.

Carraro, C. 'Square Root Kalman Algorithms in Econometrics', *Computer Science in Economics and Management*, No. 1, 1988.

Carraro, C., J. P. Herbay, Williams and Zagame. 'Competitiveness, Energy, Employment and Environmental Policies', study commissioned by the European Commission (DG XII), 1995.

Carraro, C., Herbay, J. P. *et al.* 'Le Progrès Technologique pour la Compétitivité et l' Emploi. Le cas Energie-Environment', report prepared for the European Commission (DG XII-Joule II Programme), Brussels, 1995.

Chow, G.C. 'Econometrics, New York: McGraw Hill', 1983.

Cipolletta, I. and de Nardis, S. 'Flessibilita geografica e quote di mercato delle esportazioni italiane nell' ultimo decennio', rapporto sul Commercio Estero, ICE, 1987.

Coglio, A. and Polimeni, G. 'Distribuzione internazionale delle risorse ed evoluzione della struttura dei vantaggi comparati dell' Italia', CNR Progetto Finalizzato, *Struttura ed evoluzione dell' economia italiana*, Onida (ed.), Collana Franco Angeli, 1989.

Confraria, J. *Desenvolvimento economico e politica industrial*, Ediçoes U.C. Lisboa, 1995.

Conti, G. 'L'interscambio con l' estero delle regioni italiane', rapporto sul Commercio Estero, ICE, 1987.

Corado, C. 'Costs of non-Europe and industrial location in Portugal and Spain', *Economia*, Vol. XV, 1991, pp. 411–45.

Davidson, R. and McKinnon, J. *Estimation and Inference in Economics*, Oxford, Oxford University Press, 1993.

De la Fuente, A. 'Assessing the Effects of the Internal Market Programme: A Conceptual Framework', study commissioned by the European Commission (DG II), 1995a.

De la Fuente, A. 'Los minesotos y las regiones: economia regional desde una perspectiva neoclasica', PT 46.95, Institut d'Analisi Economica, 1995b.

De la Fuente, A. and Vives, X. 'Infrastructure and Education as Instruments of Regional Policy: Evidence from Spain', *Economic Policy*, 20, 1995c, pp.13–51.

De Nardis, S. 'La specializzazione internazionale nelle maggiori economie', rapporto sul Commercio Estero, ICE, 1990.

Di Liberto, A. 'Convergence Across Italian Regions', Working Paper 68.94, FEEM, 1994.

Dias, F., Linha de Romo, Lisboa, 1946.

Edwards, S. 'Openness, trade liberalization and growth in developing countries', *Journal of Economic Literature*, Vol. XXXI, No. 31, 1993, pp. 1358–93.

Engle, R. F. and Granger, C. W. J. 'Co-integration and error correction: representation, estimation and testing', *Econometrica*, No. 55, 1987, pp. 251–76.

Engle, R.F. and Yoo B.S. 'Co-Integrated Economic Time Series: a Survey with Results', in Engle, Granger (eds.), Long Run Economic Relationships, Oxford University Press, 1991.

European Commision, *Completing the internal market*, COM (85) 310, Luxembourg, Office for Official Publications of the EC, 1985.

European Commission, *Single Market Review VI.1*: Regional growth and convergence, Luxembourg, Office for Official Publications of the EC and London, Kogan Page Publishers, 1997.

Friedman, M. 'Do old fallacies ever die?', *Journal of Economic Literature*, (JEL), Vol. XXX, December 1992, pp. 2129–32.

Fuller, E. B. *Measurement Error Models*, New York, J. Wiley & Sons, 1987.

Gao, X. M., 'Measuring technological change using a latent variable approach', *European Review of Agricultural Economics*, 21, 1994, pp. 113–29.

Garcia-Mila, T. and Marimon, R. 'Integración regional e inversión publica en España', in R. Marimon (ed.), *La economia española en una economia diversa*, Antoni Bosch, 1995.

Gaspar, V. and Pereira, A. 'The impact of financial integration and unilateral public transfers on investment and growth in EC capital importing countries', *Journal of Development Economics*, 1995.

Glaeser, E. L., Kallal, H. D., Scheinkman, J. A. and Shleifer, A. 'Growth in cities', *Journal of Political Economy*, Vol. 100, 1992.

Goicolea, A., Herce, J. A. and de Lucio, J. J. 'Patrones territoriales de crecimiento industrial en España', Working Paper 95–14, FEDEA, 1995.

Goria, A. and Ichino, A. 'Migration and convergence among Italian regions', Working Paper 51.94, FEEM, 1994.

Grauwe, de, Paul. 'Anpassungsprobleme in Ostdeutschland – eine ökonomische Analyse', in Heisenberg, *Die Vereinigung Deutschlands in europäischer Perspektive*, 1992, pp. 170 *et seq.*

Graziani, Giovanni. 'Specialisation for Eastern Europe and access to EC markets', in van Jozef M. Brabant, (ed.), *The New Eastern Europe and the World Economy*, Boulder, 1993, pp. 175–95.

Greenway, D. *et al.* 'Adjustment and the measurement of marginal intra-industry trade', *Welfwirtschaftliches Archiv*, Vol. 130, No. 2, 1984, pp. 418–27.

Gros, D. and Steinherr, A. 'Die wirtschaftliche Integration Deutschlands – zwei Versionen auf handelstheoretischer Grundlage', in Heisenberg, *Die Vereinigung Deutschlands in europäischer Perspektive*, 1992, pp. 150 *et seq.*

Grossman, G. and Helpman, E. *Innovation and Growth in the World Economy*, Cambridge, Mass., MIT Press, 1992.

Grossman, G. and Helpman, E. 'Endogenous innovation and the theory of growth', *Journal of Economic Perspectives*, Vol. 8, No. 1, Winter, 1994.

Grubel, H. G. and Lloyd, P. J. *Intra-industry Trade*, London, Macmillan, 1975.

Haaland, J. and Wooton, I. 'Market integration, competition and welfare', in A. Winters (ed.), *Trade Flows and Trade Policy After 1992*, CEPR and Cambridge University Press, 1992.

Hall, S. and Urga, G. 'Stochastic Common Trends and Long-Run Relationships in Heterogeneous Panels', Centre for Economic Forecasting, LBS, 1995.

Hamilton, C. and Kniest, P. 'Trade liberalisation, structural adjustment and intra-industry trade: a note', *Weltwirtschaftliches Archiv*, Vol. 127, 1991, pp. 356–67.

Harris, J. R. and Todaro, M. P. 'Migration, unemployment and development: a two-sector analysis', *American Economic Review*, Vol. 60, No. 1, 1970, pp.126–42.

Heisenberg, W. *Die Vereinigung Deutschlands in europäischer Perspektive*, 1992.

Helg, R. 'Specializzazione internazionale e caratteristiche industriali: un approfondimento', CNR, Progetto Finalizzato, *Struttura ed evoluzione dell' economia italiana*, Onida (ed.), Collana Franco Angeli, 1989.

Helpman, E. and Krugman, P. *Market Structure and Foreign Trade*, Cambridge, Mass., MIT Press, 1985.

Hsiao, C. *Analysis of Panel Data*, Cambridge, Cambridge University Press, 1987.

Kemp, M. C. and Wan, H. Y. 'An elementary proposition concerning the formation of customs unions', *Journal of International Economics*, Vol. 6, 1976, pp. 95–7.

Kennedy, K. 'Real convergence: the European Community and Ireland', presidential address, Statistical and Social Inquiry Society of Ireland, May, 1992.

Krauss, M. B. 'Recent developments in customs union theory: an interpretive survey', *Journal of Economic Literature*, 10, 1972, pp. 413–36.

Krugman, P. *Rethinking International Trade*, Cambridge, Mass., MIT Press, 1990.

Krugman, P. 'Endogenous innovation, international trade and growth', 1988, republished in P. Krugman (ed.), *Rethinking International Trade*, Cambridge, Mass., MIT Press, 1990.

Krugman, P. *Geography and Trade*, Cambridge Mass., MIT Press, 1991.

Krugman, P. *Geography and Trade*, Leuven University Press, 1991a.

Krugman, P. 'Increasing returns and economic geography', *Journal of Political Economy*, Vol. 99, No. 3, 1991b, pp. 483–99.

Krugman, P. 'International finance and economic development', in Giovannini, *Finance and Development: Issues and Experience*, Cambridge, Cambridge University Press, 1993, pp. 11–23.

Krugman, P. and Venables, A. 'Integration and competitiveness of peripheral industry', in C. Bliss and J. Braga de Macedo (eds.), *Unity with Diversity in the European Community*, Cambridge, Cambridge University Press, 1990.

Krugman, P. and Venables, A. 'Integration, specialization and adjustment', CEPR Discussion Paper No. 886, 1993.

Krugman, P. and Venables, A. 'Globalization and the inequality of nations', CEPR Discussion Paper No. 1015, 1994.

Leibenstein, H. 'Allocative efficiency v. X-efficiency', *American Economic Review*, 56, 1966, pp. 392–415.

Leite, A. and Gaspar, V. 'Cohesion and convergence: the economic effects of EC structural funds', *Economia*, Vol. XVIII, January, 1994.

Levine, R. and Renelt, D. 'A sensitivity analysis of cross-country growth regressions', *American Economic Review*, 82, 1992, pp. 942–63.

Lipsey, R. 'The theory of customs unions: a general survey', *The Economic Journal*, 70, 1960, pp. 496–513.

Lorenz, D. 'West- und Osteuropa – weltwirtschaftliche Probleme des Zusammenwachsens', *Wirtschaftsdienst* 1990/XII, Hamburg, HWWA-Institut für Wirtschaftsforschung, 1990.

Lorenz, D. 'Konsequenzen für den deutschen Außenhandel aus der Integration West- und Ostdeutschlands', Referat auf der Tagung des Wirtschaftspolitischen Ausschusses des Vereins für Sozialpolitik, Marburg, March 1991.

Lorenz, D. 'Konsequenzen für den deutschen Außenhandel aus der Integration West- und Ostdeutschlands', in *Wirtschaftspolitische Probleme der Integration der ehemaligen DDR in der Bundesrepublik*, Schriften des Vereins für Sozialpolitik, Vol. 212), 1991, pp. 245 *et seq.*

Lucas, R. 'On the mechanics of economic development', *Journal of Monetary Economics*, 22, 1988, pp. 3–42.

Lutz, V. *Italy: A Study in Economic Development*, Oxford, Oxford University Press, 1962.

Lyons, B. and McCloughlan, P. 'Dynamic interdependence between FDI and foreign trade in the context of the European integration process with special reference to ECE: the case of Ireland', prepared for J. Witkowska and Z. Wysokinska (eds.), *Dynamic Interdependence Between Foreign Direct Investment in the Context of the European Integration Process with Special Reference to ECE: Comparative Aspects*, Poland, Lodz, undated.

Mankiw, G., Romer, D. and Weil, P. 'A Contribution to the Empirics of Economic Growth', *Quarterly Journal of Economics*, May, 1992 , pp. 407–37.

Marimon, R. and Zilibotti, F. 'Por que hay menos empleo en España? Empleo Real vs. Empleo "Virtual" en Europea', in R. Marimon (ed.) *La economia española en una economia diversa*, Antoni Bosch, 1995.

McAleese, D. 'Industrial specialisation and trade: Northern Ireland and the Republic', *Economic and Social Review,* Vol. 7, No. 2, 1976, pp. 143–60.

McAleese, D. 'Intra-industry trade, level of development and market size', in H. Giersch (ed.), *On the Economics of Intra-industry Trade*, Tübingen, J. C. B. Mohr, 1979.

Meade, J. *The Theory of Customs Unions*, North Holland, Amsterdam, 1955.

Michaely, M. *Concentration in International Trade,* North Holland, Amsterdam, 1962.

Michaely, M. 'On customs unions and the gains from trade', *The Economic Journal*, 75, 1963, pp. 577–83.

Mobius, U. and Schumacher, D. 'Eastern Europe and the EC: trade relation and trade policy with regard to industrial products', Joint Canada Germany Symposium, November 1990.

Mobius, U. and Schumacher, D. 'Eastern Europe and the EC: trade relation and trade policy with regard to industrial products', in B. Heitger and L. Waverman (eds), 1993, pp. 113–75.

Modesto, M. and Neves, P. 'The effects of CSF 1994-1999 on the Portuguese economy', *Economia*, Vol. XVIII, January, 1994.

Mundell, R. *Tariff Preference and the Terms of Trade*, Manchester School, Vol. 32, 1964.

Murrell, P. *The Nature of Socialist Economies: Lessons from Eastern European Foreign Trade*, Princeton, 1990.

NESC. *Ireland in the European Community: Performance, Prospects and Strategy*, Dublin, National Economic and Social Council, Report No. 88, August 1989.

Neven, D. 'EEC integration towards 1992: some distributional aspects', *Economic Policy*, 10, 1990, pp. 14–62.

Neven, D. and Roller, L.-H. 'The structure and determinants of East-West trade: preliminary analysis of the manufacturing sector', in L. A. Winters and A. J. Venables, *European Integration: Trade and Industry*, Cambridge, Centre for Economic Policy Research, 1990.

Neves, J. 'Os fundos comunitarios e a economia portuguesa: uma abordagem informal', *Economia*, 1995.

O'Grada C. and O'Rourke K. 'Irish economic growth, 1945–1988', CEPR Discussion Paper 975, June 1994.

Onida, F. 'La struttura del commercio estero dell'Italia: alcuni tentativi di verifica empirica cross-sector e cross-country', CNR Progetto Finalizzato, *Struttura ed evoluzione dell' economica italiana*, Onida (ed.), Collana Franco Angeli, 1987.

Pesaran, M. H. and Smith, R. 'Estimating long-run relationships from dynamic heterogeneous panels', *Journal of Econometrics*, Vol. 68, 1995, pp. 79–113.

Picci, L. 'Lo stock di capitale nelle regioni italiane', University of Bologna, Document No. 229, 1995.

Quah, D. 'Galton's fallacy and tests of convergence hypothesis', CEPR Discussion Paper No. 820, July 1993.

Reis, J. 'O atraso economico português em perspectiva historica', Lisbon, Imprensa Nacional, 1993.

Romer, P. 'Increasing returns and long-run growth', *Journal of Political Economy*, Vol. 94, 1986, pp. 1002–37.

Sala-i-Martin, X. 'Regional cohesion: evidence and theories of regional growth and convergence', CEPR Discussion Paper No. 1075, 1994.

SEPDR. 'Preparar Portugal para o seculo XXI – Analise economica e social', State Secretariat for Planning and Regional Development, Ministry of Planning and Territorial Administration, Lisbon, 1993.

Sestito, P. 'Sviluppo del Mezzogiorno e capitale umano', *Economia & Lavoro*, Oct.-Dec. 1991, Vol. XXV, 1991.

Shioji, E. 'Regional allocation of skills', mimeo, Universitat Pompeu Fabra, 1995.

Schumacher, D. and Mobius, U. 'Zugang der DDR zum gemeinsamen Markt.', in 'Fragen zur Reform der DDR-Wirtschaft', in *Beihefte der Konjunkturpolitik*, Vol. 37, 1990, pp. 125–61.

Simões, V. 'Dynamic interdependence between FDI and foreign trade in the context of the European integration process: the case of Portugal', mimeo, 1994.

Sims, C. A., Stocka, H. H. and Watson, M. W. 'Inference in linear time series models with some unit roots', *Econometrica*, No. 58, 1990.

Slade, M. 'Conjectures, firm characteristics and market structure, an empirical assessment', International Journal of Industrial Organization, Vol. 4, 437–369, 1986.

Stokey, N. 'Human capital, product quality, and growth', *Quarterly Journal of Economics*, CVI, 1991, pp. 587–616.

SVIMEZ. 'Rapporto 1993 sull' economia del Mezzogiorno', Il Mulino, 1993.

Taiti, F. 'Le prospettive degli scambi internazionali con riferimento alla unificazione del Mercato Europeo nel 1992', rapporto sul Commercio Estero, ICE, 1987.

Viesti, G. 'L'export del Sud Italia nella seconda meta degli anni '80', rapporto sul Commercio Estero, ICE, 1991.

Viner, J. *The Customs Union Issues*, New York, Carnegie Endowment for Peace, 1950.

Werner, K. 'Die Handelsbeziehungen der ostdeutschen Länder mit dem ehemaligen RGW-Raum, Lage und Perspektiven 1991', in *Die deutsch-deutsche Integration - Ergebnisse, Aussichten und wirtschaftspolitische Herausforderungen* (Beihefte der Konjunkturpolitik-Zeitschrift für angewandte Wirtschaftsforschung, Vol. 39.), 1991, pp. 149 *et seq.*

Williams, A. M. *The European Community*, Cambridge, 1991.

Wohlers, E. 'Außenhandelseffekte der deutschen Vereinigung', in *Hamburger Jahrbuch für Wirtschafts- und Gesellschaftspolitik*, Tübingen, Vol. 31, 1992, pp. 125 *et seq.*

Young, A. 'Learning by doing and the dynamic effects of international trade', *Quarterly Journal of Economics*, CVI, 1991, pp. 369–405.

Zilibotti, F. 'Foreign investment, enforcement constraints and human capital accumulation', Economics Working Paper 69, Universitat Pompeu Fabra, 1994.

Zilibotti, F. 'Foreign investment, enforcement constraints and human capital accumulation', Economics Working Paper 69, Universitat Pompeu Fabra, 1994.